Dimensions of Anthropological Research in Northeast India

Dimensions of Anthropological Research in Northeast India

Edited by

Sarthak Sengupta
Juri Borah

GYAN

Published, 2019

Published by

Gyan Publishing House
5, Ansari Road
Daryaganj, New Delhi-110002
Phone: 011-47034999, 9811692060
www.gyanbooks.com
E-mail: books@gyanbooks.com

Printed at: G. Print Process, Delhi.

Cataloging in Publication Data—DK
Courtesy: D.K. Agencies (P) Ltd. <docinfo@dkagencies.com>

Dimensions of anthropological research in Northeast India /
edited by Sarthak Sengupta, Juri Borah.
pages cm
ISBN 9788121214926

1. Anthropology—Research—India, Northeastern. I. Sengupta, Sarthak, 1955- editor. II. Borah, Juri, editor.

LCC GN46.I4D56 2019 | DDC 301.0729541 23

Contents

Preface

Northeast region of India is the meeting place of varied ethnic, religious and linguistic groups who entered into the region in successive waves during different prehistoric and historic periods. The inhabitants of the region are mostly tribes, and the non-tribals are mostly formed by the caste-Hindus, Scheduled Castes, Other Backward Classes, and the Muslims. With the introduction of the tea industry, a large number of tribes and castes mainly from Chotanagpur, the Santal Parganas were also brought and inducted as indentured workers in the tea estates of Assam. Besides, a large number of immigrants from neighbouring countries have also entered into Northeast India in recent years.

Anthropology in Northeast India has made significant progress in terms of research and teaching. Typical of the region, with its numerous ethnocultural groups with varied bio-cultural contours and stages of development, presents a unique field for anthropological inquiry. In today's world of rapid transformation, the significance of anthropology's holistic and empirical approach is profoundly felt in India's Northeast. Though within the Northeast region itself, the intra-societal and inter-regional disparity coupled with the significant environmental and the cultural adaptive distinction between the hills and the plains regions exists, there are also considerable elements of continuity in the biological, cultural and social issues between the hills and the plains. The problem of anthropological research in Northeast India is not at the same level as other regions of our country in view of its geopolitical significance. This area is the meeting place of international borders of Bangladesh, Bhutan, China, and Myanmar; the people of the region are exposed globally and are influenced in their approach and strategies by immeasurable issues, thus, there is an urgent need for all-inclusive, socially relevant problem-oriented and methodical anthropological studies of this region. Various research organizations and university departments of the region should initiate interdisciplinary collaborative efforts in the anthropological investigation of this region. It is unfortunate that, till date,

most of these institutions function in isolation and barring few attempts, there is hardly any collaboration and teamwork among them. It is expected that such an atmosphere of group efforts will is initiated immediately especially to avoid duplication/repetition in research as well as consequent wastage of scarce resources and to improve its quality.

The field of anthropological research in Northeast India is vast and un-researched areas are numerous. The prospect of anthropology will depend upon a thoughtful understanding of its potency and certainly, it lies in the specialized knowledge it can generate. Serious introspection is the need of the day to figure out how anthropology could assume a more meaningful role in the field of human development and welfare of the people of the region. These call for unrelenting and well-planned collaborative approach of research and publication of its outcome without delay.

The present treatise is a compilation of research articles to combine the studies contributed by experienced anthropologists on the varied population groups of Northeast India. The articles, which follow do refer to the theme of the volume, and range from the topic of social structure (R. Das), through oral tradition and folklore (C.J. Sonowal), customary law and status of women (R.P.Athparia), performing art (J.Sarkar), health issues (T. Mene; Y. Gogoi and S. Sengupta; J. Borah and S. Sengupta; B. Deka and B. Patir), eco-cultural adaptation (D.G. Danda), youth dormitory (B.K. Medhi and Bimla), contemporary anthropological research in Manipur (M.C. Arun and P. Krishnakumari), naming culture in relation to siblingship (L. Therie and N.K. Gogoi), megalithic culture (P.B. Devi), cultural memory (S. Bandopadhaya) to the prehistoric past of the region (M. ManiBabu; Q. Marak).

Our endeavour in compiling this volume will be well rewarded if these research contributions can provide a glimpse of the vast and wide-ranging dimension of anthropological research in Northeast India and proved to be informative and useful, and arouse inquisitiveness in scholars and researchers of social sciences.

6 November 2018

Sarthak Sengupta

Juri Borah

Acknowledgements

A great deal of work and dedication was involved in producing this extensive volume. First and foremost, the chapter authors deserve the greatest credit for all of the effort they put into their contributions and for giving us the privilege of including their work in this collection. Their undertaking was significant, and our gratitude for their dedication cannot be overstated.

We also thank M/S Gyan Publishing House, New Delhi for providing excellent assistance during the final phases of preparation of the book in a printed form.We are deeply thankful to Dr. Samrat Sengupta who provided us with photograph to use in the jacket.

Last, of all, we must acknowledge our heartfelt thanks to our family members since without their encouragement, support and a cheerful home environment, it would have been impossible to sustain this task.

The 6 November 2018 **— Sarthak Sengupta**
Juri Borah

List of Contributors

MC Arunkumar, Department of Anthropology, Manipur University, Canchipur, Imphal, Manipur, 795003.

Rajendra Prasad Athparia, Northeastern Social Research Centre, Christain Basti, Guwahati, Assam, 781005.

Sumahan Bandyopadhyay, Department of Anthropology, Vidyasagar University, West Medinipur, West Bengal, 721102.

Bimla, Department of Anthropology, Cotton University, Panbazar, Guwahati, 781001, Assam.

Juri Borah, Department of Anthropology, Dibrugarh University, Dibrugarh, Assam, 786 004.

Rajat Kanti Das, UGC Emeritus Fellow (Retd.), Department of Anthropology, Vidyasagar University, Flat 2A, Harmony -1, Greenwood Sonata, New Town, Rajarhat, Kolkata, West Bengal, 700161.

Bikash Deka, Department of Sociology, Dibrugarh University, Dibrugarh, Assam, 786 004.

Potshangbam Binodini Devi, Department of Anthropology, D.M. College of Science, Imphal, Manipur, 795 003.

Nitul Kumar Gogoi, Department of Anthropology, Dibrugarh University, Dibrugarh, Assam, 786 004.

Yikham Gogoi, Anthropological Survey of India, Northeastern Regional Centre, Madan Raiting, Shillong, Meghalaya,793022.

Pebam Krishnakumari, Department of Anthropology, Manipur University, Canchipur, Imphal, Manipur, 795003.

M. Mani Babu, Department of Anthropology, Manipur University, Canchipur, Imphal, Manipur, 795003.

Queenbala Marak, Department of Anthropology, Umshing-Mawkynroh, North Eastern Hill University, Shillong, Meghalaya, 793022.

Birinchi K. Medhi, Department of Anthropology, Gauhati University, Guwahati, 781014, Assam.

Tarun Mene, Arunachal Institute of Tribal Studies, Rajiv Gandhi University Rono Hills, Doimukh, Arunachal Pradesh, 791112.

Basobi Patir, Department of Sociology, Dibrugarh University, Dibrugarh, Assam, 786 004

Geetika Ranjan, Department of Anthropology, Northeastern Hill University, Umshing-Mawkynroh, Shillong, Meghalaya, 793022.

Sarthak Sengupta, Department of Anthropology, Dibrugarh University, Dibrugarh, Assam, 786 004.

C.J. Sonowal, Centre for Study of Social Inclusion and Inclusive Policies, Tata Institute of Social Sciences, Deonar, Mumbai, 400088.

LhiwepeTherie, Department of Anthropology, Dibrugarh University, Dibrugarh, Assam, 786 004.

List of Tables

List of Figures

Chapter - 1

Reassessing Social Structure as a Model of Studying Northeast Indian Tribal Communities in a state of Flux

— ***Rajat Kanti Das***

Ideally, our understanding of tribal society is as a social group which manifests a collective consciousness maintains a moral order, nurtures a normative system appropriate to its proper functioning and which is reflected in its capacity to sustain a culture. As a social system, it is regulated by a structure of its own. Generally speaking, the totality of social institutions and status relationships make up the social structure of a society. It is assumed that this structure, to a certain extent, exists independently of the individuals who at a point of time hold structurally defined positions. Such individuals may be regarded as persons holding social positions and not individuals in the strict sense of the term. At the conceptual level, the social structure may be perceived as the matrix of society, emptied of humans in a symbolical sense. It involves the totality of duties, rights, and divisions of labour, norms, social and political control, all of which have been abstracted from the ongoing social life. From that point of view, the social structure represents a stereotyped model, which appears quite handy in describing a bounded social system. Such a system used to be the hallmark of a tribal society functioning within the limits of a defined territory. But, in the present context describing a tribe exclusively in terms of a stereotyped model gives little hint of the contemporary realities and future trend marked by complexities and a multitude of events beyond the range of any known tribal system. Of course, society is now conceived in terms of (i) a structure of separation and opposition as against structure of integration, and (ii) a structure of inequality rather than the structure of equality signifying an egalitarian pattern.

Alternatively, a bipolar or binary approach covering both the extremes is usually suggested to accommodate both the perspectives. Strict adherence to binary approach, however, disregards multi-layered local- societal dynamics lying beneath the populist framework. This particularly applies to tribes of Northeast India which demonstrate a plurality of levels of existence in varying degrees. Side by side, inevitable plurality of individual contexts has also come into play, where the context is understood in the way an individual distinguishes between people, his own and others, and events influencing them.

Let me start with the example of Maring tribe of Manipur, among whom I did my first full-length research. The reason why I focused on the Maring social structure was the notion that societies in specific situations (in this case territorial contiguity and social institutional network) could be regarded as original wholes. The specific situation referred to also prevails in other regions of Northeast India where tribes are in the majority. The initial understanding of the Maring society was that there was a structural component unit or social groups in the society backed by the institutional principles with normative value, which together form a system. A system, in this case, marks the total structural pattern demonstrating a stability of its own. In an ideal situation, the social structure of a tribe like Maring could be thought to be a balanced one with the constituent units maintaining a level of inter-connectedness and independence. What is actually an ideal situation? This may refer to a situation when normative control could gain the upper hand and the individual remains committed to the society in its ideal form. Methodologically, the structural analysis aims at producing an idealized model of the society. As Edmund Leach (1954) observes,

> 'Any structural description of a social system should have an idealized model which states the correct status between groups within the total system and between the social persons who make up particular groups.'

Initially, my intention was to develop an explanatory model, which may fall in the category of an ideal model, with the help of which a brief outline of the social morphology of the Maring tribe of Manipur could be worked out. One may get the impression that adopting such a model amounts to describing social groups in static terms. But actually, what I tried to do was to follow a dialectical approach. Incidentally, it was Fredrik Barth (1959) who had advocated that social groups should be seen in the light of,

> 'the dialectic between the concrete behaviour of persons, groups, and categories on the one hand, and the collective institutions of culture and society that persist regardless of changing personnel' (cf. J. Goody, 1973).

In my study, I had tried to combine socio-centric analysis in terms of kin groups with the ego-centric analysis in terms of kin roles. It was not simply the question of describing the social process by integrating all available materials from an observable source. The integration of approaches was also involved with it. It, however, must be admitted that the generalizations arrived at was not always based strictly on an analysis of observed behaviours. These sometimes-reflected people's own views and value-based judgements on their own customary behaviour. Moreover, in such a study the scope of quantification is rather limited. Even otherwise, not all aspects of the social structure are quantifiable in a systematic way.

Ideally speaking, the Maring society is composed of kin groups to provide the organizational structure. The kin groups are segmentary with corporate functions. In the past, the organizational potential of territorially and co-residence with respect to consanguineal kin groups like clan leaves little room for doubt. A type of social gradation marked the functions of clans (*chimkhur*). *Charanga* occupied the highest position, which was the clan of *Khunbu* or *Khulpu*, the founding father of a village, closely followed by the defense head *Saopullu*. The post of defense head has now been abolished and the office held by *Khumbu* has also lost much of its importance. As the *Khullakpa* (headman) has grown in structure outpacing *Khumbu*, his clan *Dangsa* has also been upgraded. In any case, claims of higher status have been hotly debated by the members of the two clans. Monopolizing important office at the village level by *Dangsa* (*Khullakpa* and *Luplakpa*) and *Charanga* (*Khumbu*) was no doubt responsible for these being placed above other clans. It is disputable whether *Khullakpa* could be regarded as the leader of a Maring village. He is, in all probability, a later introduction by the Meitei Kings. Before that, it was *Khumbu* or *Khulpu*, who was the ruler with authority in the real sense of the term. The Maring society then was roughly stratified into three groups: rich, commoner and slaves or captives. Rich were those who had the highest ascribed social status, also confirmed by the performance of status giving rituals like *Thiltlhai,* which could not be achieved by the commoners. Slaves or war captives were sometimes given as tributes and even sacrificed during the performance of the status giving ritual *Thiltlhai.* The emphasis was on compulsive behaviour giving little scope to choice making exercise.

Clearly, a principle of dominance lies inherent in the Maring social system. It manifests itself in the principle of seniority (*Piba*) being followed at almost every stage of operation of social groups. The social structure is sustained by a principle of asymmetry, which goes hand in hand with the segmentary system. Segmentation is closely interlinked with unequal distribution of statuses and differential access to available resources. Unequal distribution of statuses and unequal distribution of wealth seem to be mutually

compatible. Apparently, a potential hierarchic organization existed in the social structure itself. The difference is that hierarchies in the past were 'prestige hierarchies', which in course of time had given way to 'power hierarchies'. Today, it is later which mainly determine the level of differentiation. Moreover, hierarchic tendency gives rise to conflict, or these could be a potential source of conflict. In the society's social structure, conflicts could automatically be resolved through ritual practices and myth. Ritual action signifies the traditional way of determining hierarchies. The Maring social units also function as 'ritual units', which have a ritual content and behaviour. To a structuralist, the structure which is symbolized in ritual is the system of socially approved proper relations between individuals and groups. Because the social action is a symbolic expression of social relations, it marks the structural system of the Maring society. The proposition that social structure involves social relations between persons may not be questioned. What has, however, escaped our attention is the role of the 'Third Element' in them. The 'Third Element' has now extended into the content of social relations, which falls into the category of 'outside factors'. In the contemporary situation, it is this 'Third Element' which dictates terms on a number of occasions. The type and quality of a social relationship depend more on these factors. Also, conflicts in the behaviour of individuals may be thought to have been caused by such factors. Of course, some such conflicts are 'built-in' to the structure marked by the unequal distribution of status and wealth. Within the limits of the society's social structure, there is not much scope for the individual conflicting loyalties to surface and disrupt the fabric of the society. But the fact remains that there has always been a potential danger of disruption of social relations offered by conflict and deviation. As long as the 'Third Element' or 'outside factors' in the form of political control, westernization,and modernization, globalization, demographic features like migration, stringent government control over local resources do not assume a serious proportion, conflicts 'built-in' to the structure could be resolved or glossed over without causing any significant change in the structural form. But as pressure on land increases, population movement, growing associational ties, governmental control, and political inroads start playing decisive roles and it becomes difficult for the structurally bound people, more in a symbolical sense, to maintain the internal balance. To speak of social structure in such a situation is to treat the 'ethnic communities' or tribes as 'imagined communities' having little real consequences.

With not much land available internally and population increasing gradually, the Maring social structure has come under pressure. Consequently, pursuing traditional social relationships within the limits of the society's social structure has become a difficult task. Already there are signs of that.

Asymmetrical alliance system in the form of MBD marriage is no longer strictly adhered to. More and more 'irregular unions' and even 'incestuous marriage' have been reported. The actual choices are more like independent expressions of the basic grammar of opposition and reciprocity. Oligarchic control, which was a special feature of the Maring society, has come under sharp criticism from the younger people. The younger people have more of the political activity and the political activities they are indulging in are less conventional in the sense that that do not strictly conform to the structural order. The traditional village council has almost been reduced to the status of a virtual non-entity. Competition between individuals for economic and political power has become the order of the day, which does not always conform to traditional structural order. As the pattern of local settlement growth has been one along village line, village rather than the kin group has become the center of activities. Kinship is going to prove less effective in organizing activities at the group level. To a certain extent, maintenance of internal order depends on external forces in operation. In such a situation how far, social structure will be effective in controlling the society's affairs remains a debatable question. Now power relations are considered more central to modern systems and in a plural situation and as a result,no tribal system can remain outside the range of influence of such a system. As power in itself is fragmented, it gives rise to many subsystems accelerating structural changes. Long back, E.R. Leach (1954) in his Kachin study tried to work out a type of political system with political organizations oscillating between polar types. Though this movement was at the level of the political system, the individuals were responsible for it since they had been provided with alternatives. The various types of political system differed from one another not only in scale but also in the formal principles in terms of which they were organized. All of these were manifestations of structural change at the societal level. Power relations within the Maring society are now determined to a great extent by forces operating from outside. From the functional point of view, the political organization of the Maring belongs to a type which not only shows its link with internally organized social groupings but also with such non-internal forces as the earlier form of political control represented by the 'Meitei Kingdom' and its principalities and the present state government of Manipur representing the modern political system. Greater interaction with the Meiteis has been promoted by an increasing desire to enter the non-traditional sources of wealth. With a depleted traditional resource base, this has become a necessity. As a result, an individual is plagued with conflicting loyalties, which create a discordant note. However, in spite of the weakening of the traditional base, a sense of corporateness still continues to pervade the society. This may be understood more as a defensive strategy. On the other hand, as they are being subjected more and more to outside influence, their traditional ways of livelihood have been rendered less and less usable and

profitable. When ethnic identity rests heavily on cultural features, these must be shared giving rise to a tradition of culture as the basis of such a construction; ethnic identity also draws on the belief, which at times becomes a conviction, of sharing a common biology. Once I, accompanied by my ex-colleague and co-worker Mr. R.K. Ranjit Singh, was on my way to a Maring village on the top of a hill lying in the foreground. We were about to cross a small stream, where at a small distance apart, a group of Maring women were taking bath. They did not pay much attention to us and we also pretended to ignore their presence. As we were preparing to cross the stream, all of a sudden, almost all the women rushed towards me menacingly as if to cause physical harm to me. They were fuming and shouting at the highest pitch of their voice. My colleague intervened and after much persuasion succeeded in stopping them from making any further move towards me. But for him, it would not have been possible for me to escape their wrath. Later, he explained to me that I was made their target because of my alien physical features. Obviously, along with culture, sharing a common biological ancestry also helps in maintaining the social structural relations. Ethnic feelings grow from here, making them identity conscious. In reality, people face conflicts, tensions, struggles, alienations, which are almost inherent to class-based societies. However, any class-based explanation for the contradictions manifested by the tribal societies today may appear rather inadequate or superfluous. Though the contradictions are the moving principle in the social fabric, they are not particularly bound by the structural order as defined by the society.

Even during my study, it was difficult to formulate structural relationships between the Maring clans, which were the main social groups contributing to the overall social structure in terms of clear-cut principles because some genuine irregularities or 'inconsistencies' (Leach, 1954) were discernible in the field of inter-clan relationship. In the past, solidarity at the tribal level could be maintained through clanship ties, which cut across the boundaries of villages. But this was possible when the clans functioning as status groups had a greater control over the behaviours of individuals. For example, *Dangsa*, by virtue of its highest status, and before that *Charanga* for similar seasons had authority over a number of villages. Their authority was never questioned during those days. But today, because of a growing interaction with the Meitei society and other surrounding communities coupled with a greater degree of governmental control, exercising the same authoritative control by the clan is inconceivable. In the past, at least two other factors, besides clanship ties, made it imperative for the members to achieve a wide level of socio-cultural integration. These factors were inter-tribal feuds and shifting cultivation. Now, with the weakening of clanship ties, the disappearance of inter-tribal feuds and increasing economic ties with outside agencies,

conflicting trends have made their appearance within the society itself. The village rather than clan has assumed greater importance, with the result that intra-village relationship is now uppermost in the minds of the people. To a Maring, the village has become the center of interest now. One reason for this is the recognition of the right of individual families over residential houses. They now pay house tax to the government, the implication being individual rights on land are recognized. The new social reality reflects a type of material reality in implicit forms, but such a reality is now riddled with contradictions and conflicting interests. In the olden days, the clans were marked by a sense of corporate identity and solidarity delimited by general logical ties. In the context of inter-village feuds and warfare, only clanship ties served to maintain relationships at the tribal level. With the recognition and installation of individual rights, the clanship ties contributing to structural order making the traditional social structure less effective. Obviously, Christianity is not compatible with many of the traditional practices. In the face of all these, the traditional social order has surfaced some of the glaring ambiguities. These relate to the 'formal bounding of social units and the constitution of groups mobilized for action'. In other words, there is a clear distinction between the structural units and action groups. Weberian approach drawing a distinction between power and authority may be inducted here. At the action group level, the Maring social structure representing the way traditional social units are formally bound may not be the true indicator of the complex situation an individual today finds oneself in. The concrete encounters an individual has with the world in his or her everyday life reflect on a complex, divergent process of identifying, perceiving, sharing of meanings to the extent they serve the interests of the individual. Here social structure as a conditioning factor hardly makes an impression. The Maring social structure representing an 'ideal model' stands for an abstract whole system, which may have some analytical value. As Leach (1954), argues with some degree of conviction that an 'abstract analytical system' could be the starting point.

> 'What one must do is first analyze out the ethnographic facts by reference to abstract whole systems conceived of as existing in unstable equilibrium, and then postulate that the confusion of reality arises from the interpretation of these unstable ideal systems'

Admittedly, there is a gap between the 'real society' and 'ideal society'. Still, the people visualize a 'model' of how their society should be organized. Following Leach, it may be said that the model is not necessarily the goal towards which the people strive. It is indicative of the continuing of the group through transformations from one level to another. Such a model is not necessarily a model in equilibrium. To a researcher, it can serve as an analytical construct which may serve as the basis for holistic analysis of the structure of relations between constitutive units and between their members. Taking

this as the basic structural model, the next step may be to analyze the process whereby new patterns of behaviour are generated. Like other societies, the Maring society has changed and has been changing. Does it affect the Maring social structure? There has been 'structural realignment' in the Maring Society: smaller groups like sub-clans and lineages have grown at the cost of bigger units like clan; in the economic field corporate functions of the kin groups or village-based work groups have given way to recognition of individual rights and control; the traditional village council has been rendered almost functionless and its place has been taken over the Village Authority constituted by the State government. Still, social structure has to be involved while recognizing the Maring as a distinct group in the form of a tribe with a separate identity of its own. Probably it applies to all other tribes of the same category. The study of social structure, in this case, will involve the total network of relations, within and outside the group, at every level of scale, throughout the whole area. Among the Maring, there is a growing section representing an area in the middle in between the highland occupied by the Maring parental villages and lowland controlled by the Meiteis. They act as a link between the two, by retaining some of the basic features of the Maring society and at the same time incorporating some of the characteristics of the Meitei society. From all indications, their member is on the increase. This will have further repercussions on the Maring social structure. The real issue is how to accommodate all the diverse sections in the form of a parental group regarded as the custodian of Maring culture and dissident groups revealing dialectical differences, economic changes and political transformation within one social structure. There are indications suggesting that the core group structure is, in fact, losing control. The time has come to refrain from seeing social change as structurally ingrained. A greater effort should be given to analyzing the working of 'outside factors' in bringing about structural changes. Side by side, the stability, durability, and continuity of social structure in its original, ideal form need to be assessed correctly. The emphasis should be more on the authenticity of facts. But the facts are sometimes deceptive because they are loaded with impressions and personal reflections. Persons engaged in enforcing compliance with the norms or generating and operating a discourse on the changing social structure are to be identified with reference to their roles instituting 'ordered courses of action'. These provide new meaning to the structure. Anthropological method of studying social structure in a changing situation calls for a rigorous approach to be developed and pursued vigorously.

Levi-Strauss's communication theory to unfold the order of elements in the social structure should be an eye-opener. But as Levi-Strauss (1969) himself laments, '...it is at the very moment when anthropologist finds himself closer than ever to the long-awaited goal of becoming a true science that

the ground seems to fail where it was expected to (be) firmest. The facts themselves are lacking, either not numerous or not collected under conditions ensuring their comparability.' It is altogether a different question whether in contemporary northeast India a rigorous, scientific approach as exemplified by the study of social structure can be followed without any distortion because the facts themselves are now very much blurred and deceptive. There is not one, but a set of structures. It is Levi-Strauss (1958) again who states that any society conveys 'a set of structures corresponding to various types of orders'. This particularly applies to Northeast Indian tribal communities. It needs to be emphasized here that social structure is basically asymmetrical in nature. As it is, no principle of equality particularly works behind the structure. Today structure involves separate domains like the domain of culture, the domain of ethnicity, the domain of class, the domain of power relations, the domain of gender relations. No doubt, the primary contradiction rests on the basic structure. In the present context, however, what is significant is the way domains are interfaced. It has given the primary contradiction a new meaning, a new direction when contradiction ceases to function as a mere contradiction. From the methodological standpoint observation and empiricism may not be able to reveal all of these complexities. What is needed is a more communicative and 'dialogical epistemology'. All in all, it is a journey from the social structure as a stereotyped model to social communication in terms of dialogical exercise. Northeast India is the ideal ground for making such an experiment. The contemporary situation calls for a thorough probe into innovations and change that have gripped the tribal societies of Northeast India regardless of the conditions in which they live or are forced to live. Innovation, which stands for a new idea, a new method or a new device, covers diverse fields and adds to the complexity and plurality of the situation. But innovations and change within the context of the local social system need to be seen from the context of social structure, which keeps the system going. The dynamism pervading the system, however, rests on some individuals. As Oliver de Sardan (2005) contends, '...each innovation, each diffusion of innovation, invariably transits via *social bearers*, who occupy an important position in the social structure.' These social bearers vary from one society to another and possess a greater or lesser degree of 'social credibility' or even of 'social credit'. The social structure into which they are integrated are usually riddled with contradictions and antagonisms having structural implications. Following Oliver de Sardan (2005), it may be contended that the various social groups identified within the local society, though not possessing identical resources, are not equally constrained. They represent the same society but are guided by different values on some occasions. Oliver de Sardan further clarifies, 'the various social groups identified within the local society do not possess identical resources, are not equally constrained, and sometimes have different values. The introduction

of an innovation is very likely to serve the interests of some people while damaging the interests of others.' Innovation tends to get naturally diffused, which transcends all boundaries. Culture is, therefore, the result of borrowing that sets in motion the process of 'intercultural hybridization', which is obviously not structurally controlled or determined. Northeast India is replete with such examples. Although internal differentiation within a tribal group of Northeast India stems from differential access to resources, there is practically no tribe today without cleavage at the social level. In the present context, visualizing society as a 'whole' as is implied in social structure appears to be a rhetoric. If there is any structural reality, it is to be assessed in the context of consumer culture, ever-expanding market economy, the introduction of technologies and unchecked development and, above all, changing power structure. This brings into force the anomalies that have developed within people's system of classification. Not surprisingly, people's action sways between acceptance and rejection of social representation. On the one hand, they show social concern about their environment and display social solidarity, while on the other they practice conspicuous and modest to high consumption at the cost of environment. Can structure provide a link between the two? It is a test for structuralists who still believe in social structure with its new meaning and shift in emphasis to come to terms with the moving reality.

Note

This is an enlarged version of the paper published in the *Journal of Asiatic Society* with the title *'Social Structure as a Model of Studying Northeast Indian Tribal Communities'* in 2011, Volume LIII, No.4.

References

Barth, F 1959, *Political leadership among the Swat Pathans*, vol. 19, London School of Economics monograph on Social Anthropology, University of London, The Athlone Press, London.

Goody, J (ed.) 1973, *The character of kinship*, Cambridge, London.

Leach, ER 1954, *The political system of Highland Burma*, Harvard University Press, London.

Levi-Strauss, C 1958, *Structural Anthropology*, Basic Books Incorporation, London.

Levi-Strauss, C 1969, *The raw and the cooked: introduction to a science of mythology*, volume I, trans. JD Weightman, New York.

de Sardan, JPO 2005, *Anthropology, and development*, Zed Books Ltd., London.

Chapter - 2

Revisiting the Domain of Oral Tradition and Folklore among the Tribes of Northeast India

— *C.J. Sonowal*

Discourse on Oral tradition

If we accept the dictionary meaning of 'oral' which defines it as 'uttered in spoken words; transacted by words of mouth; spoken or verbal'; then 'oral tradition' may be interpreted as any kind of unwritten tradition (including physical monuments, religious statues or Church frescoes) and/or a tradition(s) enunciated or transmitted through words only. What tradition actually implies then? The answer is that tradition may have several ways to look at. To name a few, tradition is a culture as a whole; an established way of doing things whether or not of any antiquity. Further, it may also be seen as a process of handing down practices, ideas, or values which are belonged to the whole of the community. Thus, when we talk of oral tradition, we assert that tradition in question possesses the characteristics like being verbal or non-written. It may also belong to the people or the 'folk' where folk may have the connotation of non-educated and/or non-elite. As a tradition, it can be seen as fundamental to the people who put values in it and it is more than often transmitted over generations, observably not through any conscious action, rather by the community or the folk.

In a very simplistic way, oral tradition can be defined, as those recollections of the past that are commonly or universally known in a given culture, a process that may continue for at least a few generations (Henige, 1988:2) did, Oral tradition has been defined by Vensina (1985) as the verbal

messages which are reported statements spoken, sung or called out on musical instruments only. Josheph Ki-Zerbo (1990) defines oral tradition as being a testimony transmitted verbally from one generation to another. His special emphasis on oral tradition is put on being verbal and mode of transmission as verbal. Several sociologists and social anthropologists hold the view that not all oral aspect of human society is qualified to be termed as 'oral tradition'. For them, certain cultural aspect must fulfill a definite set of criteria to be qualified as 'oral tradition'. To name a few — the materials under this category must be held in common by a group of people, over several generations and they should, not necessarily, be similar to the 'testimony' or 'oral history'. The messages or testimony are verbally transmitted in speech or songs and may take the form of, for example, folktales, sayings, ballads, songs, or chants.

The critical discourse on oral tradition derives at the understanding that being oral in nature, the oral tradition of a society gets affected by the factors like — space and time, ever-changing social and physical environment, changing economic pursuits and related activities, and contact with and exposure to outside world and people's changing world views as a consequence of interaction of all these factors.

Classifying Oral Tradition

Following a very simplistic view, Oral tradition may be classified in the following way. But here it has to be reminded that such classification of components is not exclusive and they are always overlapping and interactive in nature.

Classification of Oral Tradition

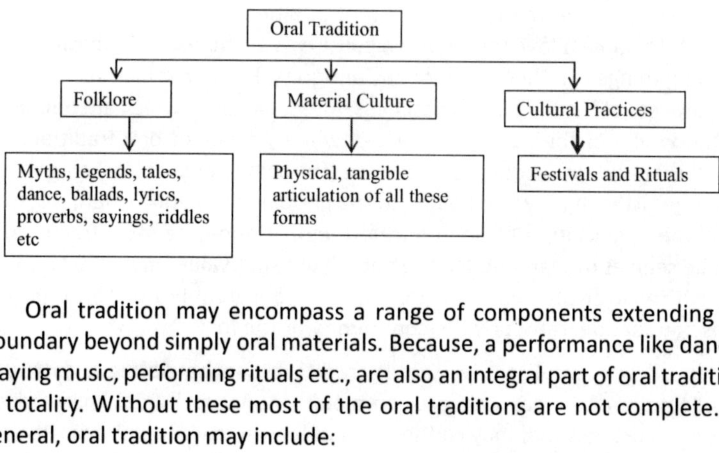

Oral tradition may encompass a range of components extending its boundary beyond simply oral materials. Because, a performance like dance, playing music, performing rituals etc., are also an integral part of oral tradition in totality. Without these most of the oral traditions are not complete. In general, oral tradition may include:

- Mythology and related hymns and chants which are sacred and though a property to the entire community, usually mastered or controlled by a certain individual with a specific capability.
- Folktales that depict the social, economic and moral aspects of the community of past years and also transmit the messages to the present generation in these aspects.
- Folklores consist of various forms of verbal expressions people used to deliver on different occasions in their social life.

Role of Oral Tradition in the Reconstruction of Cultural History

Traditional anthropologist believed that culture could be reconstructed or re-imaged using the oral tradition of a society. There have been detailed discourses from the part of these anthropologists. The outcome of such endeavour was the understanding that the evidence carried by oral traditions are fragmentary in nature. Thus, in the absence of a written record, oral tradition provides only a limited amount of information about the past. This happens due to the fact that oral tradition has a limited capability to transmit knowledge from one generation to other. Thus, people keep only those aspects of tradition which have immediate importance or meaning to the society at that particular time and space. This implies that the transmission of oral tradition goes through a continuous process of selection. Therefore, in this process of selection, only those aspects of the past are likely to be passed down which have some current relevance to the society. Since a tradition is preserved because of its present relevance, it may be passed on in a form which preserves the meaning of past events, but not necessarily the actual narrative details.

What we can find from this discussion that oral tradition is not necessarily a flawless account of any group of people. Based on the contemporary importance, the content of oral tradition to be passed down to next generation is determined. The traditions or oral materials that do not possess any meaning or value relative to that particular time tend to be wiped out due to non-performance or non-practice by the group of people. It is also evident that new components are always added to it to make the 'oral tradition' meaningful in accordance with changing social as well as physical environment.

Making Oral Tradition Culturally Meaningful

It is necessary to focus on the rich and multicoloured heritage of tribal and rural cultures to give a socio-cultural meaning to oral tradition, as the researchers on oral tradition believe. In doing so it is imperative to put emphasis on the links and relationship between the natural environment,

the daily life of people, annual calendar and life-cycle of the people, their worldviews, cosmology, social structure, knowledge and skill, traditional techno-culture and artistic manifestation.

It is important to note that change in technology, adapted cropping pattern, change in crop cycles and varieties, newly adapted economic activities and pursuits, inflow of capitalist and monetary economy and growing consumerism etc., have dominant effect to define the role and importance of involvement of a particular gender, group of people, which ultimately affects the dominant value and symbolism of any gender-specific oral tradition.

It is a universally held idea that oral traditions are derived from and based on experiences and transcendental knowledge of the cultural group. Surely, rationality takes a back seat in the origin and transmission of oral tradition. But, oral tradition has been utilized for more than reckoning past and construction of ethnohistory of any cultural group. It has also encompassed the nationalist politics and ideology. Social scientists state that in the sociological term, oral tradition provides a holistic experience of life shared collectively and territorially in all spheres, activities, and aspirations to give every being a distinct social and cultural identity. There is a contention regarding the orality of oral tradition in that many components of oral traditions have been textualized nowadays. Thus, components of oral traditions are no longer remained oral in its strict sense because there has been a data of the same and handing down of this tradition becomes easier and non-selective.

Thus, methodologically a research study on oral tradition needs:

(i) Understanding deeper structures in 'cultural texts' comprising unwritten materials (rituals, beliefs, lore, and artistic expression), also written materials (inscriptions, jottings, leaflets, books) in an integrated fashion.

(ii) Reaching out to the ordering of oral tradition in the experience and expression of people, and,

(iii) Going beyond the objectives and conceptual to the cognitive consciousness of people.

Considering all these, now the oral tradition no longer remains as tools to reckon past. It entered into the arena of post-modernist dialectics synthesizing between:

Personal – impersonal,

Self – others

Subjectivity – objectivity etc.

The significance of Oral Tradition

The significance of Oral traditions of a cultural group thus can be ascertained through the discussion made above. Putting the importance of the continuity of customs and tradition at the first place, the significance of oral tradition in a society may be assessed for its capability to carrying forward the age-old tradition and customs of the society. Through its various components, Oral tradition help proves the existence of the group in remote past. Its sayings, proverbs, and folktales etc. give meaning to the customs and traditions they follow even at the present-day situation and give a unique identity to the particular group. Along with these, the oral tradition also keeps the continuity of the ideology related to the ways of life people follow, their socio-cultural practices, their beliefs systems, and their world views.

By establishing the community in concern in its mythical past, oral tradition creates a cosmology of its own linking its subjects to the universe, nature and the earth as a whole and to a particular locality and its physical environment and natural happenings. The oral traditions also give significant directions towards work role, responsibilities, morale and ideology to be followed by the people of that particular group, sometimes in gender-specific ideologies. It also describes the usual life situation of each gender as a social actor at their different stages of life course along with the general ideas on the social and economic life of people as a whole.

If oral stories take us inside a local culture, they also point outward to other cultures; although their contents may not be historically accurate, as linguistic texts they may provide evidence of historical connections between cultures, and the values they contain may suggest similarities between those cultures.

Oral tradition can be seen as a two-way process in the social reality of a group. While oral tradition can be seen as the unwritten encyclopedia of cultural activities of people living within its ambit, it can also be seen as the domain of direction as for how people should work or act in a given situation. It provides both normative and empirical base for observation and understanding a society.

Discourse on Folklore

Folklore has been recognized as a major component of oral tradition in every human society as it is transmitted from generation to generation orally. If at all they have been written down, they have been always expressed through oral performance only. Dorson (1982) writes that the term 'folklore' emerged in an early 19th century when the antiquaries in London and Philologists in Germany began some intensive studies about the life of lower

classes. In 1846, William John Thomas, an English antiquary, set forth the term 'folklore' in the place of the contemporary phrase 'popular antiquary'. The term gained popularity with its wide scope of study areas, but not without confusions. Wendy Reich (1971) defines folklore as a patterned verbal expression which includes verbalized beliefs, besides myths, songs, stories, and legends, as repeated and shared by all the members of the society. Dorson (1959) and others' statement imply that folklore cannot be folklore until it has been in the oral tradition for quite some time. Reich (1971) puts emphasis on shared verbalization and says that folklore is transmitted through the culture, largely by word of mouth until it becomes a part of the belief system of that particular culture.

Lindgren (1939) identifies four main trends or schools of thoughts concerning folklore study – the comparative, the national, the anthropological and the psychological. Among these schools of thought, the Anthropological theory of folklore could attract a few of coveted anthropologists like Franz Boas and his students like Ruth Benedict who was chiefly responsible for assigning folklore an influential role in studies of non-literate cultures. Boas formulated the proposition that the corpus of traditional tales in a culture mirrors the traits of the material culture. The tales comprise ethnography and provide valuable clues to vanished elements of the tribal history. Boas (1891) also substantiated that tales and tale-incidents are transmitted through diffusion from tribes to contiguous tribes at points of culture contact. Ruth Benedict (1935) opines that tales constitute a fantasy world, constructed from the cultural reality. Jacobs (1959) and Herskovitz (1958) stressed that one should furnish considerable additional information about the 'givens' of the culture, cosmology, social arrangements, economic habits, linguistic structure, and value system, so alien to the reader, from constant reference points within the tale.

Theories of Folklore

As a result of constant endeavour of folklorists, classicists and other social scientists, several theoretical perspectives of looking at folklore and folklife have emerged over a period of time. Some of the dominant theories relevant to this discussion have been placed as follows:

Historical Reconstruction Theory

The proponents of this theory advocate that folklore and Folklife narratives can be used to recapture vanished historical period of the certain group of people or nation etc. in the event of scarcity of other evidence. The proponents of this theory hold that historical reconstruction is possible because it is possible to separate layers of folk traditions deposited by different races successively settling and conquering on the same terrain.

Ideological Theory

The scholars of this school of thought searched for the soul of the people revealed in the native dialects, the folktales and folksongs carried in those dialects, the literature developing the themes of the folklore, and the history glorifying the deeds of national heroes. In its extreme form, it became entwined with political ideology and virulent nationalism especially in Nazi Germany and Soviet Russia. In Germany, Hanns Naumann (1922) brought out '*Grundzuge der Deutschen Volkskunde*' through which he held the view that folklore originated among intelligentsia (*oberschicht*) and tricked down on the peasantry (*unterschicht*). On this basis, the Nationalist Government of Hitler came out as a national state which made political capital of folklore studies. In this process the Nazi concept of Volk (nation) under the term 'Herrenvolk' was projected through a massive literature of folklore in the 1930s, a mystical bond of blood and tongue, culture and tradition were created and publicized to unite different Volks.

Just opposite things happened in Soviet Russia where folklore was used as a powerful component to advance communism. But as the communism was primarily based on the support of mass peasantry and factory workers in Russia, the very ideology was reversed here, and it was propagated that folklore originated as the creative expression of the working classes. Pressurized by state interest, the folklorists of Russia propounded that:

- Folklore is an echo of the past, but at the same time, it is also the vigorous voices of the present.
- Folklore has been and continues to be, a reflection and a weapon of class conflict.

In Russia, folklore was a shared domain of the farm and factory workers and the ideas expressed through folklore were of their own, rather being presented by a few intellectual entities. Lenin declared that folklore must be considered from the 'socio-political points of view', as an aid to understanding the 'hopes and expectations' of working masses in the past. For obvious reason, the older schools of folklore were designated as Slavophiles[1], romantics, and spokesmen for 'Official Nationalism'.

Functional Theory

Through an analytical approach into the role played by folklore in a given culture, there emerged the Functional theory in folklore studies. American anthropologist Franz Boas maintained that tribal narratives mirrored the ethnography of the culture. William Bascom (1954) holds that in folklore, proverbs help settle legal decisions, riddles sharpen wits, myth violates conduct, and satirical songs release pent-up hostilities. Ethnographic examples

can illustrate the cultural functioning of different folklore genres. Validation of beliefs, conduct, and ritual is another function performed by the tribal folklore, particularly by the myth narratives. In Europe, even more, than in America, the functional theory has received strong support from the new generation of folklorists. The ethnologists have filled the gap between anthropologists and folklorists. Functionalism can be applied to material culture as well as to oral literature.

Anthropologist's Interest in Folklore

Folklore is studied in anthropology because it is a part of the culture. It is a part of men's learned traditions and customs, a part of their social heritage. It can be analyzed in the same way as other customs and traditions, in terms of form and function, or of interrelations with other aspects of culture. It presents the same problems of growth and change and is subject to the same processes of diffusion, invention, acceptance or rejection, and integration. It can be used, like other aspects of culture, for studies of these processes or those of acculturation, patterning, the relation between culture and the environment, or between culture and personality.

It can be assumed that many folktales or proverbs, like many other inventions, were rejected because they either did not fill a recognized or subconscious need or because they were incompatible with the accepted patterns and traditions of folklore or of culture as a whole. If they were accepted, they depended on retelling, in the same way, that all cultural traits in a non-literate society depend upon restatement and re-enactment. An element of material culture, such as a hoe or bow or mask, has, of course, a certain independent existence once it has been created, but for the craft itself to continue these items must be made again and again. The nonmaterial elements of culture, however, are entirely comparable in this respect to folktales or proverbs; rituals must be performed, beliefs and attitudes must be expressed, kinship terms must be used, and the privileges and obligations of kinship must be exercised. In the course of this retelling or redoing, change occurs each time new variations are introduced, and again these innovations are subject to acceptance or rejection. As this process continues, each new invention is adapted gradually to the needs of the society and to the pre-existing culture patterns, which may themselves be modified somewhat to conform to the new invention.

Finally, anthropologists are becoming increasingly concerned with the functions of folklore-what it does for the people who tell it. In addition to the obvious function of entertainment or amusement, folklore serves to sanction the established beliefs, attitudes, and institutions, both sacred and secular, and it plays a vital role in education in non-literate societies. It is not

possible to present an adequate analysis of this problem here or even a discussion of the very suggestive data bearing on it which have been accumulated from many different parts of the world. But, in addition to its role in transmitting culture from one generation to another, and to providing ready rationalizations when beliefs or attitudes are called into question, folklore is used in some societies to apply social pressure to those who would deviate from the accepted norms. Moreover, even the function of amusement cannot be accepted today as a complete answer, for it is apparent that beneath a good deal of humor lies a deeper meaning, and that folklore serves as a psychological escape from many repressions, not only sexual, which society imposes upon the individual.

Situating Tribal People in Space and Time Through Folklore

It has been discussed elsewhere in this chapter that oral tradition indicates various aspects of the social and cultural life of people in a society. The importance of folklore in a society as a whole is immense. Folklore in the form of mythology, hymns, tenets etc., provides a unique identity to a particular society or group of people. For instance, in every society, both tribal and non-tribal, there is the myth of the origin of the universe, the natural objects, the earth, and its surroundings. The creation of life and appearance of human beings as the progenitor of that particular social group have been the universal phenomena. Such stories sometimes help the society concerned to assimilate with the significant others, and contrarily, most often, it helps a social entity to draw a distinction from the significant others and also to establish its existence in the space and time. Even the migration history of various population groups has been depicted in folklore current in their socio-cultural domains.

If we look at these folk narratives and folklore, it becomes evident that it helps people establish an undeniable link between place/land and people, air and water and also a continuous existence in past and present. We can also see that when such folklore and folk narratives are more intimately related to those places of living, the claim of the people to be the son of the soil becomes more emphatic. Besides, the narratives on origin, the folklore also link the supernatural entities to the surroundings of the concerned population group which makes their existence more evident in space and time.

Khasi Cosmology and Khasi Tribes in Space and Time

We can draw the instances of tribal people from northeast to locate them in their cosmology, created and re-created. For instance, the Khasi cosmology is very much grounded in their space and time, their natural entities like hills and forest, rivers, land, and waterfalls. The Khasi mythology

speaks of the supreme god in heaven U-Blei who created the guardian spirit of the earth, Ramew, a female figure, while her husband Basa was assigned as patron god for Khasi villages. Five children of Ramew were Ka Sngi (the sun goddess), U Bnai (the moon god) and three daughters who represent water, wind, and fire. These children needed a guide or controller to control their power. But all the guides sent by the supreme god failed to do their duties. So, the sixteen clans living in the heaven discussed the situation down on the earth and the supreme god directed seven of these clans to come down to the earth to till land populate and govern the creatures called as Hynnewtrep — the seven huts. It is believed that these seven clans are now recognized as Khynriam, Pnar, Bhoi, War, Maram, Lyngngam and Diko. God ordered them to adhere to the three principles of life

(i) *ka Tip Briew Tip Blei* (secure in the knowledge of Man and God),
(ii) *Ka Tip Kur Tip Kha* (secure in the knowledge of one's maternal relations),
(iii) *Ka kamaiia ka H*ok (secure in the knowledge of one's paternal relations).

Over a period of time men on earth got tired of following god's dictation and started their own ways of life. They began to cheat, to swindle, to steal, and even to kill to fulfill their evil desire. Annoyed with men's responses, god blocked the way back to heaven by cutting down the ladder, a tree called 'Lam Sohpet Bleng'. They identify the mountain where the seven clans landed on earth as the Shillong Mountain. This mythology clearly shows how the Khasis perceive themselves as the original inhabitant on the land where they live and a clear connection and continuity right from creator to the created. This reveals their existence in space and time throughout human history.

It is very important to note here that as the Khasi mythology has a direct relation between heaven and earth (the place where they live); their other mythologies are also related to their surroundings. This may be a reason for which despite the spread of Christianity, the Khasi could retain most of the core components of their cultural life, beliefs, and practices. Another interesting aspect of the mythology is the demarcation of geographical limits and a clear indication of clans who came down to the earth. This explains the biological and cultural peculiarity of the Khasis, much separate from its surrounding communities — tribes as well as non-tribes.

Nyishi Cosmology and their Existence in Space and Time

When we look into the mythology related to the Nyishis of Arunachal Pradesh, we find that they have a very fragmented history of origin. They have no definite place of origin in their mythology. They also have no definite supreme god and a place called heaven. Their mythology, rather, is full of

description on procreation and genealogical record traced down to Abo-Tani, the progenitor of and the first human being on the earth. The Nyishis also have no definite natural entity like hills, rivers etc to which a specific mythology is attached to. Rather, their cosmology is not confined to any specific geographical locality. Those are general beliefs about the creation of earth, nature, and creature.

The Nyishi mythology talks of various evil spirits, no rule of law and very scanty evidence of social customs related to mythological accounts. Such evidence indicates a rather unorganized and lawless society among the Nyishis and the myths being created with their limited ideas of natural and supernatural relations. Their description reveals that the people were shrouded with physical insecurity, uncertain future and rampant loss of life due to difficult terrain and rapid conflict and raids. There are also some amounts of mythological account on their migration from a place different from the present-day habitat. If we look at the record of traditional beliefs and practices, one can find that those are heavily influenced by the idea of the need to satisfy the supernatural beings which are mostly malevolent to human beings. There is no denying to the fact that the difficult and volatile geographical location compelled them to create such a cultural life where the uncertainty of life always persists. The difficult terrains also prevented these people to interact between villages scattered in different hills for which they were most probably unable to develop a universal and more rational cosmology. No mention of geographical limit in mythology also supports the idea that the Nyishis migrated from a different place.

Further, the Nyishi mythology and folklore have been absolutely verbal and transmitted from generation to generation through socially recognized dignitaries — definitely not through common people. This is also another reason why the spirituality and religiosity did not penetrate the common people as we observe in various plains tribes or organized tribe like Khasis of Meghalaya.

Monpa Cosmology and their Existence in Space and Time

Contrary to such rich cultural heritage of tribes, the Monpas of Arunachal Pradesh does not have any traceable mythology about their origin. Rather, their migration history is somewhat known to us. The Monpas migrated from Tibet and they follows Tibetan Buddhism. All of their beliefs and practices are in accordance with Buddhist school of thought. Perhaps this has been the reason for which Monpas have lost their traditional history of the origin and their traditional mythology. It is believed that Monpas accepted Buddhism in 17th century AD. The traditional customs of Monpa thus got dominated by Buddhist ideology for which they no longer remember or perceive it.

Paite Cosmology and their Existence in Space and Time

Paite, a hills tribe of Manipur has been Christianized extensively at present. But the pre-Christian mythology talks of their beliefs about gods and goddesses, the spirit world and people's relation to them. Further, their various terminologies and narratives talk of their migration from a different place. The high god of pre-Christian Paite was known as Pasian or Pethian followed by Lungzai, next to his rank. Pasian is believed to be the creator of heaven, earth and everything in them. These two gods are still found relevance in certain family level rituals. These high gods are now equated with universal Christian god.

The institution of family has a very distinct place in Paite social life. The presence and function of 'Indongta', the family council, has been continuing even in Christianized Paite society. Paite mythology talks about the family goddess called 'Pusa' — she was the provider and caretaker of the family.

The pre-Christian high god of Paite has been equated with Hebrew Yahweh. The other name the Paites ascribe to god is Kouzi:n – the unseen, strong and powerful at will, good and benevolent at will and he could be communicated by the incantation of *dawi: la*. This god did not live in underworld called *misi-khua*. He was just the same as the *Melchizedek* of the Old Testament of the Bible.

It can be seen that post-Christian Paite society has discarded the major chunk of their traditional beliefs and practices related to religious aspects and mythology of origin and creation. Rather, their primary concern of customs and traditions remained more of political in nature. Having migrated from another place the people could hardly any significant imprints which might relate them to the natural and supernatural beings of their immediate surroundings.

Mishing Cosmology and their Existence in Space and Time

Among the plains tribes of Assam, the Mishings are the second largest tribal groups after the Bodos. Mishings have their own language and some unique cultural components. It is believed that the Mishings, who are also known as Miri, have been an offshoot of Hill Miri tribe presently resides in Hills of Arunachal Pradesh.

There are folklore and folk narratives which indicate that they came to the plains to Assam from the Hills of Arunachal Pradesh a few centuries back from now. Their cosmology hardly relates them to their surroundings; rather, to some extent, their progenitor is similar to that of Nyishis — the Abo-Tani. The myth of the creation of Mishing does not indicates any geographical locality. Their Aa: bang songs talk of the creation of the universe, the sky, the

water, the land etc. These folklores rather indicate how Mishing people survived, how they could learn to grow crops etc. A lot of the Aa: bang tenets talk about the spirit that lives in forest and hills. They hardly talk about rivers and plains. Though they have their own language, they lack terminology for a lot of the material implements they use on day to day life — like implements used in cultivation, materials used in construction house, dresses they use to wear etc. Rather, they use the dominant Assamese terms to denote those implements. This clearly suggests that those implements were not used by the Mishing before they came down to the plains of Assam. This also proves that they have migrated to plains of Assam at a later period and accepted the socio-economic life of the dominant plains people to a great extent. As they migrated from hills and used to spread to different places in Assam plains, they could hardly leave an evidence of a relationship between their cosmology, language (terminology) and natural entities surrounding them – like a river, lack, hills etc. Not a single folk narrative talks of any place where they reside at present.

Sonowal Kachari Cosmology and their Existence in Space and Time

Contrary to such disconnection between culture and surroundings, another plains tribe of Assam, the Sonowal Kacharis shows a great deal of relationship between their religion, culture and their surroundings. Sonowal Kacharis have a high god called Bathow. The New Year begins with the ritual performed to serve the Bathow. Though there is no extensive mythology related to the origin of the Sonowal Kacharis, there is a definite link between heaven and earth (human beings) created through the folklore of the Sonowal Kacharis called the Haidang geet. It is a widely accepted idea that the Sonowal Kacharis lost their own dialect over a period of time due to extensive assimilation with Assamese people in historical past. But their existence in their locality can be ascertained by the names of rivers, as most of the rivers are named starting with the letter 'Di' —— meaning water bodies in Kachari dialect. Thus, we come across numerous of rivers like Dihing, Dichang, Diband, Dikhow, Dimow, Digaru, Dibru, Dikrong and many more. It is believed that in remote past, all Kacharis were a single community having twelve clans. In due course of time, each of these clans started identifying themselves as a separate tribe, to name a few— Bodo, Sonowal, Tiwa, Rabha, Hajong etc.

Folklore like Haidang geet of Sonowal Kacharis also talks about their history and how and why they had to leave their homeland Hemali or Halali — a place referred to a place in and around Sadiya, the easternmost part of Assam. there are numerous cultural components and beliefs and practices among Sonowal Kacharis that indicate how directly these people have been related to the land they live in and their existence in space and time. For instance, the activities and celebrations related to cattle one day before the

spring festival Bihu is one of the great markers of the relation between dominant economic activities and culture. *Huchari*, another important component of Bihu festival is said to be originated among the Kachari community in Assam which has been now universalized in the state as a national festival of the Assamese community.

The delineation made above clearly suggest how oral tradition and folklore are indicative of past and present of a particular community in space and time. It also shows that such oral tradition shapes and is chapped by the changes that take place in the social and physical surrounding of the community concerned.

Gender and Folklore

The role of folklore is also very important in defining and shaping the social life of people of a particular society. While through folklore people in a society express their righteousness, duties, and commitments etc., it also guides society by setting certain norms. For the purpose of this chapter, we will put more emphasis on gender aspect of folklore and try to show how men's and women's lives, especially about their normative roles and behaviours expected of them by the society is depicted.

Folklore and Khasi Women's Life

In Khasi society, women are seen as the creator of family and the clan and bearer of the culture. Thus, the behaviour of women in society is perceived as very important. Women are advised to be obedient and respectful to elders, not to argue with, disobey or talk back to elders, not to laugh too much, not to say bad words, mingling with boys too much, not to stay out late and treating guests properly etc.

Traditional Khasi domain is full of such instructions through proverbs and folklore. For instance, one of such proverbs says: (*Ko kyntheiha-bakreni'anoi'ano,……U kamonkadiang un thuhkhanaei;)*

'Lady when you converse with anyone, do not smile displaying your teeth. As long as you don't know the person, excessive laughter you should suppress, for it will cheapen your womanliness.'

Another interesting proverb teaches one, especially womenfolk, how to sit and behave while eating: (Haba bamja wat……*miawtuhjatuhdohkha*)

'Sitting gesture while eating should be respectful. Sitting outstretched or a leg apart is considered as being in bad taste and a misdemeanor. If anyone sits in that way they are compared to laying a trap for the cat.'

Another such tenet says:

'Do not take or give anything from behind
Because it is like the ghost's work who had no last rites
Don't take or give anything between your fingers

Or you may get twins (one boy one girl: this is seen as very bad luck).'

The literary meaning of one such tenet is as follows:

'Shade words of shame concealed them,
Even if they ring true do not pronounce;
Make not a habit of gossip mongering,
For this takes root inauspiciousness
Departs from sulky ways and actions
Lest dignity is weakened.'

Such tenets also talk about the social behaviour of people in day to day interaction. For instance, one of such tenets says:

'Whenever elders visiting one's home, their bags shouldn't be empty while returning. The host should fill them with betel nut and leaves. The host will be blessed and praised and rewarded.'

Again, the quality of women in the societal domain is mostly negated by male chauvinism. This is reflected in the following proverb:

'la ki kynthei wat ai huspaijyndei,

. . . .

Ba kin die tad noh la kajing tip sngi.

This can be translated as follows:
Be reserved with liberties to women
For worldly wise, they can never become
The womanly grace will degenerate.
For they will unreasonably argue and castigate;
They won't dwell on the seriousness of life.
They won't know what is right and what is wrong;
It is a curse to give them too much liberty
They may want to sell their dignity.

That a woman must be controlled or guided by men and that without a control or guidance, women are like kites with broken threads, is expressed by the proverb '*Ka Phok tkut lot poh* (in Nongtalang dialect). It indicates that like a kite with broken thread, a woman without control or guidance is aimless and cannot perform desired roles.

In traditional Khasi domain, some of the gender roles are very much segregated and the infringement is not expected. The proverb *'Kynih ka 'iarkyntheiushynrang u khapylleng'* says that 'the hen crows while the rooster lays an egg.' This is an act of universal truth and nature which cannot be accepted. Likewise, there are certain roles to be performed only by men, and the alternate way is not possible. Khasi tenets *'habakynihka'iarkynthei la jot ka pyrthei,'* indicates that when the hen starts crowing, the world is heading for disaster. The crowing of the rooster is a very significantly fixed symbol which connotes activities associated exclusively with males. Of these, participation in governance is a primary example. Women are debarred from participating in the highly traditional system of governance such as *Ka Dorbar Hima, Ka Dorbar Raid,* and *Ka Dorbar Shnong.* These are different councils governing the corporate life of the Khasis. In fact, there is a belief that only those with mustache are allowed to participate in the meeting of these councils.

In a traditional domain, women are also not encouraged to speak about own qualities or speak too much. Such behaviour of women is seen as an indication of her being actually lack of qualities. The proverb *'U Phiang ubathylli u sawa jam'* says that the empty bronze pot (called *Phiang,* which is kept in Khasi kitchen*)* sounds the loudest. Important to note here that in most of these cases of proverbs and tenets, the Khasi society is rich with supported folktales and mythologies which are very appealing and meaningful.

Khasis perceive that the father brings along with him the seed critical for the genesis of life and continuity of the family and the clan. He also brings bread and luck – *ka kamaikajih bad ka lok ka rwiang*– to sustain the family. Khasi saying – *'u kpa u ba ai ia ka long rynieng; u ba kit ia ka khia ka shan'* reveals that the father not only gives structure and form but also bears the heat and burden of the day to provide for the needs of his children.

There are strong social indicators which show that women are held to be inferior to men. There are numbers of gendered terms and phrases in Khasi vocabulary which symbolize the unequal power relations between males and the females. The most widely used phrase talks about the superior male power over female – *u rangbah khaddar bor; ka kyntheisnibor* - meaning a man has 12 units of power/ energy; a woman has only one unit. Likewise, to express the superior physiological and intellectual power of men over women they say – *ka kynthei; ka khynnah,* meaning the woman, the children, thus analogically equates women with children.

Men in the Khasi family/society have a respectable position as the father in their wife's house and as uncles in their sister's house. An adage which reflects this finds a place in *Ki Jingsneng Tymmen says*

'Father the provider,

Maternal uncle the ceremony keeper.'

The traditional Khasi proverb *'ka nongpah ka nongphon'* says that a woman is 'a charmer as well as a schemer' because she attracts a man by offering something interesting (here the relationship) away from their relatives and kin – either using sexuality or charm. Further, the Khasi mythology of the origin talks about the Sun, Water, Wind, and Fire as the daughters of Ramew – the guardian spirit of the earth and she prayed *U Blei* – the high god that there should be someone to give direction and control the powers of her great powerful daughters. Till this part of the legend indicates that female figures have been assigned with a relentless commitment to serving others and while the elder daughters (water and wind) could go as they wish, the youngest one (fire) had to accept the burden of the family and custom. Furthermore, the story also reminds the fact the power and strength of females must be controlled and guided by male figures through one or the other identity.

Mishing Women as Depicted in Folklore

Mishing society has a very limited number of proverbs that speak of women's normative character, guidelines for women's normative behaviour etc. These are known as *Luchok* among the Mishing.

Mishing people question whether a lake or the fish is preferable with the help of the proverb —*'Ongam maduneipatangemmadu-nei?'* This means that people should opt for lack, instead of for a fish. Fishes may not be available all through. If the lake is there, fish can be procured at any time in future. Here a fish is compared to a girl and the lake as compared to a relationship with families from which one can get a girl for marriage if not now, later.

That the presence of a woman in the house is indispensable and without her direction nothing remains perfect is indicated by the following proverb:

'Alo kamaan Oyinge ne-ng Kama-n Okume'

It says that if one does not put salt in a nicely prepared spicy food one cannot get a proper taste of it. Likewise, despite the meticulous decoration of a house nothing looks good if the woman of the house is not there.

Similarly, the code of conduct for a widow in Mishing society says that she is not expected to wear fashionable attire lest her morale gets into trouble. The proverb 'Lo: tung*donyc kate: tere, timbosenamcsenvgsekore*' says that:

the heat exerted by the Sun appearing in the afternoon after a shower is

very uncomfortable. Likewise, there is something wrong in her morale if a widow dresses up with fashionable attire.

In the same line, there is some restriction in dealing with widow among the Mishing society. The saying *'Lo-bo Tapiyem buka-yoka, Timbone-ngemngenka-yoka'* warn people that

one should not pull Tapi grass bare hand as its sharp and serrated leaf blade may cut one's hands. Likewise, one should not tease or mingle with a widow, for fun sake also, for this may invite bad allegation.

A style frenzy woman is never appreciated in traditional Mishing society. It is believed that such woman spends her time in her makeup only instead of putting her attention towards household chores. The proverb *'Kagori isingemnayoka, Sene yamnemlayoka'* says that

dry reeds should not be used as fuel to cook food because it burns-up very quickly and food remains uncooked. Likewise, one should not marry a stylish girl as she spends lots of time dressing up leaving her duties undone.

The patriarchal and male-centric control over women in most aspects of life can be found in the following saying:

'Asi bitkmabitkampe
Mala gidungerali'

It says that

erali, a straw-like weed grown in water-logged areas, turns its direction the way water flows. This means that women can hardly go against the wish of the male members of her family, parents, and husband etc. She abides by their decision at the final count.

Men are never expected to abide by the will or advise of women. The proverb *'Neng Agom Tatnede, Longemsin Kabegmang'* says that a man who follows advice or will of a woman is worse than a blind man who cannot see anything in broad daylight. The normative ways of assessing the good or bad quality of a woman are often expressed with the help of proverb the meaning of which is

'A woman is a good cook if she can peel the bark of a tender bottle guard. Likewise, a woman is bad (a female monkey) who breaks her home once it was founded with the utmost endeavor.'

That the inner content of a girl is the worth, not the material wealth, is frequently expressed by Mishing people as follows:

'Lal sangmemindayok......Opanomme (jireni) aroti'

This says that one should not dislike a cup of black tea because only it can meet one's thirst. Likewise, one should not look down upon a poor girl, because she is the one who can manage the life of a man properly.

Paite Women as Depicted in Folklore

The Paites of Manipur have lost a lot of their proverbs as their society has undergone changes under the Christian ideology. Nevertheless, there are some proverbs and sayings which indicate how these are influential in their life. For instance, the following folklore indicates the perception and expectation people have while giving a daughter in marriage:

'Dear daughter, whom I sent off with heart's contentment,
Go and spread your clothes over your spouse;
Be content with your spouse,
And bear a good number of children.'

The lullabies sung by the mother or caretaker of a Paite child depict the traditional lifeways of Paite people as follows:

Dear baby; may you grow up speedily,
Like the luxuriant growth of yonder lu:idawug stalk;
And when you have thus grown up,
You are a great help to your mother and father, dear.

There is another lullaby as follows:

'Mothers and fathers of others have come home,
What are our mother and father doing?
They are doing nothing
But making axes and hoes.
What are axes and hoes for?
They are to make upper and lower walls of the enclosure.
What are upper and lower walls of the enclosure for?
They are to enclose Mithun cows and Mithun bulls.
What are Mithun cows and Mithun bulls for?
They are to buy new brides and old brides with.
What are new brides and old brides for?
They are to collect vegetables and fruits.
What are vegetables and fruits for?
They are to feed sows and hogs with.
What are sows and hogs for?
They are to give us fat for our hair

The proverb *Numei lehbaalchii* symbolically indicates that as yams need a suitable soil to grow, a good woman is needed to give birth to a good child. Thus, when the primary aim of a marriage is to procreate and give birth to children and bring them up well, a woman must learn the proper quality of a woman that is the expected gender roles as a woman. Thus, it remains an important learning aspect of a woman, and the social agents like the mother and relatives of the woman try to infuse gender appropriate qualities to the person concerned.

Women are frequently advised by the saying *'Nupi veihpeek a nawhei'* to act cautiously in everything she does. Women are also encouraged with moral incentives with the help of certain proverbs. For example, *'Numei suutpom a vaalomlou'* says that women with integrity are always valued in a society. Women are also praised for their indispensable contribution as indicated in Proverbs *'Numei lou in inn kisuanglou'* which literally means that one can't start a household without a woman. Likewise, proverb *'Numei naupaithaltangpai'* says that women bear a child risking all their life.

Paite society has lots of proverbs that indicate nature of gender subordination. Women's subordination is also indicated by the proverb *'Numei khualehsakhikhua' which* means that women do not have a permanent settlement; in other means, women cannot stick to one decision. The society also has a proper reason for social control by means of sanction and punishment as the proverb *'Numei gilosingkhu ah tuak'* says that a wicked woman is always punished. Proverb *'Numei giloekthakna ah thakik'* in the same tune says that a wicked woman is divorced. Again, the proverb *'Numei vakvakthusiazong'* says that a loitering woman is slandered. Putting women in a low light, the proverb *'Numei lehpuansia',* says that women and rugs can always be changed. Further, the proverb *'Numei lungsimkhutlumleh'* says that women change their mind as easily as the flip of a palm.

There are certain words or phrases to denote women who do not conform to expected gender-specific quality by the society. For instance, *'Numei pangpalen'* which means 'a woman who carelessly roam around' or *'Numei nolamawlmoh'* which means 'a woman who is too concerned about her paternal home rather than being concerned about her husband and parents in law'.

Women among Paite are kept out of decision-making domain, especially in village and community matters. More than a positive one, the negative qualities of women are widely described in proverbs among the Paite. For instance, the proverb *'Numei haangsawkhuan a kelbengngamlou,'* though common for both genders, mostly indicates that argumentative and aggressive women are not necessarily courageous. They simply show-up. When required they cannot take proper step or decision. Further, the proverb *'Numei gilou*

in suk pumkuaitan' says in the same light that a wicked woman goes a great length in her wickedness. Indicating the threat from a wicked woman the proverb *'Numei gilomeikuangtaipih'* says that a wicked woman runs with wildfire, indicating that she may create a major problem in family or society at any time. The proverb *'Nupi gilkial bel liansuang, pasalgilkiallomakek'* says that a hungry woman thinks about a day while a hungry man thinks about a year.

Women's disqualification for conflict mitigation and decision making is justified by the proverb *'Nupi gal gen'* which says that woman exaggerates conflict situation and help conflict to increase. Thus, the proverb *'Numei pau leAkpi khuan'* warns people that Woman's words should not be trusted entirely. Also, at the village level, initially women were not given any part or say in the village level decision making processes, they use to consider women's opinion as shallow as Pig's Through (*Numei thuleh Vok kuang dai*). However, today, there are several instances of representation of women in the Tribe level council also.

Nyishi Women's Position as Depicted in Folktales

Nyishi folktales are full of instances of depicting women as subordinate and meant to follow males' command. They indicate that in case the young and women do not obey elders and males, they are likely to land in trouble and invite misfortune to the family and the community as well. All such tales indicate that women's subordination in Nyishi society has been an inherent phenomenon of the society in a traditional setting.

For instance, the story of *Demum Rinke* warns people about the non-compliance of the advice of elders by the younger person. The story talks about two brothers and their younger sister who went to a distant place Nem Nepa to bring salt - *mafualu*, along with the route which was full of danger. While the two brothers got ready to go the sister insisted that she would also go with them. She was discouraged since it was a very tough journey. Rather she was advised to look after their old parents. However, she was obstinate and went with them in spite of their opposition. While coming back with salt, the sister was cautioned not to utter any noise look back whatever might happen. Thus, they were crossing back through that secret place. They almost had crossed when suddenly the younger sister saw a *Mithun*, which actually belonged to her elder brother and its name was Tapungbo. The younger sister forgot the secret direction of her brother and suddenly shouted out, 'Achi there`s our *Mithun*!'. This resulted in the attack of trees and birds on her. The brothers tried all resorts to save her, but they could not defeat the evil powers and had to leave the sister at the mercy of the evil powers. Hearing the news, her old parents also died.

In another story, women are depicted as a cause of misfortune and conflict in the life of men. The story talks about an evil female spirit Dojing Yashing who came to the life of a man living happily in disguise of a beautiful woman. She got married to the brother pretending that she would bring fortune to his life. But after few months of marriage, she started showing her ill intention. She wanted her husband to send out his beloved sister. Finally, she demanded that he should kill her. Ultimately, the brother killed his own sister. The evil spirit took hold of the dead body and ate it up and fled to the jungle. The brother entered the state of deep sorrow when he saw his sister's soul coming back asked him if he was happy after killing her. This story warns Nyishi people not enter in alliance with unknown women.

The horrifying story of the Yash and Achi Pilli talks about the unavoidable role of women in household chores. The story talks about two brothers and their sister who were living together. Once, the brothers proceeded to Nem-Nepa in the search of salt and trade leaving behind their sister at home and instructed her to keep the fire in hearth be lit up throughout day and night in their absence, for the fire could drive away all evil spirits. But, the sister could not comply with her brother's instruction. The fire extinguished and demon Appa Pilli entered her house and killed her and eat her flesh up. The demon collected her bones, dressed her skeleton in her dresses and kept it behind the door. When the brothers came back they found the skeleton of the sister. They could bring her back to life. The demon was killed and its body was roasted and made powder and scattered all over. Nyishi people believe that from the ground flesh of Appa Pilli, the blood-sucking insects like mosquito, dum-dum, and taki etc., came into being.

Nyishi stories are full of instances if the tragic effect of youngsters who did not comply with the advice of the elders. Mostly such stories talk about the ill fate of defying women. The story of Lurum Berge is of no difference. The girl was fond of going out frequently to catch fish, and she used to catch a good quantity of fishes every time. Her parents repeatedly advised her to avoid such huge fishing every day. However, she continued as before. Once she went to a river for fishing and did not return. She got trapped inside a stone. Her parents could find her out, but she could not come out through the hole of the rock. Her parents could provide only a small amount of food to her. Ultimately, she died a slow death. Nyishi people see it as the ultimate fate of women who do not listen to elders.

Proverbs available among the Nyishi indicates expected behaviour of women in their society. The proverb *'Bambu Salloo Langnepeetebea-yardaapagang loa Yartee Nyeegu Bea'* says that women should be like the big rock of ocean and the fruit-bearing tree of the hilltop. Because big rock

gives shelter to water living creature and fruit-bearing tree attract a variety of birds and animals.

Another proverb *'Sane Ranggar Nygam Puding Nyoma - Pakne Hahakya kam Tamsar Nyoma'* says that the irregular shape of female Mithun's horn cannot be put straight and likewise, the woman of bad character cannot be corrected. The selection of a good woman as a wife is crucial in the life of a man and his family. So, Nyishi people indulge in selecting a mate from known families to avert any unwanted problems. The proverb *'Nyokho Pabar Nyingking Mangkang, Bwnw nobar Nyingrang mangkang'* says that one suffers a year for the wrong selection of agriculture plots and suffers whole life for marrying a wrong woman.

Another proverb says that a bird species called 'Tadho' (a local name) has ten varieties. It is difficult to identify the basic physical character they possess. It is beautifully compared with the character of the woman. A woman has many hearts in her heart. You can't predict which heart is working and which is not, till her last breath. Further, it states that the *Mithun* (*Bos frontalis*) who is peaceful in nature and follows the master's command lives a long life. A person (woman) of good nature and eloquence ultimately wins many hearts.

Nyishi people put great emphasis on matrimonial relations owing to the face that such relations remain steady and bring people closer which in turn come forward in the time of need. Clan and marital relations are the real bonds, which the Nyishis mostly needed during the period when frequent raids, inter-village disputes, were very much prevalent. There are several proverbs that put emphasis on marital bond as social security. For instance,*'Doombu Laya bhu ham Changtam Bangcha-Beepu Lakya Bhu ham Sangbhee Bangding'* means that the matrimonial relations are for help and protect the weaker. Another proverb *'Keenu Peetung Lyeek Pechee'* reminds people that those who share the umbilical cord and stomach is considered as nearest one and must share sorrow, suffering, and pleasure. Thus, one should keep matrimonial relation intact. The proverb *'Sangtee Gyeepee - Taku Gyeepee Chegea'* says that the relationship between tree and creeper is inseparable, likewise, marital relations between two person and two families must be unaffected by any internal or external influence.

Nyishi generally believes the underlying motive of having sex (or in other word getting married) is to have children to keep the generation in continuation. The Nyishi proverb *'Deenam meh semiiyia- yonam meh alee'* literally means *'*eats for life and have sex for offspring'. Bearing children is very important for the Nyishi people, and so also the marriage. A small family is not sought among the Nyishis in a traditional setting. The proverb *'Kebung tatung alee sonyio- Nambungpatung Gorra anyio'* says that a short umbilical

cord indicates small family/less offspring and breaking off long house indicates small village.

Superiority of men over women in terms of stability of decision and ideas etc are depicted in the proverb *'Deem pumu w Dungku Nwrme Pumu w Dungku Deebw Perw Sevw, Dene Perw Sewv'* which says that like immovable mountain the male hearts change hardly, and as the courses of rivers changes frequently so are the hearts of female. But the hidden feelings and desires of women are not known to anybody as the proverb *'Dane Hara loo Teera Ranam Nygam Heyea Kapa Dun-Tungpee Hara loo Nyara Ranam Nygam Heyea Kapa Dun'* indicates.

Documentation of Folklore and its Impact

The entry of printing technology in the domain of oral tradition seems to be very late, especially in Northeast India. While customary laws were documented in Mizoram for the first time, the Paite tribal council has brought out its customary laws two years back only. While the tribes of the region have been extensively studied, there oral traditions and folklore have very little been examined under any established theoretical perspectives. Nevertheless, in last decade or so, a lot of publications have come up at the local level about the folklore and oral tradition of various tribal groups. This has opened up a new debate on whether the infringement of print media puts the oral tradition in 'parentheses' making it static and thereby irrelevant for the survival of social life. This question comes up because, by nature oral tradition is dynamic and ever-changing, selective and such selection of components of oral tradition is dependent on the meaningfulness of these components to the immediate surroundings and situations. But once they are written down, there is no scope for adding and rejecting its components and thus it becomes static. Moreover, when written down it may lose its character of being oral and transmitted orally. Another issue is related to the social significance of its performance, mastery over the tenets and the institution of worshipping, narrating and performing etc. the mythological narratives, chanting, the tales etc., have been the property of society. But its authority was always confined to certain individuals or a section of people in the society. Once it is documented, it becomes public, accessible to all whereby such components losses its sanctity and importance along with its performer. Very little has been examined in this line of inquiry so far.

In postcolonial India or elsewhere in the world, the concept of small nationality has sprung up as the smaller and distinct ethnic groups are unable to retain their identity under the framework of the nation-state. The oral tradition with the back-up of folklore becomes the ethnic marker for most of such emergent and resurgent ethnicity in the world. In case of the ethnic

groups of northeast India, this phenomenon is more prominent. Because the primary component of ethnic assertion in the region is related to identity and reconstruction of authority rather than being development oriented, construction and reconstruction of oral traditions remain one of the few crucial ways through which identity can be constructed or enhanced. From plains to hills, we can see a height of such enterprises among the tribes and other ethnic groups.

The ethnopolitics of Khasi in Meghalaya is full of such instances where customs and traditions have been given priority amidst the spread of Christianity to retain pureness and ethnic sentiment intact among these people. In fact, the very existences of these states are too great extent is based on such primordial standpoints. The Sang Khasi movements, the concept of Khasi Pacca, etc., are nothing but the issue of identity enhancement only.

Among the Mishing, we can observe the mobilization and sensitization of common people toward the need for enhancement, universalization, and sensitization of oral tradition for a greater ethnic cohesion. The use of print and audio-visual media was extensively used to spread the ethnic sentiment by propagating the folklore, oral tradition and their performances across the state. The central celebration of Ali-Aye-Lrigang, Dabur etc helped Mishing people come together irrespective of locality, status etc. The revival and modernization of folklore like *Oinitam* etc. gave a new life to aesthetic and cultural life of the people. Nevertheless, the political will of some leaders enhanced such endeavour to such an extent that the Mishing as an ethnic group became a politically determinant factor in parliamentary politics, especially in the northern bank of the Brahmaputra in upper Assam. They could get their autonomous council which they are trying to upgrade to Sixth Schedule provision of the Constitution of India.

The Sonowal Kacharis who have been converted to Vaishnavism to a great extent started its enterprise of revivalism in the year 1985 by researching its clan and lineage trees. Subsequently, some of the leaders also tried to revive their almost forgotten high god Bathow over and above the Vaishnavism. The folklore like Huchari and Haidang geet etc. were revived and researched. Frequent meetings, discussions etc., could enhance the Sonowal Kachari ethnicity to a great extent. In 1995, the Sonowal Kacharis politically got their own autonomous council, holidays declared for Bathow puja etc.

There have been constant activities among the Nyishis and Apatanis of Arunachal Pradesh to revive the traditional culture and customs by popularizing and making public and accessible the folklore, myths and stories recreating them suitable to be accepted by the present generation. They have

a tough struggle to popularize and contain their own tradition in the face of the increased hold of Christianity among them in recent years.

Technology and Folklore

As the last issue, I would like to mention the fate of the content of various folklore current in the societies due to infringement of radical change in transport and communication, telecommunication network, internet and visual media etc. There is folklore in every society which depicts the surroundings as a static entity and thus the content of folklore gets its currency. But something cannot be continued in the fast-changing world. This very aspect of oral tradition and folklore is an area of concern and a new domain of anthropological study. I will conclude it with one example.

One of the very popular Bihu songs says that the boy will whistle in front of the girl's house and she will come out silently and secretly without the consent of her family to enjoy Bihu with the boy – her lover. Some lamenting songs as well as Bihu, very popular among the Deori tribe of Assam says as follows:

> *The crow flying over the roof of my house gave me the news that my mother is very ill ... she is unable to get up from her sick bed; she is not eating and drinking. The married daughter laments that she is unable to go and attend her mother at this time of distress. She is also not getting proper news from her mother.*

In one more such instance, the married daughter pleads the dove sitting on the roof of her house to carry the message ....

> *that she is in utter distress, the dirt of her body has become very rough, she has got lice in her clothes ..... all these because she does not get time to take care of herself (she is near her mother to get help).*

A similar song says:

> *A dove is cooing on the rooftop of her house, definitely, something unfortunate has happened at her parental home. She further says ...... my poor mother, I told you not to send me to a distant place in marriage. Now, if you send me anything, it dries up on the way to me and the rope tied on the packet torn apart before it reaches me..... go dove, go, carry the message to my mother that I tie a lot of gifts for her collecting from the garden I raise, ... but there is no one to carry them to you for it is a faraway place... with utter disgrace, I throw the items on the floor of my kitchen and I weep and weep.*

Now if we see the possibility of the currency of such emotional and very popular as well as meaningful folklore, we get a negative picture. The

improved transportation facility, access to a mobile phone even in the remotest areas made all such songs irrelevant because the women of the present generation hardly find any meaning or relevance to it. Therefore, these bound to be an unusable repository in the name of folklore and oral tradition. Thus, it becomes very important to have a discourse on such issues while researching on oral tradition.

Note

1. Slavophilism, as an intellectual movement, was developed in the 19th-century Russia. The Slavophiles were determined to protect what they believed were unique Russian traditions and culture. In doing so, they rejected individualism. The role of the Orthodox Church was seen by them as more significant than the role of the state. Socialism was opposed by Slavophiles as an alien thought, and Russian mysticism was preferred over 'Western rationalism'. Rural life was praised by the movement, opposing industrialization as well as urban development, while protection of the 'mir' was seen as an important measure to prevent the growth of the working class.

References

Bascom, WR 1954, 'Four functions of folklore', *The Journal of American Folklore*,vol.67, no. 266, pp. 333-349.

Benedict, RF 1935, *Zuni mythology* (2 vols.), Columbia University Contributions to Anthropology 21. Abridged in Mead, Margaret, 1959, 'An anthropologist at work: writings of Ruth Benedict'. 226-Boston: Houghton, Mifflin.

Boas, F 1891, 'Disseminating of tales among the natives of North America', *Journal of American folklore*, vol. 4, pp. 13-20.

Dorson,RM 1982,*Folklore,andfolklife: an introduction*,University of Chicago Press, Chicago.

Dorson,RM1959,*American folklore*, The University of Chicago Press, Chicago.

Henige, D 1988, 'Oral, but oral what? the nomenclatures of orality and their implications', *Oral Tradition*, vol. 3, no. 1-2, pp. 229-238.

Herskovitz, MJ 1958, 'Sibling rivalry, the Oedipus complex, and myth', *Journal of American Folklore*, 71 1-15 Abridged in Dahomean narrative, 85-95, as 'Sibling rivalry and the Oedipus theorem'.

Jacobs, M 1959, *The content and style of an oral literature. Clackamas Chinook myths and tales,* University of Chicago Press, Chicago.

Ki-Zerbo, J 1990, 'Methodology and African prehistory', UNESCO International Scientific Committee for the Drafting of a General History of Africa, James Currey Publishers.

Naumann, H 1929 (1922),*Grundzfige der Deutschen Volkskunde*, Quelle and Meyer, Leipzig.

Reich, W 1971, 'The uses of folklore in revitalization movements', *Folklore*, vol. 82, pp. 233-244.

Vansina, J 1985, *Oral tradition as history*, James Currey Publishers, London.

Chapter - 3

Tribal Customary Laws and Rights of Women in Northeast India

— ***Rajendra Prasad Athparia***

Tribal Customary Laws in Northeast India

Customary law plays an integral role in tribal identity and has given some basic concepts and issues which revolves around them. These concepts and issues are important to understand the dynamics of their interface with modernity and its impact on women's status.

However, the encounter with the 'modern' formal law is not uniform throughout the Northeast. Most tribes of the region live according to their customary law but only a few have been constitutionally recognized. In 1963 the 13th Amendment to the Constitution recognized the customary laws of Nagaland through Article 371A. The 53rd amendment of 1986 recognized those of Mizoram through Article 371G. This recognition includes laws governing marriage, divorce, inheritance and other social and cultural practices and rights like community ownership. No Act of the Union Parliament concerning the religious or social practices, procedures, administration of justice involving their customary law and ownership and transfer of land and resources applies to them unless their legislative assemblies agree to it (Fernandes and Bharali, 2008).

In order to understand their gender dimensions, we shall define customary laws, take a look at the role, tradition and the constitution assign to them and study the reality in each state of all the tribes. We shall include a big and diverse enough number to make it representative of the region. It will lay the foundation of a good understanding of women's right in the customary laws (Fernandes et al., 2006: 23).

Impact of Modernisation on Tribal Customary Law in Northeast India

Regarding the impact of the customary law on modernism, Fernandes and Bharali have stated that:

> 'The interface of the customary law with the formal systems has to be situated in the context of an egalitarian society that also had seeds of inequality. Some inequalities such as women's subordinate status have been modernized. Among the forces influencing these changes are the individual-based formal laws, administrative systems, education, and religion. Most changes began in the colonial age. For example, the office of the village leader or *gaonburah* created two centers of power since he is rarely the same as the traditional chief. Its other examples are colonization and appropriation of their common lands and forests through military campaigns or legal fictions, and their eviction from their territories. These changes are at times accelerated by the rapid integration of their economies with the national and global markets especially today in the age of globalization. This rapid integration continues to expose them to economic exploitation because they are either excluded from the processes of trade and governance or are marginal actors in them' (Fernandes and Bharali, 2009:98)

In an individual's life, right from birth till death, are based on some customs which is observed faithfully without conscious effort. Some customary rules are being followed without being enforced by an outside authority. These are self-imposed ones. Sometimes it goes undergo modifications of change in response to the emergent needs of the changed socio-economic and ritual cultural scenario (Goswami, 1986: 5).

For example, in Garo matrilineal society, men do not own or inherit the ancestral property though he is the head of the family as according to their customary laws. Usually, women inherit it but with the change of time, they (men) to inherit especially the one who looks after his parents at old age (Marak, 2000:165).

The interface between indigenous peoples' customary laws and mainstream legal systems, at the national and international levels, is complex. There are instances of acute conflict between the systems, while there are also many arrangements in which customary law systems operate within the relatively benign oversight of the state legal and judicial systems. In addition, there are occasions where the relationship is one of mutual suspicion and disdain (Roy, 2005:21).

Constitutional Safeguards of Tribal Population

With the dawn of independence and adoption of the Constitution of free India, the British policy of isolation and noninterference was replaced by the policies of integration and development. The Constitution of India provided several types of safeguards to the tribal communities. There are the Protective Provisions to protect them from all forms of social injustice and exploitation, the Developmental Provisions promote education and developmental activities, the Reservation Provisions ensure their representation in legislative bodies and government jobs, and the Administrative Provisions under the Fifth and Sixth Schedules provide for special administrative setup to provide autonomy of self-governance according to their customary traditions.

The tribal people live in contiguous areas, unlike other communities. So, an area approach was adopted for administrative and developmental purposes. Under the Constitution 'Scheduled Areas' are declared by the President after consultation with the State Governors. These Areas have been designated to protect the interests of Scheduled Tribes regarding their land and other social issues and are governed by provisions of either Fifth or Sixth Schedule. The Scheduled Areas of the Northeast are covered under the Sixth Schedule provisions; all other Scheduled Areas are covered by the Fifth Schedule laws. The administrative structure is different in the two Schedules.

State Governors have a special constitutional protective role in all Scheduled Areas. They are empowered to make regulations prohibiting or restricting the transfer of land from tribals to non-tribals and prevent exploitation of the tribal communities. Since these Scheduled Areas are supposed to enjoy autonomy protected by the Constitution, the laws passed by parliament and the State legislatures do not automatically apply to them. Hence, the Fifth Schedule defines Governors' powers to adopt laws to these areas.

Modern Administrative Structure

Sixth Schedule

The Sixth Schedule areas are governed by Autonomous District Councils which have wide-ranging legislative and executive powers. As a result, they almost work like a 'mini Parliaments.' They have complete freedom to allow village level bodies to run according to customary laws. The verdicts of district and lower level courts can only be challenged in the high court. At present, 6th Schedule Areas exist only in four North Eastern States: (1) Assam, (2) Meghalaya, (3) Mizoram, and (4) Tripura. These Areas are administered

through Autonomous Districts / Regional Councils. Except for Meghalaya, other three states have only certain selected areas covered under Sixth Schedule.

Fifth Schedule

Unlike the Sixth Schedule areas, there are no institutional autonomous bodies in the Fifth Schedule areas. However, the PESA Act of 1996 has empowered the local village level Panchayats, particularly the Gram Sabhas in the Fifth Schedule tribal areas to act as local bodies of self-governance. But they lack the protective umbrella of a district level body (like the District Council of the Sixth Scheduled areas); as a result, their decisions are routinely ignored or overruled by the state officials.

Constitutional Protection

Tribal people have traditionally lived in close contact with nature, in the hills and forests. In this sense they are different from the rest of the mainstream people; they have historically tried to avoid contact with 'outsiders' to preserve their traditional community based living in which they feel more secure. The Sixth Schedule of the Indian Constitution offers them local autonomy through the system of autonomous district and regional councils which have extensive legislative as well as executive powers to protect land and tribal traditions. It was a path-breaking effort when launched in the 1950s and offered better protection than the Fifth Schedule provisions[1].

Rights of Women Over Land and Customary Law

The land is a state subject in India. There are lots of small civil societies and state or regional networks working on land rights of marginalized and backward people. Landlessness is invariably connected with inequality and poverty, more so in the case of women. The rights of women over land, housing, and other resources are essential not only to reduce their poverty but also to increase their financial efficiency. This shall, in turn, bring about gender equality and equity in the society. Land and housing rights are generally explained within a patriarchal framework – without giving due recognition to gender equity. It was observed during the study that women's rights over land, particularly agricultural land, are important in rural settings since it is a source of livelihood.

Agarwal (1994) argues that that the issues of women's rights in housing and land have been largely neglected in both research and policy. In almost all developing countries, large-scale surveys and agricultural census collect property-related information only by households, without disaggregating it by gender. In most of South Asia, including India, dependency upon small-

scale surveys and village studies to assess women's access to land cannot be undermined. These sources reveal that typically few women own arable land and even fewer have any effective control over them. In the Indian context, female workforce participation rates, rather than property rights, are widely used as the main indicator of women's economic status.

In the Indian context housing right is now recognized as a fundamental human right. As a primary user, a woman's requirements rank the highest in a house. Beyond being a shelter, a house has multiple dimensions for her. It is a place of livelihood. It is the point for social interaction. It serves as a refuge from social instability, sexual exploitation, and legal authority. There are seven elements as regards the rights of women towards housing. They are – establish the house, use the area, manage, dispose of, regulate, sanction and perform rituals in it. If a woman is able to exercise these rights, only then her right to the house is affirmed.

Women's right to housing has to be understood in terms of their access to and control over housing and property. 'Legal rights in housing and property' broadly refers to the security of tenure, i.e., right to own, lease, rent, mortgage or dwell in house and property, and the right not to be forcibly evicted. In general, the condition of Indian women, (both rural and urban) has been pathetic as far as their land and housing rights are concerned.

According to the approach paper to the Eleventh Five-Year Plan, women constitute 40.0 percent of the agricultural workforce. This percentage is rising due to large-scale migration by men, the preoccupation of men in nonfarm activities and rapid industrialization. An estimated 20.0 percent of rural households are de facto female-headed due to widowhood, desertion, or migration of males. The increasing number of women in agricultural work needs to be seen in the context of the concentration of unskilled women in this sector. This leads to decline in agricultural produce which leads to further poverty[2].

In defining the customary laws of the Northeast, our objective is to understand women's rights in them particularly over the property. Amid their diversity, they have some commonalities, the most important being patriarchy (Fernandes et al., 2006: 29). All the elements of customary law like the rules and regulations governing marriage, property rights and other social relations are elements of a culture as well, which is expressed in the form of laws. They protect its worldview and value system by giving a concrete form. Thus, the customary law becomes intrinsic to its identity and culture. The main features of a tribe's culture are community ownership, equity and a relatively high status (but not equality) of women (Fernandes and Bharali, 2009:95).

Customary Laws and Woman Rights

The customs and its laws vary from region to region and so is the case for North-eastern region. The Seven Sister state is diverse in the form of practicing different customs and traditions in order to retain their identity from one another, and these variations make the region unique in its own way. Ethnic and cultural diversity ensure differentiation in tribal socio-cultural and economic identity. Focusing on the status of women in tribal society also undergoes great diversity. In most of the tribes of this region women share in property rights are very minimal. They enjoy very limited or at times no control over landed properties, as these are bounded by patrilineal practices and ideologies where man enjoys the overall power in the family. But the situation and this practice of patriarchy contradict totally when it comes to matrilineal societies like the Garo, the Khasis, the Jaintias or the Lyngngams from the state of Meghalaya.

Women are often associated or considered as a homemaker. Nath in his book, *'Rural Women Workforce in India'* talks about the dual role of women both in the home as well as outside home. He says, 'In the social context, due to the low status attached to manual labour in our society and the cultural value associated with women's confinement to the home, the work of rural and urban as wage labourers, unskilled factory workers and menials are not conducive to a better status. The average woman in rural can give little attention to the upbringing up of her children. With dual roles and without any mechanical aids for house-work, she is really overworked. So also, are the women engaged in unskilled or semi-skilled work in organized and unorganized sectors attitude of unconcern about the public affairs, is responsible for the limited participation of women in activities like those of Trade Unions or political parties' (Nath, 2003:13).

The Mizoram Presbyterian Church, the largest Christian denomination in the state, is yet to okay woman ordination, a significant number of women have been included in its high committees and as Sunday school teachers. The Mizoram Legislative Assembly has also made some landmark decisions such as legislating the Mizoram Women Commission, adopting the parliamentary act known as the Protection of Women against Domestic Violence Act, 2005.

The Mizo women have also given a hats-off to the Mizo Divorce Ordinance 2008 which would put an end to certain divorce laws under the 'male-friendly' Mizo Customary Laws are unfavorable to women. The Ordinance was a major milestone in the history of Mizoram and was the result of concerted efforts of the women wings of different political parties and a number of highly learned Mizo women. Under the existing customary laws, when a man divorces his wife the latter leaves the house without virtually anything even

if she had contributed a lot to the family's assets. All this will be abolished with the new Mizo Divorce Law. Thanks to the women's campaign, the Mizoram Baptist Church has agreed to ordain women as *Kohhran Upa* or church elders even though woman ordination for pastors or priests seems a far cry.

We shall now discuss the customary law and women's status among some tribes of Northeast India in socio-political and socio-cultural spheres.

Tribes of Arunachal Pradesh

Arunachal Pradesh was once known as North East Frontier Agency (NEFA). Immediately after independence, Arunachal Pradesh was under Part-B of the Sixth Schedule to the Constitution as a tribal area of Assam. In Arunachal Pradesh, there are about 26 major tribes which are divided into a number of sub-tribes. In most of the tribes, the property is distributed amongst the sons and the daughters are only entitled to movable properties. Polygyny is practiced customarily. If a boy child is born out of extra-marital affairs automatically he belongs to the father's side and in case of the girlchild, she will belong to mother's clan. Usually, it is the youngest son who stays with the parents and inherits the ancestral house. In case of childlessness, the property is transferred to the clan and not to the woman.

Polygyny, which is one of the customary practices, is despised by women in Arunachal Pradesh. It has eventually increased, declining and worsening the status of women of these indigenous tribes. Women in Arunachal Pradesh are more independent and financially sound compared to men. In certain cases, it is the women who have more access to resources and they can even finance the men in need. But they do not have a legal standing.

In Arunachal Pradesh, a traditional court is known as '*Kebang*' plays a very important role in the lives of the common people and more so in case of women. *Kebang* is a male-dominated strong political body which gives judgments and makes decisions for the society. Women can come to *Kebang* only as an appellant, litigant or witness but never be part of it. This depicts very vividly their poor legal standing.

Inheritance of property among all the tribes of Arunachal Pradesh is based on a patriarchal system. Thus, women have no property rights. The eldest son gets the lion's share, particularly among the Apatanis, Serdukpens, and Noctes. The Gallongs have a joint- family system (Joshi, 2005: 67).

The Nyishi customary law excludes women from ownership and inheritance. However, the Bangi branch of the Nyishi permits the first wife to have a say in inheritance but excludes daughters from owning or inheriting clan property. However, they have full ownership of ornaments, utensils and

other gifts at their marriage. Also, among the Chakma only sons can inherit land though women are active cultivators. Roy and Rizvi discuss that the Wancho of Tirap district restricts inheritance to men through primogeniture. A couple without the son can, with the consent of the head of the clan, choose a young man to live with them, marry their daughter and inherit their property. In the case of Hill, Miri women cannot inherit any land or immovable property but their tradition allows a girl the right over private property or money. A widow is entitled to her deceased husband's property only if she is not separated from her in-laws. If a husband wants to divorce his wife then under such circumstances the wife is entitled to half of his property. (Fernandes et al., 2006: 31).

The concept of bride price was also evolved subsequently. In course of two types of marriage emerged i.e. *Tado Momping Benyi* and *Tado Momsi Benyi*. It is argued that bride price is the counterpart of dowry system that prevails in other parts of the country. The only difference is that under bride price system, the brides are purchased whereas, in dowry system, the parents of the bride give some assets or wealth at the time of marriage which is demanded by the groom's party. But this bride price system of the Nyishi society is far away different from the dowry system. In fact, the Nyishi by tradition regards women as a symbol of prosperity. It is believed if there is no women-folk in a family; it is devoid of good luck and prosperity (Mibang and Behera,2006: 334). Thus, the customary laws of Arunachal Pradesh are biased against women but also have provisions to ensure her security.

Tribes of Assam

Many tribal communities in Assam have personal laws. In general, women in Assam do not inherit the land. The parental property is distributed amongst the sons and not the daughters. A girl inherits property only if she doesn't have any brothers. A widow can inherit her husband's property.

The joint family system appears to be common among both tribal and nontribal communities in Assam; it is based on blood relationship. As long as the father lives, the son cannot claim any share of his property. So, the father is the center of the property and the rules supreme. Among the Dimasa-Kacharis the prevalent custom is that the sons inherit their father's property and the daughters inherit their mother's property. Though Assamese women are given an honoured position by the society, no other community in Assam follows the matrilineal inheritance system (Mohanty, 2006: 114).

The Bodos have a male preference as the line of inheritance is drawn by the son. Generally, the eldest son inherits the property of the father. Women play a role in agricultural operations and fishing, and also in rituals but have

no role in a political sphere. Women occupy a comparatively lower status than men (Mukherjee, 2003: 327).

The Karbis follows the rule of patrilineal inheritance. If there is no son to inherit family property, the daughter or daughters can inherit property under certain circumstances. If there is no heir to inherit ancestral land and other property, the right of inheritance passes on to one's brother and brother's children and to the other patri kin, in the given order. The prime considerations which govern the rule of inheritance are the fulfillment of obligatory duties and responsibilities by the sons or their substitute towards their parents. A daughter or an adopted son acts as a substitute for the son born of lawful wedlock. It is customary among the Karbis that the eldest son gets the largest share of the land. The younger sons also receive shares of land. The son who looks after aged parents sometimes gets the largest share of the property (Barooah, 2007: 55-56).

A widow has the privilege to acquire her deceased husband's share of joint property as well as self-owned property. The widow, along with her sons is entitled to the same share. She has limited authority over her husband property. It is necessary for her to take the consent of her deceased husband's other family members in order to sell valuable property like land (ibid).

Tribes of Manipur

In regards to a succession of land, being a patriarchal society, the sons inherit land after the death of their father. If the father does not have any son, the inheritance right goes to his nearest male kinship. The eldest son gets some advantages; although all the sons inherit the father's landed property almost equally. The house and the best-wet rice field will go to the eldest son and the rest are distributed among the other sons. Daughters are debarred from inheriting paternal land or landed property. Nevertheless, on the day of their wedding, they are given a necklace depending upon the capacity of their parents. If the mother has landed property (given in her marriage by her parents) that will be equally distributed among the daughters. The only provision for a daughter to inherit the property from her parents is that acquired at the time of her marriage (Singha, 2011:39).

There are four major groups, the non-tribal Meitei, the Naga, the Kuki, and others. The New Kuki group of tribes are comparatively new migrants in Manipur. Only in Churachandpur belt, they are found as dominating tribe (Ghosh and Ghosh, 1997: 83).

Among few Mao tribes in the state, it is found that daughters also inherit immovable properties such as land, paddy field etc. The condition is that those properties should not have been inherited but individually earned by the father. In Meitei community, though women can claim property, usually

they do not. Women in Maring community cannot inherit land and in case there are no sons in the family the land goes to the clan. Like other communities in Manipur, women are only entitled to immovable properties.

Tribes of Meghalaya

In Meghalaya, the Khasi, Jaintia, Garo, and Lyngngam tribes follow a matriarchal system where the children take their mother's title. Land and property are distributed amongst the daughters with the youngest daughter getting the lion share of the ancestral property. Apparently, women enjoy privileges but in reality, they have no control over the land. Property here includes money, jewellery, lands, houses, cattle and such other property owned by an individual family or clan. The limitation is that the youngest sister or youngest daughter of the family is the custodian of the ancestral property. Among the Garo tribes, the parents have an option to select any daughter as the heiress.

In the Khasi society, the youngest daughter (*Khadduh*) inherits the property. In case the youngest daughter goes out of the house to stay separately with her husband then the property goes to the daughter who looks after her parents. The property of childless couple goes either to the children of wife's sister or husband's sister, whoever it is who looks after them (Koireng, 2010:125).

As far as the law of inheritance is concerned in the Jaintia society, ancestral land passes from mother to the youngest daughter. If the youngest daughter dies then the property go to the immediate youngest daughter in the family. Thus, inheritance is generally on the female side. But it is not suggested that a Jaintia man is a man without any property. Though he has no right over ancestral properties as long as female heirs are there he can have self-acquired properties called *Yutran*. If he dies the property will pass on to his mother or in her absence to his sisters beginning with the youngest one. And if he has no female relatives, his property will pass on to his youngest daughter or anybody whom he has so willed *(Pynkam)* before or at the time of his death. In case of a married man if his wife undertakes not to remarry she will get half of the *Yutran*. The *Yutran* thus acquired will become an ancestral property of either the mother's or the wife's family in the next generation (ibid: 119-120).

Tribes of Mizoram

In Mizo community, it is customary that the son inherits the property and the youngest son gets the largest share but he has to take care of his parents during old age. In case of absence of a son or if the son is unable to take care of the parents, then, the women in the family can inherit the

property. Widows generally do not inherit property but if it is so mentioned in the will of her demised husband than she may get it. In case of divorce, women get nothing except the things that she bought/brought during the marriage.

According to Malsawma 2002, in the absence of male relatives, a woman inherits to the exclusion of distant kinsmen. In the case of more than one daughter, the youngest daughter will be given first preference as in the case of sons. When a man dies, if his wife and children can maintain themselves, none should disturb them. The widow is to take care of his property and children. If she is willing to remain in the house occupying the main bed and discharging the duties and functions of the mother then nobody should disturb her, especially if she has unmarried or divorced daughters or grand-daughters of the deceased living with her. In some cases, a woman for whom the husband's family has paid a bride price inherits property in her own right. If a man has no male issue his daughter and failing that, his widow inherits his property. If the widow remarries someone other than his brother, his property and the children's care vest in his brother (Fernandes et al., 2006: 34-35).

Under the Lushai system, if a man left behind only minor sons and a widow, a close male relative took over his property and looked after the family till a son attained adulthood. Inheritance by women was generally precluded but if there was no other heir, the daughter or widow could inherit, the former taking precedence over the latter. Also, under Lashker, the eldest son inherited his father's property but generally shared it with his youngest brother. The sons in the middle, daughters or the widow got no share. In the absence of sons, the property went to the eldest and youngest brother of the deceased (ibid).

Tribes of Nagaland

Being a patriarchal society, the sons inherits his father's property. The property was/is proportioned among the sons by the father or the elders in terms of terrace-fields, *jhuming* fields, forest land, and other immovable properties, and the parent's house is generally owned by the youngest son. There was/is also another type of inheritance called clan inheritance. When a clan or a lineage has no more descendants, the next immediate clan claims and inherits the property. Descent is traced from the paternal line.

Naga women, unlike other tribal women, have a high place in the society, work and agricultural activities. However, a married woman has almost no rights over the property of her father, except to those of unmarried daughters who have a share of the property of their father. The share of property that belongs to unmarried sister usually goes to her brothers after her death.

Women also inherit rare ornaments, expensive dresses, and wares from their mothers, sisters or aunts. Also, after the death of the husband, a woman with a son who is minor is liable of the husband's property or family property, until her sons are matured and she can also take a customary oath for the settlement of any dispute (Shikhu, 2007: 32-33). It is observed that they do not give land to the daughters because after marriage the land goes to a new family.

Among the Angami tribe, the laws of inheritance vary from village to village and community to community. In some villages, the entire son inherits the father's property and for some, it is only the youngest son, while the daughters are totally side-lined when it comes to inheritance of their father's property. At present, the youngest son inherits the lion's share of the property and daughters too, are given some share. In earlier times daughters would only acquire a few quintals of paddy and no other properties (Koireng, 2010:152-153).

In case of Konyak, the eldest son gets all the property. Movable property can be inherited by both son and daughter. In Khiamngan community rules of inheritance and succession follow down the male line. Close, cordial relations are observed among families of one clan (*yasangla*) and lineage. Among the Khiamngan women have no rights to father's property but all sons generally inherit an equal share of property from their father (Bareh, 2007: 261-262).

The Sema like any other Nagas tribe is patriarchal and in which women have no say over the inheritance of property or considered the head of the family. As regards property, widows are entitled to one-third of their husband's movable property and if one of the widow remain unmarried in the deceased husband's house, she or they may get whatever free labour was due to the deceased husband for a period not exceeding three years. After that, they may be given some free labour as a matter of courtesy but are not entitled to it. If the widow marries one of her husband's heirs, the latter enjoy the property, without dividing it for her lifetime and in some cases, widows are allowed to receive payments in cash on the score of dues to their late husband (Zehol, 1998:49).

Tribes of Tripura

The male inheriting the property is the norm for all the tribes of Tripura. In the case of a Reang tribe widow, she can inherit the property only if she has a male child. The Jamatia tribe is somewhat pro-woman and its customary practices are flexible. Sometimes it provides an opportunity to women in terms of heritance. For instance, if there are no sons, the daughter can inherit the property. Women have the right to enjoy their husband's property in

their capacity as caretakers of the property but cannot own it. In most of the Tripura tribes, women can't inherit from their father. A widow can inherit property from her husband provided she does not remarry. The Jamatia tribe, though, doesn't allow women to inherit property from the father but the father can give property as a gift to his daughter.

The Lushai women have no rights for inheritance. The Lushais are patriarchal societies and thereby the share of property goes to the sons. The youngest son gets the lion's share as it was said that the youngest will look after the parents. In case of no issue of sons, the daughters are eligible for inheriting the share of the property. In case of a polygamous husband, the son of the first wife will get the lion's share then the sons of the second wife (Bhowmick, 2005:173).

The Halams are a patriarchal community, so the sons inherit all their property and the daughters go to their in-law's house. In absence of any son, only the daughter can get the property share of her paternal parents (ibid: 170).

The Chakmas divide parental property equally among sons. If a man divorces his wife for no fault of hers, he has to return her ornaments, dresses and wedding gifts. Small children go with her. She has a right to maintenance till she remarries (Fernandes et al., 2006: 38).

Conclusion

Customary Laws among the tribes of Northeast India are considered as the precursors of all modern formal laws, essentially based on the fundamental importance of the rule of precedents. They do have their own positive side, and the tribal people reported that these modern laws are favourable to them. It is believed that the customary laws serve as the easiest and quickest way to deal with any kind of resolution at the village level. However, women do not get importance in decision-making as well as inheritance of property. Men do, however, receive all moveable property due to the customary laws prevalence in the society.

In the patriarchal society, there is always a gender bias in every field or aspect of life. Women are always portrayed as a meek, gentler sex, submissive to their husband and family. Thus, the question arises around us today whether it is the society or the customs that have given a particular image or character to the women? If she does not fulfill the criteria as women she is considered as an unfit mother, wife, sister, etc. Is it the custom or tradition that controlled the behaviour of sexes in great extends?

With the introduction of 33.0 percent reservation for women in the modern political system, a platform has been created for women and they

are motivated to take part in it. Another reason for the change is the modern education and its eventual fostering of socio-political consciousness among tribal women who have also begun to think of their inheritance rights, political rights and assert themselves in the current socio-political scenario. There have been some changes in property rights and women own lands though there are some opponents to equal rights for the inheritance of ancestral property. Even if women are given land, it is usually smaller in comparison to their male counterparts.

References

Agarwal, B 1994, *A field of one's own:gender and land rights*, Cambridge University Press, New York.

Bareh, HM 2007, *Encyclopaedia of North-East India: Nagaland*, vol. VI, Mittal Publications, New Delhi.

Barooah, J 2007, *Customary laws of the Karbis of Karbi Anglong in Assam*, Law Research Institute: Eastern Region: Gauhati High Court, Guwahati.

Bhowmik, KN 2005, *Status,and empowerment of tribal women in Tripura*,Kalpaz Publications, New Delhi.

Fernandes, W & Bharali, G 2009, 'Customary law- formal law interface: impact in tribal culture' in *Christianity and change in Northeast India*, eds TB Subba, J Puttenpurackal & J Puykunnel, Concept Publication Corporation, New Delhi, pp. 93-108.

Fernandes, W, Pereira, M & Khatso, V2006, *Customary laws in Northeast India: impact on women*, Northeastern Social Research Centre (mimeo), Guwahati.

Ghosh, GK & Ghosh, S 1997, *Women of Manipur*, A.P.H. Publishing Corporations, New Delhi.

Goswami, MC 1986, *Customary laws of the Tripura*, The Law Research Institute, Guwahati, Northeastern Council, Guwahati.

Joshi, HG 2005, *Arunachal Pradesh: past and present*, Mittal Publications, New Delhi.

Koireng, TN 2010,*Unwritten customary law of Northeast India*, DBCIC Publications, Shillong.

Malsawma, HL 2002, *Sociology of the Mizos*, Spectrum Publication, Guwahati and Delhi.

Marak, JLR 2000, *Garo customary laws and practices*, Ankasha Publishing House, New Delhi.

Mibang, T & Behera, MC 2006, *Marriage, and culture: reflections from tribal societies of Arunachal Pradesh*, vol. 2, Mittal Publications, New Delhi.

Mohanty, PK 2006, Encyclopaedia of Scheduled Tribes in India, vol. 5, Isha Books, New Delhi.

Mukherjee, SK 2003, 'Kachari: Boro' in *People of India Assam. vol. xv (part one)*,eds KS Singh, BK Bordoloi, & RK Athaparia, Anthropological Survey of India, Calcutta, pp. 326-329.

Nath, M 2003, *Rural women workforce in India*, B. R. Publishing Corporation, Delhi, pp. 13.

Roy, RD 2005, *Traditional customary law and indigenous peoples in Asia*, Minority Rights Group International, London, pp. 1-36.

Shikhu, IY 2007, *A re-discovery and re-building of Naga culture values,* Regency Publications, New Delhi, pp. 32-33.

Singha, K 2011, *Economy of a primitive tribal village in Manipur*, Concept Publishing Company Pvt. Ltd., New Delhi.

Zehol, L 1998, *Women in Naga society*, Regency Publications, New Delhi.

Online Journal and Website:

1. http://socialissuesindia.files.wordpress.com/2012/10/sixthschedule.pdf. NortheastIndia: Status of Governance in the Sixth Schedule Areas.
2. http://www.igsss.org/images/documents/42_823852496_igsssploghingpink.pdf

   Customary Law: The way things were Codified by Ezra Rosser: *Tribal Law Journal* Vol 8 http://tlj.unm.edu/volumes/vol8/8TLJ18-ROSSER.pdf Date of Access 27-11-12.

   http://www.capri.cgiar.org/wp/..%5Cpdf%5Cbrief_land-05.pdfGender Issues in Land Tenure under Customary Law by Patricia Kameri-Mbote. Date of Access 26/11/2012.

Chapter - 4

Hindu Epics in the Performing Arts: An Observation from A Buddhist Tribe of Arunachal Pradesh

— Jayanta Sarkar

The scheduled tribes in India living in close proximity of the caste-based Hindu society at many places have adopted myths and/or episodes from the two great Hindu epics Ramayana and Mahabharata in their performing arts. This can be viewed as a result of prolonged interaction between the two categories of populations at varied contexts. Processes of acculturation may be one of the relevant causes of such infiltration of the Hindu elements of culture in the performing arts and beliefs of the non-caste-based communities.

However, when such Hindu elements of culture are introduced in a scheduled tribe inhabiting away from any caste-based society; the processes of acculturation may appear inadequate in the first instance, for providing a logical explanation. I shall discuss this taking an example from the Khamti tribe of Arunachal Pradesh.

More than 42 years from now (2018) I had been camping in a village called Momong, near Chawkham administrative area in the Namsai division in the Lohit District of Arunachal Pradesh.

It was a compact village, then having 70 households, 61 of the Khamtis and 9 of the non-Khamtis with a total population of 414 of which 372 were the Khamtis and 42 non-Khamtis (Sarkar 1987:16). The Khamtis were the main inhabitants. The village was located on the bank of rivulet Teyeng and was in the midst of dense forest. The minimum communication facilities in those days made the village fairly secluded in respect of interactions with

other populations away from their habitation areas. The Khamtis are the followers of Theravada Buddhism. Each village had a small monastery, locally known as Bapuchang. Besides their daily routine of offering to the Lord Buddha and assembling at prayers, many of their creativities are centered on the Bapuchang. My camp in the village was adjacent to the Bapuchang, the village monastery.

Performing Arts

Like other Buddhist populations of Arunachal Pradesh, the Khamtis also have a very rich repository of performing arts in the form of drama and dance. These are educative in purpose and usually narrate a mythical story or illustrate a moral.

The dramas are staged on the occasions of Buddhist festivals. Two such major festivals of the Khamtis are Buddha Purnima and Sanken.

Buddha Purnima is observed in the month of Noonsam (February). On a specific day, all the villagers propitiate Lord Buddha with many offerings followed by an exchange of foods among the villagers.

Sanken is observed in the month of Noonha (April) when the idol of Buddha is brought out of the village Bapuchang and bathed for three consecutive days as a symbol of washing away all the unhappiness of the outgoing year (Sarkar, 1987:150). These two occasions are observed with great festive mood. The youth stage *pungs* (drama) generally based on the stories of Jataka, and Ramayana and Mahabharata. It needs to be mentioned that these two epics are available in the Khamti script and are preserved in the monasteries. Ramayana and the Mahabharata are known as Chau-La-Maung and Thamma-Puktram respectively.

How these two great epics could find a place in the Khamti culture needs to be examined for a proper understanding of performing arts of this Buddhist tribe.

The *pungs* are normally staged on an elevated platform near the Bapuchang. Before the actual play starts one of the members of the play addresses the audience

> "Ladies and gentlemen, please listen to me. Now we shall present before you a *pung* on....... Therefore, on behalf of all the participants humbly and in folded hand, I am proposing to present the *pung*. This *pung* is based on Ramayana/ Mahabharata and our aim of staging it is to enable the audience to earn *Punya* (virtue). While staging the *pung,* we may commit some mistakes for which I, on behalf of the participants, am requesting Devi Saraswati to forgive us. I pray for her to be with us. I also request the audience to forgive our mistakes, if we do any. I further pray

to mother Saraswati "Oh mother, you please help us, so that we can satisfy the audience".

It may not be out of context to mention that many Hindu gods and goddesses are worshipped by many population groups of present Myanmar, the original homeland of the Khamtis. Thagyamin is worshipped whose origins are the Hindu god Indra. Saraswati, known as Thuyathadi in Burmese, is the goddess of knowledge. These Hindu gods and goddesses were incorporated in the Khamti culture via other population groups in Myanmar who were under the influence of Hinduism.

In order to depict the characters of the drama, the Khamtis make masks of Rama, Ravana, Sita, Hanumana, Rakhshasa (Demon) and Lord Buddha and also some animals. These masks are made of paper, clay, and bamboo and sometimes even with tin. Generally, masks often heads are used for depicting the character of Ravana though the use of a single-head mask is not rare. Specially made costumes are also used when available in the village. The Khamtis are well known for their craftsmanship in the area.

The artists of the *pungs* are selected from males of different age groups. No female takes part in the actual performance. Before staging a drama regular rehearsal of the actors take place within the village under the direction of a person well conversant with the special stories. Rama among the Khamtis is believed to be the *avatar* (incarnation) of Lord Buddha and therefore, most of the *pungs*, based on the Ramayana have a character of Lord Buddha.

Breaking of *Aradhana*, the mighty bow of King Janaka is a popular subject matter of drama. However, the contents of these *pungs* not necessarily follow the actual content of the great epic. In fact, in many cases, these are adapted with alteration and addition so as to suitably fit within the frame of their way of life. One such play staged at Momong during my stay in the village depicted 'Once Rama saw Sita at Janakpur and fell in love with her. He started sending love letters from Ayodhya to Sita tying these in arrows. Accidentally such a letter reached to King Dasaratha, father of Sita. Janaka was surprised to see a letter sent from far away Ayodhya. In order to test the strength of Rama as a warrier, the King invited him to Janakpur to break the *'haradhanu'*.

What is very significant in the content of this drama is that after the success of breaking the strong bow, King Dasaratha advises Rama 'my son, always follow Buddha, Dharma, and Sangha and rule your kingdom according to the norms of Buddha'.

As in Ramayana, the Khamti Mahabharata describes King Yudhistira, the eldest brother of Pandavas, as the incarnation of Lord Buddha. Here too, Buddha narrates the stories of Mahabharata to his disciples. A popular drama is based on the episodes of the killing of Abhimanyu, son of Arjuna in an

unfair manner within the circle by the seven warriers of Kauravas, during the battle of Kurukshetra. The leading characters are Abhimanyu, Seven warriers, Arjuna and Duryodhana. When Abhimanyu was killed in the unfair battle, Arjuna was shocked and took a vow to kill each of the seven warriers. Arjuna takes revenge accordingly. The drama ends with the advice to Arjuna to follow the path of Buddhism.

Another drama is often staged that depicts how 'Sakuni' the maternal uncle of Duryodhana takes revenge over the latter. Sakuni advises Duryodhana to fight against the Pandava, knowing fully that Duryodhana would be defeated.

It is apparent from the subject matter of the dramas usually staged in the villages of the Khamtis that the two great epics of the Hindus have a deep impact on the culture of the Khamtis, though their Ramayana and the Mahabharata do not share all the features as among the original Hindu epics. In fact, these episodes are described as the narrations of Lord Buddha to his disciples.

The contents of the dramas clearly indicate the prevalence of syncretic elements. Rama is believed to be the incarnation of Lord Vishnu by the Hindus, while Yudhistira is conceived as the son of God Dharma. The Khamti society syncretized these two characters of the Hindu epics within their frame of Buddhism and perceived them as an incarnation of Lord Buddha. The characters of these dramas act according to the principles of Buddhism.

Presence of Hindu epics in the culture of the Khamtis in an area of Lohit District that does not have any caste Hindu populations becomes a subject of further investigation. This becomes more relevant in the context of their neighbouring Singpho tribe of Changlang District, inhabiting in the same geographical set up having no caste Hindu populations and professing Theravada Buddhism. The stories of Ramayana or Mahabharata are not apparent in the Singpho creative activities as among the Khamtis. This considerably weakens the logic of impact of Jataka stories on the performing arts of these tribes.

What could then be the probable reasons of the prevalence of such drama based on the Hindu epics among the Khamtis?

Historical Background

As the Khamtis and the Singphos have immigrated to their respective places of present habitation during the 18th century from the then Burma, at the first instance an attempt may be made to trace the probable reasons against the backdrop of the cultural history in their earlier homelands. These people migrated to their present places in Arunachal Pradesh from 1789

onward from a place called Khamti long or Bor Khamti of the Shan State in the Irrawaddy Valley of Myanmar. The people of the area were already under the influence of Theravada Buddhism. In fact, Buddhism spread from Indian sub-continent to Southeast Asia and China. Several forms of Buddhism were introduced to the various states from the 5th Century CE onwards. The Pali inscriptions found in Burma and Siam are dated to the 5th to 7th Centuries CE, the Siamese inscriptions to the 6th to 8th Centuries CE (Skilling, 1997:73-99). Over the years Theravada Buddhism had established great impact not only on the ruling class but also on the ordinary villagers and it became integrated into their culture and everyday life and ultimately became their religion.

At the first instance, it may appear that the story of Rama as narrated in the Dasaratha Jataka might have had an impact in adopting Rama episodes in their performing arts. However, a further probe into the cultural situations of the people of Southeast Asia before the Buddhism entered in the area reveal a cultural space that was immensely under the influence of Hinduism. The archaeological remains available on the temples and other places found in large part of this area depict the presence of Hindu gods and goddesses.

As a matter of fact, Hinduism was the state religion of various Southeast states from the 5th to 14th centuries. From the 9th to the 11th century, Angkor, present Cambodia was the home to a great Hindu civilization.

The Indian impact was especially strong in lowland areas, where an agricultural economy based on rice emerged, and were such powerful, organized states as Angkor in Cambodia, Ayuthaya in Siam (Thailand); and Pagan (Bagan), Hanthawaddya, and Arakan (Rakhine) in Burma were established.

Hindu influences on Burmese Buddhism have been significant. Many of Burma's most important *nats* are Hindu gods, such as Thagya Min, the Devine protector of the Buddhist religion, and Thuyathadi (Saraswati), goddess of learning (Seekings, 2006: 123).

It is generally agreed that the religious teachers who traveled along trade routes to the court of the local rulers and were instrumental in the spread of Hindu religion and culture in Southeast Asia (Ray, 2004: 587).

Ramayana in Myanmar

The Indian epic Ramayana came to Myanmar and other countries of Southeast Asia with the early Indian traders and merchants, some of whom settled down to form Hindu communities. The people of Bagan (11th AD to 13th century) knew the Ramayana story, and there was certainly an oral tradition which they received either directly from India or through the Mon people of Lower Myanmar. There is evidence in the lithic inscriptions, stone

sculpture, terracotta plaques and pictorial art of these frescoes which enable us to say definitely that Rama story, both as an incarnation of Vishnu, the Hindu God and also as Buddha Jataka story was known at that time (Kaung,2002:137-148).

The public recitations were a means of popularizing social ideals and cultural norms as envisioned in the Hindu world and provided the worshippers an accession for identifying with the heroes of the epics. Before the court Drama, a few scenes from the Ramayana might have been performed by the Hindu communities in Myanmar especially during their festivals like the Deepavali which the Hindu Brahmans think is the day when Sita and Rama returned to Ayodhya after Sita was rescued from Ravana. Yama U Ohn Maung thinks that there were recitations of Ramayana in Myanmar in Quet-seik style and some scenes performed as a nibat-khin (ibid:7).

In such social-cultural set up as Basham pointed out "The story of Rama has long been part of the cultural tradition of Buddhist Burma, Thailand and Cambodia. The Muslim Indonesians and Malays, who imported the Ramayana from India long before their conversion to Islam, still delight in the ancient Hindu story, adopted slightly to meet the theological requirements of their religion and the different cultural milieu of the Southeast Asian archipelago (Basham, 1967:10).

The homeland of the Singphos (Jingphos) was in the high lands of Kachin Hills in upper Burma. The place that had very limited wet rice cultivation was not a favourable place for the traders from India (Leach, 1964) who were instrumental in bringing both Hindu and Buddhist faiths in the low land areas that included the Irrawaddy valley, the earlier place of the Khamti people.

As a result, the Singphos remained outside the influence of both the Hinduism and Buddhism. In fact, the majority of the Singphos in Arunachal Pradesh got converted to the faith of Theravada Buddhism in the late 19th century.

These two cultural historical backgrounds lead us to infer that while the Khamtis had adopted Ramayana while in the Irrawaddy valley and carried the same tradition to Arunachal Pradesh, the Singphos had no such tradition to carry during their migration.

Against this cultural-historical background when we see the Khamtis to continue with their creative activities, based on the two great Hindu epics, in the habitats those are devoid of any Hindu populations, it becomes amply clear that only a cultural-historical approach can provide a satisfactory answer in respect of origin of these excellent performing arts in the Khamti society.

References

Basham, AL 1967, *The Mahabharata and the Ramayana*, The UNESCO Courier, December 1967, New York, pp. 10.

Leach, ER 1964, *Political systems of Highland Burma: a study of Kachin social structure*, London School of Economics and Political Science, University of London, London.

Ray, HP 2004, 'Hinduism' in *Southeast Asia: a historical encyclopedia from angkor wat to East Timor*, eds OOI Keat GIN, ABC CLIO, S Barbara, California, Oxford, England. pp. 587. Available from: http//www.abc-clio.com.

Seekings, DM 2006, *Historical dictionary of Burma (Myanmar)*, no. 59, The Scarecrow Press, Lanham Maryland.

Sarkar, J 1987, *Society, culture and ecological adaptation among three tribes of Arunachal Pradesh,* Anthropological Survey of India, Calcutta.

Skilling, P 1997, 'The advent of Theravada Buddhism to mainland Southeast Asia', *Journal of the International Association of Buddhist Studies,* vol.20, no.1, pp.93-107.

Kaung,UT 2002, 'Ramayanadrama in Myanmar', *Journal of the Siam Society,* vol. 90, pts.1&2, pp.137-148.

Chapter - 5

Suicide
A Public Health Issue with Special Reference to Arunachal Pradesh

— Tarun Mene

Introduction

Suicide is a complex phenomenon that has attracted the attention of philosophers, theologians, physicians, sociologists, anthropologists, and artists over the centuries. According to the French philosopher Albert Camus, in 'The Myth of Sisyphus', it is the only serious philosophical problem. As such, the task of academicians never concludes when it enters the realm of suicide.

Almost five decades back, Dublin (1963: v) claimed that 'The problem of suicide has so many aspects and such far-reaching implications, that no short treatise can possibly cover all of them. Any attempt to deal completely with a question that has so many ramifications would baffle the skill of the most thoughtful student of human affairs'. Firth (2000/1961) equally contended that 'Even the idea of suicide itself is both clear and susceptible to slippage, as there is no obvious line between where 'suicide' ends and 'risk-taking' behaviour or willful 'self-neglect' begins'. Similarly, Ian Hacking (2008: 1) noted, 'The meanings of suicide itself are so protean across time and space that it is not so clear that there is one thing, suicide'. As scholars from recent times, for example, Staples and Widger (2012) opined that 'It is a problem of enduring human interest, forcing us to ask questions about ourselves and our world that other human behaviours do not.' Munster and Broz (2015) simply concur, 'Suicide is a challenging object of study.' Minayo (2006) also

remarked that few studies have simultaneously examined the individual, social, anthropological, and epidemiological aspects of suicide. However, to the author, the micro and macro dimensions 'remain dissociated in polarities that prioritize either the individual or society.' What all these statements suggest is that there is no simple answer to this problem, and since it is a challenging subject, containing a subset of so many aspects; the research is still in the process of crossing disciplinary boundaries to arrive at some sort of holistic perspective.

Apart from the problems of contextualization, the economic and human cost of suicidal behaviour to individuals, families, communities, and society makes suicide a serious public health problem around the world. For the World Health Organization (WHO), research on suicide and suicidal behaviour and preventing and reducing suicidal behaviour are now part of their global agenda. If we look at the data provided by various agencies including the WHO, suicide remains a major public health problem on a global scale. In 1998, suicide constituted 1.8 percent of the total disease burden; this is estimated to rise to 2.4 percent by 2020 (Bertolote, 2002, 2009). The WHO has estimated that worldwide, close to a million people die by suicide every year, representing a global annual suicide rate of 16 per 100,000 people. Tragically, suicide is one of the leading causes of death worldwide today. Young people are increasingly vulnerable to suicidal behaviour. Worldwide, it is one of the three leading causes of death in the most economically productive age group (15-44 years), and the second-leading cause of death in the 15-19 years age group (Patton et al., 2009). At the other end of the age spectrum, the elderly is also at high risk in many countries (WHO, 2012).

Asia alone accounts for as much as 60.0 percent of the world's suicides, so at least 60 million people are affected by suicide or attempted suicide each year here. Despite this, suicide has received relatively less attention in Asia than it has in Europe and North America (Hendin, 2008:1). In India, researches on suicide and suicidal behaviour have received less attention, even though a big section of the population comprises a high-risk group in this regard. Only about 25.0 percent of suicide deaths in India are registered, and only about 10.0 percent are medically certified. Studies on large scale 'verbal autopsy' of all deaths in rural regions reveal that the suicide rate in the rural areas is three to four times higher than what is reported by the government. So, the official suicide rate reported in the country is probably significantly lower than the actual rate (Hendin et al., 2008:10, Saddichha, et al., 2010: 57, Gajalakshmi and Peto, 2007).

In India, recent data estimated that over one lakh people (1, 31,666) lost their lives by committing suicide in India. The official report estimated the suicide rate at 10.6 per 100,000. The overall male: female ratio was 68:32.

One out of every six suicides was committed by a 'housewife,' and nearly 67.0 percent of the male victims were married while 63.6 percent of female victims were married. A person having an income of less than 1 lakh have committed suicides contributed 69.7 percent of suicide victims. Hanging (41.8%) remained the most prominent means of committing suicides. 'Family problem' (other than marriage-related issues)' was the major cause of suicide, which accounted for 25.0 percent of total suicides, followed by 'illness.' Those educated to the middle and matriculate/secondary level contributed to the highest the number of suicides.Puducherry reported the highest rate of suicides (40.4), followed by Sikkim (38.4), Andaman and Nicobar Islands (28.9) and Telangana (26.5). Maharashtra (16,307) followed by Tamil Nadu (16,122) and West Bengal (14,310) reported the highest absolute number of suicides to total suicides in the country during 2014 (National Crime Record Bureau, 2014).

The available suicide estimate for India is based on data from the National Crime Records Bureau (NCRB), and the accuracy of these estimates has been questioned since they are based on police reports. Until recently, suicide was legally considered to be a crime in India, a factor which could easily have influenced those who might have been expected to report it. Also, the age-specific and gender-specific death figures, rates and risks, as well as the mode of suicide in India's diverse socio-demographic population are not well understood (Patel et al., 2012: 2343). For all these reasons, Indian suicide mortality estimates are rated 'poor' to 'fair' in the WHO's rating system (Hendin, 2008). This problem has serious implications in understanding the various aspects of suicide.

Apart from the above problems and the available information based on clinical and psychological studies, there is also an urgent need for community-specific research which is very wanting in the Indian context. There are two anthropological monographs of such a nature, one by Elwin (1943) and another by Saran (1974) that exclusively deal with the issue of suicide among tribal communities in central India. Such study provides cultural-specific information and patterns and determinants of suicide which is no less important than other studies. Similarly, in case of the tribes of Northeast India, we find a report on suicides among Lotha and Angami Naga in the writing of Hutton (1965: 18) who, referring to Mills (1922), informs us that, 'The thrifty and serious Lotha was apt to be given to suicide, which was very rare among other tribes.' Apart from this, suicide among the Idu Mishmi tribe was reported by Baruah (1960) and Bhattacharjee (1983). Very recently, Mene (2013), followed by Singh et al. (2013) conducted anthropological research among the Idu Mishmi tribe highlighting the issue, which is otherwise dealt with largely in the public health domain or else confined to clinical and

psychological perspectives (see Vijayakumar, 2010), that too mostly in the context of urban setting.

Suicide: A Public Health Issue in Arunachal Pradesh

The occurrence of suicide in Arunachal Pradesh is not a recent phenomenon, at least in case of the Idu Mishmi community, who inhabit five districts in the state. Apart from the National Crime Record Bureau (NCRB) and media reports, there are some anthropological works which address this issue which includes Mene (2012), Mene (2013), Singh et al. (2013), and another recent one by Mene (2016). These studies have sufficiently established that suicide is a public health issue, requiring immediate attention.

Mene (2012) collected 218 samples of suicide incidences that had occurred during the last four decades (1970-2010), and out of these, only two were found registered in the local police station. During the last decade, i.e., 2001-2010, the rate of suicide was 51.6 per 100,000 of the population - perhaps the highest among any indigenous community in India. The overall male: female ratio was 47:53 and the 10-29 age group remained the biggest contributor, at around 59.1 percent of the total cases. Maximum cases were reported from the Dibang Valley district, with a total of 159 cases (M-74 and F-85) and 59 cases (M-29 and F-30) from the Lower Dibang Valley District. Spring appears to be when the most suicide deaths occur. With regard to social status, unmarried Idu Mishmis committed suicide (49.6 %) more than the married (40.8 %) sections. Among different occupational groups, people engaged in the agriculture/farming and those who never had any formal education contributed the highest number of suicides. The most common means to commit suicide remained hanging. It was found that drowning and self-poisoning were the most popular means with females. The study also revealed a strong prevalence of suicidal ideation and life-threatening behaviour among the sample units. The previous suicide incidents in the locality have profoundly affected the general attitude of people towards suicide.

The case studies are revealing that the facts that determined the incidents of the Idu Mishmi suicides are, more or less, socially and culturally conditioned. Overall, many cases are found in relation to familial relations, familial love, and rejection, conjugal love and hatred, parental love and avoidance, marriage problems, family politics,and family structure, etc. As such, the study found that maximum cases are in relation to quarrel between husband and wife, disappointments in love affairs due to the social norms, disgust with life and other varied disappointments, domestic problems, and marriage-related problems.

Another study by Singh et al. (2013) found that in the incidence of suicide attempts among the Idu Mishmi population (14.22%) was higher than the

urban population in general (0.4–4.2%), and females were at higher risk. Depression (8.26%) was comparable with earlier reports, whereas anxiety syndrome (6.42%), alcohol abuse (36.24%) and eating disorders like binge eating (6.42%), Bulimia nervosa (1.38%) were also recorded in the population. Depression and gender, the study claimed, turned out to be significant determinants of suicide attempts in the studied population, and that alcohol abuse was not a significant factor.

In another publication, Mene (2013) has raised the issue of underestimation of suicide in India, and especially the cases among the Idu Mishmi tribe of Arunachal Pradesh. To the author, this is perhaps also applicable to other communities in India. In his study, he found only two cases of suicide being registered in police reports, whereas over 200 cases had already been reported within the same community. During the decade 2001-2010, the official data estimated only seven suicide cases in Dibang Valley district, while the field data explored at least 48 cases of suicide that had occurred among the Idu Mishmis tribe of the district. He found that suicide was highly under-emphasized and under reported for a number of reasons, such as lack of resources and competing priorities, combined with inefficient and incomprehensible death-reporting systems, family fear of social and legal consequences associated with suicide, etc. This has serious implications with regard to the official suicide estimates, and their validity and reliability. His study evidently shows that the reliability of the official estimate is subject to errors, ranging from inaccuracies in actual suicide cases and officially reported and variations in defining the data of the State Crime branch which in their reports, mixed up the cause of suicide with the method of suicide employed.

It is well documented that suicide is a serious public health issue among the Idu Mishmi tribe. The quantification of the under-reporting of suicides by Mene (2013) and the findings of Singh et al. (2013) not only highlight the prevalence and vulnerability of suicide but also identifies some of the significant determinants of suicide in a specific community which still continues today. These claims are further substantiated by the various reports in local dailies. For example, a recent article by Amar Sangno (2017) reported that there is a rise in suicide cases in Seppa town in East Kameng district of Arunachal Pradesh. There were at least eight suicide cases in the month of November alone, out of which five were females and two males, in the 14-18 age groups, and one old woman. There are similar reports of suicide in various parts of Arunachal Pradesh, which can be found in the local dailies from time to time. In spite of all this, we do not find any suicide prevention or intervention programs either at the policy level or local level. To add to their effort, recently Mene and Miso (2016) organized a workshop at Roing

involving people from various walks of life from the Idu Mishmi tribe and drafted an 'Action Plan,' in an attempt to curb the suicide menace at the community level. This Action Plan is already in the public domain, but not much has materialized from it, because of the lack of participation by the different stakeholders and society at large. This calls for establishing a community-based model of suicide-prevention strategy, involving researchers and public health professionals to draw attention to the issue at the highest governmental level (e.g. Ministry of Health). It considers the core elements of community renewal strategies, community education strategies, school strategies, youth and family strategies,and inter-agency communication and coordination and the establishment of the surveillance system. It has been advocated by an institution like WHO that suicide and deliberate self-harm(SDH) are major public health problems and that public health surveillance system is essential to the practice of public health, to guide prevention, monitor activities and evaluate outcomes of such activities. In most of the low, and middle-income countries like India there are no hospital-based surveillance systems for suicide attempts. This is more so for the rural areas like the case of the Idu Mishmis tribe of Arunachal Pradesh is a glaring example. It also emphasizes that the implementation needs to reflect the diverse cultural, social and economic factors specific to the area. These strategies also advocate for it to be innovative, low-cost (both financial and in human resource terms) to major stakeholders such as government officials and policy-makers, health professionals, community organizations, and police. Increasing awareness, as well as public education campaigns, could address stigma while being sensitive to local tribal traditions and values. This clearly requires a long-term coordinated approach, involving frequent consultation with researchers and various stakeholders.

The Implications of Mental Healthcare Act of 2016

Keeping aside the social and cultural factors associated with suicide, mental health disorders occur in all regions and cultures of the world. The most prevalent among these are depression and anxiety, which are estimated to affect nearly one in every 10 people on the planet (676 million). At its worst, depression can lead to suicide. In 2012, there were over 800,000 estimated suicide deaths worldwide, with 86.0 percent of these occurring under the age of 70 years. Globally, among young adults aged 15–29 years, as mentioned previously, suicide accounts for 8.5 percent of all deaths and is the second-leading cause of death in this group after road traffic injuries (World Health Statistics, 2016).

Although the mental health legislation has existed in India since the mid-19th century, it has gone through various changes over the years. Recently the Mental Healthcare Act (MHCA) 2016 came into existence. Under the Act,

every person shall have the right to access mental health care and treatment from services run or funded by the government. As such, a patient with mental illness will be able to access services and facilities such as essential medication, free of cost; insurance coverage for mental illness; funding for a private consultation if a district mental health service is not available. The Act further ensures that treatment and rehabilitation will be available in the least restrictive environment, and respect the rights and dignity of patients, including those from disadvantaged socioeconomic backgrounds. The outcome of these recommendations is that the financial, as well as psychosocial burden on caregivers, will be reduced to a large extent.

It covers a wide range of areas, including provisions relating to suicide and suicide prevention. It de-criminalize suicide and prohibits Electro-Convulsive Therapy. A person who attempts suicide shall be presumed to be suffering from mental illness at the time of having attempted it and will not be punished under the Indian Penal Code (IPC) if he survives, unlike before. Some of the important provisions particularly dealing with suicide are as under:

- *Clause 29.* (*1*) The appropriate Government shall have a duty to plan, design and implement programmes for the promotion of mental health and prevention of mental illness in the country.
- *Clause 29.* (*2*) Without prejudice to the generality of the provisions contained in sub-section (*1*), the appropriate Government shall, in particular, plan, design and implement public health programmes to reduce suicides and attempted suicides in the country.
- *Clause 124.* (*1*) Not withstanding anything contained in section 309 of the Indian Penal Code, any person who attempts to commit suicide shall be presumed, unless proved otherwise, to be suffering from mental illness at the time of attempting suicide and shall not be liable to punishment under the said section.
- *Clause 124.* (*2*) The appropriate Government shall have a duty to provide care, treatment, and rehabilitation to a person, having mental illness and who attempted to commit suicide, to reduce the risk of recurrence of an attempt to commit suicide.

Thus, the MHCA 2016 is a step towards improving access to mental health services in India and bringing the law in line with international mental health legislation and human rights standards. Effective implementation needs an extensive input in terms of skilled manpower, finance and proper coordination between multiple agencies. Some experts are of the notion that the bill might increase the stigma and hesitation to seek treatment from mental health professionals due to cultural, educational and social factors, particularly in rural settings. But at the same time, the promising provisions in this revised

legislation could mark a start of a new era for anti-stigma campaigns, allocation of resources to mental health which could help identify and prevent the toll of deaths by suicide. If appropriately implemented and financed, in addition to improved access to mental health services, the human rights of people who are psychologically unwell could be safeguarded to a greater extent.

Discussion and Conclusions

Suicidal behaviour is a complex process; with a span that can range from suicidal ideation which can be communicated through verbal or non-verbal means; to the planning of suicide, attempting suicide, and in the worst case, suicide. Suicidal behaviour is influenced by the interaction of biological, genetic, psychological, social, environmental and situational factors (Wasserman, 2001). Risk factors for suicide include mental and physical illness, alcohol or drug abuse, chronic illness, acute emotional distress, violence, a sudden and major change in an individual's life, such as loss of employment, separation from a partner, or other adverse events, and in many cases, a combination of some of these factors. While mental health problems play a role which varies across contexts, other factors such as cultural and socioeconomic status are also particularly influential. The impact of suicide on the survivors, such as spouses, parents, children, family, friends, co-workers, and peers who are left behind, is significant, both in the immediate and long-term. Although there is no single explanation as to why people kill themselves, timely intervention and easy access to health facilities can decide whether a person lives or dies. Precisely, this is the area where a public health professional could make a difference.

In the case of Arunachal Pradesh, a few papers on suicide have appeared from time to time in various journals; many cases have been reported in the local newspapers as well, but so far, no one has addressed the issue as a public health problem or outlined a definite programme for suicide prevention in the state. This chapter has intended to address this issue of suicide as a serious public health problem in the state of Arunachal Pradesh by highlighting the recent facts and figures. Since it has already been established that there is a huge underestimation of suicide cases in Arunachal Pradesh, there have been no intervention programmes implemented here so far by any agency, including the Government, which could have otherwise saved many lives. As discussed above, the relevance of the Mental Health Act cannot be ignored, particularly in the context of Arunachal Pradesh, but it appears that it is taking too long for the policy makers and the agencies concerned for the implementation to practically implement it on the ground level. The rate of suicide could be greatly reduced, especially in the already identied affected communities.

At the community level, the Idu Mishmi Cultural and Literary Society (IMCLS) and other NGOs and Associations in the region need to play a vital role. For example, Mental Health Act. 2016 has provisions to establish Mental Healthcare Centers at the district-level. This can be initiated by the Apex body of the community in consultation with the District Medical Officer and the District Administration with the State Mental Health Department at Naharlagun and formal procedures can be initiated at the earliest to avail of all possible facilities falling under Act. The Action Plan could be promising and useful in minimizing the rate of suicide of the Idu Mishmis if implemented at earliest by mobilizing all possible community resources with the help of other stakeholders. Of course, to overcome the problem, a community-based and participatory approach are necessary, but at the same time, academic inputs from a multidisciplinary perspective are also required to explore new possibilities and to evaluate any initiatives for future action in dealing with this public health problem in Arunachal Pradesh in particular, and India in general.

References

Baruah, ML 1960, *The Idu-Mishmi*, Directorate of Research, Government of Arunachal Pradesh.

Bertolote, JM & Fleischmann, A 2009, 'A global perspective on the magnitude of suicide mortality' in *Oxford textbook of suicidology and suicide prevention: a global perspective*, eds D Wasserman & C Wasserman, Oxford University Press, Oxford, pp. 91-98.

Bertolote, JM & Fleischmann, A 2002, 'A global perspective in the epidemiology of suicide', *Suicidology,* årg. 7, Nr. 2, pp. 6-8.

Bhattacharjee, T 1983, *Idus of Mathu and Dri Valley*, Directorate of Research, Government of Arunachal Pradesh, Itanagar.

Dublin, L 1963, *Suicide: a sociological and statistical study*, The Ronald Press Company, New York.

Elwin, V 1943, *Maria murder and suicide*, Oxford University Press, London.

Firth, R 2000 (1961), 'Suicide and risk-taking in Tikopia society' in *Cultural psychiatry & medical anthropology. an introduction and reader*, eds R Littlewood & S Dein, Continuum International Publishing Group – Athlone, London, pp. 314-338

Gajalakshmi, V & Peto, R 2007, 'Suicide rates in rural Tamil Nadu, South India: verbal autopsy of 39 000 deaths in 1997–98', *International Journal of Epidemiology*, vol. 36, pp.203–207.

Hacking, I 2008, 'The suicide weapon', *Critical Inquiry,* vol. 35, no. 1, pp. 1-32.

Hendin, H, Phillips, MR, Vijaykumar, L, Pirkis, J, Wang, H, Yip, P, Wasserman, D, Bertolote, JM & Fleischmann, A 2008, *Suicide and suicide prevention in Asia*. World Health Organization Report, Geneva, Switzerland.

Hutton, JH 1965, 'The mixed culture of the Naga Tribes', *The Journal of the Royal Anthropological Institute of Great Britain and Ireland*, vol. 95, no. 1, pp. 16-43.

Mene, T 2012, *Suicide among the Idu Mishmi tribe of Arunachal Pradesh*. Ph.D. dissertation, Rajiv Gandhi University, Itanagar.

Mene, T 2013, 'Underestimation of suicide deaths: a study of Idu Mishmi tribe of Arunachal Pradesh, India', *Economic & Political Weekly*, vol. xlviii, no. 52, pp. 129-133.

Mene, T & Miso, R 2016, *Action plan for suicide prevention among the Idu Mishmi tribe of Arunachal Pradesh.* Document submitted to the Idu Mishmi Cultural and Literary Society, Roing, Lower Dibang Valley, Arunachal Pradesh.

Mills, JP 2002,*The Lhota Nagas*, Mcmillan, London.

Minayo, MCS, Cavalcante, FG & Edinilsa, RS 2006, 'Methodological proposal for studying suicide as a complex phenomenon', *Cad. Saúde Pública, Rio de Janeiro*, vol. 22, no. 8, pp. 1587-1596.

Munster, D & Broz, L 2015, 'The anthropology of Suicide: ethnography and the tension of agency' in *Suicide and agency: anthropological perspectives on self-destruction, personhood, and power*, eds L Broz & D Munster, Ashgate Publishing Limited, England, pp. 3-23.

National Crime Records Bureau 2014, *Accidental deaths and suicides in India*, Ministry of Home Affairs, New Delhi.

Patel, V, Ramasundarahettige, C, Vijayakumar, L, Thakur, JS, Gajalaksmi, V, Gururaj, G, Suraweera, W & Jha, P 2012, 'Suicide mortality in India: a nationally representative survey', *Lancet*, vol. 379, pp. 2343–2351.

Patton, GC, Coffey, C, Sawyer, SM, Viner RM, Haller, DM, Bose, K, Vos, T, Ferguson, J & Mathers, CD 2009, 'Global patterns of mortality in young people: a systematic analysis of population health data', *Lancet*, vol. 374, pp. 881-892.

Saddichha, S, Prasad, MNV& Saxena, MK 2010, 'Attempted suicides in India: a comprehensive look, *Archives of Suicide Research*, vol. 14, pp. 56–65.

Sango, A 2017, 'Rising suicide cases in Seppa', *The Arunachal Times* 11 December 2017.

Saran, AB 1974, *Murder,and suicide among the Munda and the Oraon*, National Publishing House, New Delhi.

Singh, PK, Singh, RK, Biswas, A & Rao, VR 2013, 'High rate of suicide attempt and associated psychological traits in an isolated tribal population of North-East India', *Journal of Affective Disorders*. Available from: http://dx.doi.org/10.1016/j.jad.2013.07.018i.

Staples, J & Widger, T 2012, 'Situating suicide as an anthropological problem: ethnographic approaches to understanding self-harm and self-inflicted death', *Culture, Medicine and Psychiatry*, vol. 36, pp. 183-203.

Vijayakumar, L 2010, 'Indian research on suicide', *Indian Journal of Psychiatry*, vol. 52, pp. 291–296. [PMCID: PMC3146189].

Wasserman, D 2001, 'A stress-vulnerability model and the development of the suicidal process' in *Suicide: an unnecessary death*, eds D Wasserman & M Dunitz, BMJ Publishing Group, London, pp. 13-27.

World Health Statistics 2016, *Monitoring Health for the SDGs*, WHO, Geneva.

Chapter - 6

Maternal Health Seeking Behaviour of Three Tai Groups of Northeast India

— *Yikham Gogoi and Sarthak Sengupta*

The World Health Organization defines health as 'a state of complete physical, mental and social well-being and not merely the absence of disease or infirmity'. Usually, health is a part of a bi-polar conceptualization and is juxtaposed to the disease at the other pole. In this concept, two extreme points can be identified. One-point stands for disease and to other points is the health.

Health is man's natural condition. It is the result of living in accordance with natural laws pertaining to the body, mind, and environment. The acquisition of health knowledge starts with the socialization of the child. Identically it depends on the member of the family, especially the parents which again depend on their socio-economic, cultural and educational background. During the learning of health, knowledge is more habitual than rational and gets affected either adversely or favorable by his peer groups and environmental influence (Swain, 1994).

Social, cultural and economic factors are important in health knowledge and health practices of a community. It is also important to acknowledge the health practices of a community and also to acknowledge the biological base. Birth, aging, and death are biological phenomena, health knowledge and practices develop in response to them and to the suggestion which appears to go along with living. Health production activities begin with the birth of children and maintenance activities with their reusing. Our own care of our bodies and of our lifestyle is part of health maintaining work. Most important aspects of health products are the activities of the food gathering and the food preparation. In brief, it can be said that health and diseases are related

to sociological and cultural resources of a community in a specific environment. The environmental aspects are sanitation, sanitary habits of the people, food drink and level of nutrition. There are also various factors like nutrition, environment, geographical variation, socio-economic status, size and type of the family etc. which affect the health of the people.

In order to understand how to treat illness effectively, one should comprehend the cultural behaviours, attitude, value and the larger social and political milieu in which people live. In India, the women, by and large, don't enjoy equal status like that of men. Many of the cultural practices and traditional customs are very much discriminating against womenfolk. Deprivation of food sometimes starts in infancy where female babies are weaned earlier than male babies. Parents may be unaware that their differential weaning practice has the effect of reducing the amount of high-quality protein that girl infants receive. This early weaning practice of a girl leads to higher girl infant's mortality rate than the infant boys. Along with the women, the entire families suffer from the poor health status of women. Women in poor health are more likely to give birth to low weight infants. They are also less able to provide food and adequate care for their children. Finally, a woman's health affects the household economic well-being, as a woman in poor health will be less productive in the labor force. Reproductive health of a woman is also an important factor for a healthy society. It has been accepted that women health is a very important indicator of the development of any nation.

In this chapter, only three Tai population of Northeast India i.e. Ahom, Khamti, and Phake are taken into consideration. Data has been collected from different villages of Assam (Nopam village from Dhemaji district; Borphake, Pomung, Phaneng, Munglalang, Longtong, and Lingam village from Tinsukia district) and Arunachal Pradesh (Manmow, Nanam, Sengsup village from Lohit district) predominantly inhabited by them to collect a representative sample from the selected groups.

Tai speaking people of Northeast India are patrilineal. The oldest male member of the house is highly regarded and his orders are not violated. Though the men's position is high, still the status of their women in society cannot be ignored. Along with their personal activities, they bear all domestic responsibilities including the agricultural activities as well. Tai women of Northeast India are producers and nourishes while this reproductive role is perhaps one of the most valuable contributions that women make to their households' communities. Maternal malnutrition is quite common among them and especially among those having many pregnancies too close spaces. The nutritional status of pregnant women directly influenced their reproductive performance and it also affects the survival of the infant and its subsequent growth and development.

Tai people are very rich in indigenous traditional ethnomedical knowledge for healing varied maternal health problems which include the use of indigenous herbal drugs based on locally available plants and animals. Taboos and superstitious beliefs are also practiced by them in determining their health behaviour and health status. Tai womenfolk still depend on indigenous treatment and give much importance to the performance of magico-religious ceremonies for treating illness. They believe in actions of supernatural power, evil eye, and ancestral spirit as well as biological causations of disease.

Among them, once a girl attains menarche, they consider her to be of marriageable age. After marriage, conception is a natural and biological fact. They strongly believe in the existence of God. They feel happy and excited for the arrival of new member in the family. They believe that man cannot produce a child according to their choice unless God help them. God gives the life of the baby inside the womb of the mother.

Although these populations do not take much care for the expectant mother, yet she has to follow some taboos and restrictions for the wellbeing of the newborn. There is no restriction in undertaking any kind of household works for the pregnant women. However, she observes some taboos which vary from population to population. The Ahom, Khamti and Phake women feel shy to disclose her pregnancy even to her nearest relations. To them, discontinuation of menstruation is an indication of conception. Besides, vomiting and a swelling of abdomen are also considered as indications.

After marriage conception is considered as a natural phenomenon for all the Tai women. Soon after the confirmation of her pregnancy, no major restrictions are placed on her through some trivial restrictions, some social notions are not uncommon among them. A pregnant woman is treated normally like others which amply demonstrate that they do not give much attention in this regard. She has to perform all her daily household chores like cooking, cleaning, washing clothes and utensils etc. They even used to go regularly to an agricultural field. The pregnant women of these population groups work regularly in the agricultural field. Most of the women from Khamti and Phake community particularly also used to go to nearby forest to collect vegetables and firewood. The Ahom women frequently used to go for fishing even though they may be pregnant. There is no restriction for the expectant mothers for weaving, fishing and collecting food staff and firewood from the forest. The diet of an expectant mother is not special, except some food restrictions. Pregnant women sometimes expresses her desire for certain palatable food items and the husband tries to fulfill it if they are not harmful. Ahom pregnant women are not allowed to eat unripe papaya, pineapples etc. They believe that such food may cause miscarriage. A special dish of Ahom called '*Khar*' (one kind of alkaloid preparation make out of black gram

or corm of banana etc.) are not allowed to take along with curry during pregnancy. Though a small quantity of fruits sour in taste is permitted, however, large quantity or frequent consumption of sour fruits, strong spices, hot chilly are prohibited items during the period. Fermented bamboo shoot or bamboo shoot pickles is favourite item among them. However, during pregnancy, any kind of curry mixed with bamboo shoot '*Khorisa*' or '*Nam mai chum*' is not permitted as it is believed that it has abortive property.

Pregnant Khamti women are prohibited from observing or attending funeral rites. She is forbidden to visit the burial ground and is advised not to walk beneath the old and big tree. During the night she is not supposed to go to a distant place for fear of being possessed by evil spirits. Expected Khamti mothers also observe some taboos during festivals. She is forbidden to touch the items which are used in festivals or in some religious activities. She is not allowed to collect vegetables from kitchen garden, and not to go inside the granary. Expected mothers are habituated to spit out through an opening in the bamboo mat of the stilted floor with believing for easy delivery. She is also not permitted to take the meal prepared for the Monks and debarred from carrying meal for the Monk to Buddha Vihara.

Among the Phake society, though the expectant mother can perform all her daily activities still she should follow some restrictions. She cannot work with needle and thread. She is not allowed to step on the broom and the rope tied in the neck of a cow. She cannot visit any household where the death occurred until the final death ceremony is performed. Phake women and her husband are also not permitted to kill birds and animals during this period. She is not permitted to nail the wall and not allow sitting on the doorstep. She avoids a few items in her usual meal. The expectant mother is not allowed to take unripe papaya, bamboo shoot etc. as it believed that it has abortive quality. Crab is also not given to the Phake pregnant women.

Among the Tai speaking population groups of Northeast India, the incidence of pregnancy wastage is also common. This may be due to the high working load of a pregnant woman. Lack of proper medical checkup may be another reason for the relatively higher incidence of pregnancy wastage. Spontaneous wastage is recorded in maximum families of these societies and induce abortion is rare in occurrence among them.

Supporting women all through pregnancy, during childbirth and afterward is an important necessity for a healthy delivery and good health of the newborn baby. Usually, in the urban area, a pregnant Khamti woman mostly gives childbirth in Hospitals. They go for a regular medical checkup and take necessary vitamins and folic acid prescribed by doctors. But in rural areas, women rarely visit doctors. In some remote areas till date, proper medical facilities are not available at all. In those areas, they mostly depend

on traditional herbal medicines and traditional *dhais* for delivery. The *'dhai'* who is usually an aged woman, plays an important role among Khamti societies. Among the Ahom and Phake population also, it is found, that *dhai* plays an indispensable role during delivery. In Khamti and Phake societies, sometimes a trained nurse is also called for along with the *dhai* at the time of delivery. Only in case of complication, they inform doctors and nurses. For an easy and less painful delivery, profuse hot water is given to the pregnant Khamti woman to drink as soon as the pain starts and she is asked to sit in the squatting position. Among the Phakes and Ahoms too, the delivery is performed in a squatting position. They believe that the delivery is less painful and quicker in such position. The umbilical cord is cut with the help of any sharp material available at that moment. It may be sickle, knife, blade or sharp bamboo split etc.

Regarding the mode of delivery, now a day, a trend of change is observed among these people. Most of the young mothers nowadays used to go to the nearby health center for their delivery. ASHA (Accredited Social Health Activist) worker mobilizes the expected mothers and facilitate them in accessing health and its related services available at Primary Health Centers and Hospitals. ASHA worker creates awareness and provides information about the benefits of institutional delivery. At present, the mothers are coming forward to take the advantage of the Government Policy which is known as NRHM (National Rural Health Mission). As a result, more institutional delivery is observed among the villagers of the studied communities.

Place of birth and type of assistance received during childbirth have an impact on maternal health and mortality. A birth that takes place in non-hygienic conditions or births that are not attended by trained medical personnel is more likely to have negative outcomes for both the mother and the child. It is found that due to contemporary Government Policy, the incidence of institutional delivery increases but home delivery is not totally absent among the Khamtis and Phakes. These families rarely approach the ANM or a doctor of the Primary Health Centre. The reasons for the underutilization of the services of the ANM in conducting deliveries are mainly due to difficulties faced in approaching them and lack of transportation to the hospital.

After childbirth, the mother is advised to seat nearby a fireplace specially prepared for her and it may continue for few days. It is believed that mother's womb is cured early due to the heat of the fire. The fireplace is treated as a natural process of early curing. Villagers believe that the fire should be kept nearby the childbearing mother after birth not only for early curing but also for keeping away the evil spirits from doing harm to the mother and the newborn baby. This practice is observed by all the three studied populations.

After delivery, the Khamti mother especially use to take boiled food and avoid oily and spicy food. She is given chicken (*kai*) boil with black pepper (*mak phit lom*), papaya (*mak chang phu*). They are forbidden to take food items like sticky rice (*khao no*), sugar (*ku wan*), and pork (*mue*) etc. They believe that this food creates indigestion and other related problems.

The Ahom people follow some practices for the welfare of an expected infant even prior to its birth. After five months of the conception, the mother or mother in law of the pregnant woman ritually feeds her *ghee* (purified butter), honey, milk, sugar, and curd. This ritual is known as *panchamrit*. This is generally done in case of first pregnancy of a woman. The expectant mother should not step over on the rope tied in the neck of a cow and also should not attend to nature's call under any big tree. She is forbidden to climb to an elevated site; to cross river and other water bodies and also to lift any heavy object. She should not eat extremely bitter, sour, hot, alkaline and sweet food. During pregnancy, she and her husband should not kill birds and animals. All the prescriptions and prohibitions are basically meant for the overall health and welfare of the prospective baby as well as the mother. All the member of the family, especially the woman keeps a vigil on the pregnant women during the first three months; and also the last couple of months of her pregnancy. She is not allowed to go outside the house alone. All the time she takes a small knife with her; an iron knife is also kept below her mattress. They believe that it protects her from the possible evil influences of any supernatural force. She is forbidden to go under the bamboo *chung*, a raised structure made of bamboo poles for creeping vegetables as they believe that this act of the expected mother may cause the child to resemble a bamboo (having a weak physique). In case of home delivery, each and every member of the family becomes busy when the delivery pain starts. The women members immediately arrange the room where the delivery is likely to take place. All the almirahs and suitcases etc. in the room are unlocked. It is believed that such a practice helps in having a quick and easy delivery. Usually, the elderly women from the family or the neighborhood help the woman during delivery. Prior to birth, when the expectant mother senses an acute pain, the elderly women of the family put a knot in between the breast and the abdomen with a *gamucha*(towel) to prevent the upward movement of the pain. No male person including the husband is allowed to enter the delivery room. Prior to birth, a fire is lit in the room which is believed to act as a preventive measure for any possible infection as well as supernatural influence during the birth. Immediately after the delivery, an elderly ever-married woman having at least one child cuts the umbilical cord. Usually, scissors, new blade or sometimes bamboo strip is used for the purpose. After delivery, the mother is allowed to eat rice with a curry prepared with

black pepper powder. Chicken curry cooked with black pepper is given to the mother.

Among the Ahom on the third day of delivery, the mother is fed with a special curry with tender *colocasia* shoots (*kachuthur*) cooked with black pepper powder. This ritual is locally known as *kachujaalhukuwa* among the Ahoms. In case of well to do families, the *kachujaal* is prepared with chicken or duck meat. Some medicinal herbs like *Manimuni* (*Centelk asiatica*), young shoots of *Tezmuri*(*Xanthoxylum nitidum*), *Malkathi* herbs, young shoots with flower *(Spilanthesclava*) and sometimes three to five young shoots of *Bihlongoni* (a kind of fern), a kind of small herbs called *Bonjaluk* (*Oldenlandia corymbosa*) are added to the curry. It is believed that these herbs help in curing the body ache along with the accelerating the healing of womb. Fishes like *Singi* (*Heteropneasts fossilis*), *Sol* (*Chana merulinus*), *Senga* (*Chanaa stewarti*), *Sengelie* (*Chauna gachua*) are also added in the curry. Sometimes a special curry prepared with *Kuchia* fish i.e. mud eel (*Amphiopnous cuchia*) and above-mentioned herbs with black pepper is also given to mother as vitalizing medicine. A bunch of young shoots of special herb *Hugloti* (*Penilafrutesoens*Linn) are boiled or roasted in fire wrapping with banana leave is allowed to eat at least once or twice in a day and it continues up to a month. It is believed that this herb helps mother for quick healing of womb. Sometimes decoction of roots of *Hugloti* (*Penilafrutesoens*Linn) is boiled and a cupful of it with a little dilution with water is also given to mother after delivery.

Soon after the baby born, a few branches of thorny plum tree hang on the top of the each and every door and window of the house in order to prevent the entry of any ghost or devil, which is likely to cause harm to the newborn. Among the Ahoms special amulets are given to wear to the young child. Bone of some bony fish like *Borali*, a small piece of rhizome of *Boch* herb (*Acorus calamus),* a red latumoni seed (*Abrus precatorius*), a piece of dried *Rochun* or Alium (*Aliumcepa*), a red bead etc. are put to neck of young baby in order to protect from black magic and evil spirits. A small piece of old torn fishing net is hanged in front of the door of the house or in front of room where the mother lives, with a belief that evil spirit cannot enter the house. Again, to protect from the evil spirit a fistful of white mustard seeds tied in a small cloth are hanged on the wall of the mother's room or kept under the bed of the mother and child. Again, among the Ahom society, strangers are not allowed to enter the room of the mother and child, who comes from outside with a belief that they may carry evil spirits along with them. They may be allowed to enter the room after proper washing of the legs, hands, mouth and also after being consecrated them with fire of the fireplace. It is believed that evil spirits would be away in such measures.

Age at marriage and high birth order are the two important factors affecting the maternal mortality and health among the Ahom, Khamtis, and the Phakes. In these societies, women got married at an early age, soon after the first menarche. Exceptions are seen among some women who are educated and come from a good economic background. Marriage at an early age accompanied to the early age at first childbirth. This affects the maternal health of the women of the three studied populations. Again, due to high consumption period and desire of boy child the women of these three communities give birth to a high number of children. This, high number of total pregnancies affect greatly internal health of the women.

It is accepted that women health is very important indicator for development of any nation. A woman plays various roles in her life. She is daughter, sister, wife, aunt, sister in law and mother etc. Mother is the most important role for a woman. But it has been seen that reproduction is considered as a natural phenomenon in all the society. Now a day, women fight for their positions and right. Now, there has been a tremendous increase in developmental activity for women. One important battle is to fight for women's right to health and control over their fertility.

Education brings changes in the life of women. It carries the consciousness among them and make aware towards those problems and right. Women are developing day by day in India. But in some sector women are yet to be developed. Especially in the tribal area women needs more changes. Moreover, Indian society is mostly patriarchal, where preference is given to a man than women. In some areas, cultural practices and traditional customs are found which is very much discriminating and against the womenfolk. But it has been seen that the tribes of Northeast India enjoy a relatively higher position than the rest of the India. Economic status, education etc. are the some of the factors which affects the maternal health among the women of Ahom, Khamti, and Phake. In these societies, especially among the rural people, no proper maternal care is seen. Expectant mother of these societies has to perform all her daily household activities from agricultural field to the kitchen. Fertility among them is found to be relatively higher.

People of these three communities are still maintaining their traditional practices in various aspects of life. Every culture irrespective of its simplicity and complexity has its own notion regarding health and health-seeking behaviour. The health of any community, particularly among tribal groups is a manifestation of the interaction between socio-cultural and sociobiological practices. Among these three groups prevalent health practices includes use of indigenous herbal drugs, taboos and superstitions are also responsible for determining the health behaviour and health status of the tribal groups. Womenfolk are still depending on indigenous treatment i.e. the herbal

Table 6.1: Ethnomedicinal plants and their uses among the Tai speaking population groups In Northeast India

Sl. No.	*Scientific Name*	*Local Name*	*Part of plant*	*Procedure*	*Dosage*	*Disease*	*Com-munity Used*
1.	*Aerva Sanguinolenta* (L.) *(Amaranthaceae)*	*Bhung ma ya janoi* (Khamti) *Saru Arokson* (Assamese)	Shoot	The decoction is given to nursing mothers as a galactagogue.	About 25 ml. once daily for a fortnight.		Khamti
2.	*Alpinia galanga*(L.) *wild (Zinziberaceae*	*Heo chang* (Khamti) *Korphul* (Assamese)	Rhizome	Rhizome is cooked with rice and given to mother after childbirth as a tonic	Once on every alternate day for a month	General weakness	Ahom Khamti Phake
3.	*Amaranthus spinosus* L. *(Amaranthaceae)*	*Phak hon Phak Khun* (Ahom) *Pu-Lon* (Khamti) *Pu lum nam* (Phake)	Shoot	The tender shoot is given to nursing as lactagogue.	Several times as vegetable.		Ahom Khamti Phake
4.	*Ananaas comosus* (A.) *Merr. (Bromeliaceae)*	*Mak-king-hom* (Ahom) *Mak-Maha-Nat* (Phake)	Leaf	Leaves are crushed and soaked in water and liquid is given to hasten childbirth.	About 30 ml. once or twice within a gap of one hour.		Ahom, Phake
			Unripe fruit	A paste of unripe fruit with black pepper		As abortifacient	Ahom Khamti Phake
			Leaf	Decoction with black pepper	100ml. once daily for a week	The griping pain in the abdomen	Khamti

(Contd...)

5.	*Arundo donax* L. *(Poaceae)*	*Mai-oo* (Ahom, Khamti, Phake)	Rhizome	Paste with the root of *Saccharum spontanerum* (*Kuhiar*) and rhizome of Alpinia allughus, black pepper is given as lactifuge.	About 10 ml. twice daily for a fortnight		Ahom Khamti Phake
6.	*Alstonia scholaris* (L) *B.Br.* *(Apocynaceae)*	*Mai dong* (Phake) *Tun tong* (Khamti) *Chatiana* (Assamese)	Tree	Nursing mothers used to pray under the tree to increase the breast milk. Or The tender leaves are used for the treatment of mother after childbirth.	Almost every day for a month		Ahom, Phake, Khamti,
7.	*Alipinia allughas* (Retz.)*Rosc.* *(Zingiberaceae)*	*Phak bun hyeo* (Ahom) *Mun hyeo* (Khamti) *Tora* (Assamese)	Rhizome	A paste of cooked with entrails of *kanduli* fish (*Notopterus notopterus*) is given to eat with rice to women in gripping pain after childbirth. Steamed rice cooked by wrapping with leaves is given to mother for general health.	Once a day or twice Once daily for 15 days at least.	Gripping pain General weakness	Ahom Khamti Phake.
8.	*Bambusa balcooa*	*Mai chang*	Tender Shoot	By making paste	200gm. Once daily for two days on an empty stomach	As abortifacient	Khamti

(*Contd...*)

5.	*Arundo donax* L. *(Poaceae)*	*Mai-oo* (Ahom, Khamti, Phake)	Rhizome	Paste with the root of *Saccharum spontanerum* (*Kuhiar*) and rhizome of Alpinia allughus, black pepper is given as lactifuge.	About 10 ml. twice daily for a fortnight		Ahom Khamti Phake
6.	*Alstonia scholaris* (L) *B.Br.* *(Apocynaceae)*	*Mai dong* (Phake) *Tun tong* (Khamti) *Chatiana* (Assamese)	Tree	Nursing mothers used to pray under the tree to increase the breast milk. Or The tender leaves are used for the treatment of mother after childbirth.	Almost every day for a month		Ahom, Phake, Khamti,
7.	*Alipinia allughas* (Retz.)*Rosc.* *(Zingiberaceae)*	*Phak bun hyeo* (Ahom) *Mun hyeo* (Khamti) *Tora* (Assamese)	Rhizome	A paste of cooked with entrails of *kanduli* fish (*Notopterus notopterus*) is given to eat with rice to women in gripping pain after childbirth. Steamed rice cooked by wrapping with leaves is given to mother for general health.	Once a day or twice Once daily for 15 days at least.	Gripping pain General weakness	Ahom Khamti Phake.
8.	*Bambusa balcooa*	*Mai chang*	Tender Shoot	By making paste	200gm. Once daily for two days on an empty stomach	As abortifacient	Khamti

(*Contd...*)

9.	*Caryota urens* L. *(Arecaceae)*	*Mak buo, Tun buo* (Ahom) *Cham-chip* (Khamti), *Chewa Goch* (Assamese)	Root	Decoction with black pepper is given to nursing mothers lactagogue.	About 25 ml. once daily during the nursing period for several days.		Ahom Khamti
10.	*Celtis tetrandra* Roxb. *(Ulmaceae)*	*Tun-su-ku-ta* (Khamti), *Sukuta* (Assamese)	Tender leaf & shoot	Tender leaf and shoot are used as a vegetable, which is also said to be useful in loss of appetite and also to relieve pains, of the mother after childbirth.	Given in curry	Useful in loss of appetite and also to relieve pain especially after childbirth	Khami
11.	*Clerodandrum viscosum Vent (Verbenaceae)*	*Tong ping khoum*	Root	a piece of root is tied with a black thread around the loin of the expectant mother	One piece	For easy delivery	Khamti
12.	*Croton-joufra* Roxb. *(Euphorbiaceae)*	*Tun-mai-khao-che* (Ahom, Khamti) *Goch Mahudi* (Assamese)	Stem bark	Stem bark juice is boiled with flesh *Mastocembelus pancalus* (*chirika* fish) with a little common salt is given in post-natal diarrhea	About 30 ml. twice daily till cure)		Ahom Khamti
13.	*Curcuma longa*	*Khao maen*	Rhizome	Juice	15ml. daily on empty stomach for a fortnight	Blood purifier	Khamti

(*Contd...*)

14.	*Calotropis gigantea* (L.) *R. Br.* *(Asclepiadaceae)*	*Yang-ken-tha*(Ahom) *Houng Phouk* (Khamti, Phake) *Boga Akon* (Assamese)	Leaf	Leaf smeared with mustard oil and used to dry fomentation also body pain and the poultice is also applied to the lower abdomen of women after childbirth, which is said to help in contraction of the uterus.	Applied every day up to 15 days		Ahom Khamti Phake
15.	*Carica papaya* L. *(Caricaceae)*	*Mak Chang Phu* (Ahom, Phake, Khamti) *Mak Ma La Ka, Mak Mu Lita*		The latex of tender fruit is given as abortifacient Young tender fruit is given eat as abortifacient which is said to be effective only for six to seven weeks.	About 15 gm. thrice daily for a week. It is effective only when given eight weeks of pregnancy)	Pregnancy	Ahom Khamti Phake
16.	*Curcuma longa*	*Khao maen*	Rhizome	Juice	15ml. daily on empty stomach for a fortnight	Blood purifier	Khamti
17.	*Centella asiatica* (L.) *Urban* *(Apiaceae).*	*Phe-om-hoi* *Phak-om-oi-lung* (Ahom) *Phak-nang* (Khamti) *Bormanimuni* (Assamese)		The plant is cooked with mud water fishes like Clerius batrachus (Pla-duk-nam or Pa muk-nam) or Heterupneustes fossilis	About 50 gm. During the period of menstruation	Dys menorrhea.	

(*Contd...*)

		The paste is given in dysmenorrhoea		(Pk-duk ni or Pa muk hi) in general weakness and also given to women during the postnatal period, which is said to act as a general tonic and also help in contraction of the uterus.			
18.	*Curculigo orchidiodes Gertn (Amary) (Ilidaceae)*	*Tun-Khang lai* (Khamti) *Nagini* (Assamese)	Tuber	Tuber paste is given in impotency. A piece of the tuber is tied on the left arm of the pregnant women and it is said to ensure male child.			Ahom Khamti
19.	*Cajamuscajan* (L.) Mill *sp.* *(Fabaceae)*	*Tho-nyeng* (Khamti) *Rahar mah* (Assamese)	Seed and leaf	The paste is applied over the mammae as a lactifuge	Once in every alternative day		Khamti
20.	*Colocasia*	*Man* (Ahom)	Stem	Cooked with black pepper powder sometimes also add chicken or duck meat		After childbirth for quick healing of mother	Ahom
21.	*(i) Centela asiatica* *(ii) Xanthoxylum nitidum* *(Iii) Hautunia cordata* *(iv) Spilanthes clava* *(v) Cyclosorus exelca* *(vi) Hedyotis corymbose*	*(i) Manimuni* *(ii)Tezmuri* *(iii)Mosundori* *(iv) Malkathi hurbs* *(v)Bihlongoni* *(vi)Bonjaluk* *(Pa-ta-pa)*		Cooked with black pepper powder		To relief from body ache along with accelerating the healing of womb after childbirth	Ahom

(Contd...)

22.	*Dioscorea esculenta (Lour.) Bunk. (Dioscoreaceae)*	*Pao man* (Khamti) *Japanialu* (Assamese)	Bulb	The roasted bulb is given to women suffering from abdominal gripe during menstruation.	Roasted in open fire and about 50 gm. Bulbil gave twice daily.	Suffering from abdominal grip during menstruation	Ahom Khamti Phake
23.	*Euphorbia hirta* L. *(Euphorbiaceae)*	*Pe-Khep* (Khamti) *Phak-Khep* (Ahom) *Gakhiroti bon* (Assamese)	Young Shoot	Given in curries to nursing mother to improve lactation.	Once daily at least for one month.		Ahom Khamti
24.	*Euphorbia antiquorum (Euphorbiaceae)*	*Yang kin* (Ahom) *Li ngu (*Khamti, Phake) *Siju* (Assamese)	Stem	Pounded and fried with egg delivered by black hen) is given to menorrhagia.	About 20 gm. Stem with two eggs once daily for three days of menses.	Menstrual problem	Ahom Khamti Phake.
25.	*Flemigiastrobilifer a* R.Br. *(Fabaceae)*	*Tun Mung lying* (Ahom) *Tun ma lam* (Khamti) *Makhiloti* (Assamese)	Root	The decoction is given menstrual irregularity.	About 20 gm. Stem with two eggs once daily for three days of menses.	Menstrual problem	Ahom Khamti
26.	*(i) Heteropneasts-fossilis (ii) Chana merulinus (iii) Chana stewarti (iv) Chana gachua (v) Amphiopnous cuchia*	*(i) Singi fish (ii) Sol fish (iii) Senga fish (iv) Sengeli (v) Kuchia fish*		Cooked with black pepper		For the strength of women after childbirth	Ahom, Khamti
27.	*Ipomoea aquatic*	*Phak pung*	Shoot	Curry prepared with lentil (Lens esculentus)	Once daily from 6th day of childbirth for 10 days	Used as a galactagogue to nourishing mother	Khamti

(Contd...)

28.	*Ipomoeaagnatica Forsk. (Convolvulaceae)*	*Phak-in nam, Phak- Pung* (Ahom, Khamti, Phake) *Kolmou* (Assamese)	Young Shoots	Decoction with water in (*Gallinula choloropus*) with black pepper mixed with Musa balbisiana is given to women for contraction of the uterus after childbirth.	About 20 ml. once daily for a fortnight.		Ahom Khamti Phake
29.	*Jatropha gossipifolia (Euphorbiaceae)*	*Tun Khru Khram* (Ahom) *Tun Kong Nyeng* (Phake, Khamti)	Root	Decoction with the root of *Sida cordifolia* sprouted seed of *Vigna mungo*, black pepper, head of *Pharatimaposthuma* with little common salt is given to women after childbirth for contraction of the uterus.	About 100 ml. twice daily for a fortnight.	Contraction of uterus	Ahom Khamti Phake
30.	*Justicia adhatoda* L. *(Acanthaceae)*	*Cha-lung Khao (Ahom)* *Mow la* (Khamti) *Boga Bahok* (Assamese)	Root Leaf	Juice is applied as a liniment on the abdomen to hasten childbirth Warm juice is applied as a massage on lower abdomen after childbirth for contraction of the uterus.	Several times a day. Twice daily for a fortnight.	Contraction of uterus	Ahom Khamti

(*Contd...*)

31.	*Lagenaria siceraria (Molina) (Cucurbitaceae)*	*Mak moup* (Ahom Khamti Khamyang Aiton) *Jati Lao* (Assamese)	Fruit	Juice of roasted fruit is given in gripping pain and body care during menstruation.	50 ml. juice is given twice daily for three consecutive days.	Menstrual problem	Ahom Khamti Phake
32.	*Murraya koenigii*	*Tun phi phan*	Leaf	Garlic with bulbs of ginger is given to wear by children		To protect from the evil spirit and prevent from fever	Khamti, Kham-yang
33.	*Mussaenda roxburghii* Hook. F. *(Rubiaceae)*	*Nai Ya huk kai* (Ahom) *Yanai* (Khamti), *Hug Loti* (Assamese)	Leaf Root	Boiled or roasted in fire wrapping with banana leaf Decoction	Once or twice daily and continue up to one month A cup, boiled and diluted with water	For quick healing of womb after childbirth Quick healing after delivery	Ahom, Khamti
34.	*Musa balbisiana* Colla *(Musaceae)*	*Kui Huin Jang* (Aiton) *Tun Kui Huin* (Ahom) *Tun Kui* (Phake) *Kui Huin* (Khamti) *Athiakol* (Assamese)	Inflore-scence	Abnormal inflorescence of non-setting fruits with black pepper is given to women as antifertility.	Cooked and given to eat, in curry.	Anti fertility	Ahom Khamti Phake
35.	*Morus australis* Poir. *(Moraceae)*	*Nuni* (Assamese) *Block leng*(Ahom) *Mo Mun Kai* (Khamti, Phake, Aiton, Khamyang)	Leaf	Decoction with long pepper, black pepper, and flesh of *Ompok pabo* is given in anemia	About 25 ml. twice daily for a fortnight. About 15 gm. twice daily for a week.	Anemia Weakness	Ahom Phake Khamti

(*Contd...*)

				A paste of with *Alpinia galanga* fruit (*Korphul*) and shoots of *Meyna laxiifolia* is given general tonic after childbirth.	About 15 gm. Twice daily for a week.		
36.	*Mimosa pudica* L. *(Mimosaceae)*	*Mai ja rap* (Ahom) *Ya-non* (Khamti) *Ni-Lajibon* (Assamese)	Roof	Decoction is given in dysmenorrhoea.	About 15 ml. twice daily for three days.		Ahom Khamti
37.	*(i)Nicotina tabacuum (ii)Clerodendrum colebrokianum (iii)Capsicum frutescens (iv)Litsea monopetala*		Leave, shoot, bark	Pounded with leaves of *Nicotinatabacuum* & *Clerodendrum colebrokianum*, shoots of *Capsicum frutescens* and bark of *Litsea monopetala* and juice is squeezed out	10ml once daily from the first day of menses for consecutive	Menorrhea	Khamti, Phake
38.	*Natasiatus herpeticum Buch. Ham.ex. Arn. (Icacinaceae)*	*Chik kon them* (Khamti)	Root	Juice is applied as a liniment on the breast of women at the time of first childbirth. Make the breast longer and improve lactation.	At least twice daily.	Improve lactation	Ahom Khamti.
39.	*Nyctanthes arbor-tristis L. (Oleaceae)*	*Block-oo- no-cha* (Ahom, Khamti) *Sewali Phul* (Assamese)	Root	Paste mixed with honey is applied on vagina is said to help in the conception of barren women.	It is applied from the third day of menses and should continue for a week or more.	Childlessness	Ahom Khamti Phake
40.	*Ocimum basilicum* L. *(Lamiaceae)*	*Im Khim Phuk* (Ahom, Phake, Khamti, Khamyang)	Leaf	The decoction is given as emmenagogue after childbirth it is also said to be useful in menorrhagia.	About 15 ml. once daily for a fortnight.	Menorrhagia	Ahom Phake Khamti

(Contd...)

41.	*Piper betel.*	*Thao-mao-pu*	Tender	Decoction	100ml once daily for three days from the first day of menses	Menorrhoea	Khamti
42.	*Paederia scandens (Lour) Merr. (Rubiaceae)*			A piece of the root of about 8 cm. long is inserted overnight into the vaginal tube is also said to be effective in pregnancy, not more than twelve weeks.			Ahom Khamti
43.	*Ricinus communis*	*Tun Khong* (Ahom) *Tun Po Khong* (Aiton) *Tun Kung* (Khamti) *Era goch.* (Assamese)	Leaf	Leaves heated with smeared mustard oil is used to place over lower abdomen to heal womb after childbirth.	The practice is following during postnatal period for at least 12 days.		Ahom Khamti Phake.
44.	*Rubus rugosus Sm. (Rosaceae)*	*Nya-tao-lio*(Ahom) *Mak Pu* (Khamti Phake Khamyang)	Root	The extract is given to relieve pain in dysmenorrhoea.	About 5ml. twice daily for three days from the first day of menses.	Menstrual problem	Ahom Phake Khamti
45.	*Smilax perfoliata lour. (Smilaceae)*	*Thao malungrau* (Ahom) *Nam Kang hang* (Khamti, Phake) *Tikani Boruah* Assamese)	Root	Juice mixed with black pepper is given with cow's milk in dysentery of women after childbirth.	About 5 ml of juice in 20 ml. of milk twice daily till cure.	Dysentery of women after childbirth	Ahom Khamti Phake
46.	*Saraca asoca (Roxb.) (Caesalpiniaceae)*	*Tun mokngong* (Khamti)	Flower	The paste is given in menorrhagia	About 30 gm. twice.	Menstrual problem	Khamti
47.	*Vitex negundo L. (Verbenaceae)*	*Ya Pan* (Ahom) *Yang Pan* (Khamti) *Ya pan (Phake)* *Pocho tia* (Assamese)	Leaf	Roasted leaves in banana leaf in the fire pit is given to mother after childbirth for contraction of the uterus and to relieve pain	About 200 gm. Once daily for a fortnight.	Pain after childbirth	Ahom Khamti Phake.

treatment; preferably they give importance to the performance of magicoreligious ceremonies for treating illness. The women of these three communities believe in both supernatural (evil eye, ancestral spirit) and biological causations of disease. According to them, a woman is considered sick when poor health incapacitates her from undertaking the normal routine. Expectant mothers have not been found to be provided with any special food during the time of pregnancy. But she observes some taboos. They believe that they conceive only by the blessings of God. Pregnancy is considered as a natural phenomenon. They do not give much interest in having regular medical checkup and taking medicines during pregnancy.

Every culture irrespective of its simplicity and complexity has its own notion regarding health and health-seeking behaviour. The health of any community is a manifestation of the interaction between socio-cultural and sociobiological practices. People of these three communities are still maintaining their traditional practices in various aspects of life. Tai people of Northeast India are very rich in herbal medicines. Some ethnomedicinal plants used by the three Tai groups of Northeast India for treatment of different maternal problems are given before in a tabular form.

References

Swain, S 1994, 'Health disease and health-seeking behaviour of tribal people of India' in *Tribal health in India*, ed S Basu, Manak Publications Pvt. Ltd., New Delhi.

Chapter - 7

Semkhor Village and the Semsa

— ***Dipali G. Danda***

I

Semkhor is a village and the 'Semsa' is a community. The two are separate entities. Nevertheless, they together make a common entity one being in complementary to other. *'Sem'* means salt in Dimasa language and *'Khor'* means source and *'Sa'* stands to represent children. The village Semkhor derived its name from the source of availability of natural salt through some saline pits and the people who live there, named Semsa, are the children of salt. It is the Dimasa way to be associated with the natural objects and phenomena.

The name 'Dimasa' means children of the river. People often feel an emotional attachment to their immediate natural surroundings or habitat and identify themselves as plain or forest or desert people. This may be more applicable to the eco-system people *i.e.*, those who are intimately and entirely dependent on their eco-system for survival. Most of the Dimasa village is located by the side of a river and named after a river. It may be mentioned that most of the rivers in the region bear Dimasa name.

The Semsa is such a group of people who are emotionally integrated with their physical environment which has a special significance with the presence of natural saline pits. The Semsa inhabit a single village, i.e. Semkhor of the Dima Hasao District once called North Cachar Hills of Assam. Historically and culturally too the Semsa may be called a section of the bigger Dimasa tribe of Assam. They speak Dimasa language and share all important socio-cultural markers with them. In spite of so many commonnesses the Semsa maintain their identity, they practically made the Semsa a separate mating

population. The principle of tribal endogamy is one of the important boundary markers to distinguish one tribe from another as a mating population the same principle of endogamy made the Semsa a different group in spite of many common cultural features with the Dimasa. The Semsa do not consider them as Dimasa though the latter admit a distant historical connection with them.

The Dimasa is one of the largest tribes of Assam. Their major concentration is in North Cachar now called Dima Hasao District of Assam- the population strength being 1,02961 (2011 census), while the population of the Semsa is below one thousand and not recorded in the census.

II

The village Semkhor is situated in the same location for more than two hundred years. It is one of the oldest villages in North Cachar Hills. The village history is associated with the royal heritage of the Kachari king. It is in Maibong Tahsil of Dima Hasao District of Assam. The nearest town and market is Maibong which is 30 km away. The Maibong town provides all the facilities of marketing, school, hospital, post office to the people of Semkhor. The District Headquarter Haflong is 82 km away from the village. The communication system is poorly developed.

The village covers an area of 406 hectors. It lies in the high hills of Barail range. It is bounded by hills from all sides. The highest point of the village is 5,190 (1801 m). With the exception of one Dimasa village, most of the neighbouring villages are inhabited by the Naga and Kuki groups of people. This ecological setting as such acted as boundary maintenance mechanism to preserve their identity. They have a very limited economic relationship with the Naga or Kuki people in the form of trade through barter or cash transaction. They have no marital relationship with the Dimasa or any other communities.

There were five saline pits (Semdikhor) around the village in the past. But now there are three saline pits located at one end of the village down the hills. These are marked by a bamboo fence. They are the common property of the villagers. These pits have an important role in the life of the Semsa. They firmly believe that they cannot survive outside Semkhor where there is no saline pit. In remote past, some families shifted from here and established a new settlement. There they suffered from some epidemics and returned to the original village. Thus, their Semsa sentiment got boosted. In olden days saline water was used for cooking purpose. Now salt is available in the market, hence this practice has stopped. Nevertheless, the ceremonial value of these saline pits remains as ever. These pits are worshipped on certain

occasions. Especially the date of harvest festival (*Busu*) is to be fixed after a prescribed worship followed by a feast over there.

III

For subsistence, the Semsa entirely depend on the forest. Shifting cultivation is their primary means of livelihood, always supplemented by collection from the forest. Some men especially old men make their living through basket making. Raw materials needed for making baskets are procured from the forest. The Semsa has a good reputation as basket makers and their basketry products have great demand in their locality. Whether cultivation or basket making, the people depend on the forest which provides all sorts of materials for their survival. In the same way, old women make their living through weaving. They weave men's dress and sometimes in exchange the person does some cultivation work for them. They can also hire labourers with the money which they earn through the sale of the products in the village.

When the forest is the main resource to the Semsa their bio-cultural survival is closely integrated with the forest. The village is covered with a dense jungle of bamboo and elephant grass. Forest has multipurpose use to the Semsa and hence its management is also very important to them.

Forest is owned by the community. The whole area is marked for various purposes such as cultivation, grazing purpose, collection of firewood, housing materials, and edible roots and vegetables. Some area of the forest is marked for cremation and other ritual purposes. As there is ample land around, the demarcation is not strictly followed except for cultivation, grazing and ritual purposes.

For shifting cultivation purpose the forest land is marked for five patriclans living in the village. Any individual member is free to choose any amount of land according to his availability of manpower for an agricultural season. He enjoys usufructuary right over it. He may at best cultivate the same for two consecutive years and then it is kept fallow for regeneration and automatically the right over land goes back to the clan. If somebody selects a piece of forest land, nobody would encroach upon it even it is not cultivated for that particular season. They have a special way of marking a plot of land after selection. In the same way, they mark a beehive who has spotted it first. Wet cultivation or *panikheti* is also practiced by a few in a very crude manner. The land meant for wet cultivation is situated by the side of the riverbed and sometimes on the beds of the non-perennial river. They do the wet cultivation almost the same way as they do in shifting cultivation without following the standard practices like leveling, manuring, irrigation, transplantation of seed. Only remarkable feature in case of *panikheti* is the

use of plough driven by a buffalo. *Panikheti* is monocrop,only paddy is grown there while in *jhum* field a number of crops are grown simultaneously. Another important feature about the wetland, unlike *jhum* field, it is private property owned by a family and inheritance of such land transmits from father to son.

Ordinarily, where subsistence is based on shifting cultivation the village size is not much big and as such not much scarcity is felt and thus *jhum* land and village land both are community property. But Semkhor being a relatively large village and located in a single spot over centuries the people had to evolve a certain mechanism for homestead land management.

The village land is traditionally distributed among five patriclans. Among the patriclans again, these are divided into five different patrilineages. As their rules of residence do not allow married sons to live with the parents, everybody wants to give a piece of land to the married sons. In such condition, pressure on homestead land increases with every marriage. The numerically dominant clan Langthasa occupies the central part of the village. With the increase of population, the village got extended laterally and downwardly. Here homestead land (*noiyam*) is individual property. In the long run, the last son (if unmarried) or daughter inherits the homestead land and the hut, as he or she lives with the parents. If a person does not have any parental homestead land, he may construct a hut in his own land with the permission of the eldest member of the clan. Sometimes he is allowed to construct a house on others land too, where he does not have any permanent claim and he cannot give it to his own son. However, he can buy the same from the owner of that land. There is so much scarcity of homestead land that often people buy such land from the people of one's own clan too. Sometimes very old people sell their homestead land to someone who takes its possession after the seller's death. We have never come across such a situation in any other village of North Cachar Hills.

A portion of the forest not demarcated clan-wise is kept permanently reserved for grazing purpose. In the month of June after sowing of seeds all the buffalo owners fence this particular patch of forest collectively so that the movement of the grazing animals' remains restricted within the fenced boundary for the entire cultivation season. The fencing is done annually. It may be mentioned here that the Semsa do not keep cows as they do not drink milk or eat beef. Buffalo is used as sacrificial animal during post-funeral ceremony and harvest festival. Buffalo meat is also consumed by them. They raise poultry, pigs, and dogs in the village at family level.

Rest of the forest is used for collection of firewood, housing materials, edible vegetables, and other items. That is also for use of all the villagers. Bamboo is one of the important items of the forest which has great relevance in the life of the Semsa. Vegetables and various kinds of roots and other

eatable forest products for daily consumption are collected from different areas of forest depending on the availability according to the season. During the period from January to April, they collect firewood from the *jhum* field which is being ready for that season.

Clan-wise demarcation is observed for the purpose of cremation. There are five cremation grounds for five clans. In earlier days two more clans were there who left the village long back. But the cremation area still there and nobody uses it. Clan-wise forest is demarcated for Area gods for five clans where occasional and annual worship is done by the respective clan members. Thus, the forest provides them everything ex-mundane life to life beyond.

IV

The Semsa wholly depend on the forest for food for about six months in a year. Their agricultural yield can support them only for four months. They remain busy in food production activities for half of the year and during other half of the year in other subsistence activities. For some more months, they subsist on their yield and jungle products. Approximately for six months, they depend on jungle products only. Hence their means of subsistence is cultivation both *jhum* and wet aided with gathering from the forest. Some people make their living through craft and wage labour.

The Semsa ways of wage labour do not bear the same connotation which is ordinarily used in the monetary transaction or labour market. In lean season poor families often borrow paddy from relatively well-off families who have surplus food grains. It is not always paddy sometime they borrow any sacrificial animal like a pig for ritual purpose. Selling of live buffalo by part during a crisis period is also one interesting mode of transaction prevalent among the Semsa. When the animal is sacrificed the buyer of the part-buffalo got the price of his share in kind or cash.

They repay the loan of such kind by working during sowing or harvesting season. If the volume of loan is high the person in debt may ask for free labour from his own kinsmen to work along with him in the creditor's field. This sort of mutual help is always available especially at the time of house construction. Whether a single individual or a group of people works in others field it is obligatory for the owner of the field to entertain them with rice beer and vegetable curry. Often the person spends more towards the labour than the actual value of the goods lent out. The principle of maximization of profit or exploitation does not work there. The system of mutual help ensures labour supply to all members of the community during peak agricultural seasons and availability of food grains to others during lean season. Thus, the whole village appears to be a corporate unit to protect each other's interest. This kind of mutual help in the form of loan or service provides a

sort of insurance to the members of the society during the period of crises. To the Semsa labour within the village is not a marketable commodity — it is more toward a relationship needed for better human survival. Nevertheless, the Semsa are acquainted with the market system too and operate with the market principle outside the village. They attend weekly market at Maibong. The Semsa women, who do not have the adequate manpower to cultivate, buy paddy from neigbouring Dimasa villages and sell the rice to the market after de-husking them at home. Market mechanism does not influence their economic or livelihood. Their traditional economic system is based on the values of human relationship which is best suited for their survival.

V

The day starts among the Semsa very early and they remain busy from dawn to dusk. All their activities are mostly centered around the subsistence activities. However, their activities may broadly be divided into two segments: subsistence and domestic activities, and socio-cultural and ritual activities. All works relating to producing subsistence are cultivation, gathering, pursuing any craft like basketry or weaving, trade on paddy or wage labour. Domestic works include bringing water, firewood, banana leaves for daily needs, housekeeping, looking after children and domestic animals. The activities relating to the first group are mostly tangible works involving manual labour though lots of managerial skills is also involved in it. The second category of activities is intangible in nature. These include organizing the annual harvest festival, managing the village council. The ritual activities include magical divination, organizing, and participation in funeral activities and priestly functions.

It has been observed that in the village all the able-bodied people irrespective of sex are engaged in subsistence activities. Even the children are not an exception to this. The only thing the degree of participation varies according to age and nature of work. Division of labour on the basis of age and sex is not very conspicuous. The job specification depends on physical strength involved in it especially in case of cultivation work. Usually, the male head of the family selects the *jhum* plot and responsible for felling of trees.

Women take active part in the process of shifting cultivation starting from land preparation to harvesting and storing of crops. In fact, the major activities relating to *jhum* cultivation like sowing, weeding, and threshing, harvesting all done by women. However, cutting of jungle and preparation of wetland (*panikheti*), construction of watch hut in the field, guarding crops are men's job. They do not make rice from paddy after harvest. The women of the house everyday pound the paddy by mortar and pestle to get the required amount of rice for day's consumption. Small-scale trade on paddy

is conducted by the women within the village and neighbouring villages. Nevertheless, large-scale market transaction is always done by men. Gathering of edible roots and vegetables, fishes, fetching water, cooking, brewing of rice beer, looking after children and domestic animals except buffalo are women's work. It is not that the Semsa men cannot do these works. In a household where there are no female member,menfolk do all the works. They know the art of everything from carpentry, basketry, construction of house. Collection of honey and hunting games, however, are entirely masculine job. As opposed to basketry weaving is done by women only. Many old people earn the subsistence through crafts. By selling their products they earn money and by that, they employ labourers to cultivate the land. Though technologically backward, they have developed some kind of specialization in different spheres of activities. No work is hierarchically value loaded. The focus is on the physical strength. Most of the arduous job are assigned to men.

In terms of productive organization, women's role and responsibility are almost equal with that of the men. In fact, in the whole process of cultivation, their workload is more than that of their male counterparts. It gets doubled with the responsibility of home management. If we scan through the daily activities of women which starts from pounding of paddy in the morning and continues for the day till the evening with fetching of firewood and water from down the hill and then ends up with the preparation of evening meal. Without being sick they cannot stay at home while most of the men can enjoy midday siesta. Their busy work schedule is mostly seasonal. They remain most busy with the cutting of jungle for *jhum* field. On the other hand, women's work schedule remains the same all over the year. Practically they do not have leisure time to relax without being sick. Despite the heavy pressure of work, the women especially young women do take part in arranging annual harvest festival. Women, in general, are not debarred from ritual activities. They can perform magical divination; participate in funeral procession which is not very common in other tribal societies. Nevertheless, among the Semsa a woman cannot be a priest and they do not have any role in the village council.

VI

The Semsa is a patrilocal people. Semkhor village is inhabited by the people of five patriclans. Out of these five clans, Phonglosa and Langthasa form the major bulk of the population. The other three are Haflongbar, Thaosen, and Seingyun. We find the same set of clans among the Dimasa as it has already been stated that historically the Semsa is related to the great Dimasa tribe. When we had conducted our anthropological research to work

among the Semsa during the late 70s of the previous centuries their population was less than 1000 (Danda and Ghatak, 1985). Perhaps for the first time, we brought them on record in anthropological literature. The area was so inaccessible and politically disturbed that the group remained unattended by the scholars till 2000 though there was enough scope for interesting studies relating to the small population. Maybe, with the expansion of communication system, some scholars showed interest in this group. Thus, we get some sporadic references to the Semsa since 2000. In one such reference, there is a mention of the 'Semsa as dwelling outside Semkhor village' which was unacceptable at one time. The reference made by the scholars from the Botany Department of the Gauhati University in connection with the studies on sacred groves and sacred plants of the Dimasa (2013), the scholar from anthropology may be interested at this. The work of Ghosh and Limbu from North Eastern Hill University, Shillong may be cited here too (2002, 2010).

The Semsa is a patrilocal people though exactly not patrilineal. Their descent system is a combination of both patriliny and mariiiny followed concurrently as it is found among the Dimasa. This type of descent is designated as double bilineal descent. Where double descent prevails, it is associated with a number of variations all over the world (Danda, 1978).

Due to the rule of double descent systems, every Semsa or Dimasa person is born with double clan allegiance. A person inherits clan affiliation from both of the parents. But the nature of affiliation is sex-specific. For a man, the clan which he inherits from his father was father's father is considered his primary clan affiliation and the clan which he inherits from mother and mother's mother but not from mother's father is his secondary clan affiliation. Reverse is the case with the women. A woman inherits primary clan affiliation from her mother and mother's mother and the secondary clan affiliation from the father and father's father.

Patriclan is called 'sengfong.' Its nature is patrilineal, *ie,* it transmits from father to son and daughter. Matriclan is called 'jaddi' or 'julu' and it transmits from mother to daughter and son. The speciality of double descent in Semsa case, it is bilineal in nature. Patriclan affiliation is primary for a son and it remains unchanged for generations. It transmits through generations in male line i.e., from father to son, and his son etc. Pariclan affiliation for a daughter is always secondary. Her primary affiliation is with her matriclan which also continues for generations through female line excluding her mother's patri kin or clan members. Thus, in Semsa society, a person is double clanic by birth. He or she belongs to both patri and matriclan — i.e., one bears the double clan allegiance — one is primary and the other is secondary depending on the sex of the Ego. Both the clans are exogamous in nature. At the time of

marriage, a person has to avoid the primary clan of both the parents. The following diagram would explain the case of double clan affiliation among the Semsa. Clan names starting with capital letter signifies primary affiliation and clans name with small letter means secondary affiliation.

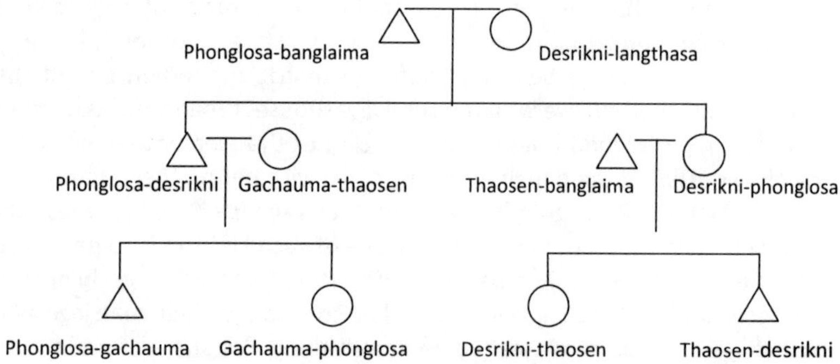

It is evident from the above diagram that primary affiliation continues from generation to generation through male and female lines. The secondary affiliation in case of both male and female lines changes in an alternate generation with marriage. Hence a man of Phonglosa clan inherits secondary matriclan affiliation from his mother. So, a son of Phonglosa-banglaina combination will be Phonglosa-gachauma as he inherits his mother's matriclan. He cannot have a spouse with Gachauma-phonglosa combination. Similarly, Desrikni-phonglosa woman cannot marry a man with Phonglosa-desrikni combination.

With the complexity of double clan system combined with village endogamy, it may appear that there may be a crisis in getting a mate within the village. In reality, it does not happen so. The society has its own mechanism to address all sorts of problems. Perhaps for that reason matriclans outnumber patriclans. In Semkhor number of patriclan is five while that of matriclan is seventeen. Thus, there is no difficulty in getting a mate from mother's father or mother's brother's patriclan.

Marriage is considered as a social bondage and it is something beyond mundane relation. If somebody dies unmarried, his/her life cycle is not complete and thus gets deprived of the chance of rebirth after death. Only exceptions in this regard are the people suffering from incurable diseases and mentally challenged ones.

The descent system not only regulates marriage it controls the residence rules of the Semsa. Though double descent is a combination of both patriliny

and matriliny, the principle of patriliny appeared to be of relatively dominant as patriclan is property owning group. Nevertheless, mother's property such as her jewelry, loom etc., is inherited by daughters. Matriclan is more effective in deciding the residence pattern after marriage. No two women belonging to different matriclans can live together in the same house or can use each other's comb or hair oil. For this reason, family can never be extended or joint by accommodating married son and his wife as mother-in-law and daughter-in-law always belong to different matriclans. When one of the spouses dies, children live with the surviving spouse. When widowed father marries for the second time if the matriclan of the stepmother, does not match with that of the daughter she is to live with her mother's mother or sister. In fact, maternal grandfather or mother's sister's husband takes care of such female children. In case of absence of such kin, she is to be looked after by the members of her matriclan. Her father looks after the children of the second wife. When grown up he has to arrange their marriage and bear the associated expenses too. However, the major share of bride price goes to the biological father (if he is surviving) or male agnates of her patriclan. Stepchildren also look after the ailing or old parents as one's children do. Social obligation along with clan obligation which is almost mandatory helps to maintain the equilibrium in the Semsa society.

VII

The Semsa presents a unique case study of small population. There is ample scope for further study among the Semsa relating to them eco-cultural adaptation. As a small community, the Semsa is self-sufficient, confined to a small pocket of Dima Hasao District of Assam. The family is the basic unit of the society and their typical double descent system along with village endogamy make the people more self-sustaining in that particular eco-cultural setting. They have a very limited socio-economic relationship with other neighbouring people. Though they have limited exposure to outside world they are not ignorant of the modern market or electoral system. Due to lack of proper communication system, the Semsa cannot avail of the opportunity of educational or medical facilities. During any crises, they fall back on their traditional system of healing and make a compromise at best possible ways with their life situation. From the heart of heat, they also aspire for better health and educational facilities and in a democratic set up their wish may also be fulfilled in near future.

References

Census of India, 2011, Provisional Population Totals. Census of India, Directorate of Census Operation

Danda, DG 1978, *Among the Dimasa of Assam*, Starling Publisher, New Delhi.

Danda, DG & Ghatak, S 1985, *The Semsa and their habitat*, Anthropological Survey of India, Calcutta.

Ghosh, AK & Limbu, DK 2000, 'The Semsa: a bio-demographic study', *International Journal of Anthropology*, vol. 15, no. 1-2, pp. 109-124.

Ghosh, AK & Limbu, DK 2002, *The Semsa*, Mittal Publication, Delhi.

Ghosh, AK & Limbu, DK 2010, *Inbreeding in the Semsa of Semkhor village in N.C. Hills*, NEHU publication.

Chapter - 8

Infant Mortality among the Dibongiya Deori of Assam: An Empirical Analysis

— Juri Borah and Sarthak Sengupta

Introduction

Infants are the important asset of a human society. According to Barclay (1958), infant includes those children in the first years of life who have not yet reached the age one. Infant mortality is an important domain of community health care and is considered as one of the most important indicators of socio-economic development (Stockwell et al., 1988). Hence, infant mortality is used to compare health status at the country or social class levels (Bicego and Boerma, 1993; Subramanian et al., 2006). The economically advanced countries are able to reduce their death rate to less than ten per thousand largely by providing their people with adequate and wholesome food, pure drinking water, better medical facilities, better sewage disposal and taking proper measures to control various diseases (Agarwala, 1988).

Based on the time period, infant mortality is divided into neonatal mortality (0-28 days) and postneonatal mortality (29 days - 12 months). Endogenous factors, e.g. the age of mothers, birth order, prematurity, weight at birth, multiple births, etc are considered as the prime causes behind neonatal deaths. On the other hand, post neonatal deaths are found to occur mainly due to exogenous factors, namely, epidemics caused by communicable diseases, such as diarrhoea, enteritis, bronchitis, pneumonia, faulty feeding pattern, poor hygiene, unsanitary surroundings, etc. (Bhende and Kanitkar, 1997).

Various studies have discussed the problem of infant mortality and also its plausible causes from time to time. The analyses basically consider the background (ethnicity, religion, and current place of residence), demographic (mother's age, age at marriage, number of children ever born, and duration of breastfeeding), and socio-economic (maternal and paternal education and occupation, and household income) variables (Adlakha and Suchindran, 1985; Bailey, 1988).

The determinants of infant and child mortality vary across different geographical and cultural groups as well as in the developed and developing countries (Mahadevan, 1986). In India, social class has been considered as a proxy for socio-economic status and poverty, and it has a substantial impact on infant health and mortality. One of the social classes in India, Scheduled Tribe (ST), has been an integral part of the country's population for a long time. A majority of the ST population lives in the Northeastern, Central, and Eastern parts of the country (Annual Health Survey, 2011-2012). Assam, the second largest state in northeastern region of India is also a homeland for diverse communities and has experienced considerable variations in health care facilities as per their place of residence.

As per the Annual Health Survey (2011-12), the infant mortality rate in Assam is 57 per thousand live births. The information on the incidence of infant mortality in Assam estimated by National Family Health Survey - 4 (NFHS, 2015-2016) was found to be considerably higher than the other states of Northeast India. However, Assam recorded the higher proportion of death of the infants in comparison to other north-eastern states of India as per the NFHS - 3 (2005-2006) report also.

Objective

In the present chapter, the bio-social correlates of infant mortality among the Dibongiya, a territorial group of Deori tribe residing in the Lakhimpur district of Assam have been discussed. Besides, an attempt is also made to assess variation on the basis of differential place of residence - rural and urban.

Material and method

The present study is confined to 405 and 99 Dibongiya Deori women respectively from rural and urban areas of Lakhimpur district, Assam. Rural areas considered for the present study are namely, Borchapori Deori *Gaon,* Kinapather Deori *Gaon*, Bhogpur Deori *Gaon,* Pichola Deori *Gaon,* Major Chapori Deori *Gaon* and the different urban settlement having Dibongiya Deori concentration are Bihpuria, Bandardewa, and Narayanpur. All these settlements are belonging to the Lakhimpur district of Assam. The respondent

women were ever married, continuing the conjugal life with husbands till the date of investigation and have a minimum of one child. Observation and interview are the key techniques adopted for the collection of data. For the purpose of collecting the relevant information, the respondents have been interviewed by using a household survey schedule and also a fertility and mortality investigation schedule. The mortality estimates used in the present study are actually the proportion of death as per the number of live births. Data were analyzed by using the computer software namely, 'Microsoft Office Excel 2007' and 'Chi-square test of Independence' in which the level of significance was set at 5.0 percent level of probability. The classification for BMI calculation is followed according to WHO, 2004.

Deori, a Tibeto-Mongoloid population group, is one of the plains Scheduled Tribes of Assam. The Dibongiya Deori is one of the sub-divisions or territorial groups (*Khels*) of Deori tribe, the name of which owes its origin from the river Dibong of their original homeland Sadiya in Arunachal Pradesh. The other territorial groups of Deori tribe are Tengapania, Borgonya, and Patorgonya. The Dibongiya Deori prefers to inhabit in relatively remote areas of different districts of upper Assam than the other two territorial groups. North bank of the river Brahmaputra is the major concentration of the Dibongiya Deori population, where they are predominantly distributed in the Lakhimpur, Dhemaji, Majuli and Sonitpur districts of upper Assam. They are sporadically distributed in the southern bank of the river Brahmaputra and are also concentrated in the Lohit and Changlang districts of Arunachal Pradesh.

Results and discussion

Proximate bio-social factors of infant mortality considered in the present chapter include mother's age at marriage, age at first childbirth, age at each childbirth, birth order, birth interval, maternal nutritional status, place of delivery, nature of delivery, family type, maternal and paternal education,and maternal and paternal occupation.

Variation in infant mortality as per the place of residence is observed because of the difference in standard of living, health condition and availability of or access to public health facilities. Mortality is reported to be higher in rural regions than in the urban areas. In a study about the situation of children in India by UNICEF (1984), it was stated that in rural areas the family system compels the women including the pregnant women to take food in less quantity and improper in quality which cause nutritional deficiency among the pregnant and nursing mothers resulting in the death of the infants in many occasions. This finding was also proven to be correct by the works of some other scholars namely,Venkatacharya (1985), Ramu

(1988), Rahman et al. (1993), etc. Though the mortality rate is always high in the infant age, yet the probability of dying is not uniform throughout the first year of life. Several studies (Ghosh, 1988; Singhi et al., 2004; Roy et al., 2008 and many others) have revealed that the risk of death is comparatively higher during neonatal infancy than during postneonatal infancy. However, sex difference in child mortality is also mentioned by scholars, in that, life expectancy at birth is substantially higher for females than for males; and females tend to survive all forms of diseases better than males. Generally, the explanations that are forwarded vary from differences in psychological stresses and living habits to physiological and genetic differences, where males are believed to be more at a disadvantage than females (Conrad, 1962; Madigan, 1968; Nayeye et al., 1971). On the contrary, many developing countries deviate from this pattern, whereby females are more at a disadvantage than males; mainly due to economic and socio-cultural reasons rather than biological ones, such as lower status of women, relative bias reflected in the standard of diet and care (Das Gupta, 1990).

Incidence of infant deaths by sex and place of residence among Dibongiya Deori is shown in Table 8.1. The incidence of mortality at an infant stage is relatively higher in the rural areas (4.35%) in comparison to an urban setup (3.64%). Yet, chi-square test of significance reveals nonsignificant variation between the two samples. Chakrabarty (1995) in a study conducted among the Jaintia of Meghalaya also observed the considerably higher incidence of infant mortality in the rural area (6.20%) than the urban area (3.19%). Chanu (2007) in her study among the Loi population of Manipur also reported the relatively higher incidence of infant mortality in the rural areas (2.09%) in comparison to the urban residents (1.02%). Variation in the incidence of infant mortality as per the place of residence is also documented by the NFHS-4 report for the state of Assam as a whole. In all the northeastern states of India considered in the NFHS-4 report namely, Arunachal Pradesh, Assam, Manipur, Meghalaya, Mizoram, and Nagaland the infant mortality in rural areas is reported to be much higher than in urban areas.

The proportion of infant mortality of the Dibongiya Deori from the rural areas (4.35%) shows conformity with that of Manipuri Meitei (4.13%; Ahmed Das and Barua, 1999), Oraon (4.56%; Ahmed Das and Konwar,2002), Sonowal Kachari (4.38%; Sengupta and Kalita, 2001 and 4.04%; Baruah and Sengupta, 2009) and Bodo (4.75%; Dutta Das and Saikia, 2010) of Assam and also Khasi (4.20%; Adak, 1993) and Pnar (4.20%; Khongsdier et al., 2001) of Meghalaya. However, the incidence of infant mortality among the Dibongiya from urban area (3.64%), the similarity is observed with the Mishing (3.80%; Baruah and Sengupta, 2009), Khamti (3.21%; Borah and Sengupta, 2013), Rengma Naga (3.25%; Rengma, 2014) and Kaibarta from Deodubi area (3.73%; Hazarika and Sengupta, 2017) of Assam and also Jaintia of Meghalaya (3.19%;

Chakrabarty, 1995). Comparatively higher proportion of infant mortality than the Dibongiya Deori irrespective of place of residence is observed among the Semsa (7.55%; Limbu and Khongsdier, 2000), Mishing (7.26%; Sengupta and Dutta, 2000), Munda (13.27%), Oraon (11.67%) and Tanti (14.82%) studied by Borkataky (2004), Tiwa (7.01%; Das, 2010), Bodo (9.89%) and Rabha (11.76%) studied by Das (2014), Ahom (5.45%; Gogoi, 2016) and Kaibarta from Sonapur area (6.04%; Hazarika and Sengupta, 2017) of Assam; Khamti (11.21%; Choudhury et al., 1991 and 7.37%; Baruah et al., 1994), Muklom Tangsa (7.79%; Sarkar, 2002) and Digaru Mishmi (10.56%), Miju Mishmi (13.22%) and Idu Mishmi (6.28%) of Arunachal Pradesh reported by Gogoi (2008); Garo (5.19%; Adak, 1993), Jaintia from rural area (6.20%; Chakrabarty, 1995), Christian (6.89%) and non-Christian (8.55%) War Khasi (Ghosh and Khongsdier, 1997), Christian (6.82%) and Niamtre Khasi (8.60%) reported by Mukherjee (2002) and Pnar from Sanaro area (14.06%; Syngkon, 2013) of Meghalaya and Lotha Naga (5.75%; Murry et al., 2005) and Ao Naga (5.18%; Sengupta and Purnungla, 2005) of Nagaland. On the other hand, the infant mortality among the Dibongiya Deori living in both rural and urban area is relatively higher than that of Bengali (2.35%) and Assamese (2.08%) population of Guwahati, Assam studied by Chakravarty (2001), Ahom (2.39%; Baruah and Sengupta, 2009) and Mishing (2.56%; Patir, 2017) of Assam; Mizo (2.30%; Adak, 1993) and Pnar from Jowai area (2.91%; Syngkon, 2013) of Meghalaya; Hmars of Mizoram (2.83%; Varte, 2006) and Meitei (2.20%) and Sekmai (3.10%) studied by Devi (1998), Loi (rural: 2.09% and urban: 1.02%) studied by Chanu (2007) and Khongsai Kuki (2.05%; Khongsai, 2012) of Manipur. However, the incidence of infant mortality of the Dibongiya Deori is marginally lower than the rate estimated by NFHS-4 for the state of Assam as a whole (48 deaths per 1,000 live births).

Among the Dibongiya Deori respondents from both the rural and urban areas, the frequency of death of male infant (rural: 4.66% and urban: 5.04%) is recorded as considerably higher than the female death (rural: 4.04% and urban: 1.98%). The same trend is noticed in both neonatal and postneonatal mortality. Among the Bengali and Assamese population of Assam, Chakravarty (2001) recorded higher incidence of death of male (0.88%) than the female (0.74%) out of all the postneonatal death. However, in neonatal stage, he observed higher incidence of the death of female (0.35%) than the male (0.26%). Das (2010) in her study among the Tiwa of Assam reported higher proportion of death of female infants (4.21%) than their male counterpart (2.80%).

The frequency of neonatal mortality (rural: 2.36% and urban: 3.18%) is comparatively higher than the post neonatal mortality (rural: 1.99% and urban: 0.45%) in both the sexes, irrespective of their place of residence. Here too, no statistically significant differences are observed between the two

considered variables. Comparatively higher proportion of death at neo natal stage than the postneonatal stage was also reported by various scholars since long. For instances, Borkataky (2004) in her study among the Munda, Oraon and Tanti of Assam reported the higher incidence of neonatal death (Munda: 8.95%, Oraon: 8.95% and Tanti: 11.11%) in comparison to the postneonatal death (Munda: 4.32%, Oraon: 3.47% and Tanti: 3.71%). Adak (1993) also reported higher incidence of neonatal death (3.39%) than the postneonatal death (1.81%) among the Garo population of Meghalaya. On the contrary, a higher incidence of postneonatal death than the neonatal death is reported among the Bengali (neonatal: 0.39% and postneonatal: 1.96%) and Assamese (neonatal: 0.80% and postneonatal: 1.28%) population of Assam (Chakravarty, 2001), Khasi (neonatal: 1.72% and postneonatal: 2.48%) and Mizo (neonatal: 0.35% and postneonatal: 1.95%) of Meghalaya (Adak, 1993) and also Meitei (neonatal: 0.98% and postneonatal: 1.22%) and Sekmai (neonatal: 0.98% and postneonatal: 2.12%) of Manipur (Devi, 1998).

Table 8.1: Incidence of infant deaths by sex and place of residence

Sex	*Live birth*	*Infant mortality*				*Total*		χ^2
		Neonatal		*Postneonatal*				
		No.	*%*	*No.*	*%*	*No.*	*%*	
Rural								
Male	558	14	2.51	12	2.15	26	4.66	0.002, p= 0.96
Female	545	12	2.20	10	1.83	22	4.04	
Total	1103	26	2.36	22	1.99	48	4.35	
Urban								
Male	119	5	4.20	1	0.84	6	5.04	0.13, p= 0.72
Female	101	2	1.98	0	0	2	1.98	
Total	220	7	3.18	1	0.45	8	3.64	

Rural – urban (x^2) = 1.22, p= 0.27

Disparity with regards to the causes of death among different communities is observed due to the diversity in geographic condition as well as variation in perception and preventive strategies towards illness condition. Incidence of infant deaths and their causes among Dibongiya Deori is shown in the Table 8.2. Among all the causes of death, having faith in evil eye is reported as the major cause in the rural area. On the other hand, delivery complicacy was recorded to be the preponderating reason of the infant mortality in the urban area. The factors responsible for the death of their infant is difficult to ascertain since many of them are not taking help from any medical expert or medical treatment during the time of their sufferings. The Dibongiya Deori women mostly prefer home deliveries. That may be one of the reasons for the delivery complications which effect on the life of their newborn in later also. In this regard, it may be mentioned here that in Meghalaya, Adak (1993) observed that the major causes of death among the

Khasi and Garo is fever and respiratory troubles respectively. In case of the Mizo living in Meghalaya, he reported the major causes of infant mortality as asphyxia and gastroenteritis. In Manipur, Devi (1998) reported jaundice, cough, and fever, diarrhea and heart disease as the main causes of infant death while it is cough and fever, jaundice and fatal accident among the Sekmai population of Manipur. Among the Assamese and Bengali population of Assam, Chakravarty (2001) recorded fever, cough, and diarrhea as the major causes of infant and child mortality. Borkataky (2004) reported the symptoms of diarrhea as the prime cause of death of the infants among the Oraon and Munda of Assam. On the other hand, the major cause infants' death identified among the Tanti (tea garden workers) is stomach trouble. Among the Tiwa of Assam, Das (2010) reported fever and pneumonia as the major cause of mortality among the infants. The cause of death during infancy among the Bodo population of Assam as recorded by Das (2014) mainly due to low birth weight, followed by pneumonia, diarrhea, respiratory problem and asphyxia. In the Rabha population also, low birth weight of the baby was documented as the major cause of infant death (ibid). However, belief in evil spirit was also reported as recurrent cause of infant mortality among the Rabha population of Assam.

Table 8.2: Incidence of infant deaths and it's causes

Causes of death	*Rural*		*Urban*	
	No	*%*	*No*	*%*
Delivery Complicacy	2	4.17	4	50.00
Respiratory Problem	4	8.33	0	0
Evil Eye	7	14.58	1	12.5
Pneumonia	3	6.25	0	0
Fever	4	8.33	1	12.5
Pox	4	8.33	0	0
Diarrhea	2	4.17	0	0
Stomach Pain	1	2.08	0	0
Jaundice	1	2.08	0	0
Urogenital Problem	1	2.08	0	0
Nonstop Crying	5	10.42	2	25.00
Neck Problem	3	6.25	0	0
Bleeding from Nose	3	6.25	0	0
Heart Problem	1	2.08	0	0
Aversion of Breast Milk	2	4.17	0	0
Vomiting	1	2.08	0	0
Unknown Reasons	4	8.33	0	0

Mothers' age at marriage, which is an indirect factor has a great role in regulating the mortality differentials of the mothers. In population growth and dynamics, a significant role is maintained by age at marriage. It has

numerous negative social and health consequences. Infant mortality of the Dibongiya Deori women according to their age at marriage is shown in Table 8.3. Among the respondents from rural area, the occurrences of infant mortality appear to be highest in those who entered into the conjugal life at the age of 19 years or even earlier (5.41%). On the contrary, in urban area, higher incidence of infant mortality is observed among the mothers in the age groups of 30-34 years (10.00%). The variation observed in this regard turned out to be statistically insignificant between the Dibongiya women from the rural and urban areas. Among the Mishing population studied by Baruah (2007), the incidence of infant mortality is quite low among those who married at relatively later ages. In Ahom population incidence of infant mortality was observed only among those mothers who married early (Baruah, 2007). Among the Khamti mothers of Arunachal Pradesh and Phake population of Assam (Gogoi, 2016), relatively higher infant mortality was recorded among those mothers who married early. Study conducted by Saikia (2015) among Sonowal Kachari women of Assam record higher proportion of infant mortality among those mothers who got married at a later age of their life.

Table 8.3: Incidence of infant deaths by mother's age at marriage

Age at marriage (in years)	*Rural*			*Urban*			χ^2
	Live birth	*Infant mortality*		*Live birth*	*Infant mortality*		
		No.	*%*		*No.*	*%*	
≤ 19	425	23	5.41	85	4	4.71	2.55, p = 0.47
20-24	410	12	2.93	90	2	2.22	
25-29	239	12	5.02	31	1	3.23	
≥ 30	30	1	3.33	14	1	7.14	

Bhende and Kanitkar (1997) opined that when a woman gives her first childbirth within the age group of 19-29 years is biologically safe for the mother as it reduces infant mortality rate. Table 8.4 shows the distribution of infant deaths by mother's age at first childbirth. Notwithstanding the place of residence, comparatively higher proportion of infant death is found among those who gave birth of their first baby at the age of 19 years or even earlier (rural: 6.34% and urban: 7.5%), followed by the age of 30 years or more (rural: 4.84% and urban: 5.56%). Here too, no statistically significant differences are observed between the rural-urban samples. Borkataky (2004) studied the infant and early childhood mortality according to mother's age at first childbirth among four tea working communities of Assam namely, the Munda, Tanti, and Oraon. Amongst all the four communities considered, incidence of infant and early childhood mortality was found to be the relatively higher when the mother's age at first childbirth is 15 years or earlier. However, a decreasing trend of mortality with the increase of mother's age at the first

childbirth amongst all the four communities was recorded by her. Das (2014) in his study among the Bodo and Rabha population of Assam also observed higher incidence of infant mortality among the mothers who experienced their first delivery at the age of 19 years or earlier.

Table 8.4: Incidence of infant deaths by mother's age at first childbirth

Age at first childbirth (in years)	*Rural*			*Urban*			χ^2
	Live birth	*Infant mortality*		*Live birth*	*Infant mortality*		
		No.	*%*		*No.*	*%*	
≤ 19	268	17	6.34	40	3	7.5	1.49, p = 0.69
20-24	465	15	3.23	106	1	0.94	
25-29	308	13	4.22	56	3	5.36	
≥ 30	62	3	4.84	18	1	5.56	

Mortality also depends on the age of the mother at which she delivers her babies. Mortality, particularly neonatal mortality, is found to be higher among children of very young mothers (Choe et al., 1999). Hobcraft et al., (1984) stated that children born to very young or to very old mothers experience more mortality compared to those born to mothers in the intermediate age groups. Ruzicka and Kane(1987) are of the opinion that the increased risk of infant death among the old mothers may be due to maternal depletion syndrome such as undernourishment, anemia and general weakness associated with the biological demands of excessive reproduction. Conversely, Ahmad et al. (1991) reported that older maternal age had tended to lower risk of child death. This may be because of the fact that with the increase in maternal age, mothers become more experienced in taking care of their children. Talwar (1988) observed that the risk of infant mortality increases among early or late childbearing women in rural Madhya Pradesh. In a study in rural Madhya Pradesh, he has shown that mother's age at the birth of the child is significantly associated with the risk of infant deaths. For mothers below the age of 20 years or above the age of 40 years, the risk of infant death is increased by 34.0 percent than the mothers bearing children between ages 20-39 years.

Distribution of infant deaths by mother's age at childbirth is shown in the Table 8.5. In both rural (7.63%) and urban (17.65%) area, the incidence of infant death is found as considerable high among those mothers who delivered their babies at the age of 19 years or earlier. The proportion of infant death seems to be low at the age groups of 20-24 years and 25-29 years among the respondents from both rural and urban area. However, it found to increase in the age group of 30 years or more (rural: 6.20% and urban: 4.84%). The differences between rural and urban sample in this regard were found as statistically insignificant. Almost similar finding with regards to distribution of infant deaths according to mother's age at childbirth was

accounted by NFHS - 4 report for the state of Assam as a whole. As per the report children born to mothers under age of 20 years (6.3%) and age group of 30-39 years (4.7%) are more likely to die during infancy than children born to mothers in the prime childbearing age group i.e., 20-29 years (4.2%).

Table 8.5: Incidence of infant deaths by mother's age at childbirth

Age at childbirth (in years)	*Rural*			*Urban*			χ^2
	Live birth	*Infant mortality*		*Live birth*	*Infant mortality*		
		No.	*%*		*No.*	*%*	
≤ 19	118	9	7.63	17	3	17.65	1.60 p = 0.66
20-24	332	14	4.22	72	0	0	
25-29	351	10	2.85	69	2	2.90	
≥ 30	242	15	6.20	62	3	4.84	

Infant mortality rates, in general, are found to depict U-shaped or reversed J-shaped curve in relation to birth order (Omran and Standley, 1976). Sathar (1985) opines that the probability of death at infancy and childhood is more in the 1st order of pregnancy. He also mentioned that the chances of survival of the infants gradually increases according to the subsequent birth, yet the risk again starts to increase after 5th birth order onwards. Analogous finding was also propped up by the study of Ruzica and Kanitkar (1973), Caldwell (1979), Arora (1980) and many others.

Table 8.6 details the incidence of infant deaths among the Dibongiya Deori women as per their birth order. Women living in the rural area record a very high incidence of infant mortality in the 4th birth order (6.25%), followed by the 1st order of pregnancy (4.99%). The frequency of infant mortality remains almost unchanged in the 2nd (3.42%) and 3rd (3.41%) birth order. Among them, there are no instances of infant mortality in the 9th-10th order of pregnancy, although relatively higher proportion is recorded in the 7th-8th birth order (4.76%), followed by 5th-6th birth order (4.49%). Among the women living in urban area substantially higher occurrence of infant mortality is noticed in the 5th-6th order of pregnancy (11.11%). No statistically significant differences are observed with regards to birth order between the women of the rural and urban area. Barua (1982) recorded that the offspring mortality is comparatively high in the first birth order and it gradually decreases with subsequent birth orders but increases sharply again with escalating birth order among the Hajong of Meghalaya.Chakrabarty (1995) in her study among the Jaintia of Meghalaya observed lowest incidence of infant and child mortality at the 1st birth order and the highest percentage of mortality was found at the 12th birth order. Chakravarty (2001) recorded higher incidence of infant and child mortality with the increase of birth order among the Assamese and Bengali population of Guwahati, Assam. In a study among the Lotha Naga women of Nagaland, Murry et al. (2005) observed relatively higher

incidence of infant mortality in the 6th order of pregnancy. Baruah (2007) in her study among the Ahom, Mishing and Sonowal Kachari of Assam observed higher proportions of infant mortality in the first birth order which decreases gradually and rises again with increased birth order. Infant and child mortality also gradually increases with increasing numbers of birth order in both the Bodo and the Rabha population of Assam (Das, 2014).

Table 8.6: Incidence of infant deaths by birth order

Birth order	*Rural*			*Urban*			χ^2
	Live birth	*Infant mortality*		*Live birth*	*Infant mortality*		
		No.	*%*		*No.*	*%*	
1	381	19	4.99	88	3	3.41	1.17 p = 0.98
2	292	10	3.42	68	3	4.41	
3	205	7	3.41	34	1	2.94	
4	112	7	6.25	21	0	0	
5-6	89	4	4.49	9	1	11.11	
7-8	21	1	4.76	0	0	0	
9-10	3	0	0	0	0	0	

Significant impact of birth interval on the infant and child mortality was cited by various scholars viz., Trussel et al. (1992), Pebley and Millman (1986), Chen et al. (1980) and many others. According to them, the probability of death is very high if the length of birth interval is short. In developing countries, children are much more likely to die if they are born less than two years of gap in comparison to the child born in longer interval (Trussel et al., 1992). In Punjab, the risk of death of infants with a birth interval of less than two years was recorded as 50.0 percent higher than the children born in the gap of two to four years (Gordon et al., 1971). It is believed that the mother can't provide proper care neither to elder nor to younger if the intervals between two births is less. The very short gap between two children is considered as problematic for the mother and her child (Bhende and Kanitkar, 1997). Significant relationship of birth order and birth interval with infant and child mortality among Scheduled Tribes in rural India during 1992 - 2006 was also reported by Sahu et al. (2015).

Table 8.7 shows the occurrence of infant deaths by birth interval. In both the rural (4.52%) as well as urban (3.85%) areas, relatively higher frequency of infant death is found among those mothers who delivered their babies within 2 years of gap. In the rural area, the proportion of death at infant stage decreases substantially with the increase in birth interval. No statistically significant differences are observed with regards to birth interval between the women of the rural and urban area. A decreasing trend of infant and child mortality with the increase of birth interval was reported by Borkataky (2004) among the four tea worker communities of Assam namely, the Munda, Tanti, and Oraon. Among the Bodo and Rabha populations of Assam, Das

(2014) observed relatively higher incidences of infant mortality in short birth intervals (<24 month) in comparison to the higher birth intervals. A significant negative relationship between the infant mortality rates and mean birth intervals among the Khongsai Kuki in both Saikul sub-division and Imphal town of Manipur were also reported (Khongsai, 2012). The study indicates that the infant mortality rate decreases along with the mean birth interval increases. Children born less than two years after a previous birth are likely to die more than two times in infancy as compared to those children whose mothers waited for two or more years between births as documented in NFHS -4 report for the Assam as a whole.

Table 8.7: Incidence of infant deaths by birth interval

Birth interval (in years)	*Rural*			*Urban*			χ^2
	Live birth	*Infant mortality*		*Live birth*	*Infant mortality*		
		No.	*%*		*No.*	*%*	
<2	752	16	4.52	156	6	3.85	5.13, p = 0.08
2-3	165	22	2.42	34	1	2.94	
≥ 4	186	10	0.05	30	1	3.33	

Nutrition is the amalgamation of processes which are essential for growth and development, health and well-being of an individual. Body Mass Index (BMI) is more nutritionally than genetically related. It is reported that BMI is closely associated with morbidity and mortality. It is reported that mortality risk increases with the increase in BMI values. Relationship of childhood mortality with the nutritional status has also been reported in a number of studies like, Gopalan and Naidu (1972), Gopalan (1973), Sengupta (1979), Mahadevan et al. (1986), Rao (1988), Bharati and Basu (1990), Chakravarty (1994), and Chakravarty (2006).

Table 8.8 demonstrates the incidence of infant deaths among the ever married Dibongiya Deori women as per their nutritional status. Noticeably higher incidence of mortality at an infant stage is observed among the overweight mothers (5.13%) in the urban area, while women from rural area who belong to the normal category (4.88%) records comparatively higher incidence of infant death, followed by the underweight mother (4.52%). In this connection, statistically significant differences between the rural and urban samples are observed. Infant mortality is completely absent among the obese mothers residing in both rural as well as urban setup. Seal et al. (2010) observed relatively higher incidence of infant mortality among the normal weighted Mishing mothers of Assam. Tengapania Deori women belonging to overweight categories also exhibit higher incidence of infant mortality (Patir and Sengupta, 2015).

Table 8.8: Incidence of infant deaths by maternal nutritional status

Nutritional status of mothers (BMI)	*Rural*			*Urban*			χ^2
	Live birth	*Infant mortality*		*Live birth*	*Infant mortality*		
		No.	*%*		*No.*	*%*	
Underweight	177	8	4.52	7	0	0	
Normal	758	37	4.88	122	4	3.28	11.38, p = 0.01*
Overweight	158	3	1.90	78	4	5.13	
Obese	10	0	0	13	0	0	

The prime important requirement for safe motherhood is the institutional delivery. The likelihood of maternal and infant mortality increases if delivery takes place at home without assistance of trained birth attendant. Infant mortality rate will come down if births take place in hygienic conditions and proper medical care is available (Visaria, 1985). Pardeshi et al. (2011) were of opinion that delivery in a medical institution promotes child survival and reduces the risk of maternal mortality.

Occurrence of infant deaths according to the place of delivery is shown in Table 8.9. It is apparent from the table that the incidence of mortality at infancy is considerably high among those who were admitted in government hospital (rural: 5.98% and urban: 5.32%), followed by the delivery at home (rural: 3.48% and urban: 2.75%). No instances of infant mortality were recorded among those who were born in the private hospital. However, the test of significance shows non-significant differences between the two samples with regards to the place of delivery. Borkataky (2004) observed higher incidence of infant mortality when the deliveries take place in home among the tea worker communities in Assam. Das (2014) also recorded higher incidence of infant mortality in home deliveries as compared to hospital deliveries in the Bodo and Rabha population of Assam.

Table 8.9: Incidence of infant deaths by place of delivery

Delivery place	*Rural*			*Urban*			χ^2
	Live birth	*Infant mortality*		*Live birth*	*Infant mortality*		
		No.	*%*		*No.*	*%*	
Home Delivery	661	23	3.48	109	3	2.75	
Government Hospital	418	25	5.98	94	5	5.32	0.30, p = 0.86
Private Nursing Home	24	0	0	17	0	0	

Table 8.10 shows the incidence of infant deaths as per the nature of delivery. Among the rural respondents, the frequency of infant mortality is higher in normal deliveries (4.37%), while the cases of caesarean delivery recorded the higher infant mortality among the women reside in the urban setup (4.55%). The test of significance fails to record any statistically significant variation in this regard. Borkataky (2004) mentioned higher incidence of infant

mortality among those Munda, Tanti, and Oraon of Assam who had suffer long labour pain during parturition. Murry et al. (2005) in their study among the Lotha Naga women of Nagaland observed comparatively higher incidence of infant mortality in case of caesarian delivery. In a study, Das (2014) observed higher incidence of infant mortality in case of caesarean delivery among the Bodo population of Assam. On the contrary, he recorded the incidence of infant mortality in the cases of normal delivery only among the Rabha population of Assam.

Table 8.10: Incidence of infant deaths by nature of delivery

Nature of delivery	*Rural*			*Urban*			χ^2
	Live birth	*Infant mortality*		*Live birth*	*Infant mortality*		
		No.	*%*		*No.*	*%*	
Normal	1053	46	4.37	198	7	3.54	0.94,
Caesarean	50	2	4.00	22	1	4.55	p = 0.33

The family may simply be defined as a group of persons united by the ties of marriage, blood or adoption, constituting a single household. It is the basic unit of social organization which is of interest to demographers as the type of family has varied socio-economic impact on the population. Better health care practices of the mothers during the period of pregnancy and also the care of the infants and children may decrease the level of infant and early childhood mortality. Srivastava and Saksena (1980) mentioned that babies born in the joint family receive more care than the babies in a nuclear family.

The two types of families observed among the Dibongiya Deori population are nuclear family and joint family. Distribution of infant deaths according to the pattern of the family types is shown in the Table 8.11. The Dibongiya Deori mothers living in joint families from the rural area have a slightly higher incidence of death at an infant stage (4.79%), while in case of women living in urban area more such incidence is found among women from nuclear families. The test of significance shows statistically significant differences between the two samples studied. The impact of family type on the mortality differential is perceived by the scholars in different ways. In Meghalaya, Barua (1980) recorded a higher proportion of infant mortality among Khasi women from nuclear families than in women from joint families. In all the tea worker communities of Assam namely, Munda, Tanti, and Oraon, child mortality was found to be the higher in the nuclear family (Borkataky, 2004). Baruah (2007) recorded a higher incidence of postnatal mortality among the Sonowal Kachari and Mishing women from nuclear families, but, the Ahom women belonging to joint families experienced a higher incidence of it. Das (2014) observed the higher incidence of infant mortality in joint

families among the Bodo, while the reverse situation was found among the Rabha tribe of Assam. Patir and Sengupta (2015) observed a higher incidence of infant mortality among the Dibongiya Deori women from nuclear families.

Table 8.11: Incidence of infant deaths by family type

Family type	*Rural*			*Urban*			χ^2
	Live birth	*Infant mortality*		*Live birth*	*Infant mortality*		
		No.	*%*		*No.*	*%*	
Nuclear	581	23	3.96	160	7	4.38	4.32,
Joint	522	25	4.79	60	1	1.67	p = 0.04*

Mother's education is found to be the most consistent and important determinant of the use of child and maternal health services (Becker et al., 1993). Maheo and Kalla (2000) mentioned that education reduces the proportions of infant and child mortality through a mixture of indirect channels, such as age at marriage, greater knowledge pertaining to fertility regulation, child care practices, etc. Table 8.12 depicts the distribution of infant mortality according to the educational status of ever-married women. In rural area, mortality at infant stage is relatively higher among those who have education beyond high school level (5.86%). However, in the urban area infant mortality records relatively higher incidence among the illiterate mothers (11.11%). In this regard, no statistically significant differences between the two samples are recorded. Sarma (1991) mentioned that the incidence of mortality is high among the Rabha women of Assam with less or no education in comparison to the educated Rabha women. The percentage of infant and child mortality to the illiterate couples from among the Jaintia women of Meghalaya was found to be comparatively much higher than that of the educated couples (Chakrabarty, 1995). Her study also recorded gradual declination of infant mortality with the increase in the level of mother's educational status. Gogoi (2001) and Baruah (2007) also mentioned about the higher incidence of postnatal mortality among the illiterate Ahom women of Assam. Among Munda, Tanti, and Oraon of Assam, Borkataky (2004) observed higher incidence of child mortality among the illiterate sections. Seal et al. (2010) documented higher incidence of infant mortality among the Mishing women in Assam having secondary level of education. Among the Khongsai Kuki of Saikul and Imphal subdivision of Manipur, Khongsai (2012) observed that the infant mortality rate tends to decline as the mother's educational level increases. Das (2014) observed the higher incidence of infant mortality among the illiterate Bodo and Rabha women of Assam in comparison to the literate section. In the Khamti population of Assam (Borah and Sengupta, 2015) no incidence of infant mortality was found among the illiterate women. But the frequency was quite high among the women with primary standard education. Saikia (2015) recorded higher proportions of

infant mortality among the illiterate Sonowal Kachari women of Assam. Patir and Sengupta (2015) observed higher proportions of infant mortality among the Dibongiya Deori women with advanced educational level. On the contrary, among the Tengapania and Bongonya Deori, higher proportions of the infant mortality among the illiterate sections is reported. Among the Ahom and Phake population of Assam (Gogoi, 2016), a decreasing trend of infant mortality with the rising of maternal education was observed.

Table 8.12: Incidence of infant deaths by maternal education

Maternal education	*Rural*			*Urban*			χ^2
	Live birth	*Infant mortality*		*Live birth*	*Infant mortality*		
		No.	*%*		*No.*	*%*	
Illiterate	298	6	2.01	9	1	11.11	2.39, p = 0.50
Primary	184	9	4.89	18	0	0	
Up to High School	365	18	4.93	62	2	3.23	
Beyond High School	256	15	5.86	131	5	3.82	

Paternal education is also concomitantly imperative for the proper nourishment of the baby. Table 8.13 shows the distribution of infant deaths by paternal education. Among the rural residents, the incidence of infant mortality in higher proportion was observed among those persons who have education beyond high school standard. In urban area, more such incidence was observed among the person having up to high school level of education. No instances of infant mortality were recorded among those persons in the urban area who are illiterate or have education up to primary level. In this regard, the variation observed turned out to be statistically insignificant between the women from the rural and urban areas. In this context, it is worthwhile to be mentioned here that works of Das (2014) among the Bodo and Rabha tribe and Borkataky's (2004) investigation among the Munda, Tanti, and Oraon also recorded higher incidence of infant mortality among the illiterate person in comparison to the literate one. Similarly, Khongsai (2012) observed the declining trend in infant mortality as the paternal educational level increases among the Khongsai Kuki in Manipur.

Table 8.13: Incidence of infant deaths by paternal education

Paternal education	*Rural*			*Urban*			χ^2
	Live birth	*Infant mortality*		*Live birth*	*Infant mortality*		
		No.	*%*		*No.*	*%*	
Illiterate	156	6	3.85	0	0	0	1.21, p = 0.77
Primary Educated	161	8	4.97	0	0	0	
Up to High School	381	8	2.10	34	2	5.88	
Beyond High School	405	26	6.42	186	6	3.23	

Children of the working women are deprived of proper care of their mothers. Since the working mother remains busy in outdoor activities, their infants cannot receive adequate breast milk from them and are provided with supplementary food. The supplementary food given to the children is neither sufficient in quantity nor nutritive enough in relation to the requirement of the children (Visaria, 1985). Moreover, the working mothers while going out have to depend on caretaker to look after the child. These caretakers while giving food to the child often do not maintain proper hygiene care.Gubhaju (1991) while working in South Asia found that working mothers experienced higher infant and child mortality due to deprived of adequate care than those who do not work. A similar result was also found in India as a whole, where working mothers have higher infant and child mortality than mothers who are not employed (Kishor et al., 1998). Table 8.14 shows the distribution of infant death according to maternal occupation. Among the Dibongiya Deori women from rural area, incidence of infant mortality is found to be higher among the homemakers (5.88%). On the other hand, working mothers experienced considerably higher incidence of infant mortality in the urban set up (6.82%). In this regard, the differences between rural and urban samples are found to be statistically significant. In Manipur, Devi (1998) recorded relatively higher incidence of infant and child mortality among the 'day labourer' women in comparison to the business and nonworker categories among both the Sekmei and Meitei population. Chakravarty (2001) observed somewhat higher incidence of infant mortality among those Assamese women who are nonworkers or economically inactive. On the other hand, among the Bengali women, Chakravarty (2001) observed that mortality is high at the highest occupational status, i.e., in Class I category. Borkataky (2004) studied the frequency of dead children according to the occupation of the mother among the four tea worker communities namely, Mundas, Oraons and Tantis. She divided the occupation of the mothers into four categories and these are medical staff, tea labourer, housewife and 'Others' that includes the women working at the creche, distributing milk at the school, sweepers, and servants in the managerial quarters and staff quarters etc. Incidence of child death is found to be quite high among the tea labourer category. In Manipur, the high infant and child mortality rates were recorded among cultivators in Saikul sub-division and housewives in Imphal town

Table 8.14: Incidence of infant deaths by maternal occupation

Maternal occupation	*Rural*			*Urban*			χ^2
	Live birth	*Infant mortality*		*Live birth*	*Infant mortality*		
		No.	*%*		*No.*	*%*	
Working	1018	43	4.22	44	3	6.82	12.68,
Non-working	85	5	5.88	176	5	2.84	p = 0.0001*

(Khongsai, 2012). In the study of Das (2014) among the Bodo and Rabha population of Assam, infant mortality is recorded as high among the women who are engaged as unskilled labours in comparison to the homemakers.

Meendik and Ramachandran (1962), Arora and Kane (1979), stated that the occupation of the father shows significant influence on infant and early childhood mortality.Distribution of infant deaths according to paternal occupation is shown in the Table 8.15. Among the respondents from rural areas, the incidence of infant mortality is found to be high among those persons who are maintaining their livelihood as a cultivator (4.81%), followed by the person running a petty business (4.73%) or engaged as a wage earner (4.64%). In the urban area, persons engaged as a wage earner (5.88%) has experienced relatively higher incidence of infant mortality, followed by the cultivators (4.88%). No incidence of infant mortality was recorded among the respondents from urban area who are running a petty business. However, irrespective of place of residences (rural: 1.50% and urban: 3.62%), the incidences of infant mortality were observed to be relatively low among those who are engaged in different government services as well as in private sectors. In this connection, statistically significant differences between the rural and urban women are observed. Borkataky (2004) in her study among the Mundas, Oraons and Tantis in Assam, infant and early childhood death was found to be relatively high among those where the fathers were engaged as labourer. Khnogsai (2012) recorded low infant and child mortality rates among those who have better paternal occupation among the Khongsai Kuki of Manipur. Among the Bodo population in Assam, Das (2014) observed high incidence of infant mortality when the fathers are unskilled labourer while among the Rabha population, he observed high proportion of infant mortality when father's occupation is business.

Table 8.15: Incidence of infant deaths by paternal occupation

Paternal occupation	*Rural*			*Urban*			χ^2
	Live birth	*Infant mortality*		*Live birth*	*Infant mortality*		
		No.	*%*		*No.*	*%*	
Petty Business	148	7	4.73	24	0	0	20.60, p = 0.0001*
Cultivator	499	24	4.81	41	2	4.88	
Service	133	2	1.50	138	5	3.62	
Wage Earner	323	15	4.64	17	1	5.88	

Conclusion

The present study witnesses relatively poor status of infant health among the Dibongiya Deori community and also concurs the impact of different bio-social factors on their health. Easy obtainability of potable drinking water is essential for maintaining the balanced health of the children. Most of the

families from rural areas are found not to have any water facilities and depend on neighbour's ring well. The Dibongiya Deori women remain busy in daily chores until the time of delivery. Since they have strong belief in supernatural forces with regards to the health of their newborn babies, they usually try to cure their baby's sufferings with some indigenous remedies. During pregnancy, although the Primary Health Centers are helpful for their routine checkup, yet they have to cover a long distance to avail such facilities from a government hospital. Most of these institutes lacks proper medical staff and as such in critical condition and they had to rush to the nearby township which is time-consuming. Establishment of the medical institution with the improved medical facility at an affordable price will be helpful for the people to move forward in this regard.

References

Adak, DK 1993, *Mortality pattern and its biosocial proximate: a study on tribal populations of Shillong (Meghalaya)*. Ph.D. thesis, Gauhati University.

Adlakha, AL & Suchindran, CM 1985, 'Factors affecting infant and child mortality', *Journal of Biosocial Science*, vol. 17, no. 4, pp. 481-496.

Agarwala, SN 1988, *India's population problems*, Tata Mc Graw Hill Publishing Company Ltd., New Delhi.

Ahmad, OB, Eberstein, IW & Sly, DF 1991, 'Proximate determinants of child mortality in Liberia', *Journal of Bio-Social Science*, vol.23, pp. 313-326.

Ahmed Das, F & Barua, R 1999, 'A demographic study of the Manipuri Meiteis of Borkula Hanchara village of Sibsagar District, Assam', *Bulletin of the Department of Anthropology, Dibrugarh University*, vol. 27, pp. 83-92.

Ahmed Das, F & Konwar, J 2002, 'A note on some demographic features of the Oraon of Tingkong Tea Estate of Tingkhong, Dibrugarh, Assam', *Bulletin of the Department of Anthropology, Dibrugarh University*, vol. 30, pp. 113-122.

Annual Health Survey 2011-2012, *Annual Health Survey, Assam – 2011-2012 Fact Sheet*, Office of the Registrar General and Census Commissioner, New Delhi, India.

Arora, DD & Kane, KK 1979, 'Feeding practices during the first five years among Central Indian communities', *Indian Journal of Pediatrics*,vol. 40, pp. 203-216.

Arora, YL 1980, 'Infant mortality and family planning', *Journal of Family Welfare*, vol.26, no. 4, pp. 73-78.

Bailey, M 1988, 'Factors affecting infant and child mortality in rural Sierra Leone', *Journal of Tropical Pediatrics*, vol. 34, no. 4, pp. 165-168.

Barclay, GW 1958, *Techniques of population analysis,* John Wiley and Sons, New York.

Barua, S 1982, 'Bio-demographic factor associated with offspring mortality among the Hajong of Meghalaya', *Journal of Indian Anthropological Society*, vol. 17, pp. 143-146.

Barua, S, Varte, R Th & Sarkar, NC 1994, 'Fertility and mortality differentials among the Khampti of Assam and Arunachal Pradesh: a study on effect of migration', *Journal of Indian Anthropological Society*, vol. 29, no. 1-2, pp. 137-142.

Barua, SK 1980, *A study on certain problems of fertility among the Khasi women of Meghalaya*. Ph.D. thesis, Gauhati University.

Baruah, P & Sengupta, S 2009, 'A study on demographic variables in three ethnic groups of upper Assam', *Bulletin of the Department of Anthropology, Dibrugarh University*, vol. 37, pp. 9-30.

Baruah, P 2007, *Demographic profile of three ethnic groups of Assam: a comparative study*. Ph.D. thesis, Dibrugarh University.

Becker, S, Peters, DH, Gray, RH, Gultiano, C & Blake, RE 1993, 'The determinants of use of maternal and child health services in Metro Cebu, the Philippines', *Health Transition Review,* vol. 3, no. 1, pp. 77–89.

Bharati, P & Basu, A 1990, 'A study on the effects of nutrition on fertility and mortality among the Mahishya of Howrah district, West Bengal', *Journal of Indian Anthropological Society,* vol. 25, pp. 185-189.

Bhende, AA & Kanitkar,T 1997,*Principles of population studies*, 6th edn, Himalayan Publishing House, Mumbai.

Bicego, GT & Boerma, JT 1993, 'Maternal education and child survival: a comparative study of survey data from 17 countries', *Social Science & Medicine*, vol. 36, no. 9, pp. 1207-1227. Available from: doi: 10.1016/0277-9536(93)90241-U.

Borah, J & Sengupta, S 2013, 'Some aspects of demographic variables among the Khamtis of Lakhimpur district, Assam', *Bulletin of the Department of Anthropology, Dibrugarh University,* vol. 41, pp. 45-56.

Borah, J & Sengupta, S 2015, 'Bio-social proximate factors of fertility and mortality: a case study among the Khamtis of Assam' in *Health education,* ed A Saikia, A.P.H. Publishing Corporation, New Delhi, pp. 29-37.

Borkataky, M 2004, *A study on infant and early childhood mortality among the tea garden workers of Dibrugarh district, Assam.*Ph.D. thesis, Gauhati University.

Caldwell, JC 1979, 'Education as a factor of mortality decline: an examination of Nigerian data', *Population Studies*, vol. 33, no. 3, pp. 395-413.

Chakrabarty, M 1995,*Differential fertility and infant mortality among the Jaintias of Meghalaya: a study on bio-social correlates*. Ph.D. thesis, Gauhati University.

Chakravarti, K 2001, *A study on differential fertility among two population groups in Guwahati*. Ph.D. thesis, Gauhati University.

Chakravarty, K 1994, *A study on nutrition, fertility, and mortality among the Ahoms of Assam.* Research project report, O.K.D. Institute of Social Change and Development, Guwahati.

Chakravarty, K 2006, 'Effects of nutritional status on fertility and mortality among slum women of Guwahati' in *Agriculture food security, nutrition,and health in North East India,* eds D Basu, BF Kulirani & B Datta Roy, Mittal Publications, New Delhi.

Chanu, TJ 2007, *A study of reproductive and child health among the Lois of Imphal Valley*. Ph.D. thesis, North Eastern Hill University.

Chen, LC, Rahman, M & Sardar, AM 1980, 'Epidemiology and causes of death among children in rural area of Bangladesh', *International Journal Epidemiology*, vol. 9, pp. 25- 33.

Choe, MK, Luther, NY, Pandey, A, Sahu, D & Chand, J 1999, 'Identifying children with high mortality risk', *National Family Health Survey Bulletin,* vol.12, pp. 1083-8678.

Choudhury, D, Behera, MC & Adak, DK 1991, 'Some bio-demographic aspects of the Khampti of Arunachal Pradesh', *Proceeding of the Seminar on patterns and problems of population growth in India with special reference to North East India,* Shillong Women College, Meghalaya.

Conrad, 1962, 'Sex roles as factors in longevity', *Sociology and Social Research*, vol.7, pp. 195.

Das Gupta, M 1990, 'Death clustering, mother's education and the determinants of child mortality in rural Punjab, India', *Population Studies*, vol.44, pp. 489.

Das, D 2010, *A study on health, morbidity and mortality among the Tiwa children of Morigaon district, Assam*. Ph.D. thesis, Gauhati University.

Das, NB 2014, *Child mortality and morbidity among the Bodos and the Rabhas of Udalguri district, BTAD, Assam*. Ph.D. thesis, Gauhati University.

Devi, NM 1998, *A study on differential fertility of the Meitei and Sekmai women of Manipur.* Ph.D. thesis, Manipur University.

Dutta Das, D & Saikia, A 2010, 'Demographic profile of the Bodo Kacharis of Lakhimpur district, Assam', *Bulletin of the Department of Anthropology, Dibrugarh University*, vol. 38, pp. 65-72.

Ghosh, AK & Khongsdier, R 1997, 'Bio-anthropological profile of Meghalaya' in *Studies in anthropology: Recent Perspective*, ed S Sengupta, Inter India Publications, New Delhi, pp. 170-200.

Ghosh, S 1988, 'Looking beyond the child', *Indian Journal of Pediatrics*, vol. 55, pp. 879-881.

Gogoi Konwar, J 2001, *Reproductive health of women: a case study in an Ahom village in upper Assam*. Ph.D. thesis, Dibrugarh University.

Gogoi, D 2008, *Population genetics of the Mishmis of Arunachal Pradesh*. Ph.D. Thesis, North-Eastern Hill University.

Gogoi, Y 2016, *Differential fertility and infant mortality in three Tai Mongoloid population groups of North-East India: a study of bio-social correlates*. Ph.D. thesis, Dibrugarh University.

Gopalan, C & Naidu, A 1972, 'Nutrition and fertility', *The Lancet* 18 November, pp. 1077-1079.

Gopalan, C 1973, 'Nutrition, fertility and reproduction', *Proceedings of the Nutritional Society of India*, vol. 14, pp. 49.

Gordon, JE, Wyon, JB & Ascoli, W 1971, 'Population pressure on families; family size and child spacing in Wray' in *Rapid population growth consequences and policy implications*, vol.2, ed D Joe, Jhon Hopkins University Press, Baltimore.

Gubhaju, BB 1991, *Child mortality and survival in South Asia - Nepalese perspective*, Daya Publishing House, Delhi.

Hazarika, J & Sengupta, S 2017, 'Fertility performance among the Kaibarta women of Assam', *Bulletin of the Department of Anthropology, Dibrugarh University*, vol. 44&45, pp. 125-132.

Hobcraft, J, Donald, J Me& Rutstein, S 1984, 'Socio-economic factors in infant and child mortality: a cross-national comparison', *Population Studies*, vol.38, pp. 193.

International Institute for Population Sciences (IIPS) and ICF 2017, *National Family Health Survey (NFHS-4), India, 2015-16: Assam*, IIPS, Mumbai.

International Institute for Population Sciences (IIPS) and Macro International 2008, *National Family Health Survey (NFHS-3), India, 2005-06: Assam*, IIPS, Mumbai.

Khongsai, L 2012, *Bio-social determinants of fertility and child mortality among the Khongsai Kukis of Manipur*. Ph.D. thesis, North Eastern Hill University.

Khongsdier, R, Nsarangbe, A & Phimu, A 2001, 'A bio-anthropological study of the Pnar of Jatinga in North Cachar Hills of Assam', *Journal of Indian Anthropological Society,* vol. 36, pp. 213-222.

Kishor, S & Parasuraman, S 1998, 'Mother's employment and infant and child mortality in India', *National Family Health Survey Subject Reports No. 8,* International Institute for Population Sciences, Mumbai.

Limbu, DK & Khongsdier, R 2000, 'The Semsa: a population genetics study' in *Contemporary research in anthropology*, ed R Khongsdier, Commonwealth Publishers, New Delhi, pp. 39-43.

Madigan, F 1968, 'Are sex mortality differentials biologically caused?' in *Population and society*, ed C Nam, Houghton Mifflin Co., Boston.

Mahadevan, K 1986, 'Mortality, biology, and society: analytical framework and conceptual model' in *Fertility and mortality-theory, methodology & empirical issues,* ed K Mahadevan, Sage Publications India Pvt. Ltd., New Delhi, pp. 239-301.

Mahadevan, K, Murthy, MSR, Reddy, RR, Reddy, PV, Gowari, VV & Raju, SS 1986, 'Culture, nutrition and infant and child mortality' in *Fertility and mortality: theory, methodology and empirical issues*, ed K Mahadevan, Sage Publications, New Delhi, pp. 314-337.

Maheo, LM & Kalla, AK 2000, 'A study on fertility among the Mao Nagas of Senapati district, Manipur', *Anthropologist*, vol. 2, no. 2, pp. 123-125.

Meendik, J & Ramachandran, KV 1962, 'Infant mortality according to social status', *Journal of Indian Medical Association,* vol. 38, no. 9, pp.477-482.

Mukherjee, N 2002, *Study on demography and growth pattern among the Khasi children of Shillong*. Ph.D. thesis,North-Eastern Hill University.

Murry, B, Sachdeva, MP & Kalla, AK2005, 'Estimates of fertility and mortality differentials among the Lotha Nagas of Nagaland', *Anthropologist,* vol. 7, no. 1, pp. 45-52.

Naeye, RL, Burt, LS, Wright, DL, Blanc, WA & Tatter, D 1971, 'Neonatal mortality, the male disadvantage', *Pediatrics*, vol.48, pp. 902.

Outran, AR & Standley, CC (ed.) 1976, *Family formation patterns and health: an international collaborative study in India, Iran, London, Philippines, and Turkey,* WHO, Geneva.

Pardeshi, GS, Dalvi, SS, Pergulwar, CR, Gite, RN & Wanje, SD 2011, 'Trends in choosing place of delivery and assistance during delivery in Nanded district, Maharashtra, India', *Journal of Population and Nutrition,* vol. 29, no. 1, pp. 71-76.

Patir, R & Sengupta, S 2015, 'Effects of some bio-cultural factors on fertility and mortality among the Deoris of Assam' in *Health education,* ed A Saikia, A.P.H. Publishing Corporation, New Delhi, pp. 70-80.

Patir, R 2017, 'A study on reproductive and child health among the Mishing of Assam', *Bulletin of the Department of Anthropology, Dibrugarh University*, vol. 44&45, pp. 133-138.

Pebley, AR & Millman, S 1986, 'Birth spacing and child survival', *International Family Planning Perspective*, vol. 12, no. 3, pp. 71-79.

Rahman, Muzibur, M, Kabir, M & Salam, MA 1993, 'The influence of socio-economic characteristics on subsequent infant and child mortality', *The Journal of Family Welfare*, vol.39, no. 3, pp. 28-34.

Ramu, GN 1988, *Family structure and fertility - emerging patterns in an Indian city,* Sage Publications India Pvt. Ltd, New Delhi.

Rao, KV 1988, Nutrition, fertility and mortality, *Nutrition News*, vol. 9, pp. 2.

Rengma, MS 2014, 'A note on fertility performance among the Rengma Nagas of Assam', *Bulletin of the Department of Anthropology, Dibrugarh University*, vol. 42, pp. 191-196.

Roy, RN, Nandy, S, Shrivastava, P, Chakraborty, A, Dasgupta, M & Kundu, TK 2008, 'Mortality pattern of hospitalized children in a tertiary care hospital of Kolkata', *Indian Journal of Community Medicine*, vol.3, no. 3, pp. 187-189.

Ruzicka, LT & Kane, P 1987, 'Infant and child mortality: the implications for fertility behaviour' in *Dynamics of population and family welfare,* eds K Srinivasan & S Mukherjee, Himalaya Publishing House, Bombay.

Ruzicka, LT & Kanitkar, T 1973, 'Infant mortality in greater Bombay', *Demography*, vol.2, pp. 41-45.

Sahu, D, Nair, S, Singh, L, Gulati, BK & Pandey, A 2015, 'Levels, trends and predictors of infant and child mortality among Scheduled Tribes in rural India', *The Indian journal of medical research*, vol. 141, no. 5, pp. 709. Available from: http://dx.doi.org/10.4103/0971-5916.159593.

Saikia, N 2015, *Fertility performance and blood group incompatibility among the Sonowal Kacharis of Dibrugarh district, Assam.* Ph.D. thesis, Dibrugarh University.

Sarkar, NC 2002, 'Bio-demographic study of the Mukloms of Changlang, Arunachal Pradesh' in *Ethnic groups, cultural continuities and social change in North East India*, eds I Baruah, S Sengupta & D Dutta Das, Mittal Publication, New Delhi, pp. 311-324.

Sarma, R 1991, *A study of some demographic aspects of the Rabhas of Boko area, Kamrup district.* Ph.D. thesis, Gauhati University.

Sathar, ZA 1985, 'Infant and child mortality in Pakistan - some trends and differentials', *Journal of Biosocial Science*, vol.18, pp. 435-447.

Seal, B, Das, R, Patir, R & Sengupta, S 2010, 'Factors affecting the reproductive performance among the Mishing women of Assam', *Bulletin of the Department of Anthropology, Dibrugarh University*, vol. 38, pp. 73-80.

Sengupta, PN 1979, 'Malnutrition, fertility and family planning', *Journal of Indian Medical Association*, vol. 72, pp. 194.

Sengupta, S & Dutta, RK 2000, 'Factor influencing fertility: a case study among the Mishing of Assam', *Bulletin of the Department of Anthropology, Dibrugarh University*, vol. 28, pp. 21-30.

Sengupta, S & Kalita, M 2001, 'Some aspects of reproductive performance of the Sonowal Kachari of Assam', *Bulletin of the Department of Anthropology, Dibrugarh University,* vol. 29, pp. 49-58.

Sengupta, S & Purnungla 2005, 'Some aspect of reproductive performance of the Ao Nagas of Nagaland', *Bulletin of the Department of Anthropology, Dibrugarh University,* vol. 33, pp. 69-76.

Singhi, S, Gupta, G & Jain, V 2004, 'Comparison of pediatric emergency patients in a tertiary care hospital vs. a community hospital', *Indian Pediatrics,* vol. 41, pp. 67-72.

Srivastava, JN & Saxena, DN 1980, 'Infant mortality differentials in an Indian setting: follow up of hospital deliveries', *Journal of Biosocial Science*, vol.13, no. 4, pp. 467-468.

Stockwell, EG, Swanson, DA & Wicks, JW 1988, *Economic status differences in infant mortality by cause of death*. Public health reports, vol. 103, no. 2, pp. 135.

Subramanian, SV, Nandy, S & Irving, M, Gordon, D, Lambert, H & Smith, GD 2006, 'The mortality divides in India: the differential contributions of gender, caste, and standard

of living across the life course', *American Journal of Public Health*, vol. 96, no.5, pp. 818-825. Available from: doi: 10.2105/AJPH.2004.060103.

Syngkon, H 2013, *Status, and determinants of child mortality among the Pnar of Jaintia hills district, Meghalaya.* Ph.D. thesis, North Eastern Hill University.

Talwar, PP 1988, 'Infant mortality - some evidence from rural Madhya Pradesh' in *Infant mortality in India,* eds AK Jain & P Visaria, Sage Publications, New Delhi.

Trussel, J, Pebly, AR & Vaughan, B 1992, 'Birth spacing with child mortality in Bangladesh and the Philippines', *Demography*, vol. 29, no. 2, pp. 305-317.

UNICEF 1984, *Child Survival*,New York, no. 119 pp. 18-19.

Varte, R 2006, *Health and nutritional status of the Hmars of Aizawl district, Mizoram*. Ph.D. thesis, North Eastern Hill University, Shillong.

Venkatacharya 1985, 'An approach to the study of sociobiological determinants of infant and child morbidity, mortality' in *International Population Conference. Florence;* IT, 5-12, June, 2. Liege B.E., IUSSP, pp. 237-253.

Visaria, L 1985, 'Infant mortality in India: level, trends and determinants', *Economic and Political Weekly*, vol. 20, no. 32, pp. 1352-1359.

World Health Organization 2004, Appropriate body-mass index for Asian populations and its implications for policy and intervention strategies, *The Lancet*, vol. 363, pp. 157-163.

Chapter - 9

The Situation of Elderly Living in Old Age Homes in Assam

— Bikash Deka and Basobi Patir

Introduction

Ageing is not a new phenomenon; it is as old as human society. It is most often seen as a biological process of decline of bodily functions. Graying hair, changing skin texture, failing eyesight, waning muscular strength or reduced vitality, all these biological signs are commonly thought of as the defining features of old age (Bond et al., 2007). However, ageing is a social process as well because the society has its profound influence on the very process of ageing. The experience of aging is dramatically different from earlier historical periods. The social and economic roles of older persons, their interactions with families and the larger social system where they live are in many ways profoundly different today from previous generations (Hooyaman and Kiyak, 2005). There is no single definition which is unanimously accepted worldwide. In the developed countries, persons aged 65 or above are normally considered as aged and are retired from jobs. The United Nations has not adopted a standard criterion but generally uses 60+ years to refer to the older population (Gurung and Ghimire, 2014). In the Indian context, a person is considered old when he/she attains the age of sixty and above because it is considered as retirement age by the Government of India and it is also considered to identify a person as old or aged in census surveys made by the Government of India. Over the past two centuries, a gradual transformation has taken place across the world; the population has been ageing due to the advancement in science and technology, improvement in health services available. Gradually the number of older people will exceed the number of younger people and amongst the older population, there will be an increase

in the oldest old (Bond et al., 2007). However, the rise in the number of old people is not the problem in the recent times. But the important factor is the declining roles, status, and caregiving of the old people in the present society.

Caregiving or caring of the aged has never been an issue or problem among the people in traditional Indian societies. Rather they were treated with respect and they had the highest authority in the family and community. Older people do maintain high levels of prestige and they are able to discipline, supervise, instruct and counsel the young people (Wilson, 1975). It is the standard practice for the younger people to turn to their elders for guidance and it was regarded as a moral duty of the children to provide support and security to their parents in old age. They were given the leadership roles and powerful positions of decision makers and advisers in the joint family and communities because their knowledge was considered to be a great value in the proper functioning of society (Mishra, 1989). The notion of honour and respect is attached to being old in traditional Indian societies (Wilson, 1975). But the situation transformed drastically in the modern times. The caregiving to the elderly people has changed to some extent. In recent times, the younger generation doesn't want to take care and responsibility to their aged parents. Moreover, they considered them as a burden to the family. This had happened because of the growing urbanization, modernization, industrialization and globalization, as mentioned by many researchers (Sati, 1988; Hossen, 2004; Lamb, 2009; Thomas and Diengdoh, 2009; Raju, 2011; Kumar and Bhargava, 2014; Bhatt and Dhruvaranjan, 2015; cited in Sahoo et al., 2015). The reasons that cause the difficulty in caregiving are migration of younger generations to towns and cities in search of job or work, changes of the family system from joint to nuclear family has shifted the authority from the older to the younger generation which made the elder depend on their children and in turn they were considered as a burden by their children (Behura and Mohanty,2005), increasing participation of the women in income earning activities, who are the traditional caregivers to the elderly and individualistic attitude and selfishness of the younger generations. Because of these changes in caregiving, in present times the elderly parents staying in an Old Age Homes (OAH) is becoming a trend and a common phenomenon. OAH is an institution where the older person is admitted in to meet his needs there. The aged spends their old age in the company of the people, who are similar to him in age, state of health mental make-up and outlook towards life (Mahapatra, 2010). In today's society,once an individual reaches his old stage, then he has the chances of someday entering an OAH. In these circumstances, there is an urgent need to give attention towards the elderly living in the institutions called OAHs, a home which is replacing the care and support of the family in modern times for a large section of elderly people.

Assam is one of the states of Northeast India. Assam is a composition of different ethnic society with their different cultures and traditions. Assamese society by tradition is a rural and agrarian society. It is characterized by powerful sentiments of kinship, locality, ethnicity, tribe, and community. Social relations in such society are remarkably firm and stable (Barooah, 1993). The cultural life of Assam is interwoven with the activities of a number of cultural institutions and religious centers such as the *Satra*, founded by the great reformer, Sankardeva, and *Namghar*(prayer house). *Satras* in Assam is an important center of religious education and activities of the Vaishnavite communities of the Assamese Hindus. In Assam, the center of all Vaishnavite religious activities is the *Namghar*. It is an integral part of the social machinery by which villagers are enabled to live together in an orderly arrangement of social relations. The elderly people held a high and respectable position in the *Namghar*. Besides, performing the religious ceremonies in the *Namghar,* the villager elderly uses it as a public place to discuss the affairs of the village. The elderly took the decisions and issues pertaining to the community were also sorted out in the *Namghar* (*ibid*). Likewise, the Vaishnavite communities, in Assam almost all the tribal communities have their own village organizations to look after the welfare of the villagers by performing both executive and judicial activities. For example, Deori communities have their own traditional prayer hall *Dewalaya* or *Morong Ghar*(club), Mising tribe have their own village council called *Kebang* or *Murong Ghar* (club), Boro tribe have their own traditional village council called *Raijw Jiraisali* or *Gamini Affat*, Karbis have their own traditional institutions *Me* (village council), Dimasa tribe's village council is called *Salis*, Tiwa (Lalung) tribe's village council is called *Khel* etc., in which the village organizations held meetings or discuss about the affairs of the village. In all the religious institutions or village meetings, an elderly male member is elected as the *Gaonbura* (headman) of the village and he presided over the meetings. Moreover, all the elderly members constitute the village meetings and they were regarded as having supreme power and also their wisdom was utilized to solve important matters. The elderly member's decisions and advice were taken and considered as valuable by the other members of the village. In Assamese society, in every sphere of their life and activity, whether it is cultural, social and political, for example, marriage, village meetings etc., the aged were the first to be considered, respected and regarded by the society. This is because the aged were highly respected and regarded as the storehouse of the wisdom of the family and society.

However, modern obligation situations in domestic life are such that the separation of young from the ageing parents could hardly avoid and virtually results in the formation of a nuclear family. The formation of nuclear family under changing socio-cultural norms in the Assamese society, the resultant

isolation of the aged leads to plightful or miserable life (Mahanta, 1995; cited in Kumar, 1995). Moreover, due to the interference of modern forces, urbanization, the spread of formal education and increasing diversification of occupation, the breaking up of age-old sentiments of the joint family system, the rapid technological changes and new forms of organization have replaced the knowledge experience and wisdom of the older persons. These changes have gradually diluted the moral ethics, emotional and losing the traditional values of authority, power and prestige within their own family (Visielie, 2012; Barooah, 1993). All these phenomena lead to many physical, psychological and sociological problems to the elderly and make them think to reside in the OAHs which were unknown in the Assamese culture. Though not recent in nature but the present circumstances show a negative trend towards giving protection to the ancient tradition and culture of caring for the elderly among the Assamese people. OAHs are increasing day by day in Assam. Though still not so common in the rural areas many OAHs have sprung up in the urban areas of Assam.

Reflection in earlier studies on the conditions of the elderly living in OAHs

OAHs are considered as a social stigma by the caretaker of the elderly (Shirmly, 2014). The children and family members do not want to send their aged parents to OAHs fearing that society will talk about them. Further, the aged also prefer to live in their own family or village because they have also a notion that someone belonging from other community or village could not love them more than what their own family could do (Visielie, 2012). However, OAHs becomes the last resort for the elderly to pass their last days only when the family fails to discharge its traditional duties of care and support to the elderly (Kumar and Reddy, 2002; Shankardass, 2010). The elderly mostly prefers to stay with their children than in the OAHs. In this regard, Devi (2005) stated that family is the best place for taking care of the old people but when it is not found then formal care giving provides a choice to the elderly. Vanitha (2014) discussed that elderly become dependent and needs the help of others due to their physical disability. Since every body, even their children do not find time for them. According to her, this is the reason for the elderly to stay in OAHs. Mahapatra (2010), points out that institutionalized care is needed for the elderly people because of the changes in the family system, life-style of the younger generation have led to changes in the living arrangements of the elderly. He also stated that the concept of OAHs has its positive impact on the quality of life and have boosted the attitude of elderly towards their lives. Dandekar (1996), mention that in the advanced countries the elderly people live in the OAHs because of poor health but in India, people mainly reside due to poverty because they cannot work and earn since they become

old. She also stated that everyone likes to live with their families however if that is not available then OAHs could be the best choice for the homeless, helpless, and childless people. Adhikari (2016) made a comparative study of elderly living in OAH and within the family. He stated that in the OAHs, the elderly suffers from various psychological and environmental problems including the feeling of neglect, loss of importance in the family, loneliness, and feeling of redundant in the family as well as society. The elderly in the OAHs was mentally ill and they felt alone. They are depressed due to irregular or infrequent visit of their family members. They lived in a truncated network of relationships in old age home. They were less interested to be associated with their fellow inmate due to differences in their behaviour. But the elderly people who were at their own family, they were mentally in a better position. The family network of relationship supported the psychological wellbeing of elderly living within the family. Kumar et al (2012), also finds in their study that elderly living in OAHs face problems of adjustment with the tight and rigid schedules, total separation from the family/social milieu, anxiety over entrusting oneself to a new environment, diminished physical capacity and very close and frequent encounters with death and ailments in the institutions. While examining the viewpoints of the OAHs residents, Mishra (2012) addressed the issues of disengagement from various roles and the different strategies adopted by them to further re-engage themselves socially. He finds that the residents not only believed in disengaging themselves from familial roles but also most of them had withdrawn themselves from family responsibilities. Further, they re-engage themselves in various activities in the OAHs, which helped many of the residents maintain their physical and mental health. Beevi (2010) finds that in compared to the elderly living in institutions, the aged who live in the household are healthier and happier. She also stated that though the elderly living in institutions have more facilities in the OAHs, the company of the peer groups and good living environment do not give much satisfaction as they miss their families very much and feel discarded, they were also segregated from their social life.

Reviews have expanded the knowledge to understand the advantage and disadvantage of the OAHs in India while the literature on OAHs in Assam is not available. Therefore, the present study is an attempt to know whether OAHs may be an alternate for elder care in Assam.

Objectives of the Study

1. To explore the socio-economic background of the elderly living in OAHs in Assam;
2. to identify the reasons for living in the OAHs;

3. to explore the issues and problems of the elderly living in OAHs; and
4. to analyze the situation of meaningful engagement of the elderly in the OAHs.

Methodology

The present study was conducted in seven OAHs located in six districts of Assam. They were situated in Lakhimpur, Tinsukia, Nagaon, Kamrup (Metro), Kamrup (Rural), Moran (Dibrugarh) and Jorhat. Out of these seven OAHs, two are paid OAHs in which the aged have to pay for their stay and five of the homes were unpaid where the aged stay free of cost. The total inmates of the seven OAHs were 110. The criterion of selection of the respondents is that we only conducted the study of the elderly who have aged 60 years or above. The criteria for exclusion is below 60 years of age and the respondents who have a mental disorder, deaf and dumb, sick during the visit and who didn't want to response or talk. The present study is a mixture of both qualitative and quantitative approach. For qualitative approach, semi-structured interview schedule with both open and closed questions was used to collect data. Moreover, in-depth interview, focus group discussion was conducted with the respondents. The respondents were questioned regarding the quality of life they were spending in the OAHs and also some questions were asked relating to their family matters. At the same time, necessary care was taken not to hurt the aged and also make them comfortable while asking some personal and sensitive questions needed for the study.

Results and Discussions

Out of 110 respondents, 33 respondents were residing in paid OAHs in which they have to pay for their stay. They have to pay from Rs.4000- 6500 for their food and lodging. 77 respondents were residing in unpaid old age homes in which they stay free of cost. They do not have to pay for their stay in the old age homes.

Socio-economic characteristics of the elderly

The socio-economic characteristics of the elderly include sex, age, marital status, family type, and religion, place of residence, educational qualification, occupation, monthly income, economic dependency, living arrangement, housing status and reasons of living of the elderly in the old age homes.

Table 9.1: Socio-economic characteristics of the elderly

Sl. No.		*Paid*	*Unpaid*	*Total*
1. Sex				
i.	Male	7(6.4%)	31(28.2%)	38(34.5%)
ii.	Female	26(23.6%)	46(41.8%)	72(65.5%)
2. Age				
i.	60-69(young old)	8(7.3%)	38(34.5%)	46(41.8%)
ii.	70-79(old-old)	16(14.5%)	17(15.5%)	33(30%)
iii.	80and above(oldest-old)	9(8.2%)	22(20%)	31(28.2%)
3. Marital Status				
i	Married	4(3.6%)	6(5.5%)	10(9.1%)
ii	Unmarried			
	Bachelor	1(1%)	21(19.2%)	22(20%)
	Spinster	8(7.2%)	13(11.8%)	21(19.1%)
iii	Widow	15(13.6%)	27(24.5%)	42(38.2%)
iv.	Widower	4(3.6%)	7(6.3%)	11(10%)
v.	Separated/ Divorced	1(1%)	3(2.7%)	4(3.6%)
4. Family Type				
i.	Joint Family	10(9.1%)	28(25.5%)	38(34.5%)
ii.	Nuclear Family	23(20.9%)	49(44.5%)	42(65.5%)
5. Religion				
i	Hindu	29(26.4%)	57(51.8%)	86(78.2%)
ii	Christian		16(14.6%)	16(14.5%)
iii	Islam	4(3.6%)	4(3.6%)	8(7.3%)
6. Place of Residence				
i.	Rural	8(7.3%)	40(36.4%)	48(43.6%)
ii.	Urban	25(22.7%)	37(33.6%)	62(56.4%)
7. Educational Qualification				
i.	Illiterate	5(4.5%)	54(49.2%)	59(53.6%)
ii.	Primary (I-V)	3(2.7%)	10(9.1%)	13(11.8%)
iii.	Middle school (V-VII)	2(1.8%)	10(9.1%)	12(10.9%)
iv.	High School (VIII-X)	7(6.4%)	3(2.7%)	10(9.1%)
v.	Matriculation	5(4.5%)	1(1%)	6(5.5%)
vi.	Higher secondary	2(1.8%)		2(1.8%)
vii.	Graduation	8(7.2%)		8(7.2%)
8. Occupation				
i.	Skilled labourer (Police, Worker in office, Engineer, Nurse, Teacher)	12(10.9%)	3(2.7%)	15(13.6%)
ii.	Unskilled labourer (Business, Agriculture, labourer in a factory, tea garden, Artisan, Daily wage earner)	2(1.8%)	37(33.7%)	39(35.4%)
iii.	Own household work	19(17.3%)	23(20.9%)	42(38.3%)
iv.	Other's household work		14(12.7%)	14(12.7%)

(Contd...)

9. Monthly Income				
i.	< 5000		41(37.3%)	41(37.3%)
ii.	<10000	2(1.8%)	13(11.8%)	15(13.6%)
iii.	<20000	3(2.7%)	1(1%)	4(3.6%)
iv.	<30000	5(4.5%)		5(4.5%)
v.	40000and above	3(2.7%)		3(2.7%)
vi	No Income	20(18.2%)	22(20%)	42(38.3%)
10. Economically Dependent				
i.	Your pension/savings	8(7.3%)		8(7.3%)
ii.	Husband pension/Savings	13(11.8%)	2(1.8%)	15(13.6%)
iii.	Son and Daughter-in-law	5(4.5%)	15(13.6%)	20(18.2%)
iv.	Daughter and Son-in-law		4(3.6%)	4(3.6%)
v.	Brother and Sister-in-law	4(3.6%)	14(12.7%)	18(16.3%)
vi.	Nephew/Relatives	3(2.8%)	3(2.8%)	6(5.5%)
vii.	No one		39(35.5%)	39(35.5%)
11. Living Arrangement				
i.	Spouse	3(2.7%)	5(4.5%)	8(7.2%)
ii.	Living with only son	3(2.7%)	1(1%)	4(3.6%)
iii.	Son and Daughter-in-law	6(5.4%)	12(10.9%)	18(16.4%)
iv.	Daughter and Son-in-law		4(3.6%)	4(3.6%)
v.	Brother and Sister-in-law	8(7.3%)	20(18.2%)	28(25.5%)
vi.	Living with unrelated persons		15(13.6%)	15(13.6%)
vii.	Relatives		1(1%)	1(1%)
viii.	Alone	13(11.8%)	19(17.3%)	32(29.1%)
12. Housing Status				
i.	Own house	20(18.2%)	14(12.7%)	34(30.9%)
ii.	Parental house	2(1.8%)	8(7.3%)	10(9.1%)
iii.	Brother and Sister house	7(6.3%)	11(10%)	18(16.4%)
iv.	Daughter and Son-in-law's house		4(3.6%)	4(3.6%)
v.	Son's house	1(1%)	3(2.7%)	4(3.6%)
vi.	Rented house	3(2.7%)	4(3.6%)	7(6.3%)
vii.	Institutionalized		3(2.7%)	3(2.7%)
viii.	Relative's house		1(1%)	1(1%)
ix.	Hospital Station		9(8.2%)	9(8.2%)
x.	Other's house/land		20(18.2%)	20(18.2%)
13. Reasons for Living in the Old Age Homes				
i.	Nobody to take care and responsibility	18(16.2%)	5(4.5%)	23(20.9%)
ii.	Adjustment problem and conflict with son and daughter-in-law, family members and villagers.	3(2.7%)	7(6.3%)	10(9.2%)
iii.	Economic exploitation	1(1%)	2(1.8%)	3(2.7%)

(Contd...)

iv.	Death of spouse and no children to take care and responsibility.	1(1%)	10(9.1%)	11(10%)
v.	Poverty and poor health and no one to take care		35(31.8%)	35(31.8%)
vi.	No son and socially not acceptable to stay with the daughter's family.	1(1%)	3(2.7%)	4(3.6%)
vii.	Housing is too inadequate to stay.	1(1%)	1(1%)	2(1.8%)
viii.	To do social work.		5(4.5%)	5(4.5%)
ix.	Not likes to be dependent.	8(7.3%)	9(8.1%)	17(15.5%)
	Total	**33**	**77**	**110**

Data in Table 9.1 reveals that out of 110 respondents, 65.50 percent are female and 34.50 percent are male. There is a feminization of the OAHs i.e. more female elderly resides in the OAH than the male. This is because of the higher life expectancy of a female in compared to male elderly (Dandekar, 1996; Mishra, 2012; Yadav, 2014; Vanitha, 2014). In regard to the age of the elderly, it is found that 41.80 percent respondents are from the age-group of 60-69 years (young-old), 30.00 percent are from the age group of 70-79 years (old-old) and 28.20 percent respondents are from 80 and above years (oldest-old). This shows that with the increase in the aged, their life expectancy tends to decreases.

Data on marital status reveals that 38.20 percent of the respondents are in the category of the widow, 20.00 percent respondents were in the category of bachelor, 19.10 percent was a spinster, 10.00 percent were widowed, 9.10 percent were married respondents and 3.60 percent belongs to the category of separated/divorced respondents. In this study, it is found that widowhood is the main reason for the women that forced them to reside in the OAHs. This is because of age differences between wife and husband at the time of marriage, women usually marry men who are older to them, lower rate of remarriage in women and due to higher longevity in women than men (Rajan, 2000; Venkateswarlu and Raju, 2007; Akbar et al., 2014; Chen, 2000; cited in Jhabwala and Subrahmanya,2000).

In terms of the type of family, it is found in the study that majority of the respondents (65.50%) belong to a nuclear family and 34.50 percent belongs to the joint family. This shows that due to the emergence of nuclear family elderly were forced to reside in the OAHs.

Regarding the place of residence and religion of the respondents, it is found that 56.40 percent belongs to urban areas and 43.60 percent respondents were from rural areas These findings is similar with (Dandekar, 1996; Rao et al., 2015) that the elderly from the urban areas are more aware

of the old age homes than the elderly from the rural areas. The majority (78.20%) of the respondents belong to Hindu religion, as it is the dominant religion of Assam, followed by Christian (14.50%) and Islam (7.30%).

Data on educational qualification reveals that majority of the respondents are illiterate (53.60%), 11.80 percent had education up to primary level, 10.90 percent had education up to middle school, 9.10 percent of the respondents had education up to high school, 7.30 percent of respondents had education up to graduation and 5.50 percent of respondents had education up to matriculation.

In regards to the occupational status, it is evident that 38.30 percent respondents have been doing their own household chores, 35.40 percent respondents were engaged in unskilled labour, followed by 12.70 percent were engaged in other's household work. Only a few were engaged in skilled labour (13.60%). From this data, it is clear that the aged who resides in the unpaid home were mostly engaged in unskilled labour than the elderly in paid homes.

In regards to monthly income and economic dependence of the elderly, it is found that most of the elderly from the unpaid old age homes have no income (20.00%) and below Rs. 5000.00 (37.30%). The respondents of the unpaid homes also had no one to be dependent (35.50%) compared to the paid homes. This shows that the respondents in the unpaid homes belong to the poor class with low income and no one to depend; therefore, they were more in numbers to reside in the OAHs in Assam. Moreover, it is also found in the study that though the elderly from the paid OAHs had their own children or relatives to be economically dependent but they were also forced to reside in the OAHs, which ultimately shows that not only the poor but also the well to do people resides in the OAHs.

Data on living arrangement of the elderly before coming to OAHs shows that most of the respondents (29.10%) were living alone, 25.50 percent are living with their brother and sister-in-law, 16.40 percent of the respondents co-resides with their son and daughter-in-law, 13.60 percent were living with unrelated persons, 7.20 percent were living with their spouse, 3.60 percent were living with their only son and 3.60 percent were living with their daughter and son-in-law.

In terms of housing status, it is found 30.90 percent of the respondents lived in their own house, 18.20 percent of the unpaid respondents lived in other's house and land, 16.40 percent lived in their brother and sister's house, 9.10 percent lived in their parental house, 8.20 percent of the unpaid respondents lived in hospitals and station, 6.30 percent lived in rented house, 3.60 percent respondents lived in son's house, 3.60 percent of the unpaid

respondents lived in daughter and son-in-law's house and 2.70 percent of the unpaid respondents lived in other institutions (OAHs).

Data on reasons for which the elderly have to join the OAHs shows that 31.80 percent of the unpaid respondents are poor, have poor health and have no money for their medical expenses, 20.90 percent of the respondents had no one to take care and responsibility, 15.50 percent said that they don't want to be dependent on their family members, 10.00 percent of the respondents said that they have no children to take care and responsibility after the death of their spouse 9.20 percent have adjustment problem and conflict with their son and daughter-in-law, other family members, and villagers, 4.50 of the unpaid respondents came to reside in the OAHs to do social work, 3.60 percent have stated that they have no sons and it is not socially acceptable to stay with their daughter's family, 2.70 percent of the respondents reported that they face economic exploitation from their family members, and 1.80 percent of the respondents said that their house is too small to reside. This study reflects that most of the elderly from the unpaid homes came to reside in the OAHs because of poverty, poor health elderly and most of the elderly from paid OAHs joined the homes because they have no one to take care and responsibility of them.

Activities of the Elderly in the OAHs

Activities are very important for an individual to keep himself physically and mentally fit. This helps them to keep mentally active, keeps isolation away, promotes a sense of pride in being able to contribute.

As people grow older, their participation in the daily activities changes because of declining physical and mental capacity and life cycle transitions such as retirement from paid works (Singh and Kiran, 2014). In the present study, similar changes have been found among the elderly before living in the old age homes. Most of the elderly from the paid old age homes were retired employee, which means that they were no more related to their daily habitual routine and also income-earning activities. Before joining the homes, the elderly from the unpaid homes were still engaged in the income earning activities. They worked as a labourer, daily wage earner and were also engaged in agricultural practices because most of them belong to the poorer class and they have no savings or pensions to support them at this age. Most of the elderly women both from the paid and unpaid homes provide domestic support in their families such as cooking and other household chores. They were also engaged in baby sitters or child care activities as they enable other members of the house to engage in skilled or unskilled labour which indirectly contributes to the financial support of the family.

In gerontological literature, the social Theory of Disengagement suggests that as people approach old age, they gradually withdraw from the social roles that previously had been important to them especially their work roles (Kunemund and Kolland, 2007; cited in Bond et al., 2007). The present study correlates with the disengagement theory of ageing. Since the elderly grow old, they lost their roles in their family, therefore; they were disengaged from their roles. They lack care from their family and due to poor health, the poverty they were forced to reside in the old age homes, thus they were further disengaged from their family members. The elderly who has no one was also disengaged from their own life because in the old age homes they got a new environment, new people, and lifestyle, which is different from their previous life. In this situation, it is important to know how they re-engage in the old age homes by disengaging from their family and previous life.

There is a common belief that as age advances, the elderly cannot perform their daily activities and they will be having much free time and due to the absence of any meaningful activity in their later life the elderly finds it difficult to adjust and lead an unhappy life in their old age (Rao,2007; Mishra, 2007). Here, an attempt has been made to know how the elderly living in OAHs spend their time and also to understand how they re-engage in the homes. When asked, it was found that they were engaged in various activities in the OAHs. Presented below are some of the activities of the respondents performed in both the paid and unpaid OAHs.

Table 9.2: Activities of the elderly

Sl. No.		*Paid*	*Unpaid*	*Total*
1. Daily activities of the elderly				
i.	Religious work		4(3.6%)	4(3.6%)
ii.	Gardening		10(9.2%)	10(9.2%)
iii.	Sweeping		4(3.6%)	4(3.6%)
iv	Work in the institutions	1(1%)	2(1.8%)	2(1.8%)
v.	Any work asked to do		4(3.6%)	4(3.6%)
vi.	Only cooking		4(3.6%)	4(3.6%)
vii.	Kitchen work other than cooking	27(24.5%)	9(8.3%)	10(9.2%)
	Weaving		2(1.8%)	2(1.8%)
viii.	Own work (Cleaning dish, washing	5(4.5%)	26(23.6%)	53(48.2%)
ix.	clothes etc)		12(10.9%)	17(15.4%)
	Nothing			

(Contd...)

2. Leisure activities of the elderly				
i.	Reading religious books, magazines,	7(6.4%)	4(3.6%)	11(10%)
	newspaperand other.	4(3.6%)	13(11.8%)	17(15.5%)
	Watching T.V.	8(7.3%)	15(13.6%)	16(14.5%)
ii.	Gossiping with friends	3(2.7%)	13(11.8%)	16(14.5%)
iii.	Simply sitting alone			
iv.	Morning walk/Evening walk	5(4.5%)	3(2.7%)	8(7.3%)
v.	Helping others		14(12.7%)	14(12.7%)
	Meditation		5(4.5%)	5(4.5%)
vi.	Writing books and novels etc			
vii.	Playing music	3(2.7%)		3(2.7%)
viii.	Sleeping	1(1%)		1(1%)
ix.		2(1.8%)	10(9.3%)	12(10.9%)
	Total	**33**	**77**	**110**

Data in Table 9.2 reveals that 48.20 percent of the respondents do only their own work like cleaning their own dish, washing clothes etc. 9.20 percent of the unpaid respondents were engaged in gardening and farming, 9.20 percent of respondents do only the kitchen work, 3.60 percent of the unpaid respondents do the sweeping and cleaning work, 3.60 percent of the unpaid respondents do the religious work, 3.60 percent of the unpaid respondents do any work asked to do by the supervisor and manager of the homes, 3.60 percent of the unpaid respondents do only cooking, 1.80 percent of the unpaid respondents work in the institution such as gatekeeper, one of the respondent is given the post of caretaker in the home and he looked after all the respondents, 1.80 of the unpaid respondents were engaged in weaving. 15.40 percent of the respondents do not do any work in the OAHs.

It is evident from the study that most of the respondents in the paid OAHs do only their own work. In the unpaid home, the respondents besides doing their own work, they also have to do other work in the institutions because they have no workers in the homes. It is also found that some of the respondents do nothing because of their ill-health and physical disability.

Activity theory of ageing, suggests that successful ageing occurs when older adults stay active. Activity is viewed as necessary to maintain a person's life satisfaction and positive self-concepts. To be happy in old age, individuals need to be active in old age. The longer older persons stay active, the longer they may enjoy good health and well-being and stay independent (Srivastava, 2010).

In the present study, it is found that the respondents who perform their own daily activities and who are also engaged in other work in the institutions were happier and healthier than the elderly who do not perform any work in the old age homes. Moreover, the elderly who do nothing also were happy and satisfied because most of them came from a poor background, poor

health, no children, ill-treatment of daughter-in-law and son and no one to take care of them. So, in this situation, the OAH is the best place for them because they took care and support of them.

Regarding the leisure activities of the elderly in the OAHs, it is found that 20.90 percent of the respondents spend their time by talking with their friends; 15.50 percent spend their time by watching T.V.; 14.50 percent respondents simply sit alone; 12.70 percent of respondents spend their free-time by helping others in the home; 10.90 percent of respondents spend their time by sleeping; 10.00 percent of the respondents spend their time reading magazines, newspapers and religious books; 7.30 percent of respondents spend their time doing exercise; 4.50 percent of the unpaid respondents spend their time by doing meditation, 2.70 percent of the paid respondents spend their time by writing novels, books and 1.0 percent of the respondents from the paid home spend his free time by playing music in his guitar.

It is found in the study that in the unpaid home, the respondents help each other since there is no caretaker in the home. They help the old who are blind or cannot walk by bringing their food, taking them to the bathroom etc. In paid OAHs some of the respondents write books and novels, one of the respondents said that by selling her books, she used to get money which she can use to pay her rent. The respondents from one of the unpaid homes said that they help others, whenever, their neighbour asks help from them.

Relationship and Adjustment of the elderly with other inmates in the OAHs and with their family ties

This study is made to know the adjustment of the respondents with other inmates. It is important to know the relationship with other inmates because in the absence of their own family members, the elderly stay in the companionship of other inmates in the OAHs. This study also shows the visits of the family of the elderly in their homes. This will give a glimpse of the elderly's situation in the OAHs. Presented below will reveal the adjustment of elderly with other inmates.

Table 9.3: Adjustment of elderly with other inmates.

Sl. No.		*Paid*	*Unpaid*	*Total*
1. Adjustment problem of the elderly with other inmates				
i.	Always	5(4.5%)	13(11.8%)	18(16.3%)
ii.	Occasionally	2(1.8%)	22(20%)	24(21.8%)
iii.	Rarely	3(2.7%)	18(16.5%)	21(19.2%)
iv.	Never	23(20.9%)	24(21.8%)	47(42.7%)

(Contd...)

2. Reasons for adjustment problem				
i.	Regarding work		9(8.2%)	9(8.2%)
ii.	Different background	3(2.7%)	9(8.2%)	12(10.9%)
iii.	Clash of personality	2(1.8%)	21(19.1%)	23(20.9%)
iv.	Regarding noise and cleanliness	1(1%)	5(4.5%)	6(5.5%)
v.	Regarding belonging		8(7.2%)	8(7.2%)
vi.	Sharing bathroom	4(3.6%)	1(1%)	5(4.5%)
vii.	Not applicable	23(20.9%)	24(21.8%)	47(42.8%)
3. Visitors of the respondents				
i.	Both son and daughter	4(3.6%)	1(1%)	5(4.5%)
ii.	Son and daughter-in-law	12(10.9%)	3(2.7%)	15(13.6%)
iii.	Daughter and son-in-law	2(1.8%)	7(6.3%)	9(8.2%)
iv.	Brother and sister	7(6.3%)	4(3.6%)	11(10%)
v.	Spouse	2(1.8%)		2(1.8%)
Vi	Nephew	2(1.8%)	4(3.6%)	6(5.5%)
vii.	Relatives	1(1%)	1(1%)	2(1.8%)
viii.	Unrelated		1(1%)	1(1%)
ix.	No one	3(2.7%)	56(50.9%)	59(53.6%)
4. The frequency of visits to old age home by relatives				
i.	Often	4(3.6%)		4(3.6%)
ii.	Occasionally	6(5.4%)	12(10.9%)	18(16.3%)
iii.	Only when you ask them	3(2.7%)	4(3.6%)	7(6.2%)
iv.	Once in a month	10(9.1%)	5(4.5%)	15(13.6%)
v.	Once a year	5(4.5%)		5(4.5%)
vi.	Once in a 2 year	2(1.8%)		2(1.8%)
vii.	Never	3(2.7%)	56(50.9%)	59(53.6%)
	Total	**33**	**77**	**110**

The data reflects that 42.70 percent said that they have never a problem with other inmates, 21.80 percent said that they have occasional a problem with other inmates, 19.20 percent said that they have rarely a problem and 16.30 percent said that they have always problems with their inmates.

From the study, it is found that though, 42.70 percent of the respondents said that they have no adjustment problem, but overall it is evident from the study that they have a problem with other inmates it may not be always but occasionally and sometimes. This difference may be due to their age itself, the more their age increases, the more they are unable to adjust with other (Vanitha, 2014). Moreover, they came from different situations and with different problems which hamper their mental stress and on the other hand it might result in low adjustment with other inmates.

Regarding their reasons for adjustment problem, it is found that 20.90 percent respondents said that due to their different personality they have problems to adjust with each other, 10.90 percent reported different backgrounds of culture, and class or religion for their adjustment with other, and 8.10 percent reported that their poor adjustment was regarding fight for their work. It was mostly found in elderly in the unpaid homes because

they have to work in the institution, 7.20 percent of respondents from the unpaid homes said that they have poor relationships concerning fight over their belongings. They claim a particular belonging to be their own. Some of them also reported that their belongings were stolen by the other inmates. 5.40 percent reported that they want to stay in peace without any disturbance from other inmates, 4.50 percent of the respondents reported that their less adjustment with other inmates was regarding the sharing of the bathroom. It was mostly found among the elderly of paid OAHs. They don't want to share the bathroom with other inmates. 42.70 percent of the respondents have no adjustment problems with other inmates. They maintain good relationships with everyone in the OAHs.

Most of the respondents consider their different personality and background to be the reasons for their adjustment problems. There is no difference between paid and unpaid OAHs; both of them face low adjustment with other inmates. Moreover, most of the respondents also said that in spite of these problems, though it is difficult to adjust, yet they have to tolerate the other inmates because they have no option and choice but have to reside in the homes with the other inmates. They also said that they want to live in peace and harmony instead of having fight for some small issues. This shows that the elderly desire to have peace in their last stage of life.

Regarding the visitors of the respondents in the old age OAHs, it is found that 53.60 percent of respondents had no visitors, 13.60 percent were visited by their son, 10 percent of respondents were visited by their brother and sisters, 8.20 percent of respondents were visited by their daughters, 5.50 percent of the respondents were visited by their nephew, 4.50 percent were visited by both their son and daughter, 1.80 percent of the respondents of the paid homes were visited by their spouse, 1.80 percent of respondents were visited by their relatives and 1.0 percent of the respondent from the unpaid home was visited by unrelated persons, (N.G.O) who kept her in the home.

The data in the study reflects that majority of the respondents have no visitors. It is also found that most of the respondents from the paid home were visited by their son and daughter-in-law and daughters. It shows that they still maintain a relationship with them. It might be because the Old age home supervisor of the paid home said that while keeping the old aged in the home, they also have to keep one guardian of the aged and they were in contact with the guardian because they have to pay the rent for them and also, they keep contact with them for the benefit of the aged. Moreover, in the unpaid home, the elderly has no visitors at all. It is found in the study that the respondents who have been visited by their family members both from paid and unpaid old age home were happier than the other respondents who don't have visitors at all. It is also found in the study that the respondents

who were unmarried and childless, they don't expect any visitor that will come to visit them in the homes.

Data on frequency of visits to the aged by their children or family members show that 16.30 respondents were visited only sometimes by their family members, 13.60 percent of the respondents were visited once in a month, 6.20 percent of the respondents have visitors only when they asked their family members to visit them, 4.50 percent of respondents from the paid homes were visited by their family members once in a year, 3.60 percent of the respondents from paid homes were visited regularly by their family members and 1.80 percent of the paid homes respondents have visitors once in two years. 53.60 percent of the respondents have no visitors at all to visit them. It is also found in the study that the respondents who have children but have no contact with them were more depressed than the other respondents who were visited by their children, childless and unmarried.

Advantages and problems faced by the elderly living in OAHs

In the present study, an attempt has been made to know the advantages and also the problem faced by the elderly living in old age homes in Assam. On the basis of in-depth interview and case study the researcher has identified various reasons of the advantages and problems in residing in old age homes in Assam, which is presented in the following table:

Table 9.4: Advantages and problems of residing in old age homes

Sl. No.		*Paid*	*Unpaid*	*Total*
1. Advantages of the old age homes				
i.	Everything is free (Food, clothes, medicine etc and no need to worry about it)		43(39.2%)	43(39.2%)
ii.	No responsibility and free time	5(4.5%)	1(1%)	6(5.4%)
iii.	Safety	4(3.6%)	7(6.3%)	11(10%)
iv.	Have friends to talk and share	13(11.8%)	11(10%)	24(21.8%)
v.	Got a shelter to reside	5(4.5%)	13(11.8%)	18(16.4%)
vi.	Nothing good	6(5.4%)	2(1.8%)	8(7.2%)
2. The problem faced by the elderly in the old age homes				
i.	Financial		5(4.5%)	5(4.5%)
ii.	Loneliness	5(4.5%)	2(1.8%)	7(6.4%)
iii.	Food	4(3.6%)	1(1%)	5(4.5%)
Iv.	Physical immobility	3(2.7%)	12(10.9%)	15(13.6%)
v.	Poor health		14(12.8%)	14(12.8%)
vi.	Adjustment problem	5(4.5%)	13(11.8%)	18(16.4%)
vii.	Don't have privacy		5(4.5%)	5(4.5%)
viii.	Feels like living in jail		6(5.5%)	6(5.5%)
ix.	Strict rules and regulations	3(2.8%)	4(3.6%)	7(6.3%)
	Total	**33**	**77**	**110**

Regarding the advantages of residing in OAHs, it is found that 39.20 percent respondents from the unpaid homes said that everything is free in the home including food, clothes; medicines, treatment and they have no need to worry about it. 21.80 percent said that they have friends of their same age to talk and share their feelings, 16.40 percent respondents said that they have got a shelter to reside, 10.00 percent respondents said that it is safe to reside in the home, 7.20 percent respondents said that nothing is good to reside in the home. They were not satisfied but had no option, 5.40 percent of respondents said that they have freetime and no responsibility in the homes. It is found in the study that most of the respondents from the unpaid homes said that everything is free in the home. Most of the respondents from the paid homes said that they have got friends of their same age to talk and share their feelings.

Mr. B.B, a bachelor, aged, 68 years who reside in the Christian run unpaid OAHs. He has no one and was staying alone. He stated that 'I am blind and was staying in the Railway Station, from where the Old age home supervisor brought me in the home. I receive a lot of care and love from my supervisor, which I even didn't receive from my parents. In this home, we get everything and we have no need to beg for food, clothing, etc.'.

Mr. R.M, a widow, aged 82 years from the unpaid home who was suffering from health problem, he has only daughters and no son and was living alone in the home stated that 'The home is taking good care of me; I have no need to worry about food, which I used to do before coming to the home. Now, if I go out of this home, what will I do? I would be begging on the street, who will take care of me, Therefore, I feel that this kind of home is very important for the needy and poor people like me'.

Mr. R.C, a widower aged 79 years, from the paid home, said, 'When a man grows old and is alone then old age home is the best place to stay because here one gets friends of the same age to talk and share own feelings. Besides, this in my home, I have to cook my own food but here we don't have to do anything, we are taken care of and we get our food timely'.

Mrs. K.U, a widow and a writer, aged 76 years, from the paid home said, 'In this home, I don't have to take any responsibility regarding the household chores, therefore, I have available time and can peacefully write books and novels in this home without any disturbance'.

This clearly depicts the advantages of old age homes in taking care of the old people who are poor and needy. It provides them with food, shelter, safety, and care which they unable to earn or get from their family members. The study also shows that the elderly has got a companion to share their feelings which they didn't get in their own homes from their family or relatives.

Regarding the problems of the elderly residing in the old age homes, it is evident from the study that 16.40 percent respondents said that they have problems in adjusting with others, 13.60 percent of the respondents said physical immobility as their main problem, 12.80 percent of respondents consider poor health as their main problem, 6.40 percent of respondents consider loneliness as their problem, 6.30 percent considers to follow the rules and regulations of the old age homes to be their problem, 5.50 percent of the unpaid old age homes reported that they feel like living in a jail in the old age homes, 5.40 percent of the respondents from the unpaid homes said that they face financial problem, 4.50 percent said that the food provided in the home is not good, 3.60 percent of the respondents from the unpaid homes said that they don't have privacy in the old age homes. 39.20 percent said that they have no problem at all.

It is found in the study that most of the respondents consider an adjustment to be their main problem. Moreover, it is found that in the paid homes, most of the elderly consider adjustment and loneliness to be their problem and in the unpaid homes, most of the elderly consider poor health and adjustment to be their problem. This is because the elderly was mostly involved in the family affairs in their home. Loss of family and homely environment might have caused them more stress and problem in the old age home.

Mr. B.R, a widower aged, 70 years, who stay in the unpaid home with two other inmates said that he felt lonely in the old age home because his two friends never talk with him. He stated that 'if only they would talk to me, then I would never feel lonely in the home but they never talk, they only sleep from day to night'.

Mrs. K.K, aged 75 years, a widow who stay in a double room in the paid home said that his roommate watches T.V anytime, therefore, she gets disturbed and cannot sleep peacefully. After telling her several times, she did not listen to her words.

Mr. K.G, a widower, aged 69 years, who stay in the unpaid home, said that he can't go out of the old age homes without permission. When he was in his villages he was independent and used to roam freely without seeking any one's permission, therefore he felt that he has lost his independent life and feels like living in a jail.

This study clearly shows that though the Old Age Homes have advantages, on one hand, it has also some disadvantages faced by the elderly living in OAHs.

Satisfaction and the issue of engagement of the elderly living in the OAHs

The elderly under various circumstances were forced to reside in the OAHs. Since they were disengaged from their family and homely environment; therefore, it made them feel depressed and unsatisfied with life. Here, an attempt has been made to know to what extent the quality of the OAHs contribute to those elderly's life satisfaction and also to find out how engaging in various activities in the home helps them to overcome their depression.

Table 9.5: Satisfaction and the issue of engagement among the old age home inmates

Sl.No.		*Paid*	*Unpaid*	*Total*
1. Satisfaction				
i.	Fully satisfied	18(16.4%)	59(53.6%)	77(70%)
ii.	Partially satisfied	9(8.2%)	16(14.5%0	25(22.7%)
iii.	Not satisfied	6(5.5%)	2(1.8%)	8(7.3%)
2. Anxiety feeling				
i.	Want to die soon because life is a burden on others	1(1%)	12(10.9%)	13(11.8%)
ii.	Distressed about the present life	3(2.7%)	8(7.2%)	11(10%)
iii.	Fear to death		2(1.8%)	2(1.8%)
iv.	Health	4(3.6%)	14(12.7%)	18(16.4%)
v.	Worried about the remaining life	11(10%)	13(11.8%)	24(21.8%)
vi.	Remembering all the good things about the past	8(7.3%)	9(8.2%)	17(15.5%)
vii.	Could not achieve the goals of life	2(1.8%)	7(6.4%)	9(8.2%)
viii.	Cannot say		2(1.8%)	2(1.8%)
ix.	Nothing to worry	4(3.6%)	10(9.2%)	14(12.7%)
3. Overcome				
i.	Keeps busy in work	1(1%)	20(18.1%)	21(19.1%)
ii.	It passes off after sometime	6(5.4%)	23(10.9%)	29(26.5%)
iii.	Spending some time with friends	13(11.8%)	21(19.1%)	34(30.9%)
iv.	Reading religious books and others	2(1.8%)	1(1%)	3(2.7%)
v.	Writing books and novels	3(2.7%)		3(2.7%)
vi.	Watching T.V and playing music	4(3.6%)		4(3.6%)
vii.	Cannot say		2(1.8%)	2(1.8%)
viii.	Nothing to worry	4(3.6%)	10(9.2%)	14(12.7%)
	Total	**33**	**77**	**110**

The data clearly reflects that majority of the respondent's(70.00 %) are fully satisfied with the life provided in the old age home, 22.70 percent respondents are partially satisfied and 7.30 percent respondents are not at all satisfied with the life in the home.

Regarding the anxiety feeling of the respondents, it is found that most of the respondents, 21.80 percent were worried about their remaining life, 16.40 percent were worried about their health, 15.50 percent said that they remember all the good things about their past life, 12.70 percent respondents said that they were worried about nothing, 11.80 percent said that they want to die soon because they felt that their life is a burden on others, 10.00 percent said that they were distressed about their present life, 8.20 percent respondents felt sad because they could not achieve the goals of their life, 1.80 percent respondents of the unpaid homes were worried about their death, 1.80 percent of respondents cannot say anything, therefore, they have no answer to this question.

In regards to the manner in which the respondents overcome their depression, it is evident from the study that 30.90 percent respondents said that they spend some time with friends to overcome their depressions, 26.50 percent said that it passes off after sometime, 19.10 percent said that they kept busy themselves in work in order to overcome their depression, 12.70 percent respondents said that they were worried about nothing, most of this persons has no one and they were living alone, 3.60 percent of the respondents from the paid homes said that to overcome their depression they watch T.V and play music 2.70 percent of the respondents said that they read religious books and other books to overcome their depression and 2.70 percent of the respondents from the paid homes said that they write books and novels to overcome their depression and 1.80 percent cannot answer this question.

Most of the respondents said that they spend their time with their friends to overcome their depression. It is evident from the study that since most of the elderly spends with friends, share their feelings and feel happy with them. Therefore, it can be said that their friends are replacing the care and love that they supposed to get from their family members. In this way, after disengaging from their family relationships, they were engaged in a new relationship with some unknown persons in the old age homes with whom they live and feel comfortable and happy.

Conclusion

Living in OAHs which was unknown in Assam, is becoming a trend in recent societies, especially in the urban areas of Assam. In fact, there are greater chances that most elderly requiring relocation in OAHs, belong to poor or low middle-income group in a state like Assam where 31.98 percent of the population remains below poverty line (Sarma, 2009; cited in Kipgen and Nattar, 2009). It is found in the study that mostly the vulnerable sections of the society reside in the OAHs of Assam. They are the poor, destitute and

the widow. Among the female, widowhood is the main reasons for their stay in the homes. It is because as found in the study that they face various problems in their later life after the death of their husband. Moreover, it is also found in the study that though the elderly from the paid OAHs had their own children or relatives to be economically dependent but they were also forced to reside in the old age homes, which ultimately shows that not only the poor but also the well to do people resides in the old age homes. Therefore, it can be said that poverty, lack of care, poor health and conflict with son and daughter-in-law and daughter were the main reasons for the elderly to reside in the OAHs in Assam.

The elderly in the homes have a low adjustment with the other inmates. It is because they came from different situations with different problems which hamper their mental stress and on the other hand causes low adjustment with other inmates. Moreover, it is found in the study that most of the elderly people have no visitors, which made them feel depressed and unhappy, especially the elderly who have children. Regarding the activities of the elderly, it is found that the elderly was engaged in various activities in the homes. The problem that the elderly face in the homes was an adjustment, health and financial. Loss of family and homely environment might have created them more stress and problem in the homes. Most of the elderly were satisfied with living in the homes because most of them came to reside in the homes due to poverty, poor health and lack of care, in this situation they are provided with food, clothing, and shelter by the OAHs, which is the most important requirement in human lives. After disengaging from their family, although most of the elderly were worried about their life it is also evident from the study that they were engaged in various activities in the OAHs which help them to overcome their depression. This shows that they were re-engaged in the OAHs meaningfully.

OAHs have both advantages and disadvantages. On the one hand, it will erode the traditional practices of care and respect given to the older people in Assam. Though in Assam, the traditional practice of caregiving and respect is still maintaining it is slowly increasing and starting from within the family itself. On the other hand, from the study, it is found that the elderly face problems in their own homes, however, it differs from persons. Some of the elderly have a conflict with their children and family members, some of them lack care from their children which forced them to reside in the OAHs. Instead of having family and children they were forced to reside in the OAHs. It is found that mostly the vulnerable sections of people reside in the OAHs. They were poor and destitute. The poor people who were engaged in the unorganized sector with no pension and savings, they were the most sufferer because of their poor health, they cannot work and earn any more,therefore, they were forced to reside in the homes. In these situations, the OAHs provide

them with food, shelter, clothing, and care, which are the most requirements in human lives. In this context, the OAHs are playing a great role in helping the poor and needy people. Moreover, it could also be said that in the absence of these old age homes, there would be more old street beggars in Assam. Therefore, the role of OAHs has saved the lives of the elderly people, especially the poor and destitute.

At the same time, no individual is happy and no one prefers to live in isolation or separation from their family members because family is the best place and no one can replace the care of the family. But the elderly people in the present study have no option but different situations and conditions forced them to reside in the OAHs. OAHs should not be considered as the option or dumping places of the old parents though it is of great help for those who have no children and destitute. Younger generations (children) should take care of their parents when they grow old because it is their parents who sacrificed their whole life for the betterment and welfare of their children. In return, it is the duty of the children to look after them at their old age. No one can replace their children and no one can make them feel happy, except the love and care of their children.

References

Adhikari, H 2016, 'Family or Old Age Home - which is appropriate for happiness of elderly at post-retirement life in India?', *Journal of Gerontology and Geriatric Research*, vol. 5, no. 3. Available from: doi 10.4172/ 2167- 7182. 1000305.

Akbar, S, Tiwari, SC, Tripathi, RK & Pandey, NM 2014, 'Reasons for the living of elderly to in Old Age Homes: an exploratory study', *The International Journal of Indian Psychology*, vol. 2, no. 1, 55-61.

Barooah, J 1993, *Single women in Assamese Hindu society*, Gyan Publishing House,Delhi, pp. 28.

Beevi, JS 2010, 'A profile of elderly women living in Old Age Homes - a study in Kerala', *International Research Journal of Social Sciences*, vol. 3, no. 2, 13-32.

Behura, NK & Mohanty, RP 2005, *Aged in changing social system: their problems*, Discovery Publishing House,New Delhi,pp 1.

Bhat, AK & Dhruvarajan, R 2015, 'Ageing in India: drifting intergenerational relations, challenges, and options' in *Sociology of ageing, a reader*, eds. AK Sahoo, GJ Andrews & SI Rajan, Rawat Publications, Jaipur, pp. 334-349.

Bond. J, Peace, SM, Kohli, FD & Westerhof,G (eds.) 2007, *Ageing in society*,Sage Publications, London, pp. 1.

Chen, MA 2000, 'Indian widows in search of dignity and identity' in *The unorganized sector: work security and social protection*, eds. R Jhabwala & RKA Subrahmany, Sage Publications, New Delhi.

Dandekar, K 1996, *The elderly in India*, Sage Publications, Delhi, pp. 108-110.

Devi, SB 2005, 'Challenges and issues informal care giving', *Indian Journal of Gerontology*, vol. 19, no. 4, pp. 447-456.

Gurung, S & Ghimire, S 2014, *Role of family in eldercare, school of healthcare and social sciences,* Lapland University of Applied Sciences, Oulu, Kemi.

Hooyaman, N & Kiyak, HA 2005, *Social-gerontology: a multidisciplinary perspectives*, Allyn and Bacon,Boston, Mass, pp. 45.

Hossen, MA2004, 'Socio-economic transition and its impact on the elderly in Bangladesh: issues, challenges, and some policy implications', *Indian Journal of Gerontology*, vol. 18, no. 1, pp. 115-134.

Jhabwala, R & Subrahmanya, RKA 2000, The unorganized sector: work security and social protection, Sage Publication, New Delhi.

Kumar, Y & Bhargava, A 2014, 'Elder abuse in Indian families: problems and preventive action', *International Journal of Scientific and Research Publications*, vol. 4, no. 10.

Kumar, VS & Reddy, N 2002, 'Social security for the elderly in India: present status and future challenges' in *Indian society, continuity, change and development*, eds. PS Reddy & V Gangadhar, Common Wealth Publishers, New Delhi.

Kunemund, H & Kolland, F 2007, 'Work, and retirement' in *Ageing in society*, eds. J Bond, SM Peace, FD Kohli & G Westerhof,Sage Publications, London, pp. 173-174.

Lamb, S 2009, *Ageing and the Indian diaspora cosmopolitan families in India and Abroad*, Indian University Press, Indian University Press, pp. 57-58.

Mahanta, BC 1995, 'A study of dependability and support in old age in the Assamese society: an ethnological perspective' in *Challenges before the elderly: an Indian scenario*, ed SV Kumar, MD Publications, New Delhi, pp. 21.

Mahapatra, S 2010, 'Second home after home for elderly: a study of old age homes in the globalization era', *Indian Journal of Gerontology*, vol. 4, no. 1, pp. 115-122.

Mishra, AJ 2007, 'Staying active and promoting well-being among the elderly, a study of the Old Age Homes in Orissa', *The Indian Journal of Social Work*, vol. 68, no. 4, 561-572.

Mishra, AJ 2012, 'Disengagement or re-engagement in later life? a study of old age home residents of Orissa', *Indian Journal of Gerontology*, vol. 26, no. 4, pp. 564-577.

Mishra, S 1989, *Problems and social adjustment in old age: a sociological analysis*, Gyan Publishing House, Delhi, pp. 4-6.

Rajan, SI 2000, *Home away from home: a survey of old age home and inmates in Kerala.* Working Paper No.306, pp. 4-17.

Raju, SS 2011, *Studies on ageing in India: a review*, Institute for Social and Economic Change, Bangalore.

Rao, AN, Trivedi, Y & Yadav, V 2015, 'Assessing the life satisfaction of elderly living in Old Age Homes of the city of Ahmadabad', *Indian Journal of Gerontology*, vol. 29, no. 2, pp. 154-169.

Rao, KV 2007, *Ageing in rural India*, Associated Publishers, Delhi.

Sati, PN 1988, *Retired and ageing people: a study of their problems*, Mittal Publications, Delhi, pp. 1.

Shankardass, MK 2010, 'Elder abuse and adult protection' in *Ageing and health in India,* eds. CS Jhonson & SI Rajan, Rawat Publications, New Delhi, pp. 187-206.

Sharma, HD 2009, 'Social and economic status of elders: issues and challenges' in *Ageing in Northeast India, Manipur perspective,* eds S Kipgen &B Nattar, Akansha Publishing House, New Delhi.

Shirmly, I 2014, *Psycho-social problems of elderly: a study of Imphal-West district in Manipur.* Ph.D. thesis, Department of Social Work, Assam University.

Singh, B & Kiran, UV 2014, 'Recreational activities for senior citizens', *IOSR Journal of Humanities and Social Science*, vol.19, no. 4, pp. 24-30.

Srivastava, V 2010, *Women ageing, social work intervention*, Rawat Publications, Jaipur, pp. 86-89.

Thomas, JC & Diengdoh, FT 2009, *Ageing in Meghalaya*, Akansha Publishing House,Delhi, pp. 11.

Vanitha, D 2014, 'Institutional care of the elderly: a study of Old Age Home in Hasan City, Karnataka, India', *International Journal of Interdisciplinary Studies*, vol. 1, no. 5, 100-107.

Venkateswarlu, V & Lakshmipathi, RM 2007, 'Exploring the social and family background of rural elderly: results of a baseline survey in Guntur district', *Help Age India-Research and Development Journal*, Vol. 13, no. 2.

Visielie, 2012, *Ageing and disengagement in Naga Society: a comparative study of rural and urban area.* Ph.D. thesis, School of Social Sciences, Nagaland University.

Wilson, MA 1975, *Social-cultural aspects of aging*, ETD Collection for AWC Robert W.Woodruff Library, Paper 534, Working Paper Number 3.

Chapter - 10

The Jirkedam:

An Indispensable Socio-cultural Organization in the Pristine Karbi Society of Assam

— ***Birinchi K. Medhi and Bimla***

Introduction

The dormitory is an integral part of the many tribal societies of the world, which has different features in different contexts. The youths of same communities live in a separate house among many tribal people to guard the village and to get systematic training. In the German language, the house is named as *junglinghaus* (youth house). It can be called by different terms such as a dormitory, youth dormitory, bachelors' hall, etc. Furer-Haimendrof (1939:20-24) prefers to identify it as *morung*, which has gained much popularity in anthropological writing on the tribes of North-East India. There are various reasons for establishing a dormitory, such as, the need of a rest house for the visitors in a village; the usefulness and convenience of the youths in a village to be organized for their availability for social works; universal human tendency to form clubs; to enable girls to have suitable husbands; to serve as defensive force; to encourage the growing boys and girls in the task of educating the younger children as the parents have no time for the training of their offspring, and so on. According to Elwin (1947: 321), keeping the children away from the parental bedroom, was the primary reason for establishing the village dormitory among the Karbis.

The dormitory institution is almost as old as the family system. This system possibly is a survival of the community houses from which private dwellings split off. Peal (1893:244) opines that the individual or separate house

for each family is a later development among the tribals. The dormitory institution, particularly in Africa and Nagaland, serves the purpose of the military organization, where raids are planned and the group guards in village warfare (ibid: 78).

According to Roy (1915: 111), the Oraon dormitory is an economic organization for the purpose of food quest, a useful seminary for training the young men in their social and other duties, and an institution for magico-religious observances calculated to secure success in hunting and augment the procreative power of the young men. The magical aspect is also found playing an important role in the establishment of an Oraon dormitory. In Mizoram among the Lushei-Kuki clan, a man who hunts a rhinoceros has to spend a day and a night in the village dormitory; otherwise, they believe that his family will die (Shakespear, 1912: 103).

As a tribal village is situated at a far distance from another habitation, so the village dormitory acts as a resting place for the travelers and tradesmen. The village meetings are also held in a dormitory and it provides a common platform for all sorts of discussion as well as many religious performances of the village. The youth of the dormitory perform agricultural activities, social activities and religious performances besides defending the village from external aggression. It is their clubhouse where they gossip, sing, dance, play, work and sleep at night. The utilitarian purpose from the socio-economic point of view is also mentioned as a cause of the origin of dormitory (Majumdar, 1930: 164). The aim or purpose of establishing a dormitory is to enable the girls to have suitable husbands as found among the Bondo tribe of Orissa, who keep the girls away from the village in a dormitory (Elwin, 1947: 311).

In Africa among the tribal populations which have rich varied cultures, the dormitory institution mainly performs two functions, i.e., training the young warriors in warfare and village defense and save the parents from the embarrassing presence of grown-up children in small houses. Among the tribes living in the Bank Island, dormitory houses are established for the male only and a boy tries to enter it at any age or initiation but on payment of a fee. Even married men neither sleep nor eat with their wives, but in their dormitory house called *sukwe* (Lowie, 1921: 260). The Crow tribe establishes dormitories for both the boys and the girls. They have also some military organizations for the men alone whose membership is not obligatory (ibid, 1921:273). There are village dormitories in many parts of South America. In Brazil, the Bororo tribe builds the dormitory known as *bahito* to keep the village boys together. They learn manufacturing weapons, singing, and dancing by participating in various festive occasions. They arrange an annual feast in the dormitory when they abduct the virgins who have no parents

and keep them in their dormitory (Fric and Radin, 1906: 388). In Sumatra, the Battak establishes both boys' and girls' dormitories known as *sopo* and *loho*,respectively. Among the Moi of Annam and the Kha of Siam, dormitories are set up to train the youths for social requirements (Boudesson, 1919:45).

The Andamanese have their triple arrangement of huts for bachelors, spinsters and married couples. Widowers and widows are placed in the first and the second, respectively. The boys and girls at the age of eleven have to undergo a probationary period, in which they have to fast occasionally and avoid food such as turtle, honey, pork, and other delicacies. It is a test of self-denial which ends at the suggestion of the chief. A ceremony is performed by the priest before entering the club and the initiated person is painted and decorated. The person has to dance before the gathering and their parents' laments for going away from home and entering the club (Lowie, 1921: 250-55). Among the south Indian tribes, the dormitory institution has a separate arrangement for boys and girls. The Kadu and Kuruba of Mysore have the same system of keeping boys and girls in separate dormitories. They call the youth dormitory *pundungerchavadi*, the abode of vagabonds (Iyer, 1909: 229).

In Chota Nagpur, the Oraon tribe has a very elaborate system of the dormitory. They keep their boys in *jonkherpa* or *dhumkuria* as it exists in the east of the district. They have a public building with office bearers to conduct the affairs of the institution. The girls are lodged in a separate house (not a public building) and in fact, its location is not supposed to be known to anyone except its inmates and to those of the boys' dormitory. The girls' dormitory, i.e., *pelerpa*, is looked after by an elderly woman known as *pelokotwar*. They do not have other office bearers. There is often a *barkadhangrin*, the elder girl acts as a leader. In Madhya Pradesh, the Bhumia-Baigha tribal youths are kept in a well-developed dormitory system, where they are trained for social life through participation in various social activities. The dormitory system also exists among the Hill Maria of Abujhmar Hills, Dhurwa, Bisonhorn Maria and Muria tribes. The Muria calls it *ghotul* where both boys and girls live together until marriage and that too with complete sexual liberty (Elwin, 1947: 316).

The dormitory system survives among most of the tribes in Orissa like the Juang, Bhuiya, Kond, Kadaba, Bondo, Didai, Poroja and Savara. The Juang and the Bhuiya build a large and highly decorated house in the center of the village for the boys and the girls have a separate house nearby. The Juangs calls it *darbar* or *mandagarh* for boys and *dhangri basa* for girls. Among the Juangs the dormitory is the nerve center of the social and economic life of the village. It is a clubhouse for the youths and a school of art and dance for

them. The character of the Bondo dormitory depends on certain tribal principles, that none of the descendants of the original settlers of a village should intermarry; therefore, boys and girls must seek partners from other villages (ibid, 1947: 302-311). 'Dormitory or *morung* is for the young unmarried men and among some tribes for unmarried girls as well is considered to be an important educational, political and social institution. All the unmarried boys and girls of the village, from the age of seven or eight, live till they are married in the bachelors' or girls' dormitories. Among some tribes, boys' *morung* where feminine entry is prohibited is held in high esteem. They learn manners, discipline, art, stories, songs, war tactics, diplomacy, religious and customary rites, and ceremonies living in it. It has been a school for the young to learn the art of livelihood, responsibility, and co-operation before the Nagas came in contact with the modern education and life. The Naga girls sleep together in a group in their dormitories where the boys, mostly their lovers, come to have a competition of songs' (Yonuo, 1974:11).

In Mizoram, the dormitory system is known as *zawlbulk*. It is organized for both the boys and girls for accommodation in the past. But later the girls were lodged in a separate house of the village. They perform the agricultural activities, songs, and dance together in festivals. In Arunachal Pradesh, almost all the tribes are having the dormitory system. The Khamptis are having separate dormitories for both the boys and the girls. The girls' dormitory is sacred, and no man is supposed to enter there. There remains an old maid who has outlived the age of romance, who keeps vigilance and prevents any proceeding which might be termed scandalous (Cooper, 1873: 147). Among the Tangsas of the Namchik and Tirap valley, the boys' dormitory known as *looping* does not exist, girls' dormitories *loop* or *likpyas* are still in existence in some villages, where the young bachelors pass their evening gossiping with the girls (Dutta, 1969: 46). The Khamptis also establish dormitories for both the boys and the girls separately. The entrance of male persons is prohibited in the girls' dormitory. An elderly lady keeps vigilance over the girls in their dormitory at night. The boys and girls come out of their respective dormitories in the morning, meet on the road and go together for field work (ibid, 1962: 264).

The Sherdukpen tribe of Arunachal Pradesh (Kameng district) accommodates boys and girls separately in some vacant houses. This institution was developed during conflict days when the Sherdukpens had to guard their villages against the Miji and Aka tribes. This is a recent example of the origin of the dormitory institution as a defensive measure against hostile tribes. The separate establishment of an elaborate dormitory system is not yet developed among the Sherdukpens. The adolescent boys and girls sleep in separate houses offered for the purpose by the village headman.

Though they sleep in separate houses, there is a constant meeting among the boys and the girls who often form lasting attachment leading to marriage. Such premarital relationship always leads to marriage (Chowdhury, 1973: 58-59).

The Apa Tani tribe in the district of Subansiri of Arunachal Pradesh called the group of village boys and girls as *patang*. This group consists of adolescent boys and girls of the same clan of a village for community labour. These group members are always ready to help in one another's fields during cultivation according to a principle of reciprocation (ibid, 1973: 148). The Wancho tribe of Arunachal too establishes dormitories for the boys and the girls separately. These dormitories are based on the unit division of a village. In each unit, there should be separate dormitory for the boys and the girls. In a village, there are two dormitories for all important purposes called as *panu* and *pasa*. The *panu* is a dormitory of the chief, where all social gatherings are held. In the past, the head-hunting expeditions were planned there and enemy heads were preserved in *panu*. The relationship of boys and girls in the dormitories is free like that of the Noctes. The romantic attachment of a boy and his girlfriend generally leads to marriage. The Adi (formerly known as Abor) tribe of Siang district in Arunachal Pradesh developed an elaborate system of bachelors' dormitory known as *mosup* for boys and *raseng* for girls. The Adis are divided into several sub-tribes and each sub-tribe has its own term to designate this dormitory institution. The term *mosup* is used by the Padam section; the Minyongs call it *dere*, the Milan,and other allied groups call it *ngaptek* and Bori and the Ashing call it *barge* (ibid, 1973: 240-250).

The Karbis

The Karbis are known as Mikirs in the Constitution of India. They called themselves *Arleng*, which means 'slanting place near hills', and thus denotes the people living in the slopes of the hills. The Karbi is one of the dominant tribe in the Karbi Anglong district of Assam and is scattered in different districts of Assam and Khasi Hills of Meghalaya. 'Traditionally the Karbi is a hill-tribe, but for different reasons, they are scattered over plain areas also. The culture of the Karbis is prominent for traits like dependence on *jhum* cultivation (*inglongarit*), the central place of bamboo in material culture, the indispensable role of rice beer in socio-economic and religious life, and for their rich folklore' (Medhi, 1988: 8-13). They are racially Mongoloid and linguistically belong to the Tibeto-Burman group. The Karbis have five clans (*kurs*), namely, Inghi, Ingti, Terang, Teron, and Timing. Ingti is the priestly clan and had a higher status in the society. The clans in Karbi society are rigidly exogamous. Marriages between the members of the same clan are strictly prohibited but there are cross-cousin marriages. The Karbis are

patrilineal and patrilocal people. The bachelors' dormitory *jirkedam* is the most important institution of the Karbis which is associated with agriculture, social and other activities. The traditional village council among them is known as *me* headed by the village chief. Traditionally Karbis are animists and their supreme god is Hemphu, but now some of them have adopted Lokhimon as their religion, i.e., the modified form of traditional animist religion, and also Christianity. The Karbis hold a number of religious festivals which are principally associated with agriculture, Rongker is the festival held every year before the beginning of cultivation; Sokkero is the festival of harvest and Chomangkan, which is the most important ceremony to appease the deceased forefathers among the Karbis (ibid: 10-11).

Origin of *Jirkedam*

There is no written record on the origin of the dormitory among the Karbis. According to their oral tradition, it is believed that in the past it was very difficult to send a message of invitation and nobody knew when a marriage was arranged between a boy and a girl of a neighbouring village. In the past, as villages were situated at far distances, the villagers had to walk a long distance in order to visit a relative or a friend inhabited in other villages. Once a marriage was fixed and the groom village decided to clear the jungle and thereby make a short path to the bride's village. One morning the boys of the groom's village cleared the jungle and constructed a path to the bride's house. The villagers were so surprised to see such a short path, as they had been traveling through a very long route. Thereby, the villagers honoured the boy by offering betel nut and rice beer and also decided to honour the boys in all social gatherings and festivals and organize the boys into a close group. These boys group according to the Karbi oral history was the beginning of the dormitory institution. The youths were known as *risomar*, '*riso*' means 'youth' and '*mar*' is the plural version. The *risomar* going to work together is called as *jirkedam*, '*jir*' means 'thread that binds together flowers of a garland', '*ke*' means 'a form of the root' and '*dam*' means 'to go'. Therefore, *jirkedam* literally means 'going together' (Terang, 1974: 106). *Jirkedam* usually means 'collective march' or collective work' (Bhattacharjee, 1986: 61). The members of the *jirkedam* are known as *jersong*.

The dormitory institution is very old in the Karbi society. There is no written history but according to their oral history in a document of a village council meeting of Amchekso village in Resak Hills, a special name was mentioned known as Harbimang, who first introduced the hierarchy of the dormitory members. The first leader, i.e., *klengsarpo* of the Ingti was Dirsu Arai Rongpi, the second leader *klengdun* was Sam Ingti and there was one Naga boy acting as *phankri* (rendering services to the two leaders) mentioned

in the document. Today the name, place, and hill mentioned in the document cannot be ascertained (Terang, 1937:45). The function of the dormitory institution is not only confined to the social services but it also serves many useful purposes in the society. The inclusion of girls in the dormitory was done at the later period. The other reason for the establishment of the dormitory by the Karbis was to avoid the children's presence in the house at night for the convenience of their parents. It is not only among the Karbis but among other tribes too. Therefore, at six or seven years of age, the children are sent to the dormitory. Nowadays the girls are allowed to sleep with the grandparents where there is no dormitory. This is not only found among the Karbis but among some other tribes also (Medhi, 2004: 25-28).

Establishment of *Jirkedam*

A *jirkedam* is usually established after the approval of the Karbi king (*ronghanglindok*) and the village headman (*Sarthe*) is sought permission in order to establish the dormitory in the village. In the Karbi village, there is one headman who gives judgment on cases related to disputes along with the village council. The territory of the *jirkedam*, in general, is the territory of the village. There are provisions for fifty-two office bearers and innumerable young members in a *jirkedam*. The Karbi dormitory institution is established after the Chongkong Ranker festival. The Karbis perform the annual festivals known as Ranker in which the Karbi great god Arnam Kethe is worshipped and offered with rice beer and sacrifices goat, chicken, etc. After the festival, the clearing and cutting of jungles for *jhum* is started in the month of December. In the month of April, before sowing of seeds a festival is observed by the Karbis known as Chongkong Ranker, after which the dormitory institution is formally established. They do not have a calendar, so the village headman tentatively fixes a date for the festivals. The main requirement of the festivals are the six goats, i.e., two she-goats and four he-goats (two black and two white), one pig, twenty-five chickens, plenty of rice and rice beer. The items are either donated by the rich families of the village or purchased from the villagers by collection of funds. The boys collect the items and girls prepare rice and rice beer. A dormitory house (*terang*) is then constructed by the boys near the headman's house. A tree is also located in the village which is neither fruit-bearing nor thorny. Underneath the tree, a pile of stone is erected to do sacrificial offerings. A day is fixed for the ceremony, especially a moonlit night, and the boys are informed to attend the observance of the ceremony. Even the people from neighbouring villages are invited for the ceremony (Medhi, 2004:30-35).

Membership

As a rule, all the unmarried boys and girls of a village become the

members of the dormitory. They sleep in the dormitory at night, participate in agricultural activities of the institution, join in the community dance and ceremonial performances organized in the village, play games and take part in other recreational activities like fishing and hunting expeditions. There is no fixed age at which the children claim admission to the dormitory. After crossing the infancy stage, the child likes to spend most of the time with the group together at night. At the age of six to eight years, the boys and girls start to sleep at the dormitory house. There are also other parents who are eager to send their children to the dormitory when they cross the infancy stage due to privacy concern of the parents.

In *jirkedam,* there are three categories of the members:

(i) The office bearers

(ii) The associate office bearers, and

(iii) The general members

There are 26 office bearers in a *jirkedam* for which no more than one of the age group of 12-13 years should be selected from a household of the village. The leader is known as *klensarpo*, who are selected on the basis of his personal qualification and character. Those boys having a good qualification with amiable character, efficiency in work, sound judging capacity and great respect towards the elders, are preferred in the selection. According to the pristine rule, the leader must not be the son of the king (*rongkhang*), officials of the king (*pinpomar*), or that of the headman (*sarthe*). The leader is generally selected from among the poor, particularly the son of the widow. This practice has been abandoned by many village headmen, who prefer to select their own sons to be the leader of the respective village dormitories. The other requirements needed for the office bearers are that he must be above 12 years of age, who must not hold the office for more than three years must have the willingness to be selected for office bearers and must not have any objections from their parents.

After the establishment of the dormitory institution in the village, head selects the office bearers with the two leaders, the *klengsarpo,* and the *klengdun.* The designations of the office bearers in order of their ranks are listed below along with the duties attached to the respective officials in brief.

Table 10.1: The office bearers of *jirkedam* with their salient features

Sl. No.	*Designation*	*Etymological meaning*	*English equivalent*	*Duties*
1.	*Klengsarpo*	eldest of all	chief executive officer	overall supervision and execution
2.	*Klengdun*	next to the eldest	assistant chief	assistance in supervision and execution

(*Contd...*)

3.	*Sodar-kethe*	big supervisor	supervisory officer	supervision of work
4.	*Sodar-so*	small supervisor	assistant supervisory officer	assistance in work supervision
5.	*Sanghorai-kethe*	big guard of the team	captain	maintenance of discipline in the dormitory
6.	*Sanghorai-so*	small guard of the team	assistant captain	do (assistant)
7.	*Chengbrup-kethe*	big drum	drummer	beating drums
8.	*Chengbrup-so*	small drum	assistant drummer	beating drums
9.	*Barlon-kethe*	big measuring rod	measuring rod carrier	measurement of land
10.	*Barlong-so*	small measuring rod	assistant measuring rod carrier	do (assistant)
11.	*Motan-are*	right-hand worker	work initiator in the right side in the field	initiation of works
12.	*Motan-arvi*	left-hand worker	work initiator in the left side	do (assistant)
13.	*Thana-are*	right-hand observer	house observer	up-keep of the dormitory
14.	*Thana-arvi*	left-hand observer	assistant house observer	do (assistant)
15.	*Langbong-kethe*	big water gourd	water carrier	supply of Water
16.	*Langbong-so*	small water gourd	assistant water carrier	do (assistant)
17.	*Me-apai*	fire fencing	firekeeper	lighting of fire
18.	*Lang-apai*	water fencing	fire brigadier	extinction of fire
19.	*Kove-thak*	betel nut divider	betel nut supplier	supply of betel nut
20.	*Bithi-thak*	betel leaf divider	betel leaf supplier	supply of betel leaf
21.	*Chinhak-kethe*	big tool basket	tool keeper	keeping tools and equipment of works
22.	*Chinhak-so*	small tool basket	assistant tool keepers	do
23.	*Arphek-kethe*	big broom	cleaner	cleaning of the dormitory house
24.	*Arphek-so*	small broom	assistant cleaner	do
25.	*Phankri-kethe*	big orderly	senior orderly (to the *klengsarpo*)	rendering service to the two leader
26.	*Phankri-so*	small orderly	junior orderly (to the *klengdun*)	do

Source: Jirkedam: A School in Deeds, 2004: 37-38.

It is to be noticed that there is always a couple, a boy with a girl, for a similar job or rather the same job. It is remarkable to note that each couple derives its designation from a local word which indicates the nature of its work. The suffix '*kethe*' and the '*so*' are used to mean big and small, literally, these two may also be interpreted as senior and junior, respectively. They are the office bearers and assistants of the *klengsarpo* and *klengdun*. The two office bearers are in a pair, works together helping each other in performing their duties. In the absence of one, the other performs the job ungrudgingly (Medhi, 2004:36-39).

The leader *klengsarpo* guides and supervise the members at work. He makes sure that the members maintain a good relationship in the dormitory and he even punish the wrongdoer. The role of *klengdun* is to assists the leader *klengarpo* in all matters like supervision of work and enforcement of law and order in the dormitory. If the members are divided into two groups for agricultural work then *klengsarpo* acts as the leader of one group and *klengdun* supervise the other. In the absence of the leader *klengsarpo*, *klengdun* acts as the leader of both the groups. But the *klengdun* cannot take major decisions, he has to consult either the village headman or the *risobasa* regarding matters such as the expulsion of a member, fixing of a date for working in a household in important festivals like Chomangkan or for working in another village. The next office bearer to *klengsarpo* and *klengdun* are *sodar-kethe* and *sodar-so*. The *sodar-kethe* executes the work to be done by the group who is assisted by the *sodar-so*. The *sodar-kethe* and *sodar-so* assist the two senior leaders in all matters and decide small issues. Inside the dormitory, the *sanghorai-kethe* and *sanghorai-so* are responsible for maintaining discipline and behaviour of the members. In case of any default or indiscipline, the matter is decided by the leaders.

The *changbrup-kethe* and *changbrup-so* are the persons who beat the drum on a special occasion. They also beat drum early in the morning and way back to the dormitory after work. It is their duty to beat drums whenever there is an occasion. On some occasions like bringing paddy to the residences from the field, the drummers beats drum throughout the day. The *barlon-kethe* and *barlon-so* are to carry the measuring bamboo pole in the field, measure the plot of land where the group will work and always lead the group while going to the field for work. The *motan-are* and the *motan-arvi* are assigned to clear the right and left the side of the jungles when the group proceeds towards the field. When the other members are away from the dormitory house, the *thana-are* and *thana-arvi* have to receive the message and serve the guests visiting the dormitory and report it to the leaders on their arrival. The *long bong-kethe* and the *longbong-so* are to fetch water from the nearby spring in bamboo tubes. This bamboo tubes are then to be tied in the two corners of the dormitory house. They have to fetch water and

supply water to the office bearers whenever necessary. In the morning they pour water into the hands of the two leaders then to the other members for washing their hands. The office bearers below the rank of *barlon-so* fetch water directly from the spring. They not only fetch water for the use dormitory but also to the households during festivals.

The office bearer *me-apai* has to light the fire first in the dormitory house. The role of *lungapai* is to keep an eye on the fire and to guard the house when everyone is asleep at night. The role of *kove-thak* and *bithi-thak* are to supply betel nut and betel leaf to every member of the dormitory. The *chinhak-kethe* and *chinhak-so* are to carry the tools like hoes, machetes, and bamboos in a bamboo basket to the field. They also have to mark the land with small bamboo poles, when the measuring rod carriers the *barlon-kethe* and the *barlon-so* measured the land. The whole plot of land is divided and sub-divided equally for the convenience of the member to work in the field. The *arphek-kethe* and *arphek-so* clean the dormitory every morning and evening. The *phankri-kethe* and *phankri-so* are orderly attached with the two leaders, but they usually carry rice and rice beer for all the members. In the morning when the members go to the field, the two office bearers move house to house in the village collecting rice and rice beer in leaf bowls and bamboo tubes. It is then kept in a small hut (*madhu*) usually constructed for the purpose. At noon all the members share the meal equally though at the time of collection the quantity and quality supplied by each household may vary. These two office bearers are usually the young members of twelve years of age.

The adolescent girls are subsequently selected as associate office bearers (*marpi*) of the dormitory. An associate office bearer should not be from the family whose siblings are in the dormitory. A girl having her brother as office bearer is disqualified for becoming an associate office bearer. The girl thus, selected is attached to each office bearer by the leader *klengsarpo* in consultation with *risobasapi*. The boy selected for a girl to be attached with him must not belong to his clan. Both of them are to be of different clans and their relationship can lead to marriage without any social obstacle. Every office bearer gets an associate office bearer to assist in his work. From the designation of an office bearer, it can be understood to which office bearer the girl is attached. The leader of the girl is attached to the leader of the boy, the *klengsarpo*, then she is called as the *klengsarpo-a-marpi*. She must be willing to accept the responsibility and to accept the *klengsarpo* as an all-time companion. She is selected on her personal qualifications like hard working, good physique, commanding ability and proficiency in dance and music. She has to control the girl members in the *jirkedam* and to assist the *klengsarpo* in the maintenance of discipline among the girls. The next girl in order of the rank is attached to the *klengdun* and she is called the *klengdun-*

a-marpi. She assists the *klengsarpo-a-marpi* in her works and acts as the substitute leader of the girls in her absence.

There are associate office bearers who are to work more than the office bearers, e.g., girls attached to the water supplier. These two associate office bearers, the *langbong-kethe-a-marpi,*and the *langbong-so-a-marpi* are to fetch water for the dormitory with the two boys. They are to supply water needed in any family of the village on festive occasions. Though they may be helped by other girls, the responsibility of supplying water remains with these two girls. The two associate office bearers, *arphek-kethe-a-marpi,*and *Aphek-so-a-marpi* attached to the two cleaners *arphek-kethe* and *arphek-so* are also to work more than their counterparts. They have to clean the dormitory platform and courtyard every morning and evening. The *arphek-kethe* and *arphek-so* entrusted for the purpose of cleaning only supply the two associate office bearers with bamboo brooms and give them company while cleaning the places. There are exceptions for *barlon-kethe-a-marpi* and *barlon-so-a-marpi* that they neither carry the rod nor measure the land though they are attached to the two measuring rod carriers*barlon-kethe* and *baron-so*. Likewise, the two associate office bearers attached to the two drummers never beat the drums.

Thus, a girl attached to an office bearer boy forms a pair and both share each of their activities. The girls have to massage the tired limbs of the boys after they return from the work. A girl even shares the bed at night to whom she is attached. There is an exchange of gifts between the girl and the boy. The relationship between a boy and a girl is known to the *risobasapi* and the inmates inside the house of the dormitory but not by the villagers. The relationships between the office bearers and the associate office bearers are kept the secret to the inhabitants of the village. Even during Chomangkan dance, the faces of the girls are covered with veils, not to be recognized while dancing with their attached office bearers. This type of arrangement is traditional and accepted as quite natural, as nobody is curious to know about such a temporary relationship in the dormitory. After completing the three years term in the *jirkedam*, these associate office bearers (girls) get married to their engaged boys preferably with the sons of their fathers' sisters. But, in case of serious love relationship the pair might elope to some other village from where they would inform their parents to arrange their marriage and if there is a dispute between the two families, the pair is caught and punished by the village council. If the girl becomes pregnant inside the dormitory, then the marriage is arranged without revealing the fact to anyone in the village and if the pregnancy is detected by the villagers, then severe punishment is given to the girl by the village council. This system of attaching girls to the boys in the dormitory is now absolutely defunct. Now, in ceremonial occasions

in the village, girls help the boys of the dormitory and while dancing together, they consider the clan exogamy (Medhi, 2004: 43-46).

All the children living in the house of the dormitory, other than the above two categories are regarded as *hazar-aso* (general members), which literally means 'young fellows'. They are the novices or new entrants who are entrusted with the duty of collecting firewood for the dormitory house. Besides this, they are to massage the feet, arm, and body of the tired office bearers after hard work. The duty of the *hazar-aso* becomes very important after the exclusion of associate office bearers (girls) from the *jirkedam*. They are not assigned to a particular activity but are encouraged to participate in all the chores of the institution. The unmarried ex-office bearers can sleep in the house at night and enjoy all the rights and privileges of this category of members and are not entrusted with any duty. The members of the institution enjoy certain rights and privileges in the village. All the members, in general, have the right to sleep in the dormitory; participate in dance and ceremonial performances organized in the institution or in the village; play games or participate in recreational activities like fishing or hunting expedition. The members of the first two categories, i.e., male office bearers and female associate office bearers, are entitled to share the earnings of the institution at the end of their three-year term, share the bed of the partner; to receive special honour and favour at social gatherings; two leaders always get the first priority.

The *jirkedam* is for unmarried young adolescents and there is no place for the married men and women. Though the married men may enter the dormitory for village council meeting or evening gossip, they are not allowed to sleep in the dormitory at night. The married women are even not allowed to enter the courtyard of the *jirkedam*. However, for the headman there is an exception; he remains as a dejure executive head of the institution. The headman is helped by the office bearer who is chosen for the duty of execution. The final judicial authority rests with him when a matter cannot be decided by the leader like the nature of punishment for the wrongdoer, change of leader, the expulsion of a member and similar other serious matters are decided by the headman. If the headman is busy with other duties then the *risobasa* acts as the head of the institution. He acts as a representative of the headman and is directly responsible to him for any misconduct or mismanagement of the institution. There is another minor official known as the *terang-asar*, who is entrusted with the duty of closing the door of the dormitory from outside at night and to open the door just at dawn.

A married woman (*risobasapi*) is to look after the girls and listen to their complaints, who discuss matters and settle disputes between the boys and the girls in consultation with the *klengsarpo*. She is allowed to visit the

dormitory at any time and she keeps an eye on its up keeping. In her absence, *basapi*, the wife of the headman, may also visit the dormitory, and mediate between the disputes of the girls and the boys especially arising out of the sexual relationship. These two women are the advisers of the girls in sexual matters. But now, the exclusion of girls from the dormitory have lessened the responsibility of the *risobasapi*, but she still pays a daily visit to the dormitory. These adult persons by virtue of their position in the village become ex-officio advisers of the *jirkedam*.

Construction and Inauguration of the Dormitory House

The architectural skill of the Karbis can be observed in the design of the dormitory house. It is a big hall of about twelvemeters in length and sevenmeters in width without any partition. The construction of the house is connected with ritualistic observance and ceremonial practices. It is the largest house in the entire village.

The site to construct a house of the dormitory is selected by the village council members based on certain factors like elevated land, slightly higher than the adjoining land; central place of the village; nearest to the headman's residence; near to the hilly spring, etc. These factors are considered due to various reasons like hygienic consideration, the purpose of village defense, constant supervision of the dormitory members by the headman and to carry water easily during feasts or ceremonies. The dormitory has to be in the middle of the village with large open space for the performance of rituals and ceremonies where a fellow member can assemble.

It is a raised bamboo chair or a bench decorated with bamboo lace and wild flowers in front of the dormitory house meant for sitting of the two leaders, i.e., *klengsarpo* and *klengdun*. It is customary to construct first the *hongthar* before construction of the dormitory house. The raw materials needed for the construction of *hongthar* are mature bamboo and cane where *klengsarpo* and *klengdun* will sit in the *hongthar* every morning and evening after work and will also be used for the judicial purpose by the leaders to settle down disputes among the members.

The dormitory house is constructed after a year of establishing the dormitory (*jirkedam*). The headman has to give permission for its construction. The villagers assist the members of the dormitory in the construction of the dormitory house. Before construction, all the necessary items are collected such as bamboo, cane, a log of wood, thatch, etc. Rice beer is offered to the villagers by the members of the dormitory during the construction of the dormitory house. After the collection of materials for construction, the leader approaches the headman for engagement of a good carpenter. The carpenter usually engages some novices for rendering help though some members may

also learn the art of helping the carpenter. After engaging a carpenter, the various tasks that are undertaken to construct the house is the erection of the post, construction of the platform, making the roof, wall, door, fireplace (*mehip*), lavatory, ceiling, furniture and other articles to use. After completion of the dormitory house, the leaders approach the headman for its inauguration. The headman fixes a date and the members get ready with all the necessary items for the offering in the name of the god for the wellbeing of the inmates of the dormitory house, such as three gourd-shells full of rice beer, three white cocks, one pig and three plantain leaves. Besides these, the members are to arrange rice, rice beer and other food items for the villagers.

The headman arrives on the auspicious day and the leaders offer him a gourd shell full of rice beer and ask him formally to start the ceremony. At first, plantain leaves are kept near the *klengsarpo* post, i.e., first post in the middle row of the dormitory house, over there a gourd shell full of rice beer is placed, then a white cock is placed over the plantain leaves near that gourd-shell, a hymn is sung by the headman to please the deity Risoarnam (god of youth). The hymn describes the origin and function of the *jirkedam*. After that, the cock is sacrificed by beheading and throwing it a bit forward of the village headman. By looking at the position of the cook an omen is observed by the headman. After that, a pig is brought and placed near the post and sacrificed chanting a hymn by the headman. The feathers of the cock are placed on the post and the post-plate. Then another cook is sacrificed near the fireplace of the dormitory and a gourd-shell full of rice beer is offered. In the meantime, the members cook the meat of the pig. The headman then performs his offering of rice beer and a cock in the third place, i.e., urinal (*phi-inkar*) and completes the ritual for the day. In earlier days the preparation of meal was done in the fireplace of the dormitory house, but now the meal is prepared in the courtyard of the headman because married men and women are tabooed to enter the dormitory house. The heads of the cocks and pig are given to the headman and two leaders (*klengsarpo* and *klengdun*) and other office bearers of the institution.

Socio-economic Activities in the *Jirkedam*

After the establishment of the *jirkedam,* it is the responsibility of the headman to train the leaders *klengsarpo* and *klengdun* giving formal instruction every morning and evening for a week, on matters relating to agriculture, maintenance of discipline and performance of various activities. The headman also sits with the other members in the evening and tells them about their duties and responsibilities towards themselves and to the society. After a week an initiation ceremony is organized by the members. They prepare rice and rice beer for the occasion and collect other items like plantain leaves, fowls, bamboo vessels, etc. A day before the festival the headman

takes the members in the nearby field and clears the jungle. In the east or south direction of this area, an altar is prepared with the mud of about half a meter in height and nine-meter in circumference. Then on the next day, the headman arrives with the *terang-asar* at dawn in front of the dormitory house. The *terang-asar* opens the door of the dormitory house and all members wake up. The water carrier office bearer (*longbong-kethe*) offer water to the *klengsarpo* and other members on the basis of their rank for washing faces and hands.

The two drummers beat their drums in the courtyard. The beats signify that all the members are lined up according to their task to be performed while proceeding to the field for work. The *barlon-kethe* stands in the front with his measuring rod, followed by the two drummers, then the two broom carrier, then the two tool carriers and then the office bearers from lower to the higher rank; *klengsarpo* takes the last position in that line. The headman then asks the *pherangki* to place the gourd full of rice beer on the altar every member offers a betel nut and betel leaves in the altar. Then he starts measuring the land with a *barlon-kethe*. Then the whole land is divided into two equal halves and each half is again sub-divided into small parts. The two halves are meant for two working groups, i.e., one headed by the *klengsarpo* and other by the *klengdun*. The small parts are meant for each member. The significance of this division is clearly explained by the headman. This is done to encourage the spirit of competition between the two groups. Small divisions are made in order to complete the work early. Then, the headman tells the members about their duties in the village. The members are organized to cultivate a land and thereby learn the art of earning a living. It has to help the villagers in their agricultural works, clearing the village roads, preparing small bridges, making arrangements for bamboo pipes to carry water from hilly spring, helping in the performance of various religious festivals, helping the villagers in times of need and to protect the village from external aggression. The headman also narrates the rules and regulation to be followed in the dormitory and the punishment for the wrongdoer (Medhi, 2004: 64-67).

A member stays in the dormitory for a period of three years; within that period the members cannot marry. The members then take oath in the name of the *Risoarnam* (god of youth) and offer rice beer reciting a hymn. After that, they sit around the altar and take rice beer and afterward return to the village in an orderly manner. In the meantime, the girls and women of the village prepare a meal for all and after taking the meal the initiation ceremony completes. 'The initiation ceremony also marks the entry of the Oraon boy to the dormitory institution. But there is only individual rite and no group teaching among the Oraon tribe. On admission to *dhumkharia* (dormitory) a boy is to go naked with an earthen jug to the spring or neighbouring village

and fetch water and mud stolen and keep the jug hidden with mango leaves (Roy, 1915:214). Most of the tribes are in habit of practicing some sort of initiation ceremony integrated to dormitory but there is also an exception in some tribes like the Trobriand Islanders (Malinowski, 1927:59).

The member of the dormitory takes part in different activities. The slash and burn or *jhum* are known as *inglongarit* cultivation among the Karbis. The usual process for *jhum* cultivation is that the whole area is cleared and jungles are cut down in winter and allow it to dry up and burn it in the month of March. Then the summer season starts and different types of vegetables mixed with and various plants are grown. The first year the *jirkedam* members might not be able to cultivate but the second year they cultivate, their land, besides helping the fellow villagers in their cultivation. The members are to work in the field of the headman and also in the field of the person who supplied two drums (*chengbrups*) to the dormitory. Then the members help in the fields of the families of which members are in the dormitory and then to the other families of the village.

In the months of March and April, the members organize a religious ceremony to start the cultivation known as *Ret-kinong* in which the headman perform certain rites before the tilling on the first day and the next day the headman along with the members of the dormitory go to the field and take a position in a row at one end of the plot of land to be cultivated. The members work for the whole day in the field; only in the evening they return to the dormitory house and sing and dance on the platform. In the first year, rice is not grown in the *jhum*, which can be sown from the second year. The different vegetables are grown in the first year by the members of the dormitory. They are also invited to work in other villages with a certain amount of wage per day. The money is kept by the leader and it goes into the common fund of the institution. After harvesting the paddy, it is brought in the dormitory house by the members. They also help the villagers in their harvest. It is customary to offer rice beer by the householder to the *klengsarpo* requesting to help his family in bringing the paddy from field to home.

The members of the dormitory also work in the construction of road and bridge, clean the village road and marketplace, etc. If the task is for two villages, then the headman of the village where the dormitory is situated, send a message to the headman of other village fixing a date for the work. The headman sends a boy as a messenger with a rope of jute or bark of a tree, if the rope is tied with one knot then the task is not so urgent, but if there are two folded rope, then it is urgent. Both the parties meet in between the village and do their work. The members of the dormitory are also engaged in fixing the bamboo pipe from the hilly spring to carry water to the village.

The girls who are the members of *jirkedam* have to tattoo their foreheads with a black vertical line at the age of 12 to 13 years, which is done by an old lady by pricking her skin with the thorn of cane and then applying a black colour made out of a wild creeper. The boys are not tattooed. The boys and girls can freely talk or meet in the village, who perform together with the agricultural works in the field, community feast, sing ceremonial songs and dance. If a girl loves a member of the dormitory, with whom she is in physical relation and if she is selected as *marpi* in the boys' dormitory, then the *marpi* hardly need any advice from the *risobasapi*. In case of a *marpi* who does not have any such relationship with any boy then she is instructed by the *risobasapi* about her duty towards the boys' at night. The idea of romantic or platonic love is almost absent among the members. For a girl a boy is handsome if he is honest, dutiful, and helpful to the needy person; likewise, for a boy, a girl is beautiful if she is dutiful, weaves cloth, bags, prepare good rice beer and if she has good health (Elwin, 1947: 428). The dormitories are taboo to married women (Sachchidananda, 1964: 357). The premarital freedom of sexual affairs in the dormitory must not lead to pregnancy. In case a boy has to marry a girl before the villagers know it otherwise he will be punished for his conduct. If a member boy who is to perform his marriage must take permission from the leader of the dormitory if he is the member of the institution. But if he has completed his three years in the dormitory, then it is not necessary to take permission. 'Sometimes an illegitimate child is born, but by custom is made legitimate by forcing the lovers to marry before the birth of the child' (Yonuo, 1974: 13).

If the member has the minor illness then it is treated in the dormitory house by the *risobasapi*, but in case of severe illness, the member is sent home for better care and treatment. If a member fell sick during sowing, weeding or harvesting, then his share has to be done by all the other members of the dormitory. In such cases, there is no payment to be made to the members of the dormitory, because of the rigid social tie among the Karbis where the illness of one person will not affect him alone but his misery is shared by all. They help him in his fieldwork, in his domestic work and also in religious offerings. 'A man suffering from protracted illness is said to be possessed of by an evil spirit. The diviner, *uche* is called upon to detect the evil spirit which has possessed the ailing soul. In serious illness, the *lodep*, a diviner of higher rank, is called upon to throw cowry shells on the ground or cut an egg for finding out the evil spirit and the direction of its coming. The sacrifices for propitiating the spirits are performed which is usually a costly affair' (Stack and Lyall, 1908:35). The diviner prescribes the treatment, i.e., propitiating the particular god by sacrificing fowls or pig with rice beer.

Besides this, the members of the institution are engaged in wood carvings like fine wooden toys representing animals like elephant, tiger or bird like

duck or chicken. Pottery among the Karbis is practiced by a few specialists. The members of the dormitory are not engaged but may occasionally visit a worker and learn the art of pottery. Basketry is an essential art found among the Karbis. The members of the institution spend their summer in making baskets of different designs, which are used for different purposes such as storing and carrying paddy; small smooth baskets for carrying firewood or bamboo vessels to fetch water; small conical baskets to carry smaller things; rice beer container with wax to keep the beer. The important musical instrument is made out of bamboos like flute and jewsharp. Drums are also made by them with a log of wood and animal hides and bows and arrows with bamboos. The girls are expert in weaving. Besides these, the other activities of the members in the dormitory house are playing games, fishing, and hunting. The ex-members can stay in the dormitory without any designation till their marriage.

The members of the *jirkedam* worship 'the god of youth', locally known as *Riso-arnam Klarkli*, in the month of June, at the end of sowing and weeding seedlings. It is a very simple rite performed in the *jhum* field. The headman performs the rite by sacrificing a fowl and by the offering of rice beer to the deity.

The Karbis worship the heaven as a god. This ritual is known as *Chojun* or *Charak*. It is a household ritual which can be performed every year by each family. The leader of the dormitory is requested by a member of the household by offering rice beer to help them in performing the ritual. Then the leader appoints two girl members and two boy members of the dormitory to help the household in preparation of rice, rice beer and in other works. This boys and girls have to work on the orders of the householder. The help of the members of the *jirkedam* is a notable feature in such family affairs. Nowadays in many villages where the girls are neither included in the institution nor are living in a group in the headman's guest house (*hangpharla*). The order of the leader *klengsarpo* not only binds the boys but the girls also. In a place where there is no *jirkedam,* the headman of that village instructs the boys and girls to help the villagers in time of need.

The Chomangkan

The Karbis burn the human corpse. *Chomangkan* also known as *Arleng Karhi*, is the greatest ritual of the tribe where the deceased forefathers were propitiated by a few households together. Sometimes a rich family performs this ritual alone. This death ritual is very expensive, which has three types known as *harne, langtuk* and *kangflafla* depending upon the status of the deceased. The family arranging the *Chomangkan* has to procure a large stock of rice and rice beer. It is customary that the head of the family approach the

klengsarpo of the *jirkedam* with a gourd full of rice beer. The person explains the purpose of his visit and requests for their help in the ritual. The leaders and the office bearers discuss the matter and then give their consent to help the host. The date is fixed and the leaders with their associates reach the host's house. The members go to the forest to bring bamboo for the ritual and girls are engaged in pounding paddy. The boys go to the forest in a single line with the drummers beating the drums. Each bamboo is cut with a machete in one stroke. The bamboos are then carried by the members on their shoulders and some are kept near the courtyard of the deceased and some are taken near the cremating place of the dead. There the boys prepare the *banjar* (decorated bamboo). It takes a week to prepare the *banjar*. The youth also plan for songs and dances for the ritual. *Langtuk*, a pit is dug outside the village boundary by the members with the maternal uncle of the deceased. The pit dug for the occasion is square in shape, each side having ten to fifteen feet and its depth is about ten feet. The perimeter at the bottom is about half that of the surface. The stairs are also to be made from the surface to the bottom of the pit. In some areas, the pit is fenced in four sides with a gate towards the stairs. A conical megalith named as *long-e* is to be erected in the name of the deceased in front of the *langtuk*. If the death ritual is for more than one person, then the megaliths have to be erected accordingly. In *Langtuk Chomangkan* one *jumbelliathon*, a dancing implement made of wood is placed near the megalith and bamboos are placed on all the four corners of the *langtuk*. The shape and size of the stones differ depending upon the deceased male, female and children. Now cemented figures are placed instead of megalith.

The date is fixed for the ritual. On the day of the ritual the members of the dormitory dances in the tune of the drums around the food prepared by the female ritual weeper (*uchepi*) for the deceased. The boys dance around the food, inviting the deceased to accept the meal. On arriving home, the boys are to prepare a rice straw effigy of the deceased. The lamentation of the female weeper continues till the ritual is over with occasional breaks. In the second day, the members of the dormitory build a small hut at the cremating place of the deceased with decorated poles of bamboo. Near the hut, they prepare a pyre, a platform with bamboo posts and splits for cremating the dead. In the evening the boys dance which is locally known as *kansopadu*. On the third day, the boys proceed towards the bamboo forest. They cut many bamboos and return to the courtyard of the deceased's residence, where they dance with a bamboo place in their hands. Then they proceed towards the pit and place a bamboo for each deceased in the center of the pit. The bamboos are placed in vertical position in all the four corners of the pit. During this, some boys move and dance around the pit holding each other's hands.

In the same day, the male members of the dormitory made an altar on the bank of the nearby river where the maternal uncle of the deceased sacrifices fowls, pigs, etc. The different dancing parties from different villages also arrive there. The boys from different villages too dance with swords and shields in their hands. In the evening the boys of the deceased's village stand making a circle and hold on each other hand for the *Chomangkan* dance. Then along with the drum beats they move and dance singing love songs. The *risobasapi* places the girls in the middle of the circle with their face covered with black scarfs. The boys and girls are in pair but should not be from the same clan and the pair must be in marriageable relation. The boys and girls dance till night followed by the dance of swords and shields by the boys till morning. On the fourth day, the girls and boys of different villages leave for their respective abodes after getting their shares of sacrificed meat. The boys of the village dormitory prepare for the last day ritual (*rongchamkedam*). The *rongchamkedam* is ended after fixing the *banjar* post and *seroso* (six small pieces of bamboo measuring about one metre in length, decorated with ornaments and green leaves) near the *pirsik* (a fully-grown bamboo with leaves) in the front courtyard of the host residence. After completion of the ritual, the youth and other male members performed various types of dances including *banjarkekan*. Then the effigy of the deceased is carried in the bier by four youths in the cremation ground (*tipit*), where some rituals are observed by the elders. The boys dance around the pyre with swords and shields when pyre is set on fire. Thus, the ritual comes to an end after cremating the pyre. In this important event of the Karbis, *jirkedam* offers great service to the family who has observed the *Chomangkan*.

The Valedictory Function

The *jirkedam* is attended for three years by a batch of the youths. After completion of the three years, a new batch replaces the old one. The *klengsarpo* and *klengdun* after their completion of their term of office, approach the headman for his permission to organize a valedictory function known as *jerchekak*. The function is organized only if the headman is convinced. If he doesn't want the members to leave the dormitory then he will simply give different reasons not to organize the function. However, if the headman agrees then he will arrange a meeting with the members of the village council to perform the function. A date is fixed and the preparation for the function starts. The girls prepare rice, flattened rice and rice beer. The boys collect fowls and pigs in large number for sacrifice. The last pig purchased is sacrificed on the way by the headman with all the formalities in the name of the god to get his benediction for making their event a success. The sacrificed pig is then roasted on the spot and is distributed to all the villagers. Then the members prepare a dome out of the earth raised over the

ground (*longle-kebui*), which is round in shape and pointed on the top. Around the dome, three drains are constructed of about one foot in breadth and between two drains there is a path of one foot in breadth. The function is invariably held in Tuesday or Wednesday. A day ahead of the function is called as *chechadi*. All the headmen of different villages accompanied with one or two youth assemble in the dormitory house on *chechadi* days. The number of the headmen will be invited depending on the capacity of the host to entertain. Each of the headmen of the other villages brings a gourd full of rice beer to be used in the function. One headman acts as the priest and offers a gourd full of rice beer to the god for making the function a success. Another gourd full of rice beer is offered by the priest singing song and praising the god Hemphu; this is called as *hanrat*. Then the priest sacrifices a pig and its head is kept in the branch of a tree in the courtyard of the dormitory house. The girls prepare the pig meat, in the while, the leaders with other office bearers and members sing and dance in pairs. Along with meal rice beer is offered to everyone. It is a time of merrymaking. The headmen of other villages stay in the village guest house (*hangpharla*); for that night the village headman and the youths sleep in the dormitory house.

In the next morning, the members lined up in front of the branch of the planted tree in the courtyard. They tie their bamboo sticks and poles used for measuring land on the tree. Two more drummers from another village attend the function. The four drummers beat the drums and they along with the other people proceed to the field where the earthen dome was made. On reaching the spot the headman of the dormitory house with measuring rod carrier with their bamboo sticks climb to the earthen heap. The headman erects two bamboo sticks on top of it in slightly bending position towards the east. Then the headman sacrifices one white cock and smears the blood on the pole and at the forehead of the members. After the ritual, he along with other assembled people return to the courtyard. Then again, the headman offers rice beer and propitiates the *Hemphu* in the courtyard. The two drummers beat their drums for the last time and conclude the playing of drums. Then a pig and a few fowls are sacrificed by the headman. The number of pigs must be equal to the number of members of the institution; the two pigs which were already sacrificed is also counted. The headman again sacrifices a white cock and smears the blood at three places on a plantain leaf placing it near the planted tree. The two drummers again smear the blood, put the feathers in their drums and place the drums near the tree which is known as *chengbrup-kewek* (hanging the drums). After that, all the fowls and the pigs are sacrificed and is prepared for the community feasts by the girls.

Inside the dormitory, the headman then started another ritual. A plantain leaf is placed in the threshold of the dormitory and upon it, a silver or bamboo

ring is kept. The headman holds a red cock, utters hymns and places the cock over the threshold. The *kove-thak* (betel nut supplier) and *bithi-thak* (betel vine supplier) distribute betel nut and betel vine leaf and the *klengsarpo* chew and spit over the red cock followed by the other members rank-wise. After that, all the members of the headman proceed towards the village path to sacrifice the cock. Some bamboo splits are placed on the road with the plantain leaf on it and rice, a ring and an egg are kept with a gourd full of rice beer. The cock is then sacrificed by the headman uttering integral hymns. The blood and feathers on the plantain leaf and it is thrown observed the omen by the headman, and after that, the egg is sliced which also indicates good or bad omen. Then they return from the village path having rice beer and roasted cock. In the courtyard of the house, they distribute meal among the guests and the assembled villagers. All the members take a meal together in a big and a flat wooden bowl made for the purpose. After ending all the rituals, the members collect the measuring rod, bamboo sticks and two drums which were placed on the branch of the planted tree during the ritual and proceed to the house and keep their tools in proper places and start preparing a meal for dinner.

The function is over now, so the next morning all the guests return to their respective villages. The headman sacrifices two pigs; one is distributed among the villagers and the other is cooked. The distribution is not equal as the members get the higher amount of meat compared to that of the households who don't have any members in the institution. The headman gets a share like a dormitory member. Then, the leader gives an account of the property of the institution like money, which is then divided among the members of the dormitory basically upon their ranks. The headman gets higher share followed by the two principal leaders than that of the other office bearers. A *marpi*, who is attached with the office bearer gets an equal share like the office bearer. The paddy, mustard seeds, and other agricultural products are divided equally among the members and those people who were closely related to the institution like the *basapi*, *risobasa*,and *terangasar*. Then the headman sings a song about the origin of the universe and the dormitory. He then requests all the members to take an active part in the village festivals in future; to repair the house when necessary; to perform all social services and to help the villagers wholeheartedly.

Conclusion

The *jirkedam* is the nerve center of a Karbi village, which is integrally related to a good number of cultural elements of the Karbi culture making the institution a culture complex. It is indispensably related to the age, sex, division of labour, family, clan, status, security, tribal solidarity, norms and values and so on. The *jirkedam* helps the Karbis, particularly in the rural

setting, to build a strong social tie through the participation in social services, music, and dances, social and religious performances, etc. It is a strong catalyst to bind up the fellow members and to accelerate the progress of the society. This institution is rigidly related to the village society and the members of the society always observe its activities and try hard to maintain its activities on the basis of their customs and tradition. The *jirkedam* helps the old, deceased, needy and downtrodden of the village; a member of the *jirkedam* not only works for the institution but also works parallelly for the viability of his family. The members of the *jirkedam* acquire much-needed factors for the tranquility and solidarity of the society like co-operation, the dignity of labour, equanimity, forbearance, tolerance, team spirit and utilized those when they come out from the institution and merge in the village society. It is a strong agent of enculturation through which the culture transmitted from the ascending generation to the descending generation.

When a teenaged boy temporarily leaves his family of orientation and becomes a part of *jirkedam*, then the *klengsarpo*, the principal leader of the institution, plays the guardian, guide, and philosopher to him. This leader is considered as the model of manhood to the members and all the members meticulously carry out his orders. In the dormitory, the peer group (*jirsong*) is provided with the necessary ideas on the Karbi life ways including the concept of incest, which are not so conspicuous in the familial environment. The adolescent members take the entire responsibility of running the institution and also render all kinds of services for balancing and accelerating their village society. The dormitory house serves the purposes of a modern school building with provisions for classrooms, meeting hall and the hostel to eat and sleep at night.

After the growth of modern education and adoption of Christianity abandoning their pristine religion by some of the Karbis, the *jirkedam* system among them becomes flaccid. The Christian Karbis are not allowed to be the part of the dormitory, because it trains the members to observe many animistic religious practices. The new form of educational centers replacing steadily the dormitories among the Karbis. The meticulous training of *jhum* cultivation, which was the mainstay of the Karbis, cannot serve the purpose to fulfill the present day needs of the people. Many of them have abandoned *jhuming* and adhered to non-traditional occupations for maintenance of their lives. The survival of an institution is directly linked up with its utility in the society. The education in a *jirkedam* helps the members to fruitfully adjust in the traditional Karbi society, which is changing very fast abandoning many pristine traits and acquiring innumerable alien elements. In such a transitional phase *jirkedam* cannot provide the required training to its members. Therefore, the *jirkedams* are naturally replaced by the modern educational institutions. The social service and community participation are very effective

and rewarding in a *jirkedam* in the traditional environment of the Karbis. The spirit of *jirkedam* can be incorporated in the modern educational centers not only among the Karbis but also in different societies in other parts of our country.

References

Boudesson, H 1919, *Indo-China and its primitive people*, Hutchinson and Company, London.

Chowdhury, JN 1973, *Arunachal panorama*, Chapala Book Stall, Shillong.

Cooper, TT 1873, *The Mishmee hills*, Henry S. King, and Company, London.

Dutta, P1969, *The Tangsas of the Namchik and Tirap valleys*, Directorate of Research, North-East Frontier Agency, Shillong.

Elwin, V 1947, *The Muria and their Ghotul*, Oxford University Press, Bombay.

Fric, V& Radin, P 1906, 'Contribution to the study of Broro Indians', *Journal of Anthropological Institute*, vol. XXXVI, pp. 388.

Furer-Haimendrof, CV 1939, *The Naked Nagas*, Methuen & Co,London.

Iyer, Ak 1909,*The Cochin tribes, and caste*, Higginbotham,and Company, Madras.

Lowie, RH 1921, *Primitive society*, Routledge and Kegan Paul, London.

Majumdar, DN 1930, 'The economic background of social institution in primitive society', *Man in India*, vol. X, pp. 1.

Malinowski, B 1927, *Sex, and repression in savage society*, Routledge and Kegan Paul, London.

Medhi, BK 1988, 'Rituals connected with birth among the Karbis', *Journal of Assam Science Society*, vol. XXXI, no.1, pp. 1-13.

Medhi, GC 2004, *Jirkedam: a school in deeds*, Everywhere, Guwahati.

Peal, SE 1893, 'The communal barracks of primitive races', *Journal of the Asiatic Society of Bengal*, pp. 244-246.

Roy, SC 1915, *The Oroans of Chotanagpur*, Bar Library, Ranchi.

Sachchinanda, 1964, 'The Morung and the Dhumkuria: a study in contrast', *Journal of Bihar Research Society*, vol. XXXX, pp. 357.

Shakespear, J 1912, *The Lushei-Kuki clan*, Macmillan, and Company, London.

Stack, E& Lyall, CJ 1908, *The Mikir*, David Nutt, London.

Terang, BL 1937, *Ru-Kasen* (Karbi),Puthighar, Nowgong.

Terang, RB 1974, *Karbi Lamtasam*, Dictionary, Diphu.

Yonuo, A 1974, *The rising Nagas*: *a historical and political study*, River Publishing House, Delhi.

Chapter - 11

Recent Doctoral Researches in Anthropology: A Preliminary Survey in Manipur

— M C Arun Kumar and Pebam KrishnaKumari

Introduction

Like in many other States, the anthropological exploration, if not research, in Manipur Anthropology started during the colonial period with the writings of political agents. The monographs or ethnographic accounts of ethnic groups, communities of the State were mainly done with the information gathered from local informants who knew a little English. These works were not scientifically explored rather were written for certain political goals. Notable works include that of TC Hudson, a British administrator and a member of the Royal Anthropological Institute who believed in E B Tylor school of thought furnished information on the social, cultural life of the people in Colonial Manipur. Academic works started with Indian anthropologists like T C Das whose work *The Purums: An Old Kuki Tribe of Manipur* (1945) initiated a debate on kinship.

In the early days of the post-colonial period, the anthropological works were sparely done. Many of them were of monographic and ethnographic researches. The establishment of Department of Anthropology in Manipur University gave a new horizon of research. There is a proliferation of research works within Anthropological domain and many disciplines adopt anthropological knowledge in various fields of research. Till date, more than sixty Ph.D. scholars and two (2) Post-doctoral research scholars have completed their works in Manipur University in various fields of research

ranging from growth studies to criminology. In Manipur University, there are three main branches of Anthropology – Social and Cultural Anthropology, Physical Anthropology and Prehistoric Anthropology. Most of the researches are mainly concentrated within these three subdivisions of Anthropology though some are interdisciplinary. We are trying to highlight recent advances in anthropological researches done in the Department of Anthropology, Manipur University.

Physical Anthropological Research

Within the physical Anthropology paradigm, a multitude of research themes is generated namely growth pattern, anthropometry, anthropogenetics, HIV/AIDS and many more covering many of the physical anthropology aspects across different communities of Manipur. Mention can also be made of the study by Konsam Renu Devi on *The Kwatha-Meitei: The culture and demo-genetic study* which was completed in 2004. This study was conducted among the Meitei community in a hilly area and historically isolated from the mainland social and political streams of the State as well as of the Meitei. The researcher used various variables – social and physical — to depict the contemporary life of this community. Oinam Bhabhini Devi (2008) gives a comparative account of physique and physiological observation between the Meitei women of urban and rural settings.

Rajkumari Meena conducted a study among Meitei community and worked on *Variation in height, weight and food intake among Meitei families in a village of Manipur valley.* Her work was completed in 2003. She studied food intake of the Meitei and tried to correlate with biological variables. *Human Biology of two districts Ethnic Populations of a lake fishing Eco-niche of Manipur,* studied by Yumnam Reena (2004) was also one of the human biological studies; she considered the ecological niche of the populations under study too.

The anthropology of sports is one of the areas where many researchers started working on. Laishram Dibamani Singh (2001) worked on *Kinanthropometry of Meitei male adolescents of Manipur in relation to Motor Performance.* The study tried to understand the Kinanthropometric variable that has a relationship with motor performance. The study focused on Meitei male adolescents. Hijam Sorojini (2003) completed her work on *Anthropometry of the Meitei women athletes of Manipur*. In her work, anthropometric variables are considered with the performances of women athletes in Manipur. In a similar way, Akoijam Bojen Meitei (2013) studied among the male elite and non-elite players of Manipur. He worked on *Kinanthropometric variables and physical fitness ability of male Elites and Non-elites players of Manipur.*

The study of newborns, in physical anthropological research, is one of the areas undertaken in the Department. Thingujam Medhabati Devi (2004) worked on *Anthropometric and Morpho-genetical studies of Meitei New-borns, Manipur.* The study used various anthropometric and morpho-genetical variables to give a picture of Meitei new-borns. Thokchom Ursa's *Prenatal growth and development of Meitei prenates* which was completed in 2016 is another dimension of such a research. The methods and techniques used by her in the study of Meitei prenates gave a new insight into the studies of biological anthropology.

Studies were also conducted among different tribal communities in Manipur. These works cover various fields. Haobijam Vokendro Singh (2005) on *Anthropo-genetic study of the Purum tribe of Manipur*, Kshetrimayum Vedamani Devi (2007) on *Gastronomy and Nutritional status of Tarao tribe of Manipur,* Pukhrambam Kiranbala Devi (2012) on *The Tangkhuls of Manipur: A bio-cultural study,* Lairenmayum Romeo Singh (2004) on *The Kom tribe of Manipur their demography, culture and bio-anthropology*.

Mention can also be made of research work of Keisham Somarani Devi's *A cross-sectional study on growth among the Poumai boys and girls* (2007). Though the growth study is one of the common studies in Northeast India in general and Manipur in particular, her work on Poumai has a merit in understanding this newly recognized tribe in Manipur. Alangbam Taruni Devi also completed her research work on *Differential Fertility of the Aimols of Manipur* in 2014 which is one of the demographically least tribes in Manipur. Maibam Monoranjam Singh (2008) also worked on one of the least tribes of Manipur. He worked on *Bio-Anthropological study among the Koirao of Manipur*. These works not only contribute to anthropological knowledge but also in understanding the ethnic groups of Manipur. Such study includes *Bio-Anthropology of the Simte tribe of Manipur,* done by Esther Lalremkim (2015).

Estimation of stature using measurements on other body parts within the larger Forensic Anthropological Study is another area of research in the Department. For finding out community or ethnic-specific measurements, Naorem Jibit Meitei (2014) worked on *Estimation of Stature from different body dimensions among Maring males of Manipur.* Maring is one of the tribal populations in Manipur.

Research works were also conducted among the Scheduled Caste community *(Lois)* of Manipur. A number of research scholars engaged themselves in *Loi* study. Heirangkhongjam Jibonkumar (2007) on *Growth and nutritional status of the Sekmai children, Manipur*, Naorem Dayabati Devi (2004) on *The Khurkhul people of Manipur: A dermatoglyphic study* gave in-depth knowledge on different aspects of the community mainly of physical and biological characteristics. The work of Laishram Gopendra Singh (2013),

Physique and health status among physically active and inactive Ningthoukhong populations of Manipur, focuses on one of the Meitei localized communities in Manipur. The Ningthoukhong population has a historical and sociological identity among Meiteis.

Another work on the dermatoglyphic study is on *A comparative study on dermatoglyphical variations between the Brahmin and Muslim of Manipur* which was done by Mangstabam Shyamchand Meitei (2007).

Research works conducted among the Muslims in Manipur include the work on *Estimation of stature from various body dimensions among Manipuri male Muslims of Manipur* which was conducted by Sarangthem Dilipkumar Singh (2012).

Studies on different populations of Manipur from comparative perspectives were also taken up seriously. The comparative works searched for the relationship, distribution of traits in different communities, ethnic groups etc. N Mamta Devi (2002) on *A study on differential fertility of the Meitei and Sekmai women of Manipur* is a study on two communities in Manipur i.e. Meitei, the major ethnic community and a Scheduled Caste community of Manipur. Maishnam Rustam Singh (2007) on *A comparative study on some genetic markers among six populations of Manipur* took up some genetic markers as points of comparison and tried to locate different communities in a larger framework.

Besides these studies on different communities, problem-oriented studies were also taken up by a number of research scholars. Mention can be made of work of Ningthoujam Yaima (1999) on *A study on the natural history of AIDS among the IDUs in Manipur with special reference to their behaviours and biomedical aspects*. Such a study was done by Haobijam Prabhabati Devi (2011). She worked on *Physique and body composition of HIV/AIDS and Pulmonary TB Co-Infected Meitei male patients of Manipur.* Thangjam Premeshwori Devi (2012) also conducted her research work on *Vehicular pollution in Imphal.*

We see a wide range of research areas of the people has been covered in Physical and Biological Anthropological research in Manipur University. The widening of research areas and the in-depth studies in these works are commendable.

Research in Pre-Historic Anthropology

Though exploratory works on Manipur's pre-historic life dates back in colonial period, systematic and scientific exploration of prehistoric life started very late. Systematic research of Prehistory of Manipur in Manipur University was done by Okram Kumar Singh in 1995. He worked on *Stone Age Cultures*

of Manipur. His descriptions of stone age cultures and extensive treatment of Hoabinhian culture in Manipur were commendable.

Mani Babu (2006) started to carve new horizon of prehistoric archaeological study with the ethnoarchaeological framework. He worked on *Pottery of the Andros of Manipur: A study on Ethnoarchaeology* for his doctoral degree. His research work focused on two things: first is to visualize the pottery of Andro within the framework of the system paradigm to identify a 'ceramic ecology' of the people and secondly to reconstruct ancient ceramic ecology of the prehistoric forerunners of Andro on the basis of the analogies between the present ethnographic pottery and the past archaeological ones.

Within the Prehistoric Anthropological context, Rangya Gachui in 2007 completed her Ph.D. work on *Potters and pottery of Oinam Mao (Poumai) and Nungbi (Longpi) Tangkhul villages of Manipur: A study in socio-cultural aspects*. Her study is confined to studying the technology used in making pottery crafts which are still practicing since time immemorial among the Oinam and Nungbi potters.

Another study on pottery in Manipur within the prehistoric anthropology paradigm was of Kh Manglembi Devi (2008). She worked on *A study of the traditional subsistence pattern of the Kabuis and its relation with the prehistoric cultures of Manipur*. Her research work focuses on the how the economic activities of Kabuis interweave with the cyclic rituals and compare the artifacts related to their subsistence economy with the artifacts discovered from different places of Manipur at different times by different scholars. Thus, most of the prehistoric anthropological researches were conducted on pottery of different communities in Manipur. The ethnoarchaeological study of the pottery and potters gained a momentum.

Social and Cultural Anthropological Research

Research works in Social and Cultural Anthropology in Manipur University are multifarious and heterogeneous starting from 1989 to date producing more than twenty Ph.D. scholars and two Post-Doctoral scholars. The topic ranges from the ethnographic study of the tribe, kinship system of different communities, continuity, and change of different tribes in Manipur, women-oriented issues, health and illness including lived experiences of HIV/AIDS, cervical cancer, reproductive health issues. The post-doctoral research works in Social Anthropology is also of different areas. One had completed on the economy and another on reproductive health services.

Chand Anth Thangmi (2004), for the doctoral degree, worked on *The Thangal (Koirao) tribe of Manipur.* It gave a detail ethnographic account of one of least tribes in Manipur. Another ethnographic account is on *the study of the socio-cultural life of the Gorkhas of Manipur*, studied by Kangabam

Ibetombi Devi (2004). The work focused on the ethnography of Nepali community in Manipur. She gave a historical introduction as well as changes occurred after inhabiting in Manipur. Hari Krishna Shiwakoti (2013) also gave community life of the Nepalis in Manipur. His work was on *The Nepali Community of Kanglatombi: A case study on cultural adaptation in Manipur.* His study gave new light to the cultural adaptation of a migrant population in a host society.

Kinship system is one of the key areas of study in Social Anthropology. However, for about two decades, the area was least focused in Manipur. However, some research scholars like Khundrakpam Shanta Devi and Thiyam Rabikanta Singh took up such studies in the Department. Khundrakpam Shanta Devi (2003) worked on *Family, marriage, and kinship of the Meiteis of Khurkhul: An anthropological study.* She studied the family, marriage, and kinship in one *Loi* village. Thiyam Rabikanta Singh (2005) also took up the area for his doctoral degree. He worked on *A study on the kinship system of the Meitei.* His research gave a new insight into the elements of matriliny in Meitei society. He used both synchronic and diachronic approaches in order to examine the change in kinship organization over history.

Migration of tribal people from hill to plain areas attracts some scholars. Shougaijam Brajeshwori Devi (2010) worked on *Mantak (Kakching) Kom village: A study on continuity and change*. She described the socio-cultural and political scenario of a tribal community living in the plain area of Manipur. She tried to find out reasons for migration of the Kom and settled in a village called Mantak in the valley. Further, she extended her study on change and continuity in this plain tribal community.

Surbala Thokchom (2012) also worked on the migration of the tribal peoples but of recent times. She completed her research work on *Social dynamics of migration among the Paomai of Manipur* in 2012. Her main enthusiasm in this work is to find the ratiocinating factors of migration among Paomai tribes in Manipur.

Another area of study in Department of Anthropology, Manipur University is Christianity and Conversion. Bringing home to such research activity is the Doctoral work of *Christianity conversion and responses- A case study of the Rongmeis,* done by Jane T. Panmei (2014). She tried to examine the responses to the conversion to Christianity among Rongmeis in Manipur.

Conflict is an area of the social problem. Study of the social problem has a tradition in the Department. Among the works in recent times, the conflict among the tribal peoples and their identity formation in Manipur touched the intellectual faculty of some scholars in Department of Anthropology, Manipur University. Helkhomang Touthang completed his research work of *Ethnic fission among the Kukis of Manipur* in 2009. His work is to historically

trace the ethnic connection of the Kuki-Chins with the Miao, Yao and the Lai peoples of northern Southeast Asia and southern China and to provide an understanding between the several conflicting tribal groups in the Kuki Chin family. He used the historical approach as well as synchronic data to examine the elements which are rooted in diverse historical traditions.

The social problem that intersects health is another area in which some researchers worked for their doctoral degree. The woe of a person living with HIV was taken up by Thuanchuiliu Dangmei (2012). She worked among the HIV/AIDS patient for her thesis, *Lived experiences of women living with AIDS: A cross-cultural study.* She worked within the phenomenological framework. The work brought out the experiences of living with chronic illness that generates the needs people identify as much as those related to the clinical features of the disease, how they give meanings to the past experience and how culture shaped their perception in cross-cultural dimension.

Interdisciplinary research work is the motto of Manipur University. The Department of anthropology always encourages such study. In this line of research work, Rajkumar Lenin Singh (2013) worked on *Anxiety disorders among the Meiteis of Manipur: A psycho-social study.* He studied the different forms of anxiety disorder among Meiteis and tried to examine various social, psychological and psycho-social factors that lead to such disorder.

Another work of interdisciplinary approach is *A study of personality profile of the Meitei maibis of Manipur* is of Lourembam Roshan Singh (2014). This research work is to evaluate the personality traits of Meitei Maibis (priestess in non-Hindu domains of Meitei religion) who are engaged in officiating festivals, rites, and rituals of Meitei society. He studied the impact of parameters like education, family type, age at marriage etc. on personality traits. Such interdisciplinary works include the work on *Pattern of child-rearing practices: A Case Study of Moirang,* of Thangam Somola Devi (2011).

Department of Anthropology, Manipur University produces research works on women and women-oriented issues since early days of the 1990s. Such works include crime, food habit and gender power, cervical cancer, reproductive health and so on. Recent works are *Women, society and culture: A case study of Thongjao, a scheduled caste village of Manipur* is a doctoral research work conducted by Thounaojam Bimola Devi (2014), *Food habit, gender and power: A case study of the Kabuis of Manipur,* by Gangmei Akhuan Rongmei (2015), *Socio-cultural aspects of Cervical among Manipuri women* by Arundhati Devi Maibam (2014). Gangmei Akhaun Rongmei examined the gender inequality among a tribal community as reflected through food culture. He discussed the relationship between power and food habit.

Research works on the reproductive health of women from the social and cultural dimension has drawn the interest of scholars in Manipur

University recently. Mention can be made of Irengbam Bijeta who works among the Muslim community in Manipur. Her thesis entitled *An anthropological study of the reproductive health of married Muslim adolescent girls in Manipur* was completed in 2017. Her work among the married adolescent Muslim women in Manipur is to understand the reproductive health experience at the backdrop of socio-cultural factors and the interface between tradition and modernity in various aspects of their reproductive health.

Another study on *Reproductive health of Meitei women: A case study of Phaknung village, Manipur* was conducted by Lairellakpam Aruna in 2013 which focus on meta-narratives on reproductive health in the light of life experiences of women in a village in Manipur.

Within the ambit of social and cultural Anthropology, there are scholars who have completed their Post-Doctoral research. Among the Post-Doctoral research works, done in Department of Anthropology, Manipur University, mention can be made of Pebam Krishnakumari who worked on *Reproductive health services: Implication on women's health in Manipur* and was completed in 2018. She throws light on how the choice women made for the treatment of reproductive health problems are based on certain social factors.

Another post-doctoral research was on *Socio-economic development and molasses entrepreneurs in Manipur: A study on scheduled caste women entrepreneurs,* conducted by P Dhaneshwari Devi (2016). She studied among Kakching community, a *Loi* group in Manipur. The work contributed to a new line of research in economic anthropology in general as well as in understanding entrepreneurship as driving force for scheduled caste development. She highlighted some of the changes brought out among the scheduled caste populations in Manipur in recent past.

Research in Social and Cultural Anthropology in Manipur University covers a wide range of social problems thus introspecting into the different aspects of social issues. The topic taken up by scholars includes issues related to problems which affect at the individual level and to the society at large. Thus, social and cultural anthropological research in Manipur University deals with various dimensions of social problems emanating in Manipur.

To conclude, a wide spectrum of research activity on various issues in different communities of Manipur can be visualized in the research work conducted in Department of Anthropology, Manipur University. With the initiation of anthropological research during the colonial era and the establishment of Department of Anthropology, Manipur University, research activity in Anthropology in Manipur is an ongoing process. The proliferation is however prominent after the establishment of a Department of Anthropology, Manipur University. The widening of research areas and the

in-depth studies in physical and biological anthropological research in Manipur University are commendable. Research in Prehistoric Anthropology in Manipur University is also laudable in terms of quality. In Social and Cultural Anthropology, various social problems were looked into. Thus, irrespective of the specialization in Anthropology research in Manipur University is variegated and sterling.

References

Akhuan, RG 2015, *Food habit, gender, and power: a case study of the Kabuis of Manipur.* Ph.D. thesis, Manipur University, Imphal.

Anth, TC 2004, *The Thangal (Koirao) tribe of Manipur.* Ph.D. thesis, Manipur University, Imphal.

Dangmei, T 2012, *Lived experiences of women living with AIDS: a cross-cultural study.* Ph.D. thesis, Manipur University, Imphal.

Das, TC 1945, *The Purums: an old Kuki tribe of Manipur*, Calcutta.

Devi, AT 2014, *Differential fertility of the Aimols of Manipur.* Ph.D. thesis, Manipur University, Imphal.

Devi, HP 2011, *Physique and body composition of HIV/AIDS and pulmonary TB co-infected Meitei patients of Manipur.* Ph.D. thesis, Manipur University, Imphal.

Devi, KI 2004, *The study of the socio-cultural life of the Gorkhas of Manipur.* Ph.D. thesis, Manipur University, Imphal.

Devi, KM 2008, *A study of the traditional subsistence pattern of the Kabuis and its relation with the prehistoric cultures of Manipur.* Ph.D. thesis, Manipur University, Imphal.

Devi, KR 2004, The Kwatha Meitei: their culture and demo-genetic study. Ph.D. thesis, Manipur University, Imphal.

Devi, KS 2003, *Family marriage, and kinship of the Meiteis of Khurkhul: an anthropological study.* Ph.D. thesis, Manipur University, Imphal.

Devi, KS 2007, *A cross-sectional study on growth among the Poumai boys and girls.* Ph.D. thesis, Manipur University, Imphal.

Devi, KV 2007, *Gastronomy and nutritional status of Tarao tribe of Manipur.* Ph.D. thesis, Manipur University, Imphal.

Devi, MA 2014, *Socio-cultural aspects of cervical among Manipuri women.* Ph.D. thesis, Manipur University, Imphal.

Devi, ND 2004, *The Khurkhul people of Manipur: a dermatoglyphic study.* Ph.D. thesis, Manipur University, Imphal.

Devi, NM 2002, *A study on differential fertility of the Meitei and Sekmai women of Manipur.* Ph.D. thesis, Manipur University, Imphal.

Devi, OB 2008, *Physique and physiology of rural and urban Meitei women of Manipur.* Ph.D. thesis, Manipur University, Imphal.

Devi, PD 2016, *Socio-economic development and molasses entrepreneurs in Manipur: a study on scheduled caste women entrepreneurs.* Post-Doctoral Thesis, Manipur University, Imphal.

Devi, PK 2012, *The Tangkhuls of Manipur: a bio-cultural study.* Ph.D. thesis, Manipur University, Imphal.

Devi, SB 2010, *Mantak (Kakching) Kom village: a study on continuity and change.* Ph.D. thesis, Manipur University, Imphal.

Devi, TB 2014, *Women, society,and culture: a case study of Thongjao, a scheduled caste village of Manipur.* Ph.D. thesis, Manipur University, Imphal.

Devi, TM 2004, *Anthropometric and morpho-genetical studies of Meitei newborns, Manipur.* Ph.D. thesis, Manipur University, Imphal.

Devi, TP 2012, *Vehicular pollution in Imphal.* Ph.D. thesis, Manipur University, Imphal.

Devi, TS 2011, *The pattern of child-rearing practices: a case study of Moirang.* Ph.D. thesis, Manipur University, Imphal.

Gachui, R 2007, *Potters,and pottery of Oinam Mao (Poumai) and Nungbi (Longpi) Tangkhul villages of Manipur: a study in socio-cultural aspects.* Ph.D. thesis, Manipur University, Imphal.

Hijam, S 2003, *Anthropometry of the Meitei women athletes of Manipur*. Ph.D. thesis, Manipur University, Imphal.

Irengbam B 2017, *An anthropological study on the reproductive health of married Muslim adolescent girls in Manipur.* Ph.D. thesis, Manipur University, Imphal.

Krishnakumari, P 2018, *Reproductive health services: implication on women's health in Manipur.* Post-doctoral Report, Manipur University, Imphal.

Lairellakpam, A 2013, *Reproductive health of Meitei women: a case study of Phaknung village, Manipur.* Ph.D. thesis, Manipur University, Imphal.

Lalremkim, E 2015, *Bio-anthropology of the Simte tribe of Manipur.* Ph.D. thesis, Manipur University, Imphal.

Manibabu, M 2006, *Pottery of the Andros of Manipur: a study on ethnoarchaeology.* Ph.D. thesis, Manipur University, Imphal.

Meitei, AB 2013, *Kinanthropometric variables and physical fitness ability of male elite and non-elite players of Manipur.* Ph.D. thesis, Manipur University, Imphal.

Meitei, MS 2007, *A comparative study on dermatoglyphical variation between the Brahmin and Muslim of Manipur.* Ph.D. thesis, Manipur University, Imphal.

Meitei, NJ 2014, *Estimation of stature from different body dimensions among Maring males of Manipur.* Ph.D. thesis, Manipur University, Imphal.

Panmei, JT 2014, *Christianity conversion and responses- a case study of the Rongmeis.* Ph.D. thesis, Manipur University, Imphal.

Rajkumari, M 2003, *Variation in height, weight and food intake among Meitei families in a village of Manipur valley.* Ph.D. thesis, Manipur University, Imphal.

Shiwakoti, HK2013,*The Nepali community of Kanglatombi: A Case Study on cultural adaptation in Manipur.* Ph.D. thesis, Manipur University, Imphal.

Singh, HJ2007, *Growth and nutritional status of the Sekmai children, Manipur.* Ph.D. thesis, Manipur University, Imphal.

Singh, HV 2005 *Anthropo-genetic study of the Purum tribe of Manipur.* Ph.D. thesis, Manipur University, Imphal.

Singh, LD 2001, *Kinanthropometry of Meitei male adolescents of Manipur in relation to motor performance.* Ph.D. thesis, Manipur University, Imphal.

Singh, LG2013, *Physique and health status among physically active and inactive Ningthoukhong population of Manipur.* Ph.D. thesis, Manipur University, Imphal.

Singh, LR 2004, *The Kom tribe of Manipur their demography, culture, and bioanthropology.* Ph.D. thesis, Manipur University, Imphal.

Singh, LR 2014, *A study of personality profile of the Meitei maibis of Manipur.* Ph.D. thesis, Manipur University, Imphal.

Singh, MM 2008, *Bio-anthropological study among the Koirao of Manipur.* Ph.D. thesis, Manipur University, Imphal.

Singh, MR 2007, *A comparative study on some genetic markers among six populations of Manipur.* Ph.D. thesis, Manipur University, Imphal.

Singh, OK 1995, *Stone age cultures of Manipur.* Ph.D. thesis, Manipur University, Imphal.

Singh, RL 2013, *Anxiety disorders among the Meiteis of Manipur: a psycho-social study.* Ph.D. thesis, Manipur University, Imphal.

Singh, SD 2012, *Estimation of stature from various body dimensions among Manipuri male Muslims of Manipur.* Ph.D. thesis, Manipur University, Imphal.

Singh, TR 2005, *A study on the kinship system of the Meitei.* Ph.D. thesis, Manipur University, Imphal.

Thokchom, S 2012, *Social dynamics of migration among the Paomai of Manipur.* Ph.D. thesis, Manipur University, Imphal.

Thokchom, U 2016, *Prenatal growth and development of Meitei prenates.* Ph.D. thesis, Manipur University, Imphal.

Touthang, H 2009, *Ethnic fission among the Kukis of Manipur.* Ph.D. thesis, Manipur University, Imphal.

Yaima, N 1999, *A study on the natural history of AIDS among the IDUs in Manipur with special reference to their behaviours and biomedical aspects.* Ph.D. thesis, Manipur University, Imphal.

Yumnam, R 2004, *Human biology of two district ethnic populations of a lake fishing eco-niche of Manipur.* Ph.D. thesis, Manipur University, Imphal.

Chapter - 12

Inequality in the Practices of Manipur Megalithic Traditions

— ***Potshangbam Binodini Devi***

Introduction

In Northeast India, particularly in Manipur, megalithism is practicing as a living tradition till date by some tribes. Each tribe performs a series of feast-of-merit with megalithic rites and rituals differently and raised various megalithic structures. The Liangmai, the Maram, and the Poumai tribes are those who still continue this tradition but with some modifications. It is a unique opportunity to observe the unequal social processes involved in raising and constructing different megalithic types by these three tribes and to record their living traditions.

To achieve the objectives, village to village survey method is employed. In addition to it, ethnographic method (particularly observation method, interview method, and case study method) is adopted in recording the methods of selection and erection of megaliths, associated rituals, and feastings etc.

The People

The author has selected three larger tribes: the Liangmai, the Maram, and the Poumai. They occupy mainly in three hill districts of Manipur. Each tribe has its own unique custom and tradition.

The Liangmai is one of the indigenous tribes of Manipur. After 2011 this tribe is completely baptized to Christianity. They are distributed in 47 villages of Tamenglong and Kangpokpi districts of this state and mostly concentrated

in the Tamei sub-division of Tamenglong district. Scattered pockets are also found in the Imphal East and Imphal West districts (Binodini, 2006: 21-23).

The Maram is the only primitive tribe and also one of the largest tribes of Manipur. Nowadays most of them are Christians whereas some of them are still following their traditional religion. They are distributed in 32 villages and mostly concentrated in the Mao-Maram sub-division of the same district. Scattered pockets are also found in Kangpokpi district. All the Maram villages come under three circles. They are: (i) the Maram Khullen Circle, (ii) the Senapati Circle, and (iii) the Willong Circle. (Binodini, 2009:16).

The Poumai is also one of the indigenous and largest tribes; and mainly concentrated in the Paomata sub-division, Senapati district, Manipur. Scattered pockets are found in other sub-divisions of the same district, and also in other districts like Imphal East. There are 78 Poumai villages, which come under three circles. They are the Paomata Circle, (ii) the Chillevai Circle, and (iii) the Lepaona Circle (Binodini, 2011:168).

The Socio-Economic and Political System

All the villages which belong to Liangmai, Maram,and Poumai tribes are governed by the traditional village council and village authority. Each traditional village council is headed by the chief of the village. The functions of the traditional village council of each tribe are broadly executive, administrative, and judicial. The councilors are the real body in whom the highest power of the village is vested. They are at the helm of the affairs of the village. They formulate the policy of the village and amend the unwritten laws, which are then rigidly followed. Each councilor is the representative of each clan of the village concerned of all these three tribes. They are selected on the seniority basis. They are equally important and expected to discharge their respective duties in the village administration. Descent is also counted through the male line.

They are primarily agriculturist. They cultivate on periodically shifted *jhum* fields and on permanent wet paddy fields with their hoes and it is the woman who takes a greater part in the whole process. They practiced and still practicing hoe culture. Hunting and fishing contribute to some extent to their food supply.

Among the Liangmais, the *Chawang* is the most powerful person. He is the owner of the land and also the chief of a village in every respect. He sometimes controls more than one village. In his role as religious head he is assisted by the village priest (*Phaimew*), and in his role as secular head, he is assisted by the members of traditional village council (*Peimei).* They have boys and girls dormitories known as *Khangchu* and *Luchu.*

The Maram village chief (*Sagong*) functions as both religious and secular head and in his function as religious head, he is assisted by the village priest (*Atingba*) and in his function as secular head, he is assisted by the members.

Unlike other tribes, the Maram has only one supreme ruler of all the Maram villages. He is their king. Each village follows the rules whatever amended by him. They have boys' and girls' dormitories known as *Hansaki* and *Lashaki*.

The Poumais has a fairly developed society and culture, and it forms a part of an interesting study. Each Poumai village is economically self-sufficient; the chief of the village (*Veo*) controls the economic affairs with the help of a council of elders (*Chikumai/Neih Pfupfumai*). In religious matter, he is assisted by the village priest (*Khaohro*).

The Megaliths

In each village of the Liangmai, Maram, and Poumai tribes there are a number of megaliths scattered here and there. They are of different morphological structures and sizes too. They are listed below:

Liangmei Megalithic Types

1. *Kasaibo Tusom* (Menhir with flat stones raised for a distinguished person);
2. *Chenku Tusom/Lungaibao Tusom* (Menhir, a commemorative stone for rich a man);
3. *Maning Taoba Tusom* (Memorial stone);
4. *TazanTatboTusom* (Cairn for highest social status);
5. *Atugra* or *Atukra* (Dolmen with a menhir, serve as Holystone/oath taking stone);
6. *Taideli Atu* (Capstone, use as gravestone);
7. *Kapen/Kapet Bam* (Cromlech, a burial pit for hunted heads);
8. *Pet/Pen Bam* (Menhir, village foundation stone);
9. *Tubaolong* (Cairn, a stone lookout);
10. *Roukhangtu* (Horizontal/upright stone, ancestor's stone);
11. *Kahu-katanmai Saimingbo* (Menhir, for the bravest and richest person); and
12. *Kareng Hang* and *Kareng Dree* (Stone walls and village gates)

Maram Megalithic Type

1. *Beitung* (Menhir with a dolmen, use as witness stone);
2. *Ranii Atu* (Cairn, use as watch tower/ resting place);
3. *Tiisum* (Menhir serve as memorial stone);
4. *Arou Atu* (Dolmen, use as gravestone);
5. *Tiirosum* (Dolmen/horizontal flat stones for use as stone seats);
6. *Amailui* (Small avenue, represent male members of 1906);
7. *Atu chagakamatei* (a Monolith serve as Holystone); and
8. *Atu ameiogijaphuigungkheikaranijangbaatuwaikheibamle* (Capstone for a burialpit of decapitated heads).

Poumai Megalithic Types

1. *Zaosochu* (Menhir of social status);
2. *Chukho* (a Cairn);
3. *PaohonChukho*(clan's stone seats associated with Dolmen);
4. *Raikhubu* (Dolmen of highest social status);
5. *Seibechu* (religious flat stone);
6. *Chadeichu* (a judiciary stone);
7. *Neisha Chukho*(religious stone);
8. *Tapu*(a Megalith for placing the decapitated head);
9. *Chuchukho,* (a stone circle, related to head hunting);
10. *Khophochu,* (Capstone for the grave);
11. *Loupfo,* (a small alignment, each stone represents a girl/woman, whom a brave man had won her hand); and
12. *Aro Adu,* (village gate and wall).

The Liangmais

The Liangmais raised twelve different structural types of megaliths. Each megalithic structure is erected with a different mode of construction. They are listed below:

Kasaibao Tusom or Tasaibao Tusom (Menhir with flat stones): It is a composite structure, having a platform of flat stones, and a standing stone (menhir), facing the entrance. It is always found in the habitation area. The *Kasaibao Tusom* is erected in honour of a distinguished person after his death.

An intending performer informs the village council about his wish to raise a *Kasaibao Tusom*. Then he, along with his co-villagers, searches a

suitable stone. Thereafter a cock is let loose on the spot with ritual, so that there may be no difficulty in dragging the stone to its selected place.

An auspicious day to raise the stone on the selected spot is fixed by the village priest (*Phaimew*). They usually set up such stone along the paths leading to village or *jhum* or wet terrace fields or water tanks or springs. For transporting such stones, they use a wooden sled. Once the stone is on the sled, it is the duty of the puller to take care of the possible slip. For pulling the stone, the Liangmais use a hard and strong creeper called *Tuchareng* (Binodini, 2011:112-114).

While the dragging process is continuing the performer's wife is not allowed to sit down on the ground until the stone reaches the selected spot. According to Liangmai tradition, if the housewife of the performer sits down on the ground the pullers feel a heavy weight to drag the stone if she walks to and fro inside the house — the stone moves on the light. Meanwhile, the performer is required to walk in front of the stone dragging party.

When the stone arrives at the appointed place, the stone pullers are refreshed by offering rice-beer. Afterward, they raise the stone properly. In the meantime, four cattle, four pigs are sacrificed and cooked. The cooked meat is then offered with cooked-rice and rice-beer to all the participants (Binodini, 2006:103-106).

Chenku Tusom/Lungaibao Tusom (Menhir): Before a wealthy Liangmai erects a memorial stone to attain the highest social status, he performs a series of feasts-of-merit associated with the megalithic rituals. The initial feast-of-merit is called *Chenku* and the stone erected to mark the occasion is also known as *Chenku Tusom/Lungaibao Tusom*.

Chenku Tusom is a menhir. It may be planted, according to the wish of the performer. Thus, such types are distributed all over the village area. The *Chenku* feast-of- merit starts with the searching for the desirable stone. This is followed by informing the intending merit-seeker's wish to the village council through the *Chawang*. The *Phaim ew* selects the stone which would bring prosperity to the merit-seeker. The auspicious day for dragging and setting up such memorial stones is fixed by the *Chawang* assisted by the *Phaimew*. The head and the base of the stone are sorted out by an expert person before setting up. They believe that the stone thus erected may cause much harm to the performer and his wealth if some mistakes are committed to erecting the stone.

A month before, the performer along with his co-villagers goes to the jungle and selects a large tree to make a sled. Along with the preparation of this sled, they also collect strong creepers (*Tuchareng*) as many as possible, which are required for dragging the stone. And ten days before the *Chenku*

feasting the merit-seeker distributes paddy to all the women of the village for pounding to meet the required amount of rice for cooking and brewing rice-beer for the feast.

On the first day, of *Chenku* feast, all the guests from neighbouring villages and kinsmen assemble, those who have brought gifts, hand them over to the merit-seeker. The selected stone had been quarried out previously from the site alongside a level path and had been left horizontally on its edge. Most of the poles and levers made of special hardwood are brought down from the performer's house. Some are also prepared on the spot if required.

Then the priest purifies the stone by pouring rice-beer over it and also loses a fowl to prevent unwanted events while dragging the stone up to its appointed place. The stone is then lashed very firmly to the sled with ropes made of creepers, tied both to the staves underneath and through the holes in the arms. Creepers for pulling the sled are then attached. For the first day, the work is stopped at the sunset.

On the second day, more creepers are attached to the sled, and in the meantime, the *Phaimew* worships the spirit of the stone. Then the performer offers food and drinks to the stone and says 'Your place is not here. We have made another for you. You must go to that place which we have made for you. Now you stand up, we will take you, be light' (Binodini, 2011:116).

The stone pullers, all adorned with the colourful ceremonial dress, take their positions systematically, all holding the rope of the sled, keep awaiting the signal to start. When the signal is given, all start to pull. Once off, the stone starts to move on slowly. The merit-seeker walks ahead of the pullers along with an elder person who holds a special leaf and keeps on saying, '*Kaichou Kaichou toulelo Ajang Hoi*' (you have enough strength, use it quickly or go quickly and pull with equal force and stride; Binodini, *op.cit*).

On the way, the stone pullers take rest and get refreshed with rice-beer. Eventually, the stone is pulled up and laid on the spot, already selected. For the day, they leave the stone as it is on the sled, checking the wedges and lashes. The performer feeds all the stone pullers. As a rule, these persons are not allowed to eat anything in their respective houses. The performer slaughters cattle or pigs to feed them, besides rice and rice-beer.

On the third day, a hole is dug in the earth by the village elders. The lashing on the stone is then cut. An expert person determines the head and foot sides of the stone. After this the base of the stone is kept in place by means of pressure applied along the poles pushed by a number of men, the other end of the stone being raised by inserting levers, raising it a fraction, wedging it, pressing it up a little more, then wedging it again. The pulling from the front, pressing from behind and propping it up with longer wedges

underneath every time, the stone is erected at last. As the stone attains the vertical position all the pullers hold the stone firmly with their hands, to steady it, while a great yell goes up signaling the accomplishment of a great task.

On the stone raising day, the merit-seeker sacrifices a number of animals like cattle, pigs, and fowls and prepares thirty to forty jars of rice-beer each containing forty liters or more. Then he feeds the guests and friends besides the persons who took an active part in pulling the stones till they get pleased.

All the young men of the village play drums, while the village girls dance. Thus, the feasting, drumming, and dancing continues the whole day and night in the house of the performer. Then the stone is given the name of the performer in whose honour the feast is celebrated.

On the fourth and last day of the feast, all the guests and relatives retreat to their own home. The merit-seeker, however, is also required to give one more feast for the people of his own village in recognition of the services rendered during the feast and for the erection of the megalith, the *Chenku Tusom*.

Maning Taoba Tusom (raised platform with an upright stone): The performer of *Chenku Tusom* is allowed to construct a new house called *Chakiwki* with *Pomnin* (house horn) and perform another feast and raise the *Maning Taoba Tusom*. It consists of some flat stones, with an upright stone erected in the centerto serve as the dwelling place for the soul of the performer after his death, during his visit or occasional peregrination around, to view his rice fields. It can be raised by the merit-seeker during his lifetime or by his son (s) after his death. The process of stone raising ceremony is same as *Chenku Tusom* and it is raised in recognition of his prosperous life.

TazanTatbo Tusom (Cairn): A merit-seeker, who had already performed a series of feasts and raised *Chenku Tusom* and *Maning Taoba Tusom*, may perform the last feast; and raise another commemorative structure called *TazanTatbo Tusom*. It is a cairn. It is found on the top of a hill. The main function of this structure is to attain the highest social status. The Liangmai consider the performer of the *TazanTatbo Tusom* is the wealthiest person in their society.

The whole process of *TazanTatbo Tusom* ceremony is similar to those described above except the selection of the stone. For this ceremony, the performer is not allowed to select the stones required for raising the heaps of stones. The stones are selected by village elders and relatives.On the last day of the feast, the village priest performs a ritual to propitiate their supreme god. In the meantime, the friends, relatives, and his co-villagers engage themselves in gathering stones. After the ritual, the piling up of stone is

started. When the construction of the cairn is completed, the merit-seeker is ritually shaved and adorned with a new female dress to symbolize his attainment of the highest status in the social ladder.

Atugra or Atukra (three Dolmens with a Menhir): It consists of a menhir and three dolmens. Their occurrence is always inside the habitation area. The main purpose of this composite structure is related to the judiciary function, particularly for oath taking. They consider it as the holiest stone, which can detect the right or wrongdoer; so holy that no one dares swear falsely on them. The *Atukra* is respected by this tribe as a god. In the past, heads taken on raids are shown to this upright stone and then kept over the dolmen.

Atukra/Atugra: In most serious cases, which could not be tried by the *Peimei*, oath-taking ceremony in front of or on the *Atukra* is resorted to. The *Peimei* normally asked both the offender and defender to bring either a dog or a cat or wooden human figure on the day of oath taking. On the oath-taking, the day the *Chawang* assisted by the *Phaimew* would ask the offender to cut the facial part of the dog (if a dog is brought). Then he would climb the dolmen and utter 'If I am a wrongdoer my mouth will be cut off/beheaded by the spirit of *Atukra*'. The defender is also asked to perform the same procedure. He would also be asked to behead the animal/wooden human figure that he brought. Then he climbs on the dolmen in front of the audience, including the village council assembled there, and says: 'I am telling the truth, if I am the wrongdoer or telling a lie, I may receive the sufferings as the cock and the human figure had, Oh! *Atukra* you punish me if I had done wrong'. It is firmly believed that the spirit of *Atukra* surely punishes the guilty person even with death. So, they always try not to undergo such oath-taking ceremony. The village authority maintains such method of the trial to maintain social justice in the village (Binodini, 2011:120).

Taideli Atu/ Taikulana Ranii (Gravestone): A wealthy Liangmai also erects memorial stone, in honour of and in memory of dead persons of his clan or his family. It is called *Taideliatu* or *Taikulana Ranii*.It consists of a raised rectangular enclosure made of a number of low dolmens, with an upright stone erected either near one end or in the center to serve as the dwelling place for the soul of the deceased person. The collection of the stone is done by the villagers and for their assistance; the host feeds them with the meat of cattle, cooked-rice, and rice-beer. This structure is given the name of the person in whose honour the feast is celebrated.

Takulana Ranii / Taideli Atu: Such monuments are built within three to five years after the death of a person. After the erection of the upright stone, rice-beer is poured over it for purification. No elaborate feast or ritual is performed in connection with this stone raising ceremony.

Pet-Bam (village foundation stone): It is a village foundation stone, raised by the founder member of a new village to commemorate the occasion. Structurally, it is a miniature monolith and found inside the village habitation area. The *Pet-Bam* is raised in the courtyard of the village founder who is also the then *Chawang* (chief) of the village.

When a village is too much populated, some villagers decide to migrate to a new place to establish a village. Among those villagers, if there are individuals who wish to become the chief of the new village, for the selection of such chief, a traditional method is observed. For this purpose, the intending persons go together to the selected place for a new settlement, each carrying a cock. There each person makes his separate hearth and sleeps that night with his cock separately. Next morning each wakes up early and listens to the first sound of the cock's crow. They firmly believe that the person, whose cock crows first in that early morning is entitled to become the *Chawang* (chief) of the new village. This is considered as the divine selection. The person, who has thus become the chief of the newly established village, must erect a monolith as the foundation stone called *Pet Bam.*

The new *Chawang* along with his clan members raises such structure ritually. This monolith is considered to be the holy stone of the village. The *Chawang* announces the ritualistic events to be observed by the villagers by standing on this stone. No elaborate feast is associated with this stone raising ceremony.After raising this monolith, the *Chawang* has to construct another megalithic structure called *Kapet Bam* along with his clan members.

Kapet Bam (Cromlech, a burial pit for hunted heads): It is a circle of stone slabs enclosing a burial pit. That pit is also covered by a flat stone directly. It is connected with the hunting of big and ferocious animals and also with the head-hunting tradition.

When a person kills a large number of wild animals individually or collectively, he/they should keep the head(s) of the hunted animal(s) in this burial pit. Like this, the human heads collected through raids are also brought here and keep inside the pit by removing its cover. Then the person(s) should inform the *Chawang* of the village that he/they had killed such, and such animals or decapitated such human head (s) and so on in detail. Then the *Chawang* informs all the male members of the village to assemble at *Kapet Bam* in full address. Soon all the male members dressed in war costume gather there and perform the war dance with the shouting of *'Hou, hou Jam, ahou jam Hou, hou, hou'*, imitating the barking dogs.

Inside the village, the person who has taken the heads of foes or animals observes personal *genna*. He goes on fasting on that day, while his family offers a feast to the whole villagers with the meat of some pig or cattle. Next day the performer is allowed to take food but some restriction is imposed on

eating some special fruits, vegetables, and beans (like bamboo shoots, soya bean, all creepers,and their products, beans, pumpkins, gourds, *etc*).

After some months, when the fleshy parts of the collected human or animal heads are completely decayed, they take out the skull(s) and bring them to the performer's home.

There he keeps the head(s) permanently in his home. No elaborate feast is done, except the purification of the skull(s) ritually by a village elder. The construction of *Kapet Bam* is followed by making a cairn called *Tabaolong.*

Tabaolong(Cairn): It is a cairn always located on the top of the hill. It is constructed by the village chief after the *Pet Bam* and *Kapet Bam* construction with the help of his clan members. It is the duty of the *Chawang* to protect his subjects from the enemies or any harmful events. The *Tabaolong* is used as a watching tower for the village. When the villagers found anything living beings missing, either cattle or human beings, they climb up on the *Tabaolong* and try to locate the missing person or cattle. In the early days, the chief of the village appointed some persons who acted as watchmen in their scheduled times so that they could detect enemies approaching the village. If enemies were advancing the watchmen would rush to the village chief and inform him about the situation, so that every possible defensive measure could be taken up easily by the village council.

Roukhang Toh/ Tarao Toh (ancestor's stone): It is also a flat stone placed horizontally or vertically after performing the last rite of a deceased person called *Takebao* or *Chakebou*. It lasts for two to three consecutive days with feastings and drinking rice-beer, but sometimes extends up to five days. It is performed by a wealthy person, usually in the month of December. In this feast, the performer offers the guests, invitees, and relatives with cooked-rice, rice-beer, and meat.

On the first day of the *Takebao* or *Chakebou*, the performer sacrifices a small fowl or a puppy ritually. The main purpose for sacrificing this small animal is that the soul of this small animal goes to the land of the dead and meets the forefathers, relatives, and ancestors of the clan of the deceased person. The host then offers grave goods for the deceased person in his graveyard ritually. After performing this, the performer may raise an upright stone or place it horizontally near the burial pit. This ceremony is performed only when the performer thinks that many sufferings are caused in his family by the soul of the deceased person (particularly relating to fertility). Among the Liangmais, there is a deep-rooted belief that the family will be more prosperous if the soul of the deceased person is pleased with the family.

Kaho Katanmei Saimingbao (Menhir): It is a monolith erected to show the outstanding fortune and actions of the bravest and the most fortunate person while he is living.

The stone to be raised for *Kaho Katanmei Saimingbao* should be searched by the paternal kinsmen of the intending performer. The selection of the stone is done by the host, assisted by a village elder. After selecting and purifying the stone, they return home before dusk. In that night, the intending performer observes omen in his dream whether or not the spirit is favourable. If unfavourable, he proceeds as before. If favourable, the stone is elected and dragged with creepers to the place where it is to be raised, generally near the inter-village path/terrace fields, so that it can be seen by the travelers.

Before dragging, the stone is again purified ritually. On this day, the village elder offers a pot of rice-beer (*Tala*), an egg, and also loses a fowl. Much care must be taken while doing so. They believe, if something is wrong in performing this ritual, the performer suffers from blindness, breaking of teeth *etc.*So, an elderly person is selected for performing such rituals.

On the stone dragging day, no cooked-rice is offered. The host offers cooked-meat and rice-beer only. When the stone is dragged to the selected spot, they leave it there till night (on the same day). The merit-seeker raises the stone, at night (on the same day), with the help of the village youths. Singing and dancing with the boys and girls continue for the whole night. Meanwhile, a clan elder of the merit-seeker comes out and announces the outstanding works are done by the merit-seeker during his life till the day of performing that ceremony for *Kaho Katanmei Saimingbao*. The clan elder says 'Mr. 'A' had 'N' times of greatest harvest in the village. He had owned 'N' number of girls as his wives; he had killed 'N' number of big games like tigers, leopards, bears, boars, deer *etc.*' Above all, he also mentioned the number of human heads taken by the merit-seeker on raids *etc.*

Next day, the merit-seeker offers a great feast. For this, he had already prepared at least thirty jars of rice-beer called *Zou-Karung* each having capacity of 20/30 liters. He also arranges a big cow, a buffalo, a *mithun*, a dog and a number of fowls for the feast.They cut the meat into pieces of considerable sizes. Some of them are distributed to the married aunts (father's sisters), sisters, daughters, and even the grand-daughters (if married) of the merit-seeker. And their husbands locally called *Tamimeikina*, serve as cooks for the feasts of *Kaho Katanmei Saimingbao.* If the merit-seeker does not have his own paternal aunts, sisters, and daughters and even close relatives, he distributes the meat to his clan's sisters, daughters *etc.*, and their husbands render services as cooks of the feast.

Kareng Hang and Kareng Dree (stone walls which serve as village gates): These are the village gates. They are always found on the boundary of the

village, may be on the north and south or on the east or west. The gate of north or east is called *Kareng Hang* and the southern or western gate is called *Kareng Dree* in Liangmai dialect.

The Marams

The Marams have eight types of megaliths, which are erected on different occasions. They are discussed under the following heads.

Beitung: It is a composite structure made of a menhir and a dolmen. Such type of megalith is raised in each Maram village when they first settled there. No elaborate ceremony was performed for the erection of *Beitung*. It is related with oath-taking functions which are associated with the following disputes like (a) Land dispute, (b) Theft case, and (c) Other crimes related to adultery, rape case or disputed paternity etc. It is resorted to only in most serious cases where all means fail to materialize. They perform three types of oath-taking function for every disputed serious crime. Both parties (offender and defender) perform the rituals one after another as directed by the *Sagong*. They are- (a) Striking on the menhir part of the *Beitung* by the butt-end of a long-bladed knife and swear 'Oh *Beitung* you punish me if I am a wrongdoer'; (b) Sacrifice a cock on the dolmen part of the *Beitung* and utters 'If I am a guilty person Oh *Beitung* I will die as the fowl has done'; (c) Cutting the tail of a cat says 'Oh the spirit of *Beitung*, you punish me. If I am telling a lie I will be deformed like the cat has' (Binodini, 2011: 146-147).

Ranii Atu: It is a cairn found in each hamlet of different *Sadungs* of every Maram village. It is constructed by the members of each *Sadung* and try to compete with one another in erecting the cairn so as to which clan could erect the best one. Such competition contributes to enhancing social value of this cairn. Besides, it serves asresting place during the normal time. Moreover, it is used as watch-tower and also vantage point during inter-village feud (Binodini, 2011: 147-149).

Tiisum: It is a menhir having the name of each donor and raised after performing a feast-of-merit. Unlike other tribes, the Marams erected menhirs in and around the settlement area. And the merit-seeker (s) should be a resourceful and blameless person(s). Besides, the merit-seeker observes one year's *genna* and lives apart from his wife for a year or more from the date of receiving the permission from the village council up to the completion of the whole procedures of stone selection, and erection. Otherwise, the stone to be erected would crack. It is not a good indication, and as a consequence, the merit-seeker's family would suffer in many ways. Moreover, the intending merit-seeker worships their supreme god to prevent the natural calamities like earthquakes or death in his family or in the families of his kinsmen or even in the village. If one of these events happens, it normally postpones the

stone raising ceremony for the duration of one month for every such event. In one village such menhirs are erected in group forming an avenue in their stone raising place locally called *Katak*.

The intending merit-seeker selects the desired stone, according to the advice of an expert person (male/female). The person who will select the stone will not take any food except drinking rice-beer and taking ginger. After selecting the stone, the merit-seeker touches the stone and utters some hymn. Then he takes out some mosses *(spa)* from the stone and returns home. At home, he/she sleeps keeping the mosses under his/her pillow and dreams on it.

During the one year's *genna* the host collects the materials required for the stone dragging and raising ceremony in cash or kind. He needs at least 2000-4000 liters of rice-beer. The pounding of rice starts before 15 days of the actual ceremony, whereas preparation of rice-beer starts a week ahead. Collection of stone dragging creepers, plantain leaves, and preparation of the sled is also done during this period.

On the stone pulling day, the merit-seeker performs a ritual on the spot, where the selected stone is quarried. A stone pulling ceremony is a spectacular event in Mara society. In fact, all the villagers, adorned in their full ceremonial dress, participated. In all, they have been in the procession at least two hundred or more.

When the signal is given, all start to pull the stone. It is indeed a very strenuous job to pull the heavy stone along the steep hill slopes and sharp bends, but the experienced stone pullers could negotiate smoothly to drag up the stone to the selected place. During the resting period, drinks are served to refresh the pullers.

The stone is thus pulled up to the selected spot (*Katak)*; they wedged it firmly to guard against the possible slip. They left the stone on the sled for some days. Once the stone is left in the *Katak,* it is prohibited to touch. The pullers left the place, but they enter their respective houses after washing their hands.

After some days, they prepare to erect the menhir. For this, they arrange long poles of hardwood and plant them on the ground to use them as a fulcrum. At the foot of the sled, on which the massive stone is pulled up, a hole about one and a half feet deep is dug and new ones are made. Inside the hole, the merit-seeker keeps some iron objects like hoe-blade/knife/sickle ritually. The Marams believe that the performer will attain alonger life as the iron objects and his fame will be everlasting as the stone.

They generally lift the stone in an inclined position for sliding the base of the stone into the hole already dug. Thus, pulling from the front and

propping it with longer wedges from behind every time, the stone is erected at last with the shouting of '*hoi*' (Photo 42). The stone is wedged underneath to make stand firmly on its own base after which the hole is filled with earth and rammed.

On this stone raising day, the merit-seeker feeds invitees, guests, and the whole villagers. He also distributes uncooked meat and rice-beer to each and every household of the village. Drumming, singing, and dancing continues the whole night by the members of the boys and girls' dormitories. On the next day also, the merit-seeker gives another feast to his co-villagers and with this, he concludes the stone raising ceremony.

Arou Atu (Gravestone): These are flat stones directly resting on the ground but capping over the grave. Sometimes it is placed on a raised platform. It is constructed in memory of their parents or any other deceased person of the family even relatives by the survivors. In rare cases, there is also an upright stone which is inscribed in Roman script stating birth and death of the deceased person.

The procedures for selecting and pulling the stone are similar to the *Tiisum,* but no purification is done in this case, but simply selects the stones and pulls them up to the burial spot and place over the grave.

Tiirosum (dolmen/horizontal flat stones use as stone seats): It is a cluster of low dolmens set up at regular intervals to serve as the public resting place, and meeting seats. In each hamlet of every village have a number of such structures. It is raised collectively by the people of each hamlet without performing rites and rituals.

Amailui (small avenue, represent male members of 1906): It is a small avenue formed by four rows of alignments of miniature menhirs. It represents the male population of Zongnamei clan of Sangkhungmei village. It was raised in 1906. Each miniature menhir represents the male member of the clan. No ritual is performed for this megalithic structure.

Atu chagakamatei (a Monolith serves as Holystone): It is a natural stone. The Marams of Willong village believes that it has been fallen down from the sky in ancient time. It plays a very important role among the traditional religion follower Marams.

Atu ameiogijaphuigungkheikaranijangbaatuwaikheibamle (Capstone for a burial pit of decapitated heads): It is a flat stone which covers a secondary burial pit. It is placed only when the *Sagong's* house is repaired.

The Poumais

Zaosochu (Menhir of social status): It is a menhir planted at their clan's stone raising place (*Chushebu*), for each clan in the form of menhir,

alignment, and avenues. Some of them are also found in and around their residential area.

Before a wealthy Poumai raises a *Zaosochu* in his name for the first time, he performs a series of five feastings. They are: (a) *Rasou*, (b) *Vaove*, (c) *Moujii*, (d) *Zhusou*, and (e) *Chiveisu*. These feasting series are performed after his request to his clan elders (*Tsiiko*), and village councilors (*Chikumai/Neih Pfupfumai*), and only when he is granted. The *Chiveisu* is performed after raising the *Zaosochu* in his name.

(a) *Rasou:* He offers rice-beer to *Kirako*, which is guided by the village priest (*Khaohro*), to protect them from any sort of suffering during the coming series of feasting.

(b) *Vaove:* Once the public announcement is made by the *Chikomai/Tsiiko,* and the *Rasou* feasting ritual is over, the *Vaove* feasting with ritual is held. For this, the intending merit-seeker worships their supreme God and Goddess called *Khaliihira* and *Teipfii Khamiru* by offering blameless cow/buffalo (*Haveijii*).

(c) *Moujii:* It is an elaborate and important feast because the host is not allowed to perform *Zhusou* (a feast for stone rising) until and unless he performs the *Moujii* feasting. After completing the arrangements, the intending merit-seeker announces the fixed day of *Moujii* feasting. In every feasting, unlike other tribes, the Poumais never offered cooked-rice. Hence the host offers cooked-meat and rice-beer only to his invitees, friends, relatives, and co-villagers.

(d) *Zhusou:* It is a ritual for stone dragging and raising ceremony. For this, the intending performer needs to work a lot. It starts with the cultivation work. Besides, they help the host in the preparation of sled (*Chukhe*), and rice-beer keeping the wooden container (*Teis*); a collection of stone dragging creeper (*churai/rurai*), and also in husking paddy, pounding rice-flour, and brewing of rice-beer.

In some village, the merit-seeker performs prayer to get an appropriate stone to be erected because such selected stone will represent the performer's life. And while selecting the stone he utters the following words *'Zhi neyejupa we nezhiyeke–a ve hiiwo'* (I like you Stone. Come, and live with me).

When the selected stone reaches the *Chushebu*, the performer returns home. The stone pullers leave the stone there after checking from its possible fall. Then all the participants are also assembled in the house of the performer. There the host serves them with rice-beer.

It continues for four/five/six consecutive days. The sacrifice of animals starts while the stone is still standing but tying with the sled at *Chuhsebu.*

In the morning of the first day of *Zhusou* ceremony, the village priest (*Khaohro*) sacrifices a small calf by touching the animal with a small stick ritually. Then all the boys below ten years of age beat the small calf with sticks. The priest also sacrifices a blameless buffalo (*Haveijii*).

The meat of the sacrificial animal is then distributed to all the houses of the village. With the sacrificed of the *Haveijii*, the process of animal sacrifice in the morning session of the first day is completed. In the evening all the villagers come and gather in the performer's house to have the cooked meat and drink rice-beer by using cups made of banana leaves (*Zaopeiso*).

The stone which is already dragged and kept in their *Chushebu* (clan's stone raising place) is formally raised on the fourth/fifth/ sixth day of *Zhusou*. If the stone raising function is completed, the merit-seeker is allowed to wear a title-clothe called *Zhoasosa/ Pheiyu.* Now he is permitted to perform *Chiveisou* and construct a decorated horn-house.

(e) *Chiveisou*: The performer of *Zhusou* feast and raised *Zaosochu* organizes *Chiveisou* to decorate his house to signify his status. In such case, the front wall and the gable of the house of the merit-seeker are particularly decorated with traditional insignia. The design and decoration of the gable are done depending on the wishes of the host. On the other hand, the decoration made on the gable of *Veo* (village chief) has a fixed one, which has two sharp pointed ends.

Chukho (a Cairn): According to the nature of structure and owner, different names are given to these structures. The procedure of construction of *Chukho* is similar to those of *Zhaoshochu.*

Paohon Chukho(clan's stone seats associated with Dolmen): It is the foundation stone of the Yumai clan and also uses as the seats.

Raikhubu (dolmen of highest social status): It cannot be constructed by any wealthy person unless he performs *Zhusou* more than three times and continues the series of feast-of-merit including *Chiveisu*.

Seibechu (religious flat stone): This stone is placed there since the time when the Saranamei village was settled there for the first time. Since that time, they have been using this stone for worshipping of a small calf on it with rituals every year.

Chadeichu, (a judiciary stone): It is a judiciary stone. The non-Christian Poumais, till today perform a cat killing ritual every year. They believe that if they perform such rituals with an expert person, and kill the cat with all villagers, then the thief will die in the same way and in the same year.

Neisha Chukho (religious stone): It is considered ritually very important. It is found in front of every chief of every village. It is used as the shouting place of the *Veo,* whenever he wants to make some public announcement.

Tapu (a Megalith for placing the decapitated head): When hunted head(s) on raids are brought the hunter keeps the hunted head on the *Tapu* and informs the village chief. The village chief comes out and beats the hunted head(s) till he gets satisfied. Then the head is returned to its original village. No ritual is performed in this connection.

Chuchukho (a stone circle, related to headhunting): It is found in the residential area of Yumai clan. It is related to the affairs of headhunting.

Khophochu (Capstone for the grave): It is always found capping a burial pit directly. No elaborate ceremony regarding the selection and erection of this gravestone is performed.

Loupfo (a small Alignment, each stone represents a girl/woman, whom a braveman had won her hand): It is a small alignment. It is raised by a sinner to remove all the sins for his misdeeds. No elaborate ritual is associated with such structures.

Aro Adu (village gate and wall): Earlier it was an important structure among the Poumais. Nowadays most of them are modified.

Results and Discussion

Varied megaliths have traditionally been erected throughout the Liangmai, Maram, and Poumai areas in Tamenglong, Kangpokpi, and Senapati, districts, Manipur. It is still practicing among these tribes under study with different rites and rituals. Each megalithic erection is associated with a grand feasting or a series of feasts-of merit. Thereafter the performer is permitted to wear a titled clothe. This permission is further extended up to the great-grandson of the merit-seeker. It is followed by the house decoration feast. Each donor of the feast of merit decorates his house with house-horn, and also carvings work on the front wall (with carved out human heads that he had taken on raids) and animal heads that were sacrificed during the feastings series or furious animals he had hunted). Such horned-house is called *Chakiwki* among the Liangmais, *Jeleiki* among the Marams and *Chikai* among the Poumais.

Erecting a megalithic structure takes some years (from the time, when a merit-seeker begins to collect the materials to the time in which he could

complete the whole process). Therefore, it takes at least three years or more to acquire the necessary items like a collection of paddies for brewing rice-beer, domestication of animals, and also the accumulation of wealth to defray the cost.

Conclusion

The inequality in the practices of megalithic tradition is clearly seen among the Liangmais, the Marams, and the Poumais of Manipur. Each of these tribes performs different procedures while raising a megalithic structure. There are twelve megalithic types in Liangmai area, eight types in Maram area, whereas there are twelve types in Poumai area. The megaliths of these three tribes have many differences in their structural and functional types. There are many differences in giving the feasts-of-merit and also in performing the rituals concerned. Above all a Liangmai merit-seeker constructs a cairn, after raising a number of menhirs (differently known as *Chenku Tusom, Maning Taoba Tusom,* and *TazanTatbo Tusom*) on different occasions, to attain the highest social status; whereas a resourceful Maram raises a menhir (*Tusiim*) to reach the highest degree in their social ladder. In contrast to these, a wealthy Poumai erects a number of menhirs after performing a series of feasts-of-merit, and finally builds a dolmen to accomplish the uppermost status

Note

This paper was presented at the International Workshop on *Human Developments and Landscapes* at Kiel University, Germany,March 20-24, 2018.

References

Devi, PB 2006, *The Liangmai Nagas: an ethno archaeological study*, Imphal.

Devi, PB 2009, *The Maram Megalithic builders*, Imphal.

Devi, PB 2011, *The Megalithic culture of Manipur*, Agam Kala Prakashan, Delhi.

Chapter - 13

Prehistoric Stone Tool and Thunderstone - Issues with Semiotic and Agency

— ***Mayanglambam Mani Babu***

Introduction

Throughout the history of mankind, humans have attempted to make sense of their environment, the natural processes and forces, thereby interpreting arbitrarily those with myths and legends. A myth, the earliest form of science (Bierlein, 1994), is a sacred story from the past which is concerned with the powers that control the human world and the relationship between those powers and human beings (Rosenberg, 1997). The *pre-modern* natives throughout the world dwell in a macro cosmic domain of myths based on invisible powers of spirits, ancestors, and natural phenomena - that infused their life-force. This is a secret world that people saw spirituality and the divine in the luminous glow of nature - whether sun and moon, fire and water, the sparkle of stars, or the iridescence of the rainbow or what not. Of these, belief on man-made stone tools (usually the ground *Neolithic Celts*) as 'thunderstone' is also one which forms a prominent chapter in human lore worldwide and probably has the historical foundation with myths linked to the psychological tendency of *cosmic plasma* phenomenon. Beginning with the allegorical and catastrophists schools of sixteenth century till the twentieth century psycho-sociological schools (of Sigmund Freud, Carl Jung, Emile Durkheim, Claude Levi-Strauss, etc.) through nineteenth and mid-twentieth century 'nature school' (of Max Muller, James Frazer, Robert Briffault, etc.) – the construct of *plasma mythology* has had its revival in twenty-first century with 'nature schools' having foundational uniformitarian assumption of mythology to nature metaphor that 'many human traditions were based on natural events' (van der Slujis, 2010:3). A few subsequent

works (Vitaliano, 1973, Piccardi and Masse, 2007) also attempted to correlate human myths and beliefs with geologic phenomena. In this regard, van der Slujis (2010) has proposed a term 'cosmo-mythology' to deal with notions about the sky in human traditions in lieu of Dorothy Vitaliano (1973)'s 'geomythology'. And since a good number of cosmic or celestial phenomena (such as, rainbow, meteoric falls, floods, etc.) do not involve plasmas, it is felt that a new 'discipline is needed that studies *any transient natural phenomena in human traditions*' (van der Slujis, 2010:3). It is seen that of the five broad categories of *transient events* with reflexes in human traditions (such as geological, orbital-dynamical, atmospheric, atmospheric-optical, and celestial), 'thunder stones' come within *geological* transient events (van der Slujis, 2010:4). And 'lightning' along with bolides, meteors, aurorae, etc. come within atmospheric transient events (*ibid.* 5). In ancient traditional societies at least five categories of objects/materials have been labeled as thunderstones - which includes *ordinary stones, especially pebbles, fossils, meteorites, tektites, prehistoric implements* (van der Sluijs, 2013).

Till this day, belief in thunderstone as celestial object hurled by *God* from the sky during thunder is almost a universal phenomenon, and humans shared its fundamental embodied existence either as a naturally produced *object* formed in storm clouds and fell with lightning, or a powerful object which is under the possession of a particular god, the 'God of thunder' who resides in the sky. In both, the cases have the infliction of power symbolism. According to legends, every time the lightning struck, a stone fell from the sky: while lightning was caused by the falling stone, fire and thunder were seen as its consequences (Blinkenberg, 1911:1; Carelli, 1997:399). These objects/stones, known worldwide as thunderstones/*ceraunia (Latin)*/*donnerstein* (German)/ *Pierre de foudre* (French) continued to be a subject of discussion into the seventeenth century. It is reported that there were plenty of previous instances of *ceraunia* being retrieved from the ground where lightning had struck. A Swiss naturalist, Konrad Gesner (1565) reported instances of falling *ceraunia* during a storm in and around Vienna during 1492 and earlier (Goodrum 2008). Libert Froidmont (the well-known Louvain theologian and natural philosopher) argued that *ceraunia* were produced when terrestrial exhalations rose into the atmosphere where they mixed with the moisture present in clouds. The resulting matter was then baked by the heat of lightning into a very hard stone that fell to the earth.

The belief in thunderstone as a universal human phenomenon, at least, validated the renowned claim of the *psychic unity of mankind* - the foundation of which was first paved by a German linguist Wilhelm von Humboldt (1776-1835), and later mooted by a German ethnologist Adolf Bastian (1826-1905). von Humboldt's assertion was that all humans shared a common nature (*Gattungs-Charakter)* despite their different languages and cultures (Bunzl

1996: 22, 31). Thus, the notion of *psychic unity* is the psychological component of a universalistic conception of human nature. Bastian's distinction between *Elementargedanke* (primary thought) and *Völksgedanke* (local 'folk' thought) was his attempt to distinguish the universal components of human mentality from the purely and particular concepts.

The construct of 'thunderstone' as a celestial object was challenged by the seventeenth-century natural historians and antiquaries[1], proposing that these *ceraunia* were not thunderstones but ancient human artifacts. An Italian naturalist Michele Mercati (1541-93) formulated the first reasoned argument supporting the idea that *ceraunia* were not produced when lightning struck the ground, but were instead *implements* made by humans. In his massive geological treatise of minerals and fossils entitled *Metallotheca*, Mercati (1717) described *ceraunia* as having the shape of a wedge or axe, exactly conform to the shape of an axe (*securis*) and also refers of '*ceraunia vulgaris, et sicilex,*' (p. 241, 243) which consists primarily of stone arrowheads. Later few naturalists [like the British geologist John Woodward (1665-1728, French naturalist Antoine de Jussieu (1686-1758), Welsh naturalist and antiquary Edward Lhwyd (1660-1709)] also made observations of their genesis to anthropogenic activities.

A natural construct in human mind owing to the mighty roar of thunder and fiery light is 'with images of the supernatural and bring forth both fear and reverence' (Parkman, 1993:90). Hence the natural phenomenon of 'thunder is almost always personified as a spirit inherent in the storm' (*ibid.),* which are seen with a number of folk mythologies (Evans, 1897; Blinkenberg, 1911; Spence, 1914; Cook, 1925; Harrison, 1927; Seligman, 1927; Eliade, 1958; Willcox, 1963; Needham, 1967; Courlander,1975; Hultkrantz, 1979; MacKenzie, 1985; Ashby, 1989; *cf.* Parkman, 1993 to cite a few). The celestial thunder personified as a supreme deity is a common belief in many North and South American tribes (Spence, 1914; Hultkrantz, 1979, Tyler, 1964; Neihardt, 1979). In the mythologies of ancient Europe and Asia also there exists the emical concept on the existence of a 'thunder god' (or 'hammer god') who possesses thunderstones - such as *Zeus-pater* (Jupiter) in southern Europe (MacKenzie 1985:3), *Thor* in northern Europe (Munro 1900), *Balei Liwen* among Penan of Indonesia (Needham 1967:275), *P'an Ku* in China (MacKenzie1985:2),*Kapohakaa*in Hawaii (Levi-Strauss 1966:96), *Shango/ Jakuta* in West Africa (Courlander, 1975:188), *Namarrgun* in northern Australia (Welch, 1982:82) and so on. Mention may also be made of Hadad or Baal Shamin (a Syrian thunder god), Semo Sanctus (a thunder god of Sabines, a member of Oscan-speaking people of the central Apennines north of Rome lived during 290 BC), Taranis (a Celtic thunder god, known from Britain, Germany, France and the province of Dalmatia) (Adkins and Adkins, 2004: 290, 302, 304). In Malay Peninsula and Borneo, often prehistoric stone

tools are perceived as thunderstones, termedas *batulintar, halintar, or batupetir* (Evans,1927: 131). In North Borneo, such objects were called *gigiguntor* (thunder teeth; Evans, 1913: 155). For both the Kelabit and Penan peoples of interior Borneo, thunderstones are believed to come into being when cosmic power from thunder and lightning hits the earth (Janowski and Barton, 2012).

As also seen in other indigenous populations of India, the belief of 'thunderstone' is also a continuing practice in almost all the tribes in Northeast India. It is known, for instance, among the Kachari (*sarak-ni-Ongthai: sarak*-heaven, *ni* - of, *on that* - stone), Karbi and Tiwa tribes (*choteracho*-thunder stone) of Assam; the Adi tribe (*lidar*-thunder stone) of Arunachal Pradesh; the Garos (*goera-gitchi: goera*-god of lighting; *gitchi*-hoe) and the Khasis (*U Sdie Pyrthat*-Thunder Axe) of Meghalaya; the Sema (*Poghupumoghii* - toad axes; Hutton, 1921), the Angami (*methie*- thunder axe), the Ao (*tsungyipo*-thunder axe; Hutton, 1921) Nagas of Nagaland; the Jamatia tribe (*fwirang* or*pherang* - thunder stones) of Tripura; Mizos or Lushai (*tek*-thunder) of Mizoram; the Meiteis (*nungmei-singjang* or *braja-singjang*), the Aimol (*chek-kral*) and among all the Naga tribes of Manipur - to cite a few. The people see *thunderstones* as concentrated in and deriving from a parallel part of the cosmos, associated with God of sky or heaven.

It is also a general belief that thunderstone possesses power, potency or life force deriving from the cosmos. As these *objects* are perceived as having the repository of extraordinary powers - there saw a number of their widely used as talisman, protective devices, and prophylactic use. The magical qualities accorded to this object being a global phenomenon, are part of a deeply rooted natural philosophy. There exist a good number of believes that individuals who owned such stones would not be hit by the lightning and might protect against lightning, and function as a kind of charm. In Ireland, polished celts turned out of ground were kept on attaching on a rafter of each dwelling hut to protect themselves from being hit by lightning (Skeat, 1912). The Jaintias of Meghalaya propitiate the Gods of Thunder to protect crops (Deb Roy, 1981). It is known among the Greeks and Romans that large-sized axe-heads (the *thunderstones*) were used to protect buildings, seemingly on a general idea of 'like *bans like* a thunderstone fallen from the sky will in future protect against thunderstorms and lightning strikes' (Faraone, 2014:2). With archaeological finds from later Greeks and Romans Bronze Age down to the medieval sites or graves, thunderstones (celts) 'were apparently thought to have some kind of magical power to protect buildings and people, especially from lightning and violent storms' (*ibid*. 1). Contrary to this, the *Ao Nagas* (of Nagaland) believe that keeping such objects in a house causes lightning to strike it (Mitra, 1931). Some of the examples of having a belief on wood of trees struck by lightning come from *Yorubas* of

Nigeria who have ordeals of drinking water from a bowl in which the skull of a person killed by lightning is dipped (Skeat, 1912). *Zulu* witch doctors sometimes make people eat an ox struck by lightning (Halliday, 1910). However, an *Ao Nagas* will not eat an animal killed by lightning (Mills, 1926: 305). It is a universal belief that a man struck by lightning is a great sinner. Such beliefs are found among *Sema Nagas* who regard death at hands of lightning as execrated ones (Hutton, 1921: 262). African tribes consider that lightning punishes criminals *(http://www.sudanvisiondaily.com)*. Among the *Maram Nagas*, it is believed that lightning punishes a person who transgresses law of intermarriage within own matrilineal clans (*Kur*) (*http:// shaining.blogspot.com/.../maram-tribe.html)*.

Many polished axes of Neolithic origin, found in abundance in most part of Northern Nigeria, are valued as magical objects (Dwyer, 1903), and 'are said to be used even now by some of the Plateau pagans for hacking off branches of the sacred trees which are protected by taboo against the use of metal' (Fagg, 1946:50). A focus of discussion at the turn of the last century was the issue with the 'reuse' of Neolithic axe-heads ('celts' or 'thunderstones') as amulets in Roman times, where the 'pre-historic axe-heads carry Greek inscriptions and sometimes Egyptianizing images that corroborate their use as amulets during the Roman Empire (and) ... nearly all of the inscribed thunderstones of known provenance come from the eastern half of the Mediterranean, although many uninscribed examples were clearly reused as amulets in Italy, France, Britain and elsewhere' (Faraone, 2014:1).

Structuring 'Thunderbolt' – the Heuristic Status

Though thunderbolts are the man-made artefacts made intentionally by prehistoric hominins for some specific purposes; - the issue now lies with an arbitrary meaning to them as of celestial *origin* hurled by thunder god from the sky during lightning and storm. Referring its heuristic status, a debate lies with whether thunderstone is to refer an *object, thing* or *material*. At the backdrop of the Aristotle's hylomorphic model of creation, making a 'thing' is resulted by bringing together 'form' (*morphe*) and 'matter' (*hyle*) Here, 'form' came to be seen as imposed by an agent with a particular design in mind, while 'matter' thus rendered passive and inert, became that, which was imposed upon. Yet, Ingold (2010) contended that the 'forms of things arise within fields of force and flows of material. It is by intervening in these force-fields and following the lines of flow that practitioners make things'. While engaging to differentiate between these two terms (*thing* and *object*), Martin Heidegger (1971) reiterated that *object* stands before us as a fait accompli, presenting its congealed outer surfaces to our inspection, and is defined by its very 'over againstness' in relation to the setting in which it is placed (Heidegger, 1971:167). A *thing*, by contrast, has the character not of

an externally bounded entity, set over and against the world, but of a knot whose constituent threads, far from being contained within it, trail beyond, only to become caught with other threads in other knots (Ingold, 2010). The *thing* thus, is a 'going on', or better, a place where several goings-on become entwined. (*loc.cit.,* 167). In the present context of debate, the piece of ground stone with broad and sharp working edge at one of its ends and a blunt tapering end on the opposite, - which the natives identified as of celestial origin – is very much appropriate to be referred as a 'thing' and not an 'object' from the perspective of embodiment. Yet, regarding this 'thing-object' issue, an opposite view was stated by James Leach (2007) –

> 'Objects are fitted into cultural contexts, while 'things' often are discussed only as the necessary material backdrop to the workings of society'... That is, because the material and the object world exist in particular relation to the person of the analyst, and this relation is so thoroughly naturalized as to appear given by the human condition, much anthropological theory has relied upon 'things' material stability of form and substance, opposing objects to the persons who act, create and utilize them (Leach 2007).

Amiria Henare et al. (2007: 5) argue that the term 'things' - 'unlike 'objects', 'artefacts' and 'materiality' . . . carry minimal theoretical baggage' which is distinguished by its peculiar vacuity (Lévi-Strauss, 1987: 55, *c.f., ibid.*).

In going further along the argument, if we refer 'thunderstone' (the piece of rock of definite shape) as an '*object*' it obviously omits the 'humans'. Owing to an ongoing interaction between humans (the actor) and the piece of stone (the object) it becomes a *thing* (that is, a Thunderstone) which can only be explained by imagining that the rock piece is endowed with an internal animating principle, the *agency*, that gives it a meaning. A piece of stone, a formless lump of matter, in simplest perception, is in its 'brute materiality' and need a concept of materiality in order to understand how particular pieces of stone are given form and meaning within specific social and historical contexts (Tilley, 2007:17). By materiality, Joshua Pollard (2004) mean 'how the material character of the world is comprehended, appropriated and involved in human projects' (pp. 48). It is natural to recognize a two-sided hylomorphic model of materiality – 'on the one side, brute materiality or the world's 'material character'; on the other, the form-bestowing agency of human beings' (Ingold, 2010). Following Heidegger, Bruno Latour's (2004) heuristic concept of 'thing' is concerned with a departure from the concept of 'matters of fact' to the 'matters of concern'.

The status of thunderbolts from their contextual and symbolical perspective is very much a material (in material culture) having anthropogenic

perception of symbol and power, and hence no more a 'natural object'/ 'thing'. Though the word 'material' (in material culture) 'embraces the class of objects known as artifacts - objects made by man or modified by man (but) it excludes natural objects'.

> Material culture is the study through artifacts of the beliefs-values, ideas, attitudes, and assumptions of a particular community or society at a given time ... the study of material culture might include a hammer, a plow, a micro-scope, a house, a painting, a city. It would exclude trees, rocks, fossils, skeletons ... natural objects are occasionally encountered in a pattern that indicates human activity ... In the broadest sense, these natural materials are artifacts-objects modified by man-and are of cultural interest (Prown, 1982: 1-2).

The use of the term 'thing' may be delineated in terms of analytic and a heuristic sense – 'the former implies a classificatory repertoire intended for refinement and expansion, the latter serves to carve out things (as an appropriately empty synonym for 'objects' or 'artefacts') as the field from which such repertoires might emerge (Henare *et.al.,* 2007:5). Thunderstone as a 'thing' is a small lump of rock through which people sets about to think as having divine power. In an analytic sense, this particular thing/object has a connection between two entities – the *stone* and the *power.* And, possession of 'power' to a thunderstone' lies with an emical belief of the people concerned, which has its cornerstone to their normative cultural ethos. However, in *heuristic* term, the status of thunderstone as a 'thing' lies with the natives' perception of divine power which has its nexus to celestial phenomena of thunderstorm and lightning caused by an imputed god.

The Issue- Agency, Semiotics, and Meaning

Obviously, the *thunderstone* debate seems to develop in two trajectories that correspond to the dichotomic divide of *natural* and *cultural* connotations within a complex interplay between *agency* and *structure* - between people as creative, strategizing subjects and those forces that shape, constrain, and even constitute their subjectivities. The most obvious symbolic belief associated with material objects has to do with value - the *inherent* and *attached* ones. Both these values are intrinsic parts to the peoples' concept of stone objects (the Neolithic celts) as that of celestial. It is seen that the duality in meaning (to a same object) emerges with symbolic embodiment to the object within a particular context – thereby giving the 'human-nature' and 'nature-culture' interaction. Such interactions refer to an understanding of people's expectations for and perceptions of nature, that led to the genesis of material objects called 'thunderbolts' after duly creating a 'symbolic' connotation to those who experienced it and assigned them with myriad

supernatural attributes. Hence, one can find emergence of a deeper connotation of bipolar *emic-etic* meaning attached to thunderstones – *one,* as a celestial or natural one - being fall from the sky during lightening, and *two,* as a man-made tool of Neolithic times or earlier. Obviously, these two areas seem to be unrelated, but can have correlations when we go deeper with the issues, like –

(i) Why and how there has a specific belief of celestial attachment to such objects of prehistoric origin and not on others? What gives them the power to influence humans, particularly as they evoke strong emotion or significantly alter behaviour?
(ii) Whether the identification of 'man-made artefacts' as 'thunderbolts' owes to the typo-technological attributes of the former in having finely made/polished surfaces with broad sharp edges at one of its ends, which obviously bear typological similarity with that of an iron-bladed cutting axe used by them?
(iii) How specifically does the social construction of knowledge and of nature of such celestial objects form the basis by which we interpret signs and ascribe their meanings? Whether these objects can be perceived as an *external symbolic storage* in consonance with the primitive/ancient human mind?

In seeking advances to our understanding of the meaning of the negotiating identities of *thunderbolt* in terms of its dyadic *culture:nature* paradigm (that is, man-made artefact and natural/celestial thunderbolt) – it is pertinent to explain it within the frame of 'agency' where we can explicate on how this 'concept' arise within human conduct (a process which Charles Sanders Pierce calls *semiotics*). Here, semiotic theory is considered as the main framework for evaluating the process of symbolization of a man-made artifact as thunderstone. The complexities of Peircean semiotics could enable in developing a situated semiotic approach to material agency (the thunderbolts). It is clear that Peirce's notion of "synechism" conveys very persuasively the way in which "people and things are conjoined through the principle of semiotic mediation" and able to show how these traditions bring into being two quite different agentic networks.

It is argued that *making* of meaning to the sign (the object identified as *thunderstone*) rather than simply *used* it has its logical basis of semiotic process of creativity as well as of materiality (i.e. the production and comprehension of signs). Here the issue lies is with the question of *agency* in terms of human and natural. The emical view of the 'thing' (the 'thunderbolts') to the indigenous populations are referred to as natural, celestial non-anthropogenic objects having their own entities; however, these are man-made artifacts from an *etical* (archaeologists') perspectives. In both

these interrelated frames, the 'form' as we see at present, is imposed by an *agent.* In this context, the conceptual paradigms of 'agency' and Piercian's semiotics framework have relevancies to go further into the similar emic coherency of this long-standing and widespread beliefs throughout known populations the world over, by partaking with the construct that 'agency is not necessarily (or even usually) a property exercised by specific people but instead can be distributed across time and space, between or among *sub-individual* and *supra-individual* units, and over types of entities, such as humans and nonhumans' (Ahearn, 2007:389). Here the issue of 'agency' is in terms of both human and natural bearings. From the natives' point of view 'thunderbolt' is signified as the natural, celestial non-anthropogenic 'thing' having their own entities; however, archaeologist's perspective is a *man-made* stone artifact.

Agency is a much-debated theme across the social sciences and within archaeological discourse also, particularly with the post-processualists (Dobres and Robb, 2000:3). Focusing more with a theoretical perspective of relationship between agency and structure (Emir Bayer and Mische, 1998), the anthropocentric view of agency is based upon a general agreement that it is a property of the human individual – 'the only true agents in history are human individuals' (Giddens and Pierson, 1998: 89). This very concept is being challenged -

> This human-centered view of agents and artefacts is not limited to those artefacts we design to be like agents. It extends to a much wider and more prosaic world of artefacts and matter, an environment of things that is conceived on our own terms, under our control and designed to serve (Knappett and Malafouris, 2008: ix).

The notion of agency is one of the most neglected in theoretical discussions of the sign, both in semiotics and in its cognate fields. The genesis of 'agency' as an important theoretical foundation in the humanistic and social sciences lies with the works of several workers (Marx, 1959; Bourdieu, 1977, 1990; Giddens, 1979, 1993; Gell, 1998; Knappett, 2005; Knappet and Malafouris, 2008; Malafouris, 2013; Latour, 1993, 1999, 2005) to name a few). Agency as a theoretical perspective in many social science disciplines sees from different angles. Its theoretical frame tries to illuminate from 'a number of perspectives, allowing one to study the distribution of agency in and across real-time social, semiotic, and material processes' (Kockelman, 2007: 387) and can investigate various dimensions, such as, 'control, composition, commitment; thematization, characterization, and reason - without squashing them together as a single, unspecified quality' (*ibid.*). Bandura's (2006) *A psychological definition of agency* refers it as an ability to act consciously and intentionally, and as a prime force in human adaptation, development

and change, on both collective evolutionary and individual levels, and human agency implies a moral agency through affective self-regulatory mechanisms. Defining agency as a 'flexible wielding of means toward ends', Kockelman (2007) brings out the importance of 'self-creation' or 'self-invention' (signifying, ritualistic, etc.) in human systems.

In the present discussion, there hold relevancy of 'agency' with Peircean-based theory of meaning, the key components of which comprise: sign, object, interpretant; iconic, indexical, symbolic; effective, energetic, representational, etc. In fact, these terms and their interrelations form the backbone of this theory (Kockelman, 2007). Obviously, meaning of an 'object' created by humans as material and symbolic structures through which the world is perceived and responded to (Moore, 1986) conveys information about social characteristics, personal feelings, and symbolic connotation. Hence, meaning is not an inherent property of things but imposed on them by mental processes. We can say that the object/thing has meaning because it is part of a code, set or structure. In fact, it's particular meaning depends on its place within the code (Hodder, 1987), having three functional components - the *technomic, socio-technic* and *ideo-technic* functions of the object (Binford, 1972). To Ian Hodder (1987) an object's meaning is the effects it has on the world and meaning will persists as long as it has found a place within the code, the sign is arbitrary. The study of 'meaning' is the field of semiotics, which recognizes a triadic relationship of *object, sign, interpretant* and any semiotic process according to Peirce (1934), relates these three components in the following way: the *representamen* (*representant*) or *sign* itself, which is the visible or sensed part of the sign; the semiotic *object*, which is what the sign stands for; and the *interpretant*, which is the sign's meaning, as determined through an interpretative process (Chandler, 2002; Colapietro, 1989; Oehler, 1987; Parmentier, 1985; Pierce, 1931-58). To Peirce, a *sign* is 'something which stands to somebody for something in some respect or capacity'. Anything can be a *sign* as long as someone interprets it as referring to something else, but 'nothing is a *sign* unless it is interpreted as a *sign*' (Chandler, 2002; Oehler, 1987; Pierce, 1931-58). When *signs* are defined in the Peircian way, it becomes apparent that *signs* saturate our biophysical and social environments, helping us to make sense of our experiences. For the semiotic approach besides *signs, icons* and *indices* (*signs* that have non-arbitrary relations to their referents) are also included. Peirce devised various complex typologies of *signs*, and some of the most important terms are (i) the '*legisign*' or a *first* order '*legislated*' or commonly agreed upon visible *representant*; (ii) the 'symbol,' a *second*-order *legisign*, or an association of general ideas that allows for interpretation of the sign; (iii) and the 'argument,' a *third* order *legisign* and symbol, or a set of signs put together in a logical pattern (Oehler, 1987, Peirce, 1985). Peirce implied that the meaning of

objects in our environment does not reside in the physical, concrete, individual objects but instead on the *signs* that are present. We respond to commonly agreed upon signs (*legisigns*) through behaviour, social actions, reactions, thoughts, and ideas.

Meaning as well power is not an inherent property of things but imposed on them by mental processes. The 'thunderbolt' issue takes meaning to be a pattern of relations among its signs, the objects, contexts, or referents, and the interpreting cognitions or actions of people engaged in or by their operation in social life. Attempts to place certain objects in the baskets of 'icon,' 'index,' and 'symbol,' similarly, miss the critical point that these Piercean terms are not types of signs but stages or moments in the hierarchical complexity of semiotic functioning; a symbol necessarily embodies an index to specify the object being signified, and an index necessarily embodies an icon to indicate what information is being signified about that object.

The Debate: The Concluding Remark

While considering the ways people interpret artifacts of prehistoric origin as material signs of celestial origin (connected with thunder and lightning) and the role these signs play in the extension of emical knowledge of *immediate* post-prehistoric humans, Peirce's semiotic theory is used. Peirce developed his model of the sign in reaction to Cartesian dualism, suggesting that meaning cannot be separated into 'objective' and 'subjective' because our understanding of all signs is embedded in experience. At its most basic level sign has a triadic structure - the *sign*, the *object,* and the *interpretant*. And the meaning of a sign 'is not contained within it but arises in its interpretation' (Chandler, 2002:32). Anything can be a sign as long as someone interprets it as referring to something else, but 'nothing is a sign unless it is interpreted as a sign' (Chandler, 2002; Oehler, 1987; Pierce, 1931-58; 2:172). Such a view has formed the basis of contemporary discourse studies, where the signs' contexts of use are investigated in order to study the different meanings a sign may have (e.g. Keane, 1997; Lee, 1997; Lee and Urban, 1989; Parmentier, 1987, 1994; Singer, 1984; Tambiah, 1984; Urban, 1991).

There are problems with the concepts of meaning and power of 'thunderbolts' which obviously centered on the issue of interpretation. It is held that the 'meaning' of a behaviour/action is determined by the nature of the intention that - the satisfying-meaning is the content of the intention. The Peircian perspective is that the *representamen*, objects, and *interpretants* create arguments that shape the peoples' behaviour, emotions, and thoughts as they progress along the augmentation of an artefact as celestial thunderbolts. The present example of 'Thunderbolt' as symbolic behaviour may come with a number of referential frameworks.

To get at the meaning of Thunderstone, one needs to focus on how material objects convey knowledge through peoples' experience of them. This raised our awareness of how interpretations of thunderstone are constrained by their physical as well as mental settings. Appraising thunderstone as a material culture item built cognitively, has relevance with Malafouris's argument that 'material culture (is) concerned with figuring out the causal efficacy of materiality in the enactment and constitution of a cognitive system or operation' (Malafouris, 2004: 55). While meaning of thunderstone may be conveyed through indexicality, it is because of this iconic relationship that may help us to understand how people give emical meaning to this object as of celestial origin. Here, a subtler argument comes forcefully of the genesis of thunderstone to the believers that, is it the human mental or emotional states that attract them to the particular sign (the object), or the sign (the physical states of the object) that attract them to particular mental or emotional posits? Both these paradigms, though arbitrary in nature are interwoven and have feasibilities to consider that the natural forces owe their credit to an extension on the peoples' mind to supernatural origin as the product of thunderstorms, the missile weapons of angry gods. As people happen to get these 'objects' amidst vast virgin forest, hilly terrains or turned up by farmer's plows in the *jhum* fields - their visual brains establish lexicons of shapes, colours, etc., followed by a number of queries in their minds - such as, how such a beautifully shaped, lustrous and uniform object comes in that particular site[2]. And envisioning the typologically analogical features of these 'objects' to that of an iron axe (having a broad sharp edge at one of its end and a blunt tapering end towards its opposite) and recognizing that these are not made and used by any living populations known to them – the native people set about their mind of the object's origin to the natural act obviously the celestial power, with due percepts that a) during lightning and thunderstorms there saw damage of surrounding environment by way of cutting large trees and sometimes take human life to death, b) these cutting and damaging acts could have been made with implements having sharp edges (like axes or daos). Here, the human cognition is fundamentally *cultural* involving symbolic communication, and such belief reflects vast network of complex cognitive skills.

Another involvement of cognitive extension in thunderstone is its construct as an organism that could experience the mundane stages of 'life' and 'death/spent/used'. Those objects in the first domain still retained its destructive or prophylactic power and the opposite in case of the second one[3].

Obviously, the visual processing systems of human brain have the potentials to act as an informative device of thinking about the features of an object (the stone artefacts) and of making connections of it with the natural

phenomena of lightning/thunder and consequently with symbolic manifestations to the object. Here we can see a linkage between the visual cortex plasticity (and the cognitive fluidity) and the environment (both the natural and cultural) on the one hand, and the material object allegedly produced by such acts on the other - which is of utmost significance as a guiding force in tracing the anthropogenic genesis of thunderstones. The very analogical typological character of thunderstone with that of an iron axe blade attracts the people in sensing the former as a missile weapon hurled by god from the sky. Thunderstone, thus produces knowledge through its *indexicality* (to use Peirce's term), which is itself analogous (or 'iconic') with a cutting tool used by the concerned people in their daily chores.

Embodiment of power and ideology that surrounds thunderstone involves structured and restructuring of sign system by agents giving forth its symbolic meaning. The cultural construct that surrounds the object developed actively by agents still forms part of the semiotic code in terms of its structuring and restructuring. Hence, once created, thunderstone forms a powerful effective medium for acting back and restructuring social practices through which to legitimate the social order precisely because of its materiality. As one moves forward with the issue, semiotics can facilitate a broader, more in-depth understanding of people's expectations for and perceptions of nature. The Peircian perspective is that the representatamen, objects, and interpretants create arguments that shape man's behaviour, emotions, and thoughts as we progress along the trail. Yet, this semiotic sequence model may not follow in an imputed sequence in case of the thunderstone issue and it may also be in a reverse direction.

It may be perceived that the indigenous concept of thunderbolt fulfills the triadic relationship denoting *qualisign, sinsign,* and *legisign*. The hierarchy upon which Peirce bases this idea precludes a consideration of the stone object as shaped exclusively by the 'social' since materiality entails qualities (*qualisigns*) embodied by individual things (*sinsigns*) which appear as representations or interpretants (in *legisigns*). The Peircean semeiotic as a device, however, provides a useful insight to the present issue of thunderbolts in considering how these 'act' and also to think about the signification process as a succession of capable, contextual and conventional states of being. In doing so, it provides a unique way to locate and define the manifold where agential forces of materiality and humanity come together. It is pertinent to say that the morphological/typological and colour attributes of the so-called thunderstones (as a natural celestial object) is apprehended somatically through an experiencing analogy with contemporary ethnographic iron axe blades and hence duly embodied as the second order of legisign (the symbol). By virtue of their placement within specific contextual settings, it seems that how interpretants as the third order of legisign might be differentially

produced by the ground between sign and object in the given society. Here one can see an intricate attribute-based coding scheme to classify a discrete property of form and colour, where aspect of design symmetry is treated as a phenomenon intimately shaped and directed by the products and system of materialization. Under these cognitive milieus of material creation, the objects are served as *interpretants* thereby enabling certain forms of relationality.

It is also seen that general typological character of the stone object (with broad/straight/semicircle sharp edge) gave rise to a strong tendency to operate it as decent indexical legisigns. In this sign possibility, a general rule exists whereby the form acts as a decent (indexical) sinsign, more specifically a 'replica', and hence clearly specifies the ground between object and sign. Here we might suggest that the semeiotic functioning of thunderbolt shape/ form directs forcefully to the subsequent conventions of governing its materiality.

To resolve the present deliberation, the symbol systems centered towards the materializing thunderstone reflects the logic of thought processes of the post-prehistoric hominid mind reflecting three fundamental forms of referential associations - (a) *Icons* point to their referents by typological analogy of the stone objects (thunderstones) with iron blades of an axe used by the people in their daily chores, (b) *Indices* are mediated by some redundant physical or temporal association between *sign* and *object* (that is, thunder/lightning will create an *object* which looks like an iron blade of an axe which possess magical power), and (c) *Symbols* are mediated by arbitrary, formal, or agreed-upon links, irrespective of the physical characteristics of either the *signifier* or the *signified.* Here, the *symbol* (the object hurled by the thunder god, or otherwise) necessarily embodies the *index* (of celestial origin fell from the sky during lightning and thunder) to specify the object being *signified* (as 'thunderstone'). At the same time, the *index* necessarily embodies an *icon* to indicate what information is being signified about that object (the 'thunderstone'). The present discussion could also speak a cognitive move of the people towards the conceptualization of stone objects (particularly the Neolithic axes) to a celestial rootage, duly mediated by a relatively coordinated form of human agency, cognitive fluidity, and the cumulative negotiations and interactions with the natural phenomena. As we move forward in exploring the human-nature interaction, semiotics can facilitate a broader, more in-depth understanding of people's expectations for and perceptions of nature.

Notes

1. Matthew Goodrum (2008) has given a general assessment on the concept of natural historians, antiquaries and historic archaeologists over the issue of Thunderstone.

2. An example from west Australia also shows that - unusual objects having distinctive appearance in shape, colour, and design are believed to have been left behind by mythological dream time in its travel across landscape (Gould, 1980:135). The indigenous West Australia Ngaatjatjarra speaking tribes referred these items (comprising tektites, pieces of bakelite plastics, old eyeglass lenses and other oddments of European origin) as *Yiruputja* which are saved and incorporated into bundle (termed as *Mapanpa*) and are used by the sorcerers owing to their belief of having magical power. Such another example is the 'Kimberley point' made out of glass, bottles, telegraph insulators and isotropic rocks (*ibid*.141) used widely by the aborigines of NW Australia.
3. It is very much a living tradition of the indigenous valley people of Manipur, the Meiteis, among whom there is a folk belief in the existence of thunderstones has a strong footing. These are still in use for magical acts, prophylactic and protective use, and many more. A preliminary exploratory work by the present author reveals that those *thunderstones* under the possession of some of the local shamans (*maibas*) happens to be those Neolithic axe and adze celts, fully-ground having lustrous look (made usually fine-textured rock types). When compared the three randomly picked up Neolithic celts (from the Prehistory laboratory, Department of Anthropology, Manipur University) with those three *thunderstones* (which are under the possession of three different *maibas*) in some typological attributes, such as shape, dimensions, state of preservation, edge-angle (such as, clay, profile, goniometer methods) etc., there shows no significant differences between the two categories of object. Again, when the three Neolithic celts are shown to a local shaman (Mr. M. Mani Meitei (75 yrs.) of Kakching village, Manipur) all are identified as 'thunderstones' – one celt of which was keyed out as 'lived' and the other two as 'dead/spent/used' one. The shaman could diagnose the very statuses of these *thunderstones* by keeping each one on his right palm and feel the pumping like pulse from the object. A more accurate procedure of such differentiation is usually made by performing a ritual act at the abode of Lainingthou Sanamahi, a Meitei household deity, placing the *object* (Thunderstone) to be proven over a piece of plantain leaf overnight with a belief that if the position of the *object* is change next morning, it is identified as a *lived* thunderstone, and if not it is a *dead/spent/used* one. Owing to the want of space and also the area lies beyond the present purview, the details could not be highlighted.

References

Adkins, L & Adkins, RA 2004, *Handbook to life in ancient Rome*, Updated Edition, Facts on File, Inc, New York.

Ahearn, LM 2007, Comments on Paul Kockelman's paper 'Agency - the relation between meaning, power, and knowledge', *Current Anthropology,* vol. 48, no. 3, pp. 375-401.

Ashby, G 1989, *Never and always: Micronesian legends, fables, and folklore*, Rainy Day Press, Pohnpei, F.S.M.

Bandura, A 2006, 'Toward a psychology of human agency', *Perspectives on Psychological Science*, vol. 1, pp. 164-180.

Bierlein, JF 1994, *Parallel myths*, Ballantine Books, New York.

Binford, LR 1972, *An archaeological perspective*, Academic Press, New York.

Blinkenberg, CHR 1911, *The thunder weapon in religion and folklore*, Cambridge University Press, Cambridge.

Bourdieu, P 1977, *Outline of a theory of practice*, The Press Syndicate of the University of Cambridge, New York.

Bourdieu, P 1990, *The logic of practice*, Stanford, CA.

Bunzl, M 1996, 'Franz Boas and the Humboldtian tradition: from *Volksgeist* and *National character* to an Anthropological concept of Culture' in *Volksgeist as method and ethic: essays on Boasian ethnography and the German anthropological tradition*, ed G Stocking, University of Wisconsin Press, Madison.

Chandler, D 2002, *Semiotics: the basics*, Routledge, New York.

Carelli, P 1997, 'Thunder and lightning, magical miracles. on the popular myth of thunderbolts and the presence of stone age artefacts in medieval deposits', in *Visions of the past. trends and traditions in Swedish medieval archaeology,* Lund Studies in Medieval Archaeology 19, eds H Andersson, P Carelli & L Ersgård, Riksantikvarieämbetet Arkeologiska Undersökningar Skrifter, Stockholm, nr 24. pp. 393–417.

Colapietro, VM 1989, *Peirce's approach to the self: a semiotic perspective on human subjectivity*, State University of New York Press, Albany.

Courlander, H 1975, *A treasury of African folklore*, Crown Publishers, Inc., New York.

Deb Roy, HL 1981, *A tribe in transition - Jaintias of Meghalaya*, Cosmo Publications, New Delhi.

Dobres, MA & Robb, J 2000, 'Agency in archaeology. paradigm or platitude?' in *Agency in Archaeology*, eds MA Dobres & J Robb, London, pp. 3-17.

Dwyer, PM 1903, 'On the thunderstones of Nigeria', *Man*, 103 (*cf.* Fagg, 1946).

Eliade, M 1958, *Patterns in comparative Sheed and Ward,* Sheed and Ward, London.

Evans, J 1897, *Ancient stone implements, weapons, and ornaments of Great Britain,* Longmans, London.

Evans, IHN 1913, 'On a collection of stone implements from the Tempassuk District British North Borneo', *Man*, vol. 13, pp. 154–158.

Evans, IHN 1927, *Papers on the ethnology and archaeology of the Malay Peninsula,* Cambridge University Press, Cambridge.

Emirbayer, M & Mische, A 1998, 'What is agency?', *American Journal of Sociology,* vol. 103, no. 4, pp. 962-1023.

Fagg, B 1946, 'Archaeological notes from Northern Nigeria', *Man,* vol. 46, pp. 49-55.

Faraone, CA 2014, 'Inscribed Greek thunderstones as house-and body-amulets in Roman Imperial Times', *Kernos*, [Online]. Available from: 27 | 2014, URL: http://kernos.revues.org/2283;DOI: 10.4000/kernos.2283. [9 January 2017].

Gell, A 1998, *Art, and agency. an anthropological theory*, Oxford University Press, Oxford.

Gesner, K 1565, *De rerumfossilium, lapidumetgemmarummaximefiguris &similitudinibus liber* (Zurich), 64r-66v. (*c.f.*Goodrum 2008).

Giddens, A 1979, *Central problems in social theory. action, structure, and contradiction*, University of California Press, Berkeley & Los Angeles.

Giddens, A 1993 (1976), *New rules of sociological method*, Stanford, CA.

Giddens, A & Pierson, C 1998, *Conversations with Anthony Giddens: making sense of modernity,* Stanford University Press, Stanford, CA.

Goodrum, MR 2008, 'Questioning thunderstones and arrowheads: the problem of recognizing and interpreting stone artifacts in the seventeenth century', *Early Science and Medicine,* vol. 13, pp. 482-508.

Halliday, WR 1910, 'The force of initiative in magical conflict', *Folklore*, vol. LXVI, no. 21, pp. 147-167.

Heidegger, M 1971, *Poetry, language, thought*, trans. A Hofstadter, Harper & Row, New York.

Henare, A, Holbraad, M & Wastell, S 2007, 'Introduction: thinking through things' in *Thinking through things - theorizing artefacts ethnographically*, eds A Henare, M Holbraad & S Wastell,Routledge, Taylor and Francis Group, New York, pp. 1-31.

Hultkrantz, A 1979, *The religion of the American Indians*, Facts on File, New York.

Hodder, I 1987, 'The contextual analysis of symbolic meanings' in *The archaeology of contextual meanings*, ed I Hodder, Cambridge University Press, Cambridge, pp. 1-10.

Hutton, JH 1921, *The Angami Nagas*,Macmillan and Co. Ltd, London.

Gould, RA 1980, *Living archaeology*, Cambridge University Press, Cambridge.

Ingold, T 2010, 'The textility of Making', *Cambridge Journal of Economics*, vol. 34, pp. 91-102.

Janowski, M & Burton, H 2012, 'Reading human activity in the landscape' *Indonesia and the Malay World*. Available from: DOI:10.1080/13639811.2012.709005.

Keane, W 1997, *Signs of recognition: powers and hazards of representation in an Indonesian society*, University of California Press, Berkeley.

Knappett, C 2005, *Thinking through material culture: an interdisciplinary perspective*, University of Pennsylvania Press, Philadelphia.

Knappett, C & Malafouris, L 2008, 'Material and nonhuman agency: an introduction' in *Material agency - towards a non-anthropocentric approach*, eds C Knappett & L Malafouris, Springer, New York,pp. ix-xix.

Kockelman, P 2007, 'Agency - the relation between meaning, power, and knowledge', *Current Anthropology*, vol. 48, no. 3, pp. 375-401.

Latour, B 1993, *We have never been modern*, Harvester Wheatsheaf and the President and Fellows of Harvard College, USA.

Latour, B 1999a, *Pandora's hope: essays on the reality of science studies,* Harvard University Press, Cambridge, MA.

Latour, B 1999b, 'On recalling ANT' in *Actor-network theory and after*, J Law & J Hassard, Blackwell, Oxford, pp. 15-25.

Latour, B 2004, 'Why has critique run out of steam? from matters of fact to matters of concern', *Critical Enquiry*, vol. 30, no. 2, pp. 25–48.

Latour, B 2005, *Reassembling the social: an introduction to actor-network-theory,* Oxford University Press, Oxford.

Leach, J 2007, 'Differentiation and encompassment - a critique of Alfred Gell's theory of the abduction of creativity' in *Thinking through things - theorizing artefacts ethnographically*, eds A Henare, M Holbraad & S Wastell,Routledge, New York, pp. 167-188.

Lee, B 1997, *Talking heads: language, metalanguage, and the semiotics of subjectivity*, Duke University Press, Durham, NC.

Lee, B & Urban, G (eds) 1989, *Semiotics, self, and society*, Mouton de Gruyter, Berlin.

Levi-Strauss, C 1966, *The savage mind,* University of Chicago Press, Chicago.

Lévi-Strauss, C 1987, *Introduction to the work of Marcel Mauss*, trans. F Barker, Routledge and Kegan Paul, London, (*Cf.* A Henare, M Holbraad and S Wastell, 2007: 5).

MacKenzie, DA 1985, *India*, Avenal Books, New York.

Malafouris, L 2004, 'The cognitive basis of material engagement: where brain, body, and culture conflate' in *Rethinking materiality: the engagement of mind with the material world*, eds E DeMarrais, C Gosden & C Renfrew McDonald Institute for Archaeological Research, Cambridge, pp. 53-61.

Malafouris, L 2013, *How things shape the mind*, Cambridge University Press, Cambridge.

Marx, K 1959 (1932), *Economic and philosophic manuscripts of 1844*, Progress Publisher, Moscow.

Mercati, M 1717, *Metallotheca. Opusposthumum, auctoritate, etmunificentia Clementis Undecimi Pontificis Maximi et tenebris* in *lucemeductum*, ed JM Lancisi (Rome), 241 (cf. Goodrum, 2008).

Mills, JP 1926, *The Ao Nagas*, Macmillan and Co., London.

Mitra, SC 1931, 'Kolarian beliefs about Neolithic Celts', *Journal of Anthropological Society of Bombay*, vol. XIV, no. 6, pp. 783-790.

Moore, H 1986, *Space, text, and gender: an anthropological study of the Marakwet of Kenya*, Cambridge University Press, Cambridge.

Munro, CH 1900, 'The Oak and Thunder God', *Journal of the Anthropological Institute of Great Britain and Ireland,* vol. 30, no. 3, pp. 22-44.

Needham, R 1967, 'Blood, thunder, and mockery of animals' in *Myth and cosmos*, ed J Middleton, University of Texas Press, Austin, pp. 271- 285.

Neihardt, JG 1979, *Black Elk speaks*, University of Nebraska Press, Lincoln.

Oehler, K 1987, 'An outline of Peirce's Semiotics' in *Classics of semiotics*, eds M Krampen, K Oehler, R Posner, TA Sabeok & T von Uexkuell, Plenum Press, New York, pp. 1-21.

Parkman, EB 1993, 'Creating thunder: the western rain-making process', *Journal of California and Great Basin Anthropology*, vol. 15, no. 1, pp. 90-110.

Parmentier, RJ 1985, 'Signs' place in media res: Peierce's concept of semiotic mediation' in *Semiotic meditation: socio-cultural and psychological perspectives*, eds E Mertz & RJ Parmentier, Academic Press, Inc., Orlando, pp. 23-48.

Piccardi, L & Masse, WB (eds) 2007, *Myth and geology,* Geological Society Special Publication 273, The Geological Society of London.

Parmentier, RJ 1987, *The sacred remains myth, history, and polity in Belau*, University of Chicago Press, Chicago, IL.

Parmentier, RJ 1994, *Signs in society: studies in semiotic anthropology*, Indiana University Press, Bloomington, IN.

Pierce, CS 1931-58, *Collected Writings*, 8 vols, eds. C Hartshorne, P Weiss & AW Burks, Harvard University Press, Cambridge.

Peirce, CS 1934, *Collected papers of Charles Sanders Peirce,* vol. 5, eds. C Hartshorne & P Weiss, Harvard University Press, Cambridge.

Prown, JD 1982, 'Mind in matter: an introduction to material culture theory and method', *Winterthur Portfolio,* vol. 17, no. 1, pp. 1-19.

Rosenberg, D 1997, *Folklore, myth, and legends: a world perspective*, NTC Pub. Group, Lincolnwood, Ill.

Singer, M 1984, *Man's glassy essence: explorations in semiotic anthropology*, IN Indiana University Press, Bloomington.

Skeat, WW 1912, 'Snakestones and stone thunderbolts as subjects for systematic investigation', *Folklore Quarterly Review*, vol. 23, pp. 45-80.

Spence, L 1914, *The myths of the North American Indians*, George G. Harrap & Company, London.

Tambiah, SJ 1984, *The Buddhist saints of the forest and the cult of amulets*, Cambridge University Press, Cambridge.

Tyler, HA 1964, *Pueblo gods and myths*, University of Oklahoma Press, Norman.

Tilley, C 2007, 'Materiality in materials', *Archaeological Dialogues*, vol. 14, pp. 16–20.

Urban, G 1991, *A discourse-centered approach to culture*, University of Texas Press, Austin, TX.

van der Sluijs, MA 2010, 'Plasma mythology – a research programme', *Chronology & Catastrophism Review*, pp. 3-10.

van der Sluijs, MA 2013, *Theories on the rocks - in a flash (part one)*. Available from: www.thunderbolts.info/wp/2013/02/28/theories-on-the-rocks-in-a-flash-part-one-2/. [26 January 2018].

Vitaliano, DB 1973, *Legends of the earth: their geologic origins*, Indiana University Press, Bloomington.

Welch, D 1982, *Aboriginal rock art of Kakadu National Park, northern territory of Australia,* Big Country Picture Company, Darwin, Singapore.

Willcox, A 1963, *The rock art of South Africa*, Thomas Nelson and Sons, Johannesburg.

Chapter - 14

Fleshing the Skeleton: Understanding Prehistoric Cultures in Garo Hills

— Queenbala Marak

The Garo Hills region in India's Northeast is believed to have been occupied since the prehistoric times as evidenced by archaeological finds reported since the 1960s. For more than two decades, researchers from the Department of Anthropology at Gauhati University annually explored various sites and documented the finds therein. Mention may be made of Professors M. C. Goswami, A. C. Bhagabati, T. C. Sharma, H. C. Sharma, S. K. Roy, D. K. Medhi and A. A. Ashraf, and their postgraduate and doctoral students. In recent times, works have been undertaken by A. A. Ashraf and D. Bezbaruah of Gauhati University; S. Sharma of IIT, Guwahati and Q. Marak of North-Eastern Hill University, Shillong. In all, a total of over 40-50 sites were reported from West Garo Hills, three from East Garo Hills and one from South Garo Hills. However, the exact number of sites is difficult to state due to its overlap and continuity. Not only for its numerous finds, but also for the wide variation in tool typo-technology it is likely that Garo Hills could hold the key for prehistoric population and cultural studies of the region.

Much of the earlier works focused on providing a typo-technological study, which included a list of artifacts and the probable traditions to which they belonged. Some of the important doctoral theses giving a detailed typo-technological approach to tools found in prehistoric sites include the works of H. C. Sharma (1972) and M. Sonowal (1987) who were students of T. C. Sharma; and H. Mahanta (1995), a student of H. C. Sharma. Noteworthy initial publications in journals include those of Walker (1931), Goswami and Bhagabati (1959), T. C. Sharma (1974, 1980, 1985, 1988), H. C. Sharma (1975, 1976), Sharma and Sharma (1968, 1971), Sharma and Singh (1986) among

others. Veering from the set path, D. K. Medhi (1980) under S. N. Rajguru's guidance gave a geomorphological explanation to these finds; while S. K. Roy (1977), under T. C. Sharma's guidance studied not the stone tools, but Neolithic pottery from Garo Hills and other areas, and found continuity with the present. Later A. A. Ashraf (2010[2004]), a student of S. K. Roy, applied a novel approach – the technometric analysis – on the tools collected from Makbilbisik and Bibragre.

It is clear that a large number of raw data has been garnered in the region spanning for more than six decades. What is required today is to try and understand the artifacts – the meaning behind the types of tools found, and where and how it was found. This chapter will hence focus on reconstructions of people and cultures in prehistoric Garo Hills. In doing so, it will use data from available secondary sources, and primary data from the author's field studies. It is hoped that the bare skeleton which the present state of prehistoric Garo Hills is will be fleshed to some extent, and certain pertinent questions answered.

Archaeological Sites

Maximum numbers of sites have been reported from the Ganol-Rongram valley and its surrounding hill ranges in the West Garo Hills district. These sites include prehistoric sites revealing pre-Neolithic and Neolithic stone tools and pottery, as well as megalithic sites. The former is seen in great profusion, while the latter is seen sporadically. Additionally, the former is undoubtedly of prehistoric character, but the latter whatever may be its origin intrudes into historic and contemporary cultures. In the following, a list of prehistoric sites from Garo Hills is given (Table 14.1).

Table 14.1: List of Prehistoric sites from Garo Hills

Sl. No	*Names of Site*	*Location*	*Findings*	*Source*
1.	Bibragre [Bibragiri]*	WGH	Hoabinhian tools	Ashraf, 2006
2.	Charam Abri	WGH	Total tools found 1567 in Charam Abri and Michingrenchep**. Tools include choppers, hand axes, cleavers, scrapers, points, borers, blade tools, burins and microliths	IAR, 1974-75
3.	Chibragre (Chibragiri)*	WGH	Hand axes, cleavers, choppers and chopping tools	IAR, 1971-72

(*Contd...*)

4.	**Chitra Abri**	**WGH**	**Neolithic axes, adzes, grinding stones, scrapers, points, borers, awls, spear-heads, cores and hammers and potsherds**	**IAR, 1966-67; IAR, 1967-68**
5.	(a) Didami	WGH	Choppers, cleavers, discoids, scrapers, points, borers, backed knives, blades, flakes and cores	IAR, 1984-85
	(b) Didami III	WGH	Cleavers, scrapers, side/round/end scrapers, points, borers, knives, cores, blade flakes, lanceolate, axes, awls, hammers, choppers, hand axes, discoid and pickaxes	IAR, 1995-96
6.	Ganol Abri	WGH	Palaeolithic; large quantities of cores, waste flakes and unfinished tools suggest that it was a factory site.	IAR, 1981-82
7.	Ganolgre (Ganolgiri)*	WGH	Neolithic axes, adzes, grinding stones, potsherds (handmade and pale grey), Hoabinhian tools	IAR, 1971-72
8.	Gawak Abri	WGH	Tools not specified; Potsherds	IAR, 1979-80; Sharma and Singh, 2017
9.	Ida Chiring	WGH	Tools not specified	IAR, 1979-80
10.	Matchakolgre (Matchakolgiri)*	WGH	Neolithic axes, adzes, grinding stones, Hoabinhian tools	IAR, 1966-67
11.	Masigingsep** (Miching Granchep)	WGH	Cleaver, scraper, side/round/end scraper, points, borers, knife, cores, blade flakes, lanceolate, axes, awls, hammer, chopper, hand axes, discoid, and pickaxes	IAR, 1974-75; IAR, 1995-96
12.	Muksak Abri	WGH	Choppers, hand axes, cleavers, scrapers, points, blade flakes and cores	IAR, 1981-82
13.	(a) Misimagre (Mishimagiri)*	WGH	>600 heavily weathered and rolled stone tools, belonging to Early, Middle and Late Stone Age and Neolithic	IAR, 1969-70; IAR, 1978-79
	(b) Misimagre-I (also Watri Abri)	WGH	>100 tools belonging to Early, Middle and Late Stone Ages and Neolithic	IAR, 1969-70
	(c) Misimagre-III	WGH	Cleaver, scraper, side/round/end scraper, points, borers, knife, cores, blade flakes, lanceolate, axes, awls, hammer, chopper, hand axes, discoid, and pickaxes	IAR, 1995-96
	(d) Misimagre-IV	WGH	Choppers, cleavers, discoids, scrapers, points, borers, backed knives, blades, flakes and cores	IAR, 1984-85
	(e) Misimagre I – IX	WGH	> 7000 chipped axes, short axes, microliths, scrapers, points, blade tools etc. Factory site; Fragmentary potsherds	Marak *et al.*, 2017

(*Contd...*)

14.	**Muksak Abri**	**WGH**	**Choppers, hand axes, cleavers, scrapers, points, blade-flakes, and cores in addition to simple flakes, broken tools, and chips.**	**IAR, 1981-82**
15.	Makbil Bisik	WGH	Hoabinhian tools	Ashraf, 2006
16.	(a) Nangalbibra	EGH	Pebble tools *in-situ*; pebble tools of chopper-chopping complex,	IAR, 1977-78
	(b) Nangalbibra-A	EGH	Choppers, chopping tools, and flakes	Sharma and Roy, 1985
	(c) Nangalbibra-B	EGH	Scrapers of various types, points, arrowheads, flakes, and cores	Sharma and Roy, 1985
17.	Rengsangre (Rengchangre/ Rengsangiri)*	WGH	Neolithic axes, adzes, and grinding stones	Goswami and Bhagabati, 1959; IAR, 1966-67
18.	Rombhagre (Rambhagiri)*	WGH	Early and Middle Stone Age tool	IAR 1971-72
19.	Rongdu	WGH	Palaeolithic choppers, scrapers	IAR 1966-67
20.	Rongru Abri	WGH	Neolithic axes, adzes, grinding stones, handmade pottery	IAR, 1966-67; IAR, 1981-82
21.	(a) Rongram	WGH	Neolithic axes, adzes, grinding stones, potsherds together with Hoabinhian tools (Sumatraliths)	IAR, 1966-67; IAR, 1971-72; Sharma, 1980
	(b) Rongram Terrace	WGH	Edge ground tools chipped pebble axes of Hoabinhian tradition and a large pounding stone	Sharma, 1988
22.	(a) Selbalgre-1 (Selbalgiri)*	WGH	Axes and potsherds	IAR, 1967-68
	(b) Selbalgre-2	WGH	Hand axes, picks, discs, chipped celts, ground celts, shouldered celts, awls, scrapers, borers, blades, knives, knife-blades, points, spear-heads, arrow-heads, fabricator, wedges, hinge-flakes, chisels, cores, hammerstones, microliths, and pottery	IAR, 1967-68
	(c) Selbalgre-3, also known as Makbil chiring	WGH	Implements from Early and Late Stone Ages. Tools-less rolled in comparison to others.	IAR, 1967-68
23.	Siju	SGH	Handaxe, cleavers made on limestone along with a chopper on dolerite pebble, and a Neolithic celt	IAR, 1976-77
24.	Thebrongre (Thebrongiri)*	WGH	Middle and Late stone tools	IAR, 1971-72
25.	Waribokgre (Waribokgiri)*	WGH	Palaeolithic and Neolithic tools and discs	IAR, 1974-75
26.	Waramgre (Waramgiri)*	WGH	Hand axes, points, scrapers of Mousterian character, small flake tools, blades, microliths etc.	Sharma, 1974

* The names wrongly spelled in literature are mentioned in parentheses.

** The correct name of the site is Masigingsep.

Note: WGH=West Garo Hills, EGH=East Garo Hills, SGH=South Garo Hills

A quick survey of the sites reveals that these sites are found located at three different locations – (a) on the hills, such as Charam Abri and Muksak Abri (*abri* = hills), (b) on the river terraces, such as Rongram terrace, and (c) near rivers and streams, such as Ida Chiring (*chiring* = stream) and Makbil Bisik (*bisik* = water source).

Ashraf (2010[2004]) stated that unlike the Khasi Hills where the people appeared to have occupied the hill ridges, in Garo Hills they occupied either the gullies or river/stream confluences. He cites the sites of Makbil Bisik, Tebronggre, Masigingsep and Waksambo for the former; and Bibragre and Nangalbibra for the latter.

A thorough exploration of Misimagre, Bibragre and Selbalgre in 2015-2017 by a team from North-Eastern Hill University (Shillong) revealed that there appeared to be certain spots that people usually preferred and selected – (a) sites near water bodies – these could be gullies (after Ashraf, 2010[2004]) or even confluence sites; (b) sites on hill slopes overlooking water bodies – these are at various gradients and distance – and not the locations at the ridge or pinnacle; and (c) sites that directly received the morning or afternoon sun. It is highly likely that the prehistoric people in Garo Hills preferred to live on hill slopes, very much like the contemporary times, giving them a vantage point on many quarters, including security from wild animals and warring neighbours (if any).

Prehistoric Traditions

It is clear from Table 14.1 that tools reported from the sites are numerous and diverse. Not only in terms of typology but technologically too, these tools reveal a wide variation in tool making activities. In Misimagre, recovered tools show a clear blade technology (with typical blade flakes and burins), chipping technique and rudimentary grinding, microlithism, as well as Hoabinhian tools (Marak et al., 2017). Similarly, in other sites such as Selbalgre, authors have reported tools form Early and Late Stone Ages (IAR, 1967-68), suggesting that several different traditions existed here.

The Palaeolithic Conundrum

In an earlier publication (Marak, 2010), I stated that tools belonging to all the cultural phases (Palaeolithic, Mesolithic and Neolithic) are seen in Garo Hills, which is rarely the case elsewhere in the region. The same has also been reported by several other authors too (Sharma, 1967; Sharma, 1972). However, today after two decades of looking and re-looking at the tools, I am at a stage of incongruity. I place here a brief recap of the 'Palaeolithic' studies done.

In 1967, T. C. Sharma reported two implements showing significant Palaeolithic characteristics, and four years later with his student, H. C. Sharma reported the discovery of Palaeolithic tools in Garo Hills (Sharma and Sharma, 1971). However, Ghosh (1978) scoffed at the idea and strongly opposed the occurrence of Palaeolithic artifacts in Garo Hills and defined the tools as 'Neolithic debitage'. In order to validate the existence of this cultural phase, H. C. Sharma (1972) studied the various Quaternary deposits developed in different river valleys of the Garo Hills and gave a geological and stratigraphic support to the Palaeolithic cultures. He made the following classification for the Pre-Neolithic period.

Table 14.2: Sharma's Pre Neolithic Stage for Garo Hills

Sl. No.	*Pre-Neolithic period*
1.	Pebble tool – Chopper-Chopping tool tradition
2.	Core tool – Handaxe-Cleaver tool tradition
3.	Flake tool tradition
4.	Blade tool tradition
5.	Microlithic tradition

Source: Sharma (1972).

Later along with S. K. Roy, Sharma further elaborated the presence of this culture when they reported the finds of tools such as choppers, chopping tools and flakes *in situ* in a cemented gravel deposit in Nangalbibra (Sharma and Roy, 1985). H. D. Sankalia, the doyen of Indian archaeology, visited Garo Hills in the 1980s and was also convinced that the tools procured were indeed 'palaeoliths' (Sankalia, 1981). Soon after, D. K. Medhi (1990) too argued that the chipped stone tools of Garo Hills were not simply debitage, as advanced by Ghosh, but purposefully knapped artifacts, at least in part.

Picking up from Sankalia's 'palaeoliths', I have no doubt that the majority of the non-Neolithic tools found are scrapers and blades with characteristic Levallois flakes as well as blade and burin technology, besides tools which 'suspiciously look' like Palaeolithic choppers and hand axes. However, to place these palaeoliths as belonging to a Palaeolithic culture is rather far-fetched, especially since these tools have not been found in stratigraphical context. The problem with the Palaeolithic culture of Garo Hills just like in Northeast India is the chronology, context, and stratigraphy (Hazarika, 2012). The lithic evidence is not supported by fossil remains (since this region is highly acidic and contains fossilization), proper stratigraphy and context (Bhuyan and Marak, 2014).

Trial trenches in the region revealed a single occupation layer of Neolithic except in two sites (Selbalgre and Rongram), shown below.

Table 14.3: Trial Trench at Selbalgre

	Culture	*Material remains*
Layer 1	Neolithic	Chipped and ground stone axes, 1 scraper, plain handmade grey pottery
Layer 2	Microlithic	Non-geometric microliths, fluted core, hammerstones, micro flakes

Source: Mahanta, 1995.

Table 14.4: Trial Trench at Rongram

	Culture	*Material remains*
Layer 1	Neolithic	Chipped and ground stone axes
Layer 2	Hoabinhian	Edge ground tools, mullers

Source: Sharma, 2003.

Thus, in the absence of stratigraphy, associated finds, and contextual evidence, it is difficult to state with certainty whether Garo Hills did have a Palaeolithic habitation, even though it is clear and beyond doubt that paleoliths or Palaeolithic-like tools were very much in usage – and possibly were one of the most popular tools. In a personal communication, Professor A. A. Ashraf of Gauhati University opines that it is highly likely that much of what we have classified as Palaeolithic tools in the context of Northeast India as well as Garo Hills might be in reality belonging to the Hoabinhian tradition of Southeast Asia which is an epi-Palaeolithic culture and is found widespread in the region. This statement bears some credit since Northeast Indian ecological adaptations in the present bear similarity to that of Southeast Asia, and hence the logic can be stretched to the prehistoric period as well.

The Microlithic-Hoabinhian Interface

There appears to have been a Mesolithic phase (possibly a late Mesolithic phase) marked by microliths (both geometric and non-geometric) from sites like Selbalgre, Misimagre, Charam Abri and Waramgre; and a Hoabinhian phase identifiable due to finds of typical Hoabinhian tools at sites like Bibragre, Ganolgre, Matchakolgre, Makbil Bisik, Rongram etc. The test excavations conducted at Rongram and Selbalgre by teams from Gauhati University also prove the same (Tables 14.3 and 14.4).

The preceding section reveals two early Holocene traditions, both pre-Neolithic in nature – a microlithic and Hoabinhian tradition. The microlithic tradition is a pan-Indian phenomenon witnessed in the Mesolithic period in India as well as across the world (Africa, Southwest Asia, India and Europe). On the other hand, the Hoabinhian tradition is a typical Southeast Asian phenomenon and marked not by small tools (like the microliths) but by large-

sized tools showing minimum flaking, unifacial flaking, and rudimentary grinding. Not only do the products of these two traditions differ in terms of shapes, sizes, and technology, but they also differ in terms of ecological adaptations.

The coming together of two diverging tool traditions is rather interesting. Firstly, we see a very popular blade tool technology along with fluting technique – possibly in the manufacture of the blade tools and microliths. Blade flakes can be produced by using both percussion and pressure methodology. The hardness of the rock, i.e., dolerite (5.5-6.5 on the Mohs scale) indirectly suggests the use of percussion method (Marak et al., 2017). It is also likely that on medium to small-sized fluted cores, punching technique might have been applied in order to remove flakes (*ibid.*). Secondly, a large number of short axes, edge ground tools, and Sumatraliths have been reported clearly indicating the presence of the Hoabinhian culture.

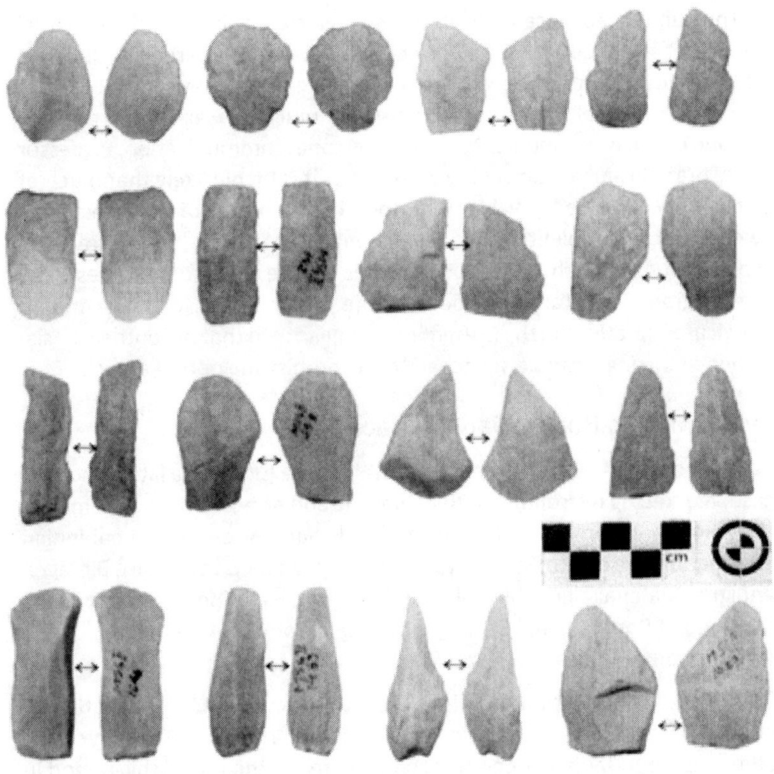

Source: author.

Figure 14.1: Microliths from MSG-IX

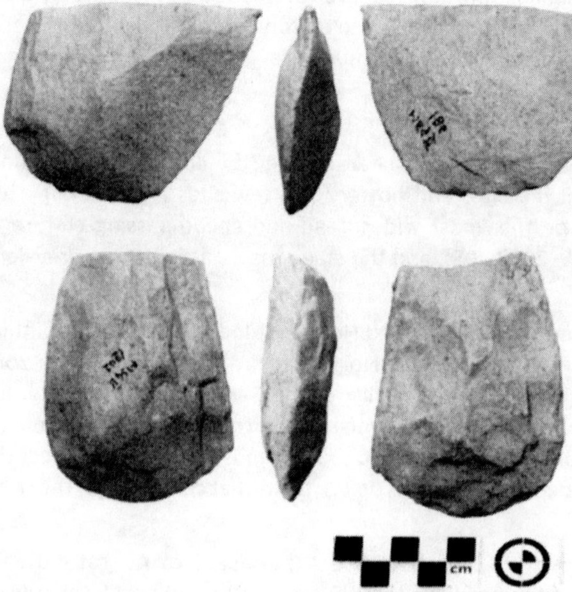

Source: author.

Figure 14.2: Short axes from MSG-IX

An interesting point rose by Mahanta (1995), is that these microliths, that he referred to as 'miniature tools', are found not in isolation in a separate stratigraphical horizon but associated with the Hoabinhian which he referred to as 'special variety tools'. He graded them as a separate flake blade industry of Mesolithic and a part of the Hoabinhian complex.

The findings of microliths and hoabins at the same stratigraphic layer are also attested by my recent findings at Misimagre (Figures 14.1 and 14.2), where from a trial trench set up at MSG-IX, both microliths and a few hoabins (esp. short axes) were recovered from the same layer

The only similarity in such a 'techno-complex' is the raw material where both the tool types are made on dolerite, the overwhelmingly preferred material. Since the technology involved in the manufacture of the tools are so diverse, it would not be wrong to assume the coming together of technology through population movements. Perhaps the Hoabinhian people living in the region came in contact with the microlithic-users and borrowed the technological know-how due to the latter's effectiveness in terms of portability as well as usage. It is pertinent to mention here, that reports of hoabins come from the majority of sites, while reports of microliths are a

minority. A similar diffusionist approach was also put forward by Glover and Presland (1985) when they tried to reason why a few microliths were found in the Hoabinhian homeland of Indonesia.

Neoliths and Pottery

The Neolithic phase is characterized by chipped and ground tools in almost all the sites and pottery in a few sites (Table 14.5). This stage appears to be the 'most widespread and encompassing culture in Garo Hills' (Marak, 2010:395), and the stage that is accepted as prevalent by all scholars.

T. C. Sharma (1981) divided Northeast India into three Neolithic zones, viz., (1) Garo Hills zone, (2) North Cachar Hills and Kamrup zone, and (3) Naga Hills zone. The speciality of the Garo Hills Neolithic culture is the raw material – dolerite – the same rock which is used for the manufacture of all other tools. On typo-technological grounds, the Garo Hills Neolithic tools can be grouped into two types (*ibid.*): (a) the flat celts, and (b) the shouldered celts.

Rita Deka (2015) under the supervision of Ashraf classified the ground stone tools of Garo Hills thus – (a) adze, (b) axe, (c) shouldered celt (curvilinear and rectilinear), (d) chisel, (e) scraper (side, end, round, gauge), (f) TMT and others. This classification was done on the basis of morphometric analysis of tools. Her study revealed clearly that once grinding technology came in, it was applied purposively on different parts of the tool to get a cutting edge.

An interesting aspect was marked by S. K. Roy (1981) when he suggested that much of the Neolithic celts found were likely reduced in size – that the tool users repeatedly re-ground the tools when its efficacy was breached. This statement finds support in Sharma's recent work on Gawak Abri (2013), where she postulates that edge-grinding took place on a large scale on the tools from the site.

On the basis of technology, it is however clear that the neoliths of Garo Hills can be grouped into (a) chipped tools, (b) chipped and ground tools, (c) fully ground tools, and (d) polished tools. Chipped tools are those where chipping or flaking can be seen all over with no grinding feature (Figure 14.3). This is taken to be the first stage of Neolithic technology. Ground tools, on the other hand, are those where some or complete grinding has been applied as seen by a smooth exterior all over (Figure 14.4). Polished tools are those which appear to have a polish or sheen on it either intentionally, or after consistent and long use.

Source: author.

Figure 14.3: Chipped tools from MSG-IX

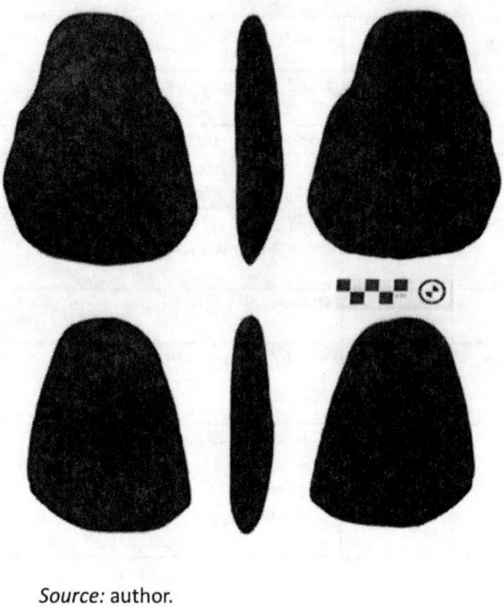

Source: author.

Figure 14.4: Ground celts from Garo Hills

As a result of ethnoarchaeological studies, it is clear that the Neolithic people of Garo Hills showed a remarkable resemblance to the present occupants of the region. Roy (1981) states that a comparative study of agricultural implements from the Neolithic and ethnographic context (i.e., the shifting cultivator Garos), reveals a homogeneity in function. The constraints that the people of this area face today appear to be more or less the same for the Neolithic peoples as well. Therefore, he states that the present people are modern but economically Neolithic (pp. 1893).

In 2005, I tried to reconstruct past economy in terms of the implements found in the archaeological context vis-à-vis modern implements through an experiment and taking clues from ethnographic milieu (Marak, 2005). In a later publication (Marak, 2014), I detail the experiment conducted in two separate plots A and B (approx. 12 x 12 feet each). Even though the output, i.e. crop production was same, a difference was witnessed in work efficiency. The experiment proved beyond doubt that parallels can be drawn between the past and present in the context of Garo Hills.

Though not found as abundantly as stone tools, a few broken pieces of pottery have also been reported from the sites of Chitra Abri, Ganolgre, Gawak Abri, Misimagre, Rongru Abri, Rongram, and Selbalgre. The details are given in Table 14.5.

Table 14.5: List of sites with pottery finds

Sl. No	*Names of Site*	*Location*	*Findings*	*Source*
1.	Chitra Abri	WGH	Handmade pale grey ware	IAR, 1966-67; IAR, 1967-68
2.	Ganolgre	WGH	Handmade pale grey ware	IAR, 1971-72
3.	Gawak Abri	WGH	(a) Coarse black pottery (b) Finer black ware with thin grey slip	Sharma and Singh, 2017
4.	Misimagre	WGH	(a) Plain red ware – core is dark grey (b) Plain brown ware – core is light grey	Marak *et al.*,2017
5.	Rongru Abri	WGH	Handmade pottery – details not given	IAR, 1966-67; IAR, 1981-82
6.	Rongram	WGH	Handmade and pale grey ware	IAR, 1966-67; IAR, 1971-72 Sharma, 1980
7.	Selbalgre	WGH	(i) Pale grey-brown ware – can be divided into 2 types based on the thickness (ii) Redware, grey ware, grey and red ware	(i) Mahanta, 1995; (ii) Roy, 1977, 2004

Note: WGH=West Garo Hills

It is clear that the pottery found in Garo Hills is handmade and coarse and has no slip (except reported by Sharma and Singh, 2017), or burnish or

decoration. The 'cord-impressed ware' taken to be a marker of Neolithic in Northeast India is missing. Undoubtedly, all the potsherds found from Garo Hills are handmade, and fragmentary in nature. Recently an OSL date of 2.3±0.2ka was procured from Gawak Abri (Sharma and Singh, 2017) indicating that the Neolithic population using handmade pottery lived approximately 2000 years ago. A small potsherd that we had sent for OSL recovered from MSG-IX could not procure an exact date due to the fragmentary nature of the sherd, but an approximate time-frame was given – about 700-1000 years ago.

Tool Making Sites

The finds of cores and other tool-making tools (TMT) including a large number of chips and waste flakes indicates that tools were positively made in Garo Hills. However, there are two scenarios on tool making activities – Firstly, they were made by users 'on the go', i.e, whenever the need arose, so the tool-user became the knapper; this could be the reason why in almost all sites, hammer stones and a few cores were reported. Secondly, they were made in a 'factory' or a site specifically meant for tool making.

On a recent exploration in Misimagre, we came across a large number of chips, TMTs, waste flakes, etc. Therefore, we decided to conduct a test excavation to see whether the site of Misimagre was a factory site. For this, a specific location at MSG-IX was selected. The test dig (1x1) revealed approx. 7000 artifacts. The finds from the 1x1 test pit were rather revealing since these tools were found in association with each other. The artifacts were collected from a single habitation layer composed of brown silty soil up to a level of 67cms when the non-implementiferous layer was breached. Table 14.6 shows the type of artifacts found during the excavation. The maximum amount of waste flakes, small chips etc. were collected from the excavated area, which along with the cores, blanks and broken tools point towards the fact that the site of MSG-IX was a factory site where mass tool manufacture took place.

Table 14.6: Stone artifacts from MSG-IX

Sl No	*Types of Artifacts*	*No*	*%*
Tools			
1	Chipped Axes	23	1.66
2	Short Axes	23	1.66
3	Scrapers	336	24.19
4	Blade	409	29.45
5	Borer	15	1.08

(*Contd...*)

6	Burin	16	1.14
7	Pick	9	0.65
8	Microlith	207	14.90
9	Point	5	0.36
10	Indeterminate	346	24.91
	Total	1389	100.00
Cores			
11	Broken	27	26.73
12	Core (both single and multi-platform)	60	59.41
13	Fluted	14	13.86
	Total	101	100.00
Debitage and TMT			
14	Blank	67	1.26
15	Waste Flakes	683	12.50
16	Small Chips	4710	86.24
	Total	5460	100.00
	Grand Total	*6950*	*100.00*

Source: Marak et al., 2017

Reports of cores and hammerstones by previous authors in sites like Chitra Abri, Didami, Didami III, Ganol Abri, Muksak Abri, Misimagre, Nangalbibra B, and Selbalgre II indicate that some amount of tool making, modification or repair did take place. However, our excavation at MSG-IX and the amount of debitage (78.56%) collected from a 1x1 test pit conclusively proven beyond doubt that the people in Garo Hills were making tools in a large scale at least at the site of MSG-IX.

Cultural Reconstructions

Reconstructions of past culture are rather a difficult task – especially since the only remains comprise of stone tools and pottery. The gravity of the situation increases since the majority of the tools and site discoveries have been done on the basis of surface finds and without any context. Nevertheless, with the help of ethnography, experimentations, and informed analogies, some reconstructions of how and in what manner people in prehistoric Garo Hills lived are attempted in the following.

Hunters and Gatherers

Ashraf (2010[2004]) theorized that in Khasi Hills in the prehistoric period, hunting might have been the primary strategy and gathering secondary, on the basis of frequency distribution of various functional tool types (of the point and projectile types) in Sawmer and Barapani in Khasi Hills; He further

states that the situation in Garo Hills might have been different (i.e., less hunting) due to the lack of the above tools. Digging tools like pickaxes, which indicate a gathering or rudimentary economy was completely absent in the two sites (*ibid.*), while they were found plenty in Garo Hills.

In Khasi Hills, the post-Pleistocene hunters lived a more or less nomadic way of life in the higher altitudes as evidenced by findings from sites along the ridges. They were possibly expert hunters who lived basically on a meat diet using projectile weapons. Around the same time or slightly later, there might have been several groups/bands living in Garo Hills. Based on tool frequencies, Ashraf surmises that there were separate bands living in Makbil Bisik and Bibragre – one with a preponderance of Hoabinhian tools (over 50.0%) and in the latter a negligible amount of Hoabinhian tools (11.0%). These bands in Garo Hills unlike their counterparts in Khasi Hills might have lived majorly by gathering due to the fact that majority of the tools belong to the cutting category (*ibid.*).

Ashraf's Hunter and Gatherer theory, when tested against tool types found in different sites of Garo Hills, appears to stand strong. In our 2017 exploration of Misimagre, we found no projectile points; whereas in the test excavation a negligible amount of points was found (0.0007%). Of course, this does not mean that the people in Garo Hills did not hunt or hunted less, but that they might have focused more or equally on the gathering of wild foods such as roots, shoots, tubers, fruits etc. of which was abundantly found. Finds of tools like picks indicate heavy-duty digging for roots and tubers. Additionally, for hunting, they might have used other raw materials found available in their environment like bamboo, for instance. This could be easily and most conveniently given shape to get spears of various shapes and sizes. If we look at the ethnographic present, the spear (*selu*) appears to be an important weapon of hunting and war, while the bow and arrow (which is of much importance in Khasi worldview) are practically absent in the Garos. Furthermore, the major strategy of hunting for the Garos is trapping and they lay traps of various kinds – large and small, complex and simple – to catch big and small animals. Therefore, drawing on similar analogies, we can assume that in prehistoric Garo Hills hunting strategies might have been limited to trapping methods, or the judicious use of bamboo as a hunting weapon.

Creek to Hill to Creek Cultivation

From the preceding sections, it is clear that continuity exists in terms of agricultural practices from the past to the present (Roy, 1981; Marak, 2005, 2014), however without shedding any light on the types of crops cultivated. From the ethnographic present, and secondary data from other parts of

Southeast Asia, it is likely that crops first cultivated might have been roots and tubers and other locally available food crops like squash (i.e., pumpkin), beans etc. When rice cultivation enters into Garo Hills is difficult to conjecture, but it is likely that by the late Neolithic period, rice cultivation might have been present in the region with rudimentary tools (like digging sticks and stone hoes) and on a preliminary scale.

Roy (1981) questions whether the cultivation of rice came down from the hills to the plains or followed the reverse direction. To this, Ashraf (personal communication) opines that cultivation first began in the fertile creeks from whence it went up the hills. From an archaeological point of view, this Creek to Hill theory appears likely. Ashraf cites the large chipped and ground tools (over 10-15cms in length) collected from different sites as an example, which he feels were possibly used in creek cultivations, where some amount of digging would be required to sow and plant. However, as cultivation process moved upwards to the hill slopes, due to the method applied (i.e., slash and burn), simple dibbling would be sufficient for sowing and planting of seeds as well as cereals like rice. Therefore, the bulk in stone axes and adzes would successively become smaller; finally taking the shape of celts as small as 5-10cms, and similar to the present-day iron hoe (*gitchi*) used by the Garos.

In an exploration in village Tusekgri in the year 2017, we came across two large chipped axes in the wet paddy fields (in the creeks). This is not to suppose that the two chipped axes were used in creek cultivation, for they could have been brought to the present location either through natural or human agencies. But a large number of chipped axes in our 2015-17 exploration does indicate indirectly an economy that might have supported some rudimentary cultivation of crops, possibly in the fertile marshy areas (such as gullies, creeks etc.). If we look at other regions in Southeast Asia, cultivation first appeared to have begun in the marshy locations near water bodies like lakes, streams, and rivers of root crops, tubers etc. Ecologically, since Garo Hills is not different from Southeast Asia, a similar strategy might have been adopted.

If cultivation moved from creeks to hills (for root crops and others), a modification to Ashraf's Creek to Hill theory can be made by looking at the ethnographic present. I suggest a Creek to Hill to Creek theory for the movement of cultivation (including rice crops). Rice cultivation appears to have started on the hills with simple tools like digging sticks and stone hoes for dibbling according to local lores. Even today, rice cultivation on the hills is done with simple tools like digging sticks (*matta*) and iron hoe (*gitchi*), which look like Neolithic celts. This cultivation is seen as an indigenous method for the present day Garos. Subsequently, Garos learned the art of cultivation in

the plains, valleys and even creeks from their neighbours, the Hajongs, and others, using the plough, which is the new form of cultivation today. The term 'Hajong', for the non-Garo tribal group by the same name, is said to have been given to them by the Garos who were astounded by how the new people tilled the land like *jo"ong* (worms). Thus, knowledge of cultivation likely moved from the creeks to the hills and back to the creeks with a new technology.

However, drawing analogies between past and present traditions, it is likely that the Neolithic people in Garo Hills adopted a rudimentary form of cultivation – that of slash and burns cultivation. This statement finds support from Roy's (1981) ethnoarchaeological work, my own experimental work (Marak, 2005, 2014) and Sharma's (2013) work on Gawak Abri.

Pottery Culture

After the discovery of Daojali Hading in Dima Hasao, Assam in the 1960s by a team from Gauhati University, T. C. Sharma (1967) stated that cord-marked handmade pottery is the distinctive pottery type associated with Neolithic culture in Assam and in other parts of Northeast India. He concluded that cord-marked pottery of Assam belongs to the Eastern Asiatic Neolithic tradition based on the similarities. O. K. Singh (2008) studied the ethnographic present in Manipur (Oinam potters) and opined that cord-marked pottery might have entered from south China through Assam.

Is cord-marked pottery the marker of Neolithic in Northeast India? Ashraf negates it and says that it is not the sole distinctive pottery type associated with neoliths of Assam. In his explorations, with his student A. Duarah, at the foothills region of Assam, he found handmade coarse grey ware which appeared to be the prime pottery type associated with neoliths in the site of Bambooti (Ashraf and Duarah, 2013-14). Potsherds collected from the excavations were OSL dated to 3000 years BP (Duarah, 2014), clearly indicating that – first, pottery cultures were unique and localized in the Neolithic times in Assam; and second, that Neolithic intrudes into the iron using stage. This unique amalgamation of Neolithic intruding into iron using stage was very lucidly explained by Ashraf (1990) when he theorized the stage of Ferrolithic in the context of Parsi Parlo in Arunachal Pradesh.

Taking a cue from Bambooti pottery, it becomes clear that Neolithic pottery in Garo Hills (which was used secondarily to stone tools) also followed a localized tradition – grey or red ware with no designs and no cord marks. The potsherds mentioned in Table 14.5 have been found in excavations in context with neoliths, and therefore these are undoubtedly of Neolithic origin. It is also likely that the people might have used non-ceramic and organic materials for storing and cooking such as dry gourds and bamboo stems,

much like the present Garos, for storing water, seeds, beer as well as for cooking just as in the Southeast Asian Hoabinhian homeland.

In the excavation at MSG-IX, two fragmentary pieces of potsherds were found with some portions of the rim intact – which made it possible for us to reconstruct the shape of the pot (Marak et al., 2017). The first type appears to be a pot with neck, while the second type appears to be an open-mouthed pot without a neck.

From the ethnographic present, after a systematic typological study, I had surmised elsewhere (Marak, 2016, 2017) that all Garo pottery is either one or the other traditional type – (a) Type 1 – Pot with neck, and (b) Type 2 – Pot without neck, also referred to as open-mouthed pots. Each of these two types could be further classified on the basis of size and function. Thus, a pot without a neck (i.e. Type 2) could be variously classified into *dikrong*, *samdik*, *matchamdik*, *sangkho* etc. shown in Table 14.7.

Table 14.7: Types of Open-mouthed Pots in Ethnographic Context

Type of Pot	*Size (in diameters approx.)*	*Used for*
Dikrong	5cms	Storing Seeds
Samdik	15-30cms	Cooking curry
Matchamdik	30-50cms	Ceremonial cooking
Sangkho	<50cms	Ceremonial cooking

Source: Marak, 2016, 2017.

A comparison of the ethnographic and archaeological contexts reveals continuity in terms of the types of pottery (i.e., shape). Thus, as the size of the pots increase the nomenclature and function changes. The technology of making a *dikrong* remains the same as that of a *sangkho*, but not only do these two differ in size drastically, but also in function.

Megaliths as a Living Tradition

Megaliths refer to large stone structures standing alone or with a group of other similar stones. In reality, however, the meaning of megalith is not always connected with large stones (Yondri, 2006; Marak, 2012), but can be applied to non-lithic structures set up for a particular purpose. Megaliths are found plenty in the Khasi-Jaintia Hills but practically remain unknown from the Garo Hills. A preliminary exploration reveals that megaliths do exist in Garo Hills region, but whether they are of prehistoric or historic origin remains to be seen.

At the outset, it is clear that morphologically, they belong to two groups – (a) large lithic structures, and (b) large wooden structures. The former is only of one type, i.e., menhir. Menhirs are long, elongated, standing stones;

and in the context of Garo Hills, they are found either alone or in a cluster. The latter takes the form of carved wooden posts and are connected to the modern-day Garo worldview.

Functionally, however, they can be any of the following:

(a) Village foundation stones – These are known as *asong* and put up when a new village is set up. Such stones are seen in Boldakgre, Mandalgre, and Selbalgre (Figure 5). They are also sometimes known as *kosi*. At Selbalgre, two sets of *asong* are seen – which are popularly referred to as *jikma* and *jikse* – which represent the two founding clans of the first settler (the clan of the wife and husband). On the other hand, in Mandalgre (East Garo Hills) several such clusters are seen. These are connected to the folk story of Sande Manda a folk hero who supposedly set up the huge cluster of stones in order to show his strength.

(b) Boundary stones – These are set up as a boundary marker between villages and are referred to as *a"mal*. Many of the old villages have such a boundary marker demarcating the villages. Boundary stones are considered sacred and are generally left untouched, with natural vegetation growing around them.

(c) Sacrificial stones – These are known as *kosi* and are places where sacrifices are made for different gods and goddesses. In days bygone, according to local lore, human sacrifices were made, which are now replaced by animal sacrifices. These rituals are connected to health and prosperity of the village and its inhabitants. Variously, foundation stones are also referred to as *kosi* sometimes – clearly indicating its function.

(d) Wooden structure – These are post-funerary memorial posts set up in memory of the deceased. Known as *kima*, they can be seen abundantly in villages like Sadolpara and Chidaogre. *Kima*s are usually sculpted out of a single block of wood and some basic shapes are given to represent the face. Additionally, clothes, ornaments, and other adornments are also placed on it.

It is clear that unlike the stone tools, megaliths continue to have a living tradition in Garo Hills. These structures (including the wooden *kima*) are considered sacred and therefore either avoided or left untouched by inhabitants. It is believed that the *asong*, *kosi* and *a"mal* have malevolent spirits living in it or in its vicinity, such that people refuse not only to touch or clean them but also go near them. It is believed that being in its mere presence will lead to bad dreams, sickness, untoward incidents, and even death.

Source: author

Figure 14.5: Village foundation stones at Selbalgre

Source: author.

Figure 14.6:* Kima *as a memorial post

Conclusion

The number of prehistoric sites discovered in Garo Hills attests to its importance in the past. No doubt, the Rongram-Ganol valley was occupied by prehistoric people on a large scale – who not only lived here, made their own tools and used them for different economic strategies but also had interactions with their neighbor-occupants. This is why inter-site similarities and differences exist in tool typo-technology – suggesting the presence of several groups/bands/clans who occupied contiguous sites. This is likely the route how dispersion of people, tools, and knowledge of tools took place. Handmade coarse pottery too appeared towards the end (which intruded into Historic), but it was the stone tools that were overwhelmingly used.

When we collate the data from all secondary and primary sources some interesting conjectures can be made. A few characteristic features of prehistoric people and cultures can be surmised, thus:

First, Garo Hills lacks a uniform prehistoric cultural tradition. Not single but multiple tool traditions existed represented very uniquely by a microlithic-Hoabinhian interface at Misimagre, an overtly Hoabinhian phase at Makbil Bisik, followed by the popular Neolithic at many sites including Gawak Abri. A microlithic-Hoabinhian interface is unheard of in the context of Northeast India, while the Neolithic is seen almost everywhere. The pre-Neolithic phase in Manipur, Arunachal Pradesh, as well as Tripura, is strongly marked by the Hoabinhian.

Second, there is no doubt that a pre-Neolithic stage existed. The non-neoliths found in almost all the sites are not all 'Neolithic debitage', rather they were intentionally made, and for a variety of purposes. For instance, in MSG-IX, microliths were intentionally made from fluted cores; and blade flakes from larger blade cores. However, to extend this pre-Neolithic stage to Palaeolithic is far-fetched, in the absence of associated finds.

Third, a single raw material (i.e. dolerite) was used throughout the ages for multiple tool traditions – to prepare blades, microliths, hoabins as well as neoliths. Dolerite is a hard-basaltic rock that is tough to manipulate; nevertheless, it was preferred over other rocks. This indicates that the same group of people (with multiple traditions) occupied the region through ages, and some form of conformity in terms of ideology led them to use dolerite.

Fourth, the different tool traditions found in the region can be explained by 'localization' of cultures that might have taken place for two reasons – as an adaptation to the immediate ecology, and for purposes of specific functions. It is likely that some amount of innovation in order to adjust to the environment, such as raw material (its scarcity or abundance) might have played an important role.

Fifth, not only are the prehistoric sites contiguous to present-day settlements, but continuity can be seen both in terms of stone tool typology and usage, as well as pottery, to the present. This is an indirect indication that possibly the prehistoric people of Garo Hills and the present occupants shared the same ideologies, in terms of ecological adaptations, socio-cultural adjustments (such as selection of a village or setting up of a village and its subsequent abandonment, agricultural practices, judicious use of crafts etc.), if not the same genes. However, it is clear that Neolithic pottery tradition not only shows a strong continuity but intrudes into Historic phase.

References

Ashraf, AA 1990, *Prehistoric Arunachal: a study of the prehistory and ethno-archaeology of Kamla Valley*, Directorate of Research, Arunachal Pradesh, Itanagar.

Ashraf, AA 2006, 'Autochthons of Meghalaya in anthropo-archaeological perspectives', *Humankind*, vol. 2, pp. 31-36.

Ashraf, AA 2010 (2004), *Stone age traditions of Meghalaya: a study of variation and continuity*, BAR international series 2176, Archaeopress, Oxford.

Ashraf, AA & Duarah, AG 2013/2014, 'Bambooti: a late Neolithic site in the foothills of southwestern Assam', *Bulletin of the Department of Anthropology*, vol. XV, pp. 23-32.

Bhuyan, G & Marak, Q 2014, 'The Paleolithic stone age conundrum in North-East India: a review', *Nrtattv: The Anthropology*, vol. 3/4, no. 5/6, pp. 67-81.

Deka, R 2015, *The ground lithic artifacts and spatial variation: a study based on collection from Northeast India*. Ph.D. thesis, Gauhati University.

Duarah, AG 2014, *Survival of prehistoric traditions in the foothills region of Southern Assam with reference to its highland counterpart*. Ph.D. thesis, Gauhati University.

Ghosh, AK 1978, 'What happens when cultural and biological adaptability of man fails? a case study with the Paleolithic period in the Garo hills' in *Cultural and biological adaptability of man with special reference to North-east India*, ed RK Kar, Department of Anthropology, Dibrugarh University, Dibrugarh, pp. 6-15.

Glover, IC & Presland, G 1985, 'Microliths in Indonesian flaked stone industries', in *Recent advances in Indo-Pacific prehistory: proceedings of the international symposium held at Poona,December 19-21, 1978*, eds VN Misra & P Bellwood, Oxford and IBH, pp. 185-196.

Goswami, MC & Bhagabati, AC 1959, 'A typological study of shouldered Celts from Rengchangiri (Garo Hills)', *Journal of the University of Gauhati*, vol. 12, no. 2, pp. 17-24.

Hazarika, M 2012, 'Lithic industries with Paleolithic elements in Northeast India', *Quaternary International*, vol. 269, pp. 48-58.

Indian Archaeology: A Review 1966-67, 1967-68, 1969-70, 1971-72, 1974-75, 1976-77, 1977-78, 1978-79, 1979-80, 1981-82, 1984-85, 1995-96.

Mahanta, HC 1995, *A study on the stone age cultures of Selbalgre*. Ph.D. thesis, Gauhati University.

Marak, Q 2005, 'The use of analogy in the interpretation of prehistoric cultures: a Study among the Garos of Garo hills, Meghalaya', *South Asian Anthropologist*, vol. 5, no. 2, pp. 167-172.

Marak, Q 2010, 'Stone age archaeology in the Garo hills: some issues', *Proceedings of NEIHA*, 31st Session, pp. 393-404.

Marak, Q 2012, 'Megaliths of North-East India', *A handbook of anthropology*, ed. TB Subba, Orient Blackswan, New Delhi.

Marak, Q 2014, 'Experimenting with stone tools: the Garo neoliths', in *50 years after Daojali Hading: emerging perspectives in the archaeology of Northeast India: essays in honour of Tarun Chandra Sharma*, eds T Jamir & M Hazarika, Research India Press, New Delhi, pp. 182-191.

Marak, Q 2016, *The art of making pottery in Garo Hills, Meghalaya*, Project report, Sangeet Natak Akademi, New Delhi.

Marak, Q 2017, 'Pottery technology in Garo hills: an ethnoarchaeological interpretation', in *Oral traditions, continuities and cultures in Northeastern India and beyond*, eds NY Modwel& S Sarkar, INTACH, New Delhi.

Marak, Q, Bhuyan, G, Meitei, AM & Sangma, TD 2017, *Misimagre: a prehistoric factory site from Garo Hills*, RIP, New Delhi.

Medhi, DK 1980, *Quaternary history of the Garo Hills, Meghalaya*. Ph.D. thesis, Deccan College Postgraduate and Research Institute, Poona.

Medhi, DK 1990, 'Prehistory of Assam', *Asian Perspectives*, vol. XXIX, no. 1, pp. 37-44.

Roy, SK 1977, *A study of ceramics from Neolithic to mediaeval period of Assam: an ethnoarchaeological approach*. Ph.D. thesis, Gauhati University.

Roy, SK 1981, 'Aspects of Neolithic agriculture and shifting cultivation, Garo Hills, Meghalaya', *Asian Perspective*, vol. XXIV, no. 2, pp. 193-219.

Sankalia, HD 1981, 'From history to prehistory in Assam', in *Cultural contours of India, part II*, ed VS Srivastava, Abhinav, Delhi, pp. 1-5.

Sharma, HC 1972, *Prehistoric archaeology: stone age cultures of Garo Hills, Meghalaya*. Ph.D. thesis, Gauhati University.

Sharma, HC 1975, 'Archaeological findings in Meghalaya', *Bulletin of Department of Anthropology, Gauhati University*, vol. IV, pp. 20-25.

Sharma, HC 1976, 'Stone age sites in Garo Hills, Meghalaya', *Bulletin of the Department of Anthropology, Gauhati University*, vol. V, pp. 82-93.

Sharma, HC 1988, 'Discovery of Hoabinhian cultural relics in Northeast India', in *Adaptation and other essays: proceedings of the archaeological conference*, eds NC Ghosh & S Chakrabarty, Research Publications, Santiniketan, Viswa Bharati, pp. 139-139.

Sharma, HC 2003, 'Prehistoric archaeology of North-East', in *The anthropology of North-East India*, eds TB. Subba & GC Ghosh, Orient Longman, New Delhi, pp. 11-30.

Sharma, HC & Roy, SK 1985, 'On the discovery of a pebble-tool industry in the Garo Hills, Meghalaya', in *Recent advances in Indo-Pacific Prehistory: proceedings of the international symposium held at Poona, December 19-21, 1978*, eds VN Misra & P Bellwood, Oxford and IBH, New Delhi, pp. 89-94.

Sharma, HC & Sharma, TC 1968, 'A report on the investigation into the prehistoric archaeology of the Garo hills', *Bulletin of the Department of Anthropology, Gauhati University*, vol. XVI-XVII, no. 2, pp. 73-84.

Sharma, HC & Sharma, TC 1971, 'On the discovery of stone age sites in Central Garo hills', *Journal of Assam Science Society*, vol. 14, no. 1, pp. 18-26.

Sharma, S 2013, 'Social information from lithic tools: the Neolithic tools of Garo hills, Meghalaya', *Pratna Samiksha: A Journal of Archaeology*, vol. 4, pp. 73-82.

Sharma, S & Singh, P 2017, 'Luminescence dating of Neolithic pottery in Northeast India', *Current Science*, vol. 113, no. [10 Aug 2017].

Sharma, TC 1967, 'Assam in prehistoric times', *Kamarupa Souvenir*, Assam Science Society, Gauhati, pp. 83-89.

Sharma, TC 1974, 'Recent archaeological discoveries in Northeastern India', *Puratattva*, vol. 7, pp. 17-19.

Sharma, TC 1980, 'Prehistoric archaeology in Northeastern India: a review in progress' in *Eastern Himalayas*, eds TC Sharma & DN Majumdar, Cosmo, New Delhi, pp. 102-135.

Sharma, TC 1981, 'Neolithic pattern of North-Eastern India' in *Madhu: recent researches in Indian Archaeology and art history*, ed. MS Nagaraja Rao, Agam Kala Prakashan, Delhi, pp. 41-52.

Sharma, TC 1985, 'Problems of the Upper Paleolithic in Northeastern India', in *Recent advances in Indo-Pacific prehistory: proceedings of the international symposium held at Poona, December 19-21, 1978*, eds. VN Misra & P Bellwood, Oxford and IBH, New Delhi, pp. 171-173.

Sharma, TC & OK Singh 1986, 'Studies on prehistoric archaeology of Garo hills', *Journal of Assam Science Society*, vol. 11, pp. 36-50.

Singh, OK 2008, *Pottery through the ages in Manipur*, Amusana Institute of Antiquarian studies, Imphal.

Sonowal, M 1987, *Studies on the flake and blade industries of the Garo Hills, Meghalaya*. Ph.D. thesis, Gauhati University.

Walker, GD 1931, 'Garo manufacturing of bark cloth', *Man*, vol. 27, no. 5, pp. 15-16.

Yondri, L 2006, 'A short review of the megalithic functions in Indonesia' in *Archaeology: Indonesian perspective: R. P. Soejono's festschrift*, eds T Simanjuntak, M Hisyam, B Prasetyo & TS Nastiti, LIPI press, Jakarta, pp. 295-302.

Chapter - 15

Rat-hole Mining in Meghalaya: Consequences and Concerns

— ***Geetika Ranjan***

Habitat and culture share a symbiotic relationship. In the present era of globalization which rings in the buzzwords like generalized culture (Henderson, 1966) or 'culture' as a common canopy term, the specificities in a culture become inconspicuous due to an emphasis on terms like global or universal.

What remains pertinent in a timeless scale is the fact that a region, an area determines and is determined by the culture of the population which inhabits that place. The natural setting of a place moulds the culture of that place and hence the problems and challenges of a region differs from the other regions. This is an important fact to reckon with in order to suitably address the challenges thrown up by a region, ignoring which may lead to more difficult consequences.

Against this backdrop, I shall put forth the issue of coal mining in the state of Meghalaya, one of the eight states of Northeast India.

We all know that geographical and cultural distance of the northeast from the so-called mainland India is an issue which continues to rake up concerns and debates around words like insurgency, autonomy, segregation, independent statehood or as in the case of Nagaland, independence from India. It is in the same vein and against this backdrop that the issue of coal mining in Meghalaya becomes pertinent to understand.

India is rich in minerals. Many states in India have a rich reservoir of coal. After India gained independence it was all set to meet the huge challenge

of being on its own feet. The focus came on the development of the basic industries in India in the early 1950s. This required massive, large-scale mining of coal and other metals. The huge energy needs of a populous country like India were being met by coal. Coal has been put to commercial use in India, since long past. After India became independent, the five-year plans gave special focus on increasing coal production. Different Governments implemented different policies towards the production, control, and usage of coal. Prime Minister late Mrs. Indira Gandhi nationalized coal mining, whereas years later the present Prime Minister, Mr. Narendra Modi changed this policy and encouraged denationalization, permitting private companies to mine coal for commercial purposes.

Looking at these regulations one realizes that these are apparently applicable at the national level in India but have little or no meaning when it comes to the tradition of coal mining in Meghalaya.

Meghalaya is rich in coal. 'The coal reserve in the state is estimated to be about 640 million tons but its production has been increasing at a snail's pace because mining is being carried on in an unscientific, unplanned manner.' (Tan et al., 2014: 652). A very large amount is exported to Bangladesh as well as too many parts of India. In India, there are two categories of coal - Gondwana coal and Tertiary coal. Meghalaya and other states of northeast India have rich deposits of sub-bituminous tertiary coal. It is used for different enterprises, as fuel for cement, bricks, tea, fertilizer industries.

Table 15.1: Estimated coal reserve in different districts of Meghalaya

Location Area (sq. km)	***Area (sq. km)***	***Reserve (in million tones)***
Khasi Hills		
Laitryngew.	31	2.738
Cherrapunji	36	19. 0
Laitduh	0.12	0.12
Mawbehlarkar	0.10	0.12
Mawsynram Rongsakham	Coal seams with average	0.30
Jathang and Mawsngi area	the thickness of 2.4 m	
Lumdidom	0.2	0.20
Langrin	Four seams with a thickness of 0.6, 1.21, 0.9 and 1.10 m	97.61
Pynursla- lyngkyrdem	2	0.50
Mawlong- Shella-Ishamati	8	9.0
Garo Hills West Darranggiri	47	127

(Contd...)

Siju	Coal seam about 11 km in strike length	125
Pendengru-Balphakram	13	107
Jaintia Hills		
Bapung	3 coal seams cover an area of 46	33.66
Lakadong, Umlatdoh	3	1.5
Sutnga	0.16	0.65
Jarain	2.8	1.1
Musiang Lamare		2.31
Loksi		3.6

(*Source:*neidatabank@hub.nic.in)http://www.moef.nic.in/sites/default/files/SoE%20report%20of%20Meghalaya_0.pdf

The Issue of Concern

Mining in Meghalaya is carried out in the most unscientific manner, causing harm to the environment as well as those working in this kind of mining endeavour. It is known as Rat-hole mining. Rat-hole mining in Meghalaya is controlled by private individuals. The State Government had no control over it. Lack of necessary checks that can come from the State has rendered the rat-hole mining in Meghalaya as an unsystematic, unregulated affair.

The act of mining, the post-mining exercise, as well as the management of the mined areas - all convey the poor, most unregulated and highly dangerous nature of this kind of mining. This is the reason why such a mining is considered illegal. In rat-hole mining, the method of extracting coal is a rather rudimentary one. In this kind of mining, the ground is first cleared of vegetation. Pits, rather holes or burrows are dug to ultimately reach the level of the coal. When the coal reserve inside the pits has been extracted horizontal holes are dug on the walls of the pits through which the labourer enters to reach the coal level. These holes (like rat made burrows) are so small (in some places, they are as small as 1-meter width) that a very slender built labourer can crawl inside the hole up to about hundred meters. This is a very difficult and risky work. Coal is extracted with hands and with traditional equipment. The labourer comes out on to the surface, carrying a basket or wheeled cart of coal. Huge heaps of coal can be seen on the ground at Sutunga area of Jaintia Hills waiting to be loaded on the trucks for trade.

The labourers working in the coal mines of Meghalaya are mostly migrants from Assam, Nepal, Bangladesh, and Bihar. The rat-hole mining is highly exploitative in nature as it engages children to carry out the extraction of coal from the risk-prone deep interiors of the mines. As the holes through which one has to crawl in order to extract coal are very narrow, children are

used to undertaking this activity. Impulse, an NGO estimates that around 70,000 children, in the age group of 7 to 17 years are working in these mines and there is no security of their lives (Impulse, 2012). This type of mining is illegal and is not registered. There is no security cover and the labourers carry out risky chores without any safety measures. Mine deaths are common.

The entire process of extracting coal entails risk to life. The labourer has to enter the slippery and fragile pits and extract coal through the dark tunnels. Death due to falls and asphyxiation occur. The poor labourers are seen working without proper footwear (like gumboots) and headgear. Fragile handrails of the wood made ladders are not dependable supports to assist the labourers in ascent and descent. The slippery ladders make the walk on them a highly precarious exercise and the situation becomes worse in the rainy season, which is quite a long one in Meghalaya. Deaths of the labourers or their loss of limbs are also caused due to caving in of the mines. Wooden pillar is used to prevent the mines from caving in, but these fall off very often.

Rat-hole mining has been in practice since long past in Meghalaya. Apart from endangering the lives of children and other workers working in the coal mines, the rat-hole mining has proved to be extremely detrimental for the environment - water sources, water bodies and overall fauna and flora of the vicinity where it is being practiced. This type of mining is being carried out without any Environment Clearance from the Ministry of Environment and Forest or without availing mining lease from concerned authority (Mohrmen, 2014). As stated earlier, rat-hole mining is totally unregulated. Not only the extraction of coal, but it's on surface management too speaks volumes about the unregulated manner in which the entire process is carried out. The coal which has been extracted is loosely piled up in the large expanse of the ground area has led to excessive pollution of air, water, and soil. Meghalaya has a rich forest cover, which is getting destroyed due to coal mining. Rat-hole mining is carried out in a poorly organized manner. The gravels, rocks, soil etc that has to be cleared in order to procure the coal, are left as unattended and unmanaged heaps near the coal mine pits, ruining the natural vegetation. Large-scale denudation of forest cover, scarcity of water, pollution of air, water and soil, and degradation of agricultural lands are some of the conspicuous environmental implications of coal mining in Jaintia Hills (Das Gupta, 1999). The green cover made by trees and shrubs is getting depleted due to mining. Studies bring out that coal mining has been detrimental for the environment badly affecting the vegetation, reducing the density of trees, shrubs, and herbs in the areas where this mining is being carried out (Sarma and Barik, 2011). While the hazards of rat-hole mining were being experienced by the workers working in this endeavour, as well as by the environment, a concerted

effort was made by the All Dimasa Students Union and the Dima Hasao District Committee for taking up this matter and for approaching the National Green Tribunal.

Commercial exploitation of coal in Meghalaya started in the Khasi Hills during the 19th century. Since most of the coal deposits were small and isolated and it was not amenable for scientific mining to be conducted in the organized sector and mining operations were left to the local miners to take up coal mining as a cottage industry. In due course of time, the tribal miners accepted coal mining as one of their customary rights (Directorate of Mineral Resource, 1992; cited in Sarma, 2005:2).

Coal mining practice in Meghalaya is being carried out without any environment clearance from the Ministry of Environment and Forest, which is a necessary step in the direction of ensuring the protection of the environment from mining hazards. In Meghalaya, coal mining is completely under the control of private individuals, the indigenous tribes - mainly Khasi and Jaintia. Meghalaya falls under the 6th Schedule of the Constitution of India, which grants major autonomy to the traditional institutions of these tribes. The natives claim that they are the sole authorities on the ownership and regulation of their land and its resources, a right which is ensured by the 6th Schedule of the Constitution of India. Thus, they are not bound by the Government as far as their land rights are concerned. They hold that ownership and utilization of land is their customary right and mining on their land is their prerogative. How they go about it is their concern entirely. This assertion kept coal mining in Meghalaya outside the purview of all mining regulations.

Due to the above-mentioned situation, coal mining has been carried out recklessly, in the most unscientific ways, driven by the single focus on maximum coal production. Mukhopadhyay (2013) clearly brings out the scenario of coal mining in Meghalaya. She mentions the reasons that attribute to the rapid unregulated depletion of coal. There is a huge demand for coal from Bangladesh and coal from Meghalaya is exported there. The other states in India are also demanding for coal as fuel in their growing industrial endeavours. Another reason for the hurried extraction of coal in Meghalaya is the pressure induced on the private coal mine owners by the State and non-State actors that have made the coal mine owners apprehensive of coal mining to be overtaken by the public sector.

The Sixth Schedule of the Constitution is many times seen as a protective shield by the indigenous mine owners in Meghalaya, there is a persistent realization that one cannot rule out the possibility that the Constitution may get amended and the Government may take over the ownership of the coal mines. Another 'driving force for rampant coal mining is poverty. Wherever

the landowner needs some emergency cash and expects that there may be coal, forest cover is cleared and a shaft of diameter varying from 3m to 10m is sunk. The hole is dug into the coal seam and goes deeper and deeper for several kilometers following the seam. These burrows or holes are big enough to accommodate just one person to crawl in with tools and basket or wheeled cart to carry out coal to the depots located near the main road' (Mukhopadhyay, 2013:4).

While some coal mine owners in Meghalaya speak of autonomy granted under the 6th Schedule, it is worth observing that the provisions of the Schedule are interpreted as per convenience. The Schedule explicitly mentions the need for licenses or leases for the purpose of prospecting for, or extraction of, mineral. Further, the lease does not give unrestrained freedom to anyone to carry out coal mining. All these factors lead to unrestrained, rampant unscientific coal mining in this area.

The Plight of Migrant Labourers

Coal mining in Meghalaya carried out by private coal mine owners is a less capital-intensive enterprise. Use of rudimentary methods for mining, without any proper paraphernalia for protecting the labourers from physical harm, as well as the sole authority of private landowners, who make the workers work on their terms and conditions, which are not in synchrony with the established coal mine working conditions, renders the whole exercise a rather cost-saving one.

Poverty is a big reason why labourers from near and far come to work in the coal mining industry of Meghalaya. They are mostly migrants from Nepal, Bangladesh and from other parts of India. Ethnographic studies (Upadhyay and Ranjan, 2014, 2016, 2017) carried on the Nepalese migrant workers in the Jaintia Hills of Meghalaya; reveal the plight of the Nepalese migrants from Nepal. They inform about the trauma they have to undergo not only while working in the coal mines, where they face a consistent risk of meeting frequent accidents, but also when they become victims of abuse and harassment by the border police when they cross the India-Nepal open border. There are frequent media reports on labourers losing their lives. The attraction for good money draws the people to work as labourers in these mines.

Working in the Meghalaya coal mines exposes the workers to dangers of different kinds. They do not have any security cover and the concept of getting a compensation for meeting accidents and loss of life does not function in their case. They are not covered under any labour laws. As the majority of the coal mine workers are migrants from outside Meghalaya, they are the vulnerable outsiders, very often facing threats to their lives in ethnic conflicts.

They have little or no say before the coal mafia - which represents a formidable nexus between muscle power and money power.

Ordinarily, mining techniques can be broadly divided into two, based on how coal is extracted under each. One is the surface mining and the other is the sub-surface or underground mining. The opencast mining entails surface mining and is a less risky method of mining, compared to the underground mining like the Rat-hole mining. The coal mining technique which is mostly employed in the open cast mining. It is carried out in a more scientific and regulated way than rat-hole mining. In open cast mining, the disposal of waste on the surface is done in a proper manner in order to prevent acid mine drainage. Here, the workers face lesser risk of meeting accidents and loss of life as they do not work deep inside the pits unlike in the case of underground mining, in which the worker has to go underground and face the risk of falling ill due to inhalation of toxic gases, which eventually leads to death of the worker. In underground mining exercises, frequent deaths of laborers are also caused due to caving in of the roofs of the mines.

Rat-hole mining and transportation of coal were banned in Meghalaya in 2014 on the orders of the National Green Tribunal. This was a major move in the direction of safeguarding human and environmental resources from the hazards of illegal mining. Voices of disapproval have been raised ever since. Mine owners, as well as their supporters, have been protesting against the ban, blaming the Government for taking away their customary rights on their land. The matter has become political and voices from ruling political leaders as well as from the aspiring ones are more concerned about garnering vote banks.

Post-ban scenario reveals that the ban has not been effective and clandestine coal mining activities are going on in the interiors of Meghalaya. In fact, there are reports which inform about the open flouting of the ban in some areas of Meghalaya. One report mentions:

> 'There is a rampant disregard to NGT guidelines. In spite of the ban, the law enforcers have failed to keep a check on coal mining related activities and NGT guidelines,' said CSWO President Agnes Kharshing who made a spot visit to West Jaintia Hills and West Khasi Hills district, 'We visited three places and we have seen that mining, transportation of overloaded coal in trucks is still going on'. Ms. Kharshing claimed further adding that the truckers are plying without proper documents and evading revenue of the state. She further alleged that the coal is being dumped anywhere and everywhere even near streams and river beds and is being sold openly on the national highway which is not allowed (The Northeast Today, 22 April 2017).

It was interesting to see the Bharatiya Janta Party (BJP) announcing the scrapping of the National Green Tribunal (The Northeast Today, 30 August 2017), before Meghalaya went to polls in February 2018. Keeping aside the political tug-of-war over the ban on rat-hole mining in Meghalaya, it is pertinent to look at the issue from a larger perspective. While it is undoubtedly, a much-needed step to put a stop to the illegal mining in Meghalaya, it is equally important, that a sustainable programme for rehabilitation of those who have lost their livelihoods in the account of the ban, should be made. Further, if the ban has to be made truly effective, in letter and spirit, then the Government has to look into its proper implementation.

References

Das Gupta, S 1999, *Studies on vegetal and microbiological processes in coal mining affected areas*. Ph.D. thesis, North Eastern Hill University, Shillong, India.

Tan, KG, Low, L & Tan, KY 2014, *Annual analysis of competitiveness, simulation studies and development perspective for 35 state and federal territories of India 2000 - 2010*, World Scientific Publishing Co., Singapore.

Henderson, RN 1966, 'Generalized cultures and evolutionary adaptability: a comparison of urban Efik and Ibo in Nigeria', *Ethnology*, vol. 5, no. 4, pp. 365-391.

Impulse 2012, An exploratory study of children engaged in Rat-hole Mining in the coal mines of Jaintia Hills district, Meghalaya.Available from:http://aeasouthasia.org/source/Study%20on%20Children%20Engaged%20in%20Rat%20Hole%20Mining.pdf.

Mohrmen, HH 2014, 'NGT ban on Rat Hole Mining: a blessing in disguise',*The Shillong Times* 28 April. Available from: http://www.theshillongtimes.com/2014/04/28/ngt-ban-on-rat-hole-mining-a-blessing-in-disguise/.

Mukhopadhyay, L 2013, 'Sustainable development - apath-dependent analysis to the Rat-hole coal mining in Jaintia Hills district, India'. Available from: https://economics.ucr.edu/repec/ucr/wpaper/13-06.pdf.

National Green Tribunal, Available from: http;//envfor.nic.in/rules-regulations/national-green-tribunal-ngt.

Sarma, K & Barik, SK 2011, 'Coal mining impact on vegetation of the Nokrek Biosphere Reserve, Meghalaya, India', *Biodiversity*, vol. 12, pp. 54–164.

Upadhyay, R & Ranjan, G 2016, 'Occupational risks in Mining: the case of Nepalese migrant workers in the coal mines of Jaintia Hills, Meghalaya', *Oriental Anthropologist*, vol. 16, no. 1, pp. 87-98.

Upadhyay, R & Ranjan, G 2017, 'Return of the Nepalese migrants working in the coal mines of Jaintia Hills, Meghalaya' in *Contemporary anthropological research in Eastern and North Eastern India*, ed S Sengupta, Gyan Publications, New Delhi, pp. 237-258.

Chapter - 16

Anthropology of Naming Culture among the Chakhesang Nagas

— Lhiwepe Therie and Nitul Kumar Gogoi

Introduction

The basic premise of identification for anything that must be communicated intelligibly is through 'names'. Though an arguably, very arbitrary connotation to view it under the prism of cultural diversity for an 'object' in question can often be made meaningful only through its usage. "The word *name* is often used to mean a term which can refer to anything, as when we say: '*Banana* is the name of the fruit,' or '*Murder* is the name of a crime'. In this sense, the word *name* is virtually synonymous with the word *noun*; indeed, in some languages, the same term can be used for both, e.g French *nom*" (Bright; 2003). Hence something that is given a name also should be understood in the cultural context. In this context, 'names' would be placed broadly in terms of 'proper noun' and more specifically to personnel's names. Borrowing the works of Tschaepe (2003), he cited Merleau-Ponty's work expounding, "... 'first-naming' is not only significant but performs a very specific function within language use that implies dynamics of power and identity insofar as the first name not only grants one a specific identity as a language user but also directs who that person is and will be through the name's physiognomy and reference to the world."

In locating the terrain of inquiry, an account can be observed from the official names being used to replace birth-given names or the social media names being used to personified themselves metaphorically. To question the validity of such names is often meted with the famous Shakespearean

colloquial expression of, 'What is in a name?'. A question often left open to many interpretations and repudiate the singular norm to understand names. This open the content or intent of 'naming' or 'names'. It allows one to posit questions on many levels; Does mere declaration of names on an official record changes the identity of an individual? Are 'names' just 'labels' to identify an individual? Does it reflect the relation or expression with the free world of individualistic-will? Does naming has any relationship with the societal perception or isolated to a certain degree of social control? An attempt will be made in this chapter to explore the naming culture among the Chakhesang Nagas and their names in relation to siblingship.

Research Area

The Nagaland State is the 16th State of the Indian Union formally recognized on 1st December 1963 and located at an approximate latitude of 25°6┐N and 27°4┐N and between the approximate longitudinal lines of 93°20┐E and 95°15┐ E. It is one of the seven sisters States of Northeast India which shares an international border with Myanmar in the East, Arunachal Pradesh and part of Assam bounds the north and Manipur in the south. Nagaland consists of 16 major tribes which are more or less recognized distinctly with the 11 administrative districts: Kohima is the home for Angami and Rengma, Mokokchung for Ao, Zunheboto for the Sumi, Peren for Zeliang, Kiphire for Sangtam and Tikhirs, Longleng for Phoms, Wokha for Lothas, Tuensang for Chang and Khaiumnugaim, Mon for Konyaks. Dimapur as an urban place is a mixture of all tribes but pre-dominantly Sumi, and lastly Phek for the Chakhesang and the Pochury.

The Chakhesang inhabiting in Phek district is the research area; which is one of the major tribes of Nagaland with a population of 1,63,418 comprising of 83,743 males and 79,675 females at the sex ratio of 951 females per 1000 males. This constitutes 8.26 per cent of the total population of Nagaland spreading across 2026 sq. km area and situated 1524 meters above sea level. The average literacy rate stands at 78.05 per cent in the 2011 census. For a very long time, the Chakhesangs were identified as the Eastern Angami in the colonial writings and it is only in 1946 the tribe came to be recognized as a separate tribe. And on 21st December 1973 a separate district, Phek district was carved out of Kohima to home the Chakhesangs and the Pochury. The district is bounded by Myanmar in the east, Kohima in the west, Zunheboto, and Kiphire in the north and Manipur in the south. The term 'Chakhesang' is a combination of three initials which bears its linguistic significance in identifying the words: *Cha* derived from *Chokri*, *Khe* from *Khezha or Kuzha* and *Sang* from *Sangtam.*

The meaning of Names among the Chakhesang Nagas

To establish the domain of 'names' among the Chakhesang Nagas, the two major linguistic sub-tribe: the Chokri and the Khezha, is considered. In this regard, the relation of the word to its exclusivity and the combination of words to make it meaningful is engaged to make sense of 'names'. Word in itself may not produce the desired meaning while giving a name '...unless these are meaningfully combined to form what we called words in a language. These words represent the form of the language concerned. But words which appear as one may be constituted by more than one or more than one smaller component's (Misra: 2000-83). Based on the meaningful combination of words it further percolates down to translate the perceptive worldview in which an ethnic group is set. For example, the words like Ocean or Sea is often left out in the vocabulary of the Chakhesang as no large body of water is heard or perceived prior to the advancement of communication. So, a rather, very generic term, *dzukuzho* mildly translates as 'big water' is used to refer to any large body of water. Here the reference is made just to connote the relation between words and perception of worldview. 'The worldview or cosmology of a people reflects how they think, visualize, conceptualize, and interpret the world or universe in which they live. A people's worldview gives them a sense of direction and purpose' (Mmadike: 2014-12). This postulates an axiomatic basis upon which spatiotemporal variation also needs to be considered in understanding the 'naming culture'.

In analyzing the 'naming culture' among the Chakhesang Nagas, the practices followed after the birth of the child will be discussed briefly. A child, upon his/her birth, is usually named within a week's (0-7 days) time. The names are given by the parents or elder members of the family. This 'first-given' name is usually retained by the child throughout his or her lifetime. The norm of naming is associated with the Chakhesang Nagas as the community endorses that 'names of a child born' be given in one's own dialect i.e Chokri or Khezha. The verbal reminder for naming children in one's own dialect has been given time and again during a public gathering held by the apex civil society of the Chakhesang community called The Chakhesang Public Organisation. A day is set to name the child in which an elder member of the family or well-wisher or a church leader is invited to pray for the new member of the family over lunch or dinner. Also, a small token of the offering is given to the church seeking the prayer of the congregation as the child finds its place as a member of the church. This rite of passage allows the child to gain recognition and starts existing as a member of the community.

For categorizing the identity of gender through distinct social constructed names even the Chakhesang Nagas share its own uniqueness in the universal pattern of categorization, as the names given to male and female marks a

clear classification. In its morphology, names have suffix being added allowing such identification. '-le', '-lu', '-no', '-ne' or '-u' are often the general suffix used in female names. Some of the samples of names are *Nutane, Huvesalu, Wenyile, Dzuthono or 'Kehe-u'*. Male names usually do not have a suffix *Nuta, Huvesa, Wenyi, Dzutho* or *Kehe*. The same name with exact meaning can be used for both male and female, however, in case of female the suffix at the end of the name suggests the category of gender.

In illustrating the significance of names among siblingship, the case of the first author's siblings is accounted. The decoding of syllables for each 'names' produces different meanings, however, the true essence of the 'names' can be unraveled only with the combination of those syllables. The sequence of the procreational chain in terms of birth is established below with translation of each syllable as well as the intended meaning from first born till the fifth child.

1st born child! *Chiekute*!*Chie+Ku+Te* !Learn + Strong+ Walk ! 'Walk with understanding and strength '

2nd born child! Neiwetso-u ! *Nei+We+ Tso-u* ! Happy + Good + End ! 'and Happiness and goodness follow on until the end '

3rd born child! Lhiwepe ! Lhi+We+Pe ! Live+ Good+ Add ! 'and become better as you live on'

4th born child! Tekhewe ! *Tekhe + We* ! Blessing+ Good ! 'and blessings and goodness enrich you'

5th born child! Wedie ! *We+Die*! Good + Big ! 'and may goodness and greatness follow through'

In making sense of these names mentioned above, the meaning of names is elaborated and represented in a larger translation with regard to siblings. The 1st child marks the point of an origin upon with the meaning of the 2nd born child is appended to produce a larger meaning. *In walking with understanding and strength, happiness and goodness must follow till the end.* As we extract the meaning of the 3rd born child's name we find that it further adds meaning to the siblings- that all of the born siblings must *become better as they live on*. The 4th born child then extends the *blessings being endowed* to all the siblings through the name. Lastly, the 5th sibling concludes with the larger expression of incorporating all the siblings that achieving *goodness and greatness be upon all the siblings till the end*.

The meaning of the names may not always necessarily have a connection and we do not in any way claim that this is exclusive; that all procreational siblings among the Chakhesang Nagas will bear a correlation with each other. In fact, the names may be individual-centered or event specific. However, we find that there is a larger pattern of 'naming processes' in terms of siblingship.

Names like *Weri or Vera, Riwe, Rayi, Rapfü* or in case of feminine *Riwe-u or Ravelu* are the names often given to the first-born child and this broad translation of the names are given below:

Rite → *Ri+ Te*→ Lead + Walk → Leading Ahead,
Rayi→ *Ra+Yi*→ Lead Ahead,
Rapfü→ *Ra + Pfü* → Lead + Win→ Lead and Win,
Vera→ *Ve + Ra*→ Good + Lead → Be victorious and lead

Mthobeli Guma while studying the meaning of names among the Basotho found the significant relation between names and personhood and posited '... it is believed that a given name does not only serve as an identity but also determines the type of person the individual will be. Names are believed to have an influence on the character of the bearer' (Guma: 2001). Similarly, even among the Chakhesang Nagas, the role of leading is given to the 1st born child, which is expected of him/her to be reflected in their character, and expectation of the next child being born is to follow suit. On account of names being given to the 2nd born child which manifest the role of leading challenges the 'name' of the 1st born child. As such this creates a competition and the conflict in its meaningful quest for assuming the best among siblingship. The second siblings usually do not get this name as it competes with the meanings of the first-born child.

The composition of names also encompasses the ambit of human emotions and thrives to satisfy one's psychological needs. The Chakhesang Nagas also give names denoting events or beliefs. The name of the first author's mother denotes an event which serves as a reminder of the past tragedy and an assurance to lead ahead with life. At the time of her birth, a tragedy be fell their family. The only brother who was aged about four harvests old (4-5 years old) passed away after having contracted a viral disease. Her parents were devastated and given that he was the sole heir to their family legacy, living in a patriarch society. Her parents were still grieving the loss of their son when she was born. So one of the close elders of the family named her *Zumotsolu* → *Zu+ Mo +Tsolu* → Ergo (thereon) + oblivious + End → *'From there on, be oblivious and live on until the end.'* The broad translation of this name captures the sad event. The consolation is intended to find peace and solace with her birth by giving her the name. The fallen calamity on her family is somehow made to find acceptance with her name 'from here on', it signifies a new beginning and the prospect of moving forward, 'be oblivious' in this context mildly translates as being unaware of the pain and not the event, and 'live on till the end' signifying the better days ahead of life. Another name which, as Guma (Guma: 2001) puts it, as a 'recording system' is *Kekhangulo or Kuchongoyi* → *a prayer answered* is one that indicates the action of the past. This name is usually given by parents or family members

who have earnestly asked or longed for a child or of a specific gender either male or female. It reflects the personality of the past action and does not bear the meaning of the specific character. However, the earnest prayers of the parents are considered an action inexplicable to the human understanding which is accorded as significant in the personal life.

The Naga political movement and the advent of Christianity are two events which need to be incorporated if one were to understand any ethnic group of Nagaland. In context, the latter underscores the purpose of understanding even the 'naming culture' among the Chakhesang Nagas. Concomitantly with the arrival of Christianity the biblical names like Andrew, John, David, Esther, Joseph, Daniel, Ruth, Samson, Jonah, Moses among others were introduced. In addition to this, the transliterated biblical names in local dialects like Johan, Mosa, Jakob, Felica among others were also used in the naming culture. These names were given derived from the biblical status of faith, love and other attributes represented in the holy book. The idea of the sacrament that personal qualities are being acquired through these names is denoted. It also indicates a transformation in the cultural fabric where faith in the divine God is given importance.

Conclusion

Though much of the 'naming culture' process and relationship with other kinship, surnames or supernatural relationship has not being mentioned in this chapter, it provides a glimpse to the question of 'What is in a name?'. Without disqualifying the intent of meanings behind 'names' the notion of exploration in the naming culture is introduced. The phrases like *'Zeshii pfo da shii* or *Piizamujute* 'mildly translates as 'he/she has taken after her name' or *'Po-Zu kuluve' or 'Pfu-Zuu lido we'* mildly translates as 'father and mother have good insights/idea' are often heard when names of children are heard. This indicates that names are not the only reflection of the individual whose personhood is observed but even the parent's cognition ability to decipher the world also appears. The names defining the person are also used to educate the children *'Eza mujumoshi ho/ Eze medji mo shiidiro'* translate as *'You have to follow your name'*. These phrases are used to teach a child or at times even adult to correct them of their mistakes by posing the meaning of names in relation with their actions which needs to be corrected. It focuses our attention towards the training process of an individual in which the trivial matters of life are also considered to 'names' being given. The socially constructed distinction of engendered names is categorized with marked clarity just as it is expected for man and woman to behave in their social life. This further constitutes from individual species to a siblingship of the naming process. A bond of relationship between family is established where the intended meaning of names is placed down to all the children.

The notion of 'names' may appear incoherent to some culture or individuals who are less associated with their core ethnic group. However, to the Chakhesang Nagas, a frame of 'value' to names is situated in which the condition is premised upon the identity that one asserts-in this case of the Chakhesang and the Christianity. 'Names' in themselves may project a gaze of 'devaluation', a sense of rebellion if postulated outside of one's free-thinking; however, the shaping and reshaping of coherent meaning is provided with an affiliation to a larger collectivity, to siblingship, to events, to phenomena, to beliefs and so on. A dialogue is created between the imaginations of the personhood with the manifestation of the character through names. This dialogue creates a roadmap in which the desired character of 'personhood' is imagined by the social unit, endorsing a certain set of social behaviour from the individual.

References

Bright, W 2003, *What is a name? reflections on onomastics, language, and linguistics*, pp. 4.4: 669-681, delivered as a lecture at the Institute of Linguistics, Academia Sinica on 24 February 2003.

Guma, M 2001, 'The cultural meaning of names among Basotho of Southern Africa: a historical and linguistic analysis', *Nordic Journal of African Studies*, vol. 10, no. 3, pp. 265-279.

Misra, KK 2000, *Textbook of anthropological linguistics*, Concept Publishing Company, New Delhi.

Mmadike, IB 2014, 'Anthropolinguistics study of Álá names in Igbo', *ISOR-Journal of Humanities and Social Sciences(ISOR-JHSS)*, vol. 19, no. 10, ver. IV, pp. 11-19.

Tschaepe, MD 2003, *Halo of identity: the significance of first names and naming*, Janus Head, Trivium Publications, Pittsburgh, PA, pp. 67-78.

Chapter - 17

From History to Memory: Religion, State and Traditional Crafts in Sikkim, India

— Sumahan Bandyopadhyay

Sikkim is resplendent as a jewel in the crown of Northeastern states of India. This is not only because of her exquisite natural beauty but also due to her colourful, both literally and metaphorically, presence with the treasure of rich cultural heritage. Sikkim is known as *Beyal Demazong* i.e the land of hidden treasure. This is really so in all senses. The name Sikkim is said to be derived from two words- *su* means new and *khim* means habitat. This appellation was given by the Gorkhas, who invaded Sikkim in 1780 A.D.

Sikkim became the 22nd state of India following 38th amendment of the Constitution of India in 1975 (Datta, 1991; Shukla, 1976). Now the state has a population of 610,577 (2011 Census, Government of India) sprawling over an area of 7,096 square Kilometers. The state is divided into four districts having a mountainous terrain and dense forest dissected by rivers and their tributaries. The third highest mountain peak in the world, Mt. Khangchendzonga (Kanchenjunga) is also located in this state. The population of the state is comprised mostly of the Lepchas, the Bhutias and the Nepalese who are the largest ethnic group in the state (Risley, 1985; Singh, 1993)[1]. Sikkim presents diverse ecological conditions sometimes very harsh to human existence (Bhasin, 1989). The population density is only 86 per sq.km in this state, compared to the national average of 382 individuals per sq.km.

Before accession to Indian state, Sikkim was ruled by the kings who had the title of *Chogyal,* meaning religious king[2]. The first Chogyal Phutsong Namgyal, belonging to immigrant Bhutia community from Tibet, was crowned in Yuksum in West Sikkim by three lamas headed by Lhatsun

Chenpo in 1642 A.D. This incident at one hand established monarchy in Sikkim, on the other it was followed by the spread of Tibetan Buddhism in the state which was quite conspicuously under the influence of Bon religion (Roy Burman, 1979; Bansal, 1994). Immediately after that incident, the first monastery in Sikkim was set up at Sangagholing in 1649 A.D. (Waddell, 1894). Lama Lhatsunis is held in high esteem by the Sikkimese. He played a great role in establishing Lamaism in Sikkim by consecrating the Chogyal of Sikkim. Until the end of kingship in Sikkim, the ritual of coronation was done by the head lama of the Pemayangtse monastery of Nyingmapa sect to which Lhatsun belonged[3]. Lhatsun became a legendary figure in Sikkimese oral tradition because of the unbelievable feats and supernatural power he was believed to have wielded. Still, the image of Lhatsun is seen in the Nyingmapa monasteries by the side of the image of Guru Rinpoche who is said to have visited the territory in the eighth century and is considered to be one of the great masters of Lamaism. The small clay idol of Lhatsun Chenpo (mostly coloured in green) is sold in the market as a piece of craft. Thus, the craftwork in Sikkim is very much rooted in the legends and history of the land.

The examples of Sikkimese workmanship, as exemplified by their folk art are pervasive in their daily life as well as in the religious domain. From the known sources it is established that the Lepchas were the earliest inhabitants of the state. Then the Bhutias came. They descended from Tibet where they were already indoctrinated to the Buddhism. The Lepchas also came under the influence of Buddhism in spite of keeping a living practice of their traditional tribal religion. Buddhism became divided into various sects. The major sects were *Nyingmapa* and *Gelukpa*. The former grewupin Sikkim under royal patronage as the predominant sect. These sects of Buddhism centered on the monastery (*gonpa,* also called *gompa*). In different parts of the state, hundreds of *gonpa* were set up. The monastery buildings, large or small constitute a regular feature of the Sikkimese culture and mostly located in the solitude of hilltop flanked by tall trees. The tortuous road that spirals around the hill is hemmed with poles in which flags of different colours flutter in the strong wind of the hills. The buildings and its material objects bear the marks of folk artistic skill of the people. In the monastery, the main building has a large hall which is the hub of ritual activities. There is an altar of Buddhist pantheon attached to the wall of the hall. This hall can be said a living museum of arts and crafts inspired by Buddhism. The Sikkimese people who follow Buddhism keep a separate space inside their house with a wooden altar of Buddhist deities which are worshipped daily. All their ritual activities and major festivals follow Tibetan Buddhist calendar. The Buddhism here through its monastic tradition plays an important role in the perpetuation of the craft tradition. However, the craft tradition of Sikkim has gone much beyond the confines of the monastery.

A craft tradition may have a close relationship with a particular region due to its concentration in the said region. One prominent example is Kashmir (Savasere, 2010). In Kashmir, the craft of weaving has been described as urban activity (ibid). There were certain clusters in the urban areas where the craftsmen used to reside. In Sikkim craft cannot be said to be an urban activity. Instead, it grew centered on the monasteries. It can be equated with a 'territorialization of heritage' (Butler, 2006). There was designated *lama* (Buddhist monks) called *lharipa* who were specialist craftsmen, but some members of the Lepcha and Bhutia communities acquired skill in craft works. They used to practice these craft work to earn their livelihoods. On the other hand, the lamas were trained in various crafts for use in the monastery, including a painting of *thanka*, mask making, wood carving etc. The crafts that flourished under the patronage of monasteries (originally following religious prescriptions, and later with active support from the government) came out of the confines of the monastery into the market as art objects. This trajectory of development of production of craft objects depicts the transformation of craft from religious object to art object. This process which started in the mid-twentieth century gathered momentum in the post-annexation era when the tradition was recast in the mould of folk art relating to the Sikkimese ethnic identity. In this context, the monastery had a great role in keeping the tradition alive, and it continues to do so since craft objects like the *phumpo, kalling, gyalling*, etc. are still used only for the ritual purpose in the monastery. Now we can see two parallel institutionalized centers for craft productions: one perpetuated by the monastery, another by the state.

Katter (1995) has mentioned that there is an inherent connectedness between or among the objects and its makers and perceivers. Craft represents the work of individuals who are connected with the community (Staub, 1988). The craft objects express the values shared within a specific community. The gendered worlds of men and women may be defined with reference to the particular craft work. In Sikkim, mask-making is associated with male craft worker, whereas the weaving is a feminine activity. Katter (*ibid*) has also studied what happens to the crafts when they are exposed to the global market and different cultures. She concludes that the forms, materials, and themes represented in the craft tradition are influenced by the contact culture. Besides region, craft tradition is often community specific. In India, there are a number of tribal and non-tribal communities who practice characteristic craft work. Dasgupta (2012) describes Ghadwa metal craftsmen of Bastar region of central India and mentions that the traditional art of the Ghadwa responds to the market very flexible. These *dokra* artisans of Bastar have brought changes in the traditional form of objects and have been producing new objects like candle stands, etc. These attract the tourist's outsiders and collectors who appreciate them and purchase them at a high

price. Meanwhile, the Ashanti tribe is famous for goldwork, silk weaving, brass casting, wood carving, etc. These were originally developed by regal and palace organization (Rattray, 1924; Johnson, 1979). Johnson (1979) has mentioned that modernization has brought many adverse effects on the Ashanti craft.

Unlike these above examples, the craft production in Sikkim shows a different trend. Here the craft production is traditionally not an individual activity for the market, since before the exposure of Sikkim to the outside market forces; the craft production was limited to the demands of the monastery and domestic consumers living locally around the monastery. If we dig still deeper into the archaeology of craft works in this state, we notice that the crafts produced the visuals engage with an ideology of Tibetan Buddhism that had gained access into the country inhabited by a multitude of ethnic groups. Here the craft played a unifying role in bringing the diverse groups together, both materially and symbolically (Waddell, 1972). This was replicated among the Tibetan refugees that had been a diasporic population in many parts of the world (Korom, 1997). Korom (1997) dealt with the Tibetans who were in exile with the Dalai Lama and struggled for existence. In this regard, their craft has become a tool of their cultural adaptation or adjustment[4]. Korom wrote:

> '...Tibetans artists and performers utilize their aesthetic skills to negotiate their identities in exile...' (Korom, 1997: 4).

Therefore, it cannot be blankly said that the monasteries perpetuated the craft traditions, but also that craft has also played a substantial role in the spread and establishment of monasteries in Sikkim. This importance of craft was later realized by the state with the growth of heritage boom and it provided the state with an opportunity to reframe its authority through this 'secular religion' that heritage is sometimes called (c.f. Horne, 1984; Duncan, 1995). One may have a shadow of an Althusserian paradigm of state apparatus on the craft production (Butler, 2006). Thus, the craft in Sikkim has performed a multitude of roles. It is perpetuated by the monastery and later transmuted through the state. Again and again, it has helped its sustaining institutions to survive. Thus, the craft should not be seen in a lineal trajectory, but rather that its development and spread is linked with the changing ideology of economy, identity, and state.

Craft

The word craft is said to be derived from the Old Norse word meaning strength and a craftsman is one who is a practitioner of manual skill (Chartland and Chartland, 1988). Valentine (1973:7), remarks that '... anything which involves using the hands can legitimately be called a craft.' Often the words

folk art and handicraft are used interchangeably (Gangopadhyay, c.f. Ghosh, 2013:15). For Henry Glassie (2000), this domain of craft works has been broadened to include many new hitherto 'non-traditional' creations under the name traditional art, also ethnographic art (Rose, 1990; Rossitto, 1994). This may also be termed 'ethnological art' as mentioned by Hazel (1963). In essence, the craft tradition of Sikkim bears semblance to the all the categories of classification. However, one should notice the difference in the focus on a particular aspect of this aesthetic material expression in these different terminological exercises. When the folklorist studies the particular form, then the preferred appellation is folk art or folk craft, which is handicraft in common parlance, though by handicraft both traditional and non-traditional craft work is meant. But the word tradition here takes up a negotiated meaning, as apparent from Glassie's study. Glassie included the idol makers, pottery, cane mat makers, metal craftsmen, *jamdani* cloth weavers along with the pictures as seen on the body of the rickshaw and the truck in his category of traditional art. The last examples of this art can only be meaningfully accommodated in this category if we try to understand the form and theme of art as embedded in the socio-religious context in which they occur. We shall return to these issues in a more rounded manner after an attempt to classify the craft works found in the monasteries in Sikkim with some concomitant extensions to the household.

The craft of the Sikkimese people can be divided on the basis of various criteria. A common approach to such classification is the generic divisions (Chakraborty, 2011). In such classifications, the craft items have been classified into folk paintings, metal crafts, bamboo, cane and jute art, clay craft, wooden craft, and weaving. In the present study, I have considered multiple bases in classifying the crafts. The bases include materials used in the production of the craft items, purpose or functions or use of the craft and the context of the production and nature of the craft. The raw materials that are used are wood, metal, fabric/cloth, paper, clay, paint, conch, organic substances. This classification results in the following:

1. Wooden Craft: Mask, *chesum (*altar of the gods and goddesses), *chokse* (small table), *chentu* (central table), *draguresan* (wood carved dragon bird), *tashitagey* (eight auspicious signs), *nga* (small drum).
2. Metal craft: *Radung* (large flute), *gyalling* (flute), *ghanti* (bell), *ting* (bowl), *mendekhorlo* (dish), *phumpo* (jar), *mera* (small decorated brass bowl for offering water to the gods and goddesses), *bajra* (literally meaning thunderbolt, it is the like scepter carried about by head lama).
3. Cloth/Fabric-made Craft: *Du* (cylindrical decorative flag found hanging from the ceiling in the main hall of the monastery), *pheney* (decorative flag), mask, *gyaltsen* (flag), *thanka.*

4. Papercraft: Mask
5. Craft made of organic material: *Kalling* (a flute made from shin bone of human), *nga* (small drum covered with animal skin),
6. Clay craft: Mask, idol
7. Conch shell craft: *Dhung* (conch shell flute)

Besides these are also *torma* from rice powder mixed with vegetable oil. The crafts in the monasteries can be classified on the basis of their function or purpose or use. This classification runs as the following:

1. Decorative craft objects: *Thanka, torma,* paintings on the wall, *du, phney, draguchesum,draguresan, tashitagey.*
2. Musical instruments: *Gyalling, kalling, radung, dhung, ghanti, nga,* cymbal.
3. Utilitarian objects: *Ting, phumpo, mendekhorlo.*
4. Symbolic objects: *Bajra,* a prayer wheel.

The objects can also be classified on sacred –secular level that is on the basis of their ritualistic use. Accordingly, there are some objects which can be used only in ritual services. *Torma, ting, bajra* etc fall in this category. The things that have non-ritual use include *chesum, chokse,* and *tue* of different types. Certain objects exist which can be used both for ritual and non-ritual purposes. *Thanka* and masks are included in this category. In this connection, it must be mentioned that the above classification shows some overlapping and mainly an etic one. For example, the objects that we have placed under the category of decorative ones bear a deep religious significance. The *lharipa* is the designated lama for the craft works in the monastery. The meaning of this term is a painter of god. Therefore, the decoration is not the actual purpose of the craftwork it has important ritual connotations. Noted artist and scholar Meera Mukherjee writes about her visit to Tabo monastery. She stated

> The Lamas paint *Tankas* here. They are painted on cloth tightly stretched on wooden frames. The ...Painting these *Tankas* is a way of attaining 'Nirvana'. Monks used these *Tankas* as a medium of '*Dhyan*' (Mukherjee, 1994:17).

From the nature of the craft objects, these may be further of two major types:

1. Simple craft: Here the craft is made of a single material like wood or metal. The wooden mask or wood carving, metal bowl, *ghanti, dhung* fall in this category.
2. Composite Craft: When more than one material is used in the making of the craft object then it is composite craft. *Kalling, thanka,* idol are examples of this type of craft.

From the above discussion, it is quite clear that craft tradition of Sikkim has flourished with an active association with the monastery. The monastery played the role of a cradle where the craft tradition was nurtured and protected under the sacred spell of the monastery, as the lamas doing the craftwork do not consider its commercial operation, but something that gives religious merit. Under this protective enclosure, the craft has been kept unaffected for centuries. In the second phase, the government took initiative to protect and spread crafts of the state. Now the craft work is passing through the third phase of its development in Sikkim. In this phase market and media are playing a crucial role. These changing phases can well be understood from the following case study describing three generations of craftsmen.

'D.B. (M/45) lives in the Tinchim village in the North Sikkim district. He lives with his wife, daughters and son S.B. His father Dr. B is an octogenarian lama in the Phodong Monastery which is located nearby. D.B was born in Tibet and inducted into lamahood at a very early age. He is a master craftsman who has impeccable skill in wood carving. He is also revered by the people for his supernatural power as the people in the village believe that he can stop the rain.

D.B. works as craft instructor in the government craft center in Gangtok. He is a master of wood carving. He has learned this craft from his father. However, he could not acquire all his father had been able to instruct. Therefore, his father has decided to teach all he knows to his grandson S.B. S.B. a mere child, is very fond of his grandfather. His family members and relations believe that the child is being grown up to emulate his grandfather' (Bandyopadhyay, 2014: 80).

The case study does not end here. But I could collect this much in 1999. Twelve years after this fieldwork when I visited Sikkim for the second time, I could not meet S.B. However, I could talk with D.B. By this time D.B.'s father passed away. S.B. has grown up into adolescence. But I was eager to know about him. This opportunity suddenly came when I was sent a documentary for review. This documentary was shot for a period of nine years. When the first shot was taken for this film, I happened to be present there as an expert in the team. In the documentary, there is an interview of young S.B. I would add the sequel to the earlier case study from this documentary (Bandyopadhyay, 2014).

> 'S.B. is grown up as a lama. He wears monk's robe while in the village. However, when he goes outside, he sports trendy clothes. He goes to disco. He has a girlfriend. His room is packed with the posters of Bollywood and Hollywood stars. He buys a gift for his girlfriend from Bodhgaya where he visits on the pretext of last rites for his departed grandfather. But he does not see any contradictions in his activities.

Because he believes that Buddhism is about the deep faith one nurtures at the core one's heart. It has nothing to do with the personal life of an individual. He is of opinion that the attitude of the people has totally changed today. The austerity and uninterrupted meditation of yesteryears are not possible today. Therefore, it is not possible now to become one like his grandfather.' (Bandyopadhyay, 2014: 80-81).

The above case study illustrates the process and changes in craftwork.

(i) The lamas used to expertise in craft work.

(ii) Monastery used to play an important role in the perpetuation of the craft by making arrangement for the training of craft work, commissioning craft work on behalf of the monastery.

(iii) The handing down of tradition followed the family line from father to son and then to grandson;

(iv) The craftwork ultimately did not remain confined to the family only, DD took service in the government training center. Here he used to impart knowledge of craft that he has acquired from his father.

(v) The attitude of people has changed with regard to Buddhist teaching the secular and sacred worlds have been overlapping yet separately conceived by people in their daily practice.

We understand the implications of this change of attitude in their innovative modification of the craft items in the government-run craft centers. So, two sets of agencies are now working towards the perpetuation of the craft objects – one represented by the monastery and another by the government-funded institutes.

Monastery and its Role

A monastery is called *gonpa* or *gompa* in Sikkim. The meaning of the word *gonpa* is the solitary place. Actually, it is a place for meditation for the lamas. The monastery at a minimum must be a building with a large central hall in which the Buddhist pantheon is ensconced on an altar attached to the wall of one side and elevated from the ground. In front of this altar, there are wooden seats in two rows meant for the lamas who regularly attend the ritual service in the monastery. Along with the main building of the monastery, there are some other buildings used for different purposes like hostels and school for the apprentice lama, lama quarters, storerooms etc. In 1894, Waddell reported that there were thirty-five monasteries in Sikkim (Waddell,1894). According to Kandell and Sailsbury (1971), the number of monasteries in Sikkim is sixty-seven. Dasgupta et al. (2014) gave us a list of seventy monasteries in Sikkim. However, popular travel guide (1991) returns

the number of the monastery in Sikkim as one hundred and forty (Dasgupta et al., 2014).

Before the entry of Buddhism to Tibet in fifth century A.D., the popular religion of Tibet was *Pon* or *Bon*. It was a shamanistic religion with beliefs in numerous spirits. Monasteries were also present in *pon* religion. Charles Bell visited one such Ponist monastery and found many similarities with the later Buddhist monasteries. It is said that Guru Padma Sambhav (Guru Rimpoche) built the first monastery at Samye, thirty miles away from Lhasa sometime during mid-seventh century A.D. (Roy Burman,1979). 'Ethnographic Tibet was larger than the political Tibet' and Sikkim was very much a part of this Tibet (Roy Burman, 1979). Tibetan Buddhism spread to Sikkim much earlier than the formal enthronement of Chogyal (the title of Sikkim king) in the seventeenth century. Mukherjee (1994) made a very important comment in this regard. Her view was that art played an important role in the spread of Buddhism.

> 'It is my impression that the artisans were engaged in the spread of Buddhism through the medium of art' (Mukherjee, 1994: 9).
>
> She added that:
>
> 'With the spread of Buddhism in India, Burma, Siam, Indonesia, China, Korea, Japan, and Central Asia, man's material surroundings have been transformed into great forms of art. In wood, in clay and ceramics, in stone, in metal, in lacquer, in silk, cotton, bamboo, horn, bones and such other mediums, form massive structures and figures down to the tiniest objects of daily use, have been created' (ibid).

So, it can be said that art has an important place in the Buddhist ethos. In the monastery, the lamas used to get training in craftsmanship. They are even allowed to earn their bread by doing craftwork. I met a lama in the Pemayangste monastery who was an expert painter and also works outside the monastery. In fact, in the Tibetan form of Buddhism, trading and other services to the layman outside the monastery are not banned for the lamas. Craftsmen monks certainly enjoy a higher status than the lay craftsmen. The craftsmen often possess multiple skills in crafts work. For example, Roy Burman (1979) wrote that the carpenter is also a skilled painter, builder, and calligrapher. However, metal craft work is not considered a respected profession as it is associated with the making of weapons. Therefore, the metal craftsmanship is mostly occupied by the Nepalese. In Sikkim, we also come across Nepali metal craftsmen called *gara* who prepare the metal utensils and musical instruments for the monasteries.

Tibetan Buddhism in Sikkim is divided into a number of sects. The main sects are *Ninmapa* (old unreformed sect, also spelled as *Nyngmapa*),

Kargyupa (semi-reformed sect) and *Gelukpa* (reformed sect). *Ninmapa* sect has predominance in Sikkim. The headquarters of this sect is a Pemayangste monastery. Each sect has their own principal deities, the hierarchy of lamas, architectural styles, characteristic attire or robe including the difference in their hat, and ritual services. The organizational structure of the monastery as mentioned earlier is definite and codified. In the main prayer hall of the *gonpa*, the seats of the lamas are arranged according to their status in the monastery order. This also reflects the organizational structure of the monastery. In *Ninmapa* monastery, the spiritual head of the monastery is called *Dorji Lobpen. Om-dze* or *udze*, the choir leader or precentor comes next to him. The organizational structure can be presented in the following table:

Table 17.1: Organizational structure in the Ninmapa monastery.

Position	***Function***	***Remark***
Dorjee Lobpen	The spiritual head of the monastery	
Umdze or *Omdse* or *Odze*	Choir leader or precentor	He reads the sacred scriptures first
Chhotimbo	He maintains discipline in the monastery	He has an administrative responsibility to designate particular lama for ritual service outside when villagers approach the monastery for this purpose.
Chikhyapo	Executive head and looks after the secular activities in the monastery	
Uchangpo	Assistant to the Choir leader or Assistant Precentor	He arranges reading of sacred scriptures on a special occasion. He is also in charge of preparing torma or offering cake at the time of festivals.
Ngerpo or *Chi-ngerpo*	Treasurer	Besides keeping records of finance, material objects, and food, he also maintains public relations on behalf of the monastery.
Chenzigpo	Looks after the mask, costumes, dress in possession of the monastery.	
Kon-nger	Daily cleaning, a ritual offering of water and lamp, and works as a guard	
Chhabdibo	Probationary monks	

Besides these, there are some other categories of monks who are not included in this hierarchic order. *Chham-po*or *Cham* also called the *Chham-pen,* organizes dance during the festival. *Lharipa* is the craftsman lama. *Adda lama* can be equated with the public relations manager. Waddell (1972; 1st edition in 1894) gives the organizational structure of the yellow hat sect. Here the *Dorjee Lobpen* is the professor or master in charge of law and conducts in the monastery. In his description, he also mentioned about the presence of the painter monks in the monastery organization.

The monks are to attend three types of rituals in the monastery. These are (i) Daily rituals (ii) special ritual events and (iii) Annual festivals. Daily rituals vary from sect to sect. The rituals are more delicate in the reformed sects than the unreformed one. There are a number of rituals for the monks in the monastery from waking to retiring to bed. The first assembly called *snatsogs* is held before sunrise. The second assembly is called *t'sa-gtin* is held around nine o'clock in the morning. Altogether five such assemblies take place in a day in the yellow hat sect. In the Ninmapa monastery, daily rituals start with the assembly in the monastery in the morning. Then another congregation takes place at around 8 A.M. which is followed by another at ten o'clock. There are three more ritual congregations at afternoon, evening and at night. All these daily rituals are summoned with the blowing of conch shell or beating of a drum. It is seen that the nature of musical calls varies from one summoning to other. At the time of ritual service, different musical instruments like *nga*, *kalling*, cymbal, *ghanti,* and conch are played. The ritual offerings are made in utensils of different shapes and designs.

Apart from daily rituals, special days are observed in the monastery. In the Pemayangste monastery, three days in Tibetan calendar observed for special rituals. These are the 8th day (*Tshegy*), 10th day (*Tshechu*) and 15th day (*Tshechingso*). On these occasions, apart from offerings, scriptures are read throughout the whole day. The metal thunderbolt (*Dorjee*) is carried

Table 17.2: Festivals observed in the monastery, which attracts a huge congregation of people

Festival	*Month*	*English Month*	*Description*
Saga Dawa	*Zhipo*	May-June	i. Observance of Buddha Purnima ii. Scriptures are cleaned and carried in procession.
Pang Lhabsol	*Dawa Dunpo*	August - September	Worship of Kanchenjonga
Lhabab Ducchen	*Dawa Gupa*	October-November	Seeking blessing of god
Ka Gyad	*Dawa Chhupo*	November-December	Worship of *Mahakala*

about by the head lama and it is kept before his seat at the time of the ritual. The annual festival calendar reflects the involvement of the monastery in the national life of the people.

At these festivals, colourful lama dance (*cham*) is performed. The lamas (dressed in gorgeous attire) perform masked dances. The masks (some of which are hundreds of years old) are worn at the time of lama dance. Each dance is based on a story of Buddhist scriptures. These dances are an integral part of their ritual activity. Dominique Casajus (1987) has discussed the role of Inadan craftsmen in the Tuareg society in northern Niger. Inadanis peripatetic and engaged in various craft activities: wood carving, weapon manufacture, jewelry, leather craft. Casajus (1987: 309) writes:

> 'The role of the peripatetic Inadan is essential to the way in which the whole of Tuareg society functions; it has been shown that without the participation of these peripatetic's social institutions such as war and marriage cannot exist among the pastoral Tuareg'.

The same can be said about the crafts of the monasteries, without which the rituals and festivals could not have been possible. The monasteries have built up a system that nurtures the use and perpetuation of craft objects in Sikkim. The daily rituals necessitate the use of objects from musical instruments to ornamented utensils. The paintings on the wall, *thanka*, flags are regular features of the monastery. The lama dances exhibit an elaborate display of the masks which are taken out of the storerooms of the monastery. Large monastery size *thankas* are kept hanging in front of the main building of a monastery at the time of rituals. The monastery organization has a definite structure that the controls the affairs of the monastery and assigns particular roles to the lamas. It is so structured that the craftsmen have a respectable place in the monastery. They are not simple craft worker, but doing the respectable job of 'painter of god'. Additionally, the craftwork is a kind of sacred activity for them, as it is a form of meditation for attaining 'nirvana', the highest goal in the life of any Buddhist. Thus, craftwork carries ritual merit for the people.

The lay followers of Buddhism have their own altars in their houses. These altars are also engraved and painted with bright colours. The householders offer water and show lamps daily to the deities. In their houses, one finds auspicious signs, masks, and *thankas*. The craft objects which have flourished and been preserved under an institutionalized structure of monastery have their daily utility among the lay followers. Here the monastery acts as a core from which craft objects have spilled over to the sacred and secular domains of the lay individuals. This process has been furthered by the involvement of the government agencies.

Craft Centers

Craft centers now play a vital role in spreading the craft tradition of Sikkim. There are thirty-two craft centers spread over across the state at present. In 1999, this number was only nineteen. This gives one an impression of how fast the demand for craft centers and craft products is increasing. The craft center is basically training *cum* production center. Here the Sikkimese youth are trained in various traditional crafts. The center has its headquarters in Gangtok, which is under the Directorate of Handicrafts and Handloom of Government of Sikkim. It was established in 1957. The centers provide the training of different trades of craft work. The headquarters center at Gangtok has the maximum number of trades open for the trainees. These training sections in the Gangtok center include *Thanka* painting, wood carving, mask making, cane and bamboo work, multi-craft, Lepcha hat making, handloom, carpet, and soft toys. I worked at the Pelling center. It was established in 1982. It had the streams of carpet making, weaving, blanket making and wood carving on the offer. The website of the DHH shows that the Pelling center has three sections: Carpet, Handloom, and Wood Carving. Thus, it can be inferred that no new section has been introduced. It may be said that there is a tendency here to stick to the tradition. In its objectives the DHH declares the following goals:

1. To be a major center of learning and training in the traditional Arts and crafts of the state.
2. Preserve and revive the languishing ethnic Traditional Arts and crafts of the state.
3. Develop Sikkim into a leading handicraft and handloom destination both in India and globally.'

One may notice the reflection of these objectives in the realities on the ground. It has performed little experimentation with the traditional forms in its centers located at the interior parts of Sikkim, but it has steadily increased the number of centers in order to spread across the length and breadth of the state. This policy would certainly help to preserve and revive the declining crafts. At the same time, the state is willing to utilize this resource for generating employment. The students coming out of the craft training centers must sell their products to the market. To materialize the sixth objective state above, the craft items that are on display for sale show a wide range of flexibility suiting to the test of the outsiders and tourists. Many of these craft objects are creative innovations of the traditional craftsmen and based on the traditional skills and themes. It renders the objects produced by them an ethnic insignia. Thus the traditional craftworks which were 'ethnographic crafts' now maybe re-christened as 'ethnic craft'. The variation of products such as small ladies' handbags, purses, ties, hats (made of cloth, bamboo

strip, feathers), flower vases made of bamboo, pen stands, yak dolls, *thanka*, autograph pads, masks of small and large sizes (made of wood or clay), dress items etc. would certainly attract the attention of the buyers from different cultures (at the same time, this range of crafts products with respective training support is only available at the Gangtok, the most visited destination in Sikkim). This strategy of producing a variety of craft items has been a common adjustment tactic for survival and/ or increasing sales. Dasgupta (2012) has mentioned this trend among the *dhokra* metal craftsmen. Bandyopadhyay (2011) has shown how the traditional *serpai* craft of an obscure village of Birbhum district of West Bengal has transformed itself to overcome the economic crisis that befell on the craftwork as the demand for *serpai* had begun to show a slow. Using the traditional knowledge of making this craft, *serpai* craftsman began to manufacture items for meeting the needs of the urban literate buyers, by switching over to pen stands, ashtrays, indoor plant pots etc. Here, tradition indicates more the indigenous process of manufacturing the craft. An item of folk art also operates within the frame that holds a traditional worldview, though when it comes to the market it becomes symbolic goods with an implicit connection of associatedness with its context of production as ethnic art. This domain is created by the institutional, discursive and historical perspectives that constitute the world of this ethnic art (Becker, 1982; Bundgaard, 1999; Chatterji, 2012). Thus, the object gains a social approval. 'That a craft object, when gets social approval its life is increased' is shown with reference to the *tant sari* of Dhaniakhali (Bandyopadhyay, 2012). In case of the craft items produced in response to market demands in Sikkim like the dolls, purses, pen stands, etc., the indigenous methods of production, motifs used, patterns of design are very much within the ambit of techno-economic capabilities and the ideological universe. Thus, the craft centers have adopted a flexible strategy accommodating tradition and modernity in the same spirit with appropriate importance to both of them.

Conclusion

Sikkim has developed as a state with a considerable number of Buddhists compared to the proportional percentage of Buddhist population in the country. The monastery acts as the fulcrum of institutionalized ritual activities in Buddhism. Apart from purely spiritual or transcendental exercises, the monastery plays important role in the cultural life of the people. The varied forms of craftworks have been nurtured by monastery for centuries. The inmates of the monastery were trained in the art. The craft works were more than an economic activity done for certain utilitarian or subsistence purpose. Craftwork was given a high status and it was a means of salvation. Thus, by binding a material domain with an ideological domain, the craft tradition

was given a boost. The cultural capital of craftsmanship grew in the particular socio-religious habitués of Buddhism and monasteries. This cultural capital is embodied, objectified and institutionalized (Bourdieu, 1986). With the changing demographics, socio-economic, and political landscape, the nature of craft production had to undergo certain changes. Lamaism condones individual monks living a family life on his own. The lama could earn an income by doing some work apart from his service to the monastery. With the increasing number of monks would be more competition for survival from the earnings from ritual services to the commoners. So, a need was felt to explore new avenues of earning. Since the order did not prohibit outside vocation, some of the lamas would engage themselves with the craftwork outside. Again with the opening of Sikkim to the outside world the demand for cultural goods which I would call 'ethnic art' increased. Apart from commercial gains, the crafts continue to reflect, the very identity of Sikkim. It has been seen that when a traditional art faces new socio-economic conditions, the general trend is to adjust itself by modifying it according to the demand of the market. However, the cultural production remains embodied in various ways - thematically, form-wise, and procedurally (Bandyopadhyay, 2011, 2012). All these mechanisms indicate some symbolic association with the actual or imagined original product. The social life of the material object is thus enhanced (Appadurai, 1986). The details of craft delineated above show how the craft is enmeshed in the life of Sikkimese people. It is a part of their memory. In this way, the 'memory approach' to heritage objects seems very pertinent in this regard (Butler, 2006), as opposed to the 'historical approach' to heritage, which placed the material objects in the temporal perspective that justified the authenticity of the materials. As per Lowenthal's,*The Past is a Foreign Country* (2015, 1st edition in 1985), the relation between the heritage object and its viewer is redefined. Now when we look at the craft objects that are used, manufactured and preserved in the monasteries, they may invite an image of the past, but beyond the precincts of the monastery, it is largely an invented tradition bearing a 'memory' link to the past. This 'memory capital' now provides the authenticity to the objects, and government supports the growth of the traditional arts by establishing a number of craft centers across the depth and breadth of the country to cash in on these ethnic memorials. Crafts produced by the Lepcha, the Bhutia and the Nepalese contribute to the formation of characteristic Sikkimese craft promoted by the state agencies. Thus the crafts linked to the 'memories' of the Sikkimese people are in many ways the carry expression of Sikkimese identity. This identity is plural in a sense that there are ethnic identities of Lepcha, Bhutia, Limbu, Tamang etc., again there are religious identities of Buddhist, Hindus, Christians. Among the Buddhist, there are different sects who have separate identities. All these identities find expressions in the craft tradition of the people in Sikkim. However, with the

passage of time, many changes have crept into the life and culture of the people. Now, tradition and change are negotiated to give credence to the cultural artifacts. The craft works of Sikkim represent a unique blend of traditional and post-traditional cultural production in the form of ethnic art.

Notes

1. The Lepcha and the Bhutia are two major tribal groups in Sikkim.
2. For the details of the political history of Sikkim, please see Basnet, 1974; Jha, 1985; Kotturam, 1983; Sinha, 1975.
3. In fact, Buddhism was the state religion in Sikkim until its merger with Indian Union. Moreover, Sikkim is the only state in the country to have Ecclesiastical Department in the government.
4. One may notice a situational similarity when the Bhutias fled into Sikkim after a sectarian fight broke out in Tibet in 16th and 17th century. These Bhutias actually founded Tibetan Buddhism in Sikkim and completed the state formation. With them, they brought the tradition of craftwork which played an important role in the spread of Buddhism (Mukherjee, 1994).

Acknowledgements

I acknowledge the Indian Anthropological Society, Kolkata that provided me the opportunity to work in Sikkim in the project funded by the Ministry of Culture, Government of India.

References

Appadurai, A (ed.) 1986, *The social life of things*, Cambridge University Press, Cambridge.

Bandyopadhyay, S 2011, 'Serpai shilpa' (The craft of Serpai)' in *Lokojo shilpa*, ed BK Chakrabarty, Parul Prakashani, Kolkata.

Bandyopadhyay, S 2012, 'Weaving in a West Bengal village: an interface between indigenous knowledge and technological development' in *Traditional knowledge system and technology in India,* eds BK Mohanta & VK Singh, Pratibha Prakashani, Delhi.

Bandyopadhyay, S 2014, 'Rain on the mirror', *The Indian Journal of Anthropology*, vol. 2, no.1, pp. 79-82.

Bansal, BL 1994, *Bon: its encounter with Buddhism in Tibet*, Eastern Book Linkers, Delhi.

Basnet, LB 1974, *Sikkim: a short political history*, S. Chand & Co., New Delhi.

Becker, HS 1982, *Art worlds*, University of California Press, Berkeley.

Bhasin, V 1989, *Ecology, culture, and change: tribals of Sikkim Himalayas*, Inter-India Publication, New Delhi.

Bourdieu, P 1986, 'The forms of capital' in *Handbook of theory and research for the sociology of education,* ed J Richardson, Greenwood, New York, pp. 241-258.

Bundgaard, H 1999, *Indian art worlds in contention: local, regional and national discourses on Orissan Patta paintings,* Curzon, Surrey.

Butler, B 2006, 'Heritage and the present past' in *Handbook of material culture*, eds C Tilley, W Keane, S Kuchler, M Rowlands & P Spyer, Sage Publications, London, pp. 463-479.

Casajus, D 1987, 'Crafts, and ceremonies: the inadan in Tuareg society' in *The other nomads- peripatetic minorities in cross-cultural perspective,* ed A Rao, B Verlag & K Wien, pp. 287-313.

Chakraborty, BK (ed.) 2011, *Lokojo shilpo*, Parul Prakashani, Kolkata.

Chartrand HH & Chartrand, HH 1988, 'The crafts in the post-modern economy', *Journal of Cultural Economics,* vol. 12, no. 2, pp. 39-66.

Chatterji, R 2012, *Speaking with pictures*, Routledge, New Delhi.

Dasgupta, BK, Sarkar, J, Danda D & Bandyopadhyay, S 2014, *Monasteries in Sikkim – persistence of cultural tradition,* Indian Anthropological Society, Kolkata.

Dasgupta, S 2012, 'Ghadwa art and artisans of Bastar in the light of development' in *Many faces of development,* eds RK Das & DK Midya, INCAA, Jhargram, pp. 115-132.

Datta, A 1991, *Sikkim since independence,* Mittal Publications, New Delhi.

Duncan, C 1995, *Civilizing rituals inside public art museums,* Routledge, London.

Ghosh, P 2013, *Folk art of Bengal,* Dasgupta & Co. Pvt. Ltd., Kolkata.

Glassie, H 2000, *Traditional art of Dhaka,* Bangla Academy, Dhaka.

Jha, PK 1985, *History of Sikkim: analysis of British policy and activities*, O.P.S. Publication Pvt. Ltd., Calcutta.

Johnson, M 1979, 'Ashanti craft organization', *African Arts*, vol. 13, no. 1, pp. 60-97.

Kandell, AS &Sailsbury, YS 1971, *Mountain kingdom: Sikkim,*W W Norton& Company Inc, New York.

Katter, E 1995, 'Multicultural connections: craft & community', *Art Education,* vol. 48, no. 1, pp. 8-13.

Korom, FJ (ed.) 1997, *Tibetan culture in the Diaspora,* Verlag Der Osterreichischen Akademie Derwissenschaften, Wien.

Kotturam, G 1983, *The Himalayan gateway: history and culture of Sikkim,* Sterling Publishers, New Delhi.

Lowenthal, D 2015(1985),*The past is a foreign country – revisited*, Cambridge University Press, London.

Mukherjee, M 1994, *In search of Viswakarma*, Meera Mukherjee, Calcutta.

Rattray, RS 1924, 'Arts and crafts of Ashanti', *Journal of the Royal African Society,* vol. 23, no. 92, pp. 265-270.

Risley, HH 1985 (1894), *The gazetteer of Sikkim*, B. R. Publishing Corporation, Delhi.

Rose, R 1990, 'Visual arts: ethnographic arts', *Pacific Arts,* no.1/2.

Rossitto, R 1994, 'Individual style in ethnographic art, the Nasilai pottery', *Pacific Arts,* no.9/10.

Roy Burman, B 1979, *Religion and politics in Tibet,* Vikas Publishing House Pvt Ltd., New Delhi.

Savasere, R 2010, 'Cradle of craft', *India International Center Quarterly*, vol. 37, no. 3/4, pp. 286-307.

Shukla, SR 1976, *Sikkim: the story of Integration*, S. Chand & Co. (Pvt.) Ltd., New Delhi.

Singh, KS (ed.) 1993, *People of India: Sikkim,* vol. 39, Seagull Books, Calcutta.

Sinha, AC 1975, *Politics of Sikkim: a sociological study*, Thomson Press (India) Ltd., New Delhi.

Staub, S (ed.) 1988, *Craft and community: traditional artist in contemporary society,* The Balch Institute for Ethnic Studies, Philadelphia.

Valentine, MD 1973, *Practical encyclopedia of crafts,* Sterling Publishing Company, New York.

Waddell, LA 1894, *The Buddhism of Tibet or Lamaism,* W.H. Allen and Company, London.

Waddell, LA 1972, *Tibetan Buddhism*, Dover Publications, Inc., New York.

Index

N

T